ESSAYS ON MORAL DEVELOPMENT

VOLUME I

The Philosophy of Moral Development

ESSAYS ON MORAL DEVELOPMENT

Volume I

The Philosophy of Moral Development

Moral Stages and the Idea of Justice

LAWRENCE KOHLBERG

1817

HARPER & ROW, PUBLISHERS, SAN FRANCISCO

Cambridge, Hagerstown, New York, Philadelphia
London, Mexico City, São Paulo, Sydney

FIRST EDITION

Designed by Jim Mennick

Library of Congress Cataloging in Publication Data

Kohlberg, Lawrence, 1927–
　　THE PHILOSOPHY OF MORAL DEVELOPMENT.

　　(Essays on moral development; v. 1)
　　Includes bibliographies.
　　1. Moral development. 2. Justice (Philosophy) I. Title. II. Series: Kohlberg, Law-
rence, 1927–　　Essays on moral development; v. 1.
BF723.M54K62 vol.　155.2′34s [155.2′34]　80-8902
ISBN 0-06-064760-4　　　　　　　　　　　　　　　　　　　AACR2

81　82　83　84　85　10　9　8　7　6　5　4　3　2　1

Contents

Acknowledgments

THESE ESSAYS are the result of continuing dialogue in a very real intellectual and moral community, Harvard's Center for Moral Education. I am very much in debt to each of its members. Ann Higgins and Clark Power, members of the Center, edited this volume. Clark has contributed not only through his insight into religious development but through his presence as a fine and gentle spirit. Ann has contributed not only through the clarity of her thought but through her sustaining and cherished company during the years in which this volume has evolved. Lastly, I would like to acknowledge the support of my mother, who has encouraged my writing since adolescence and finally has a book to see.

Some of these essays were written during the period 1970–1974, when I was freed from some of my academic duties by a National Institute of Mental Health Research Scientist award. The remainder were written in the period 1974–1980, when the Danforth Foundation supported my writing by releasing me from a portion of my teaching load. I wish to express my appreciation to these agencies, and particularly to Geraldine Bagby, Vice-President of the Danforth Foundation, for their support.

Preface to *Essays on Moral Development*

You are reading one of three volumes on moral development, as follows:

Volume I. The Philosophy of Moral Development: Moral Stages and the Idea of Justice

Volume II. The Psychology of Moral Development: Moral Stages and the Life Cycle

Volume III. Education and Moral Development: Moral Stages and Practice

Each volume is intended to stand independently of the others, but the flow of ideas and arguments logically suggests reading the volumes in the order listed.

Audience and Purpose of the Three Volumes

The three volumes are aimed at the same general audience and have the same general purpose. In writing, I have partly had in mind a special audience, the graduate students in psychology, philosophy (theology), and education whom I teach and who attend a course called "Moral Development and Moral Education." I have also had in mind a more general audience, all those potentially interested in a theory of moral education that combines (1) a philosophical theory of justice with (2) a psychological theory of the process of moral development to produce (3) an educational theory prescribing a reasonable practice of moral education in the schools.

In thinking of the more general audience, I have viewed moral education as of interest to more than a few specialists and graduate students. The major required readings for my graduate course (which these volumes supplement) are Plato's *Republic*, Emile Durkheim's *Moral Education*, Jean Piaget's *Moral Judgment of the Child*, and John Dewey's *Democracy and Education*. These books on moral education were not written for professional researchers or graduate students but for literate people interested in the great questions of society. Although my writings enter into the realm of technical research more than do these great books, and lack their grandeur of thought or style, I have tried to write them in a way that would be understandable to any literate person who might read these other books.

In writing and organizing these essays, I have also tried to keep in mind the awareness these great writers had that moral education is "interdisciplinary" and that it requires an integration of psychological, philosophical, and sociological (or political) perspectives.

Order in the Writing of the Three Volumes

Volume II, on psychology, represents both my earliest thinking and writing and my latest. The basic conception of six psychological stages of moral development goes back to my 1958 doctoral dissertation. It took, however, twenty years of longitudinal study to validate empirically the conception of the stages. This twenty-year period was not simply a matter of collecting dilemma interviews from my original subjects every three years. Rather, it was a period of revising and refining the stage definitions and the method of assessing them, a process just completed in the year of the first volume's publication. In addition to the longitudinal data themselves, Volume II reflects revisions of ideas in response to the discussions with my psychologist colleagues.

Volume III, on practice, represents the next set of ideas I worked on. When I started my dissertation in moral psychology, I was aware of a tradition of thought about moral education originating with Plato. In the contemporary world, however, it seemed as if only optimistic Sunday school educators and Boy Scout leaders thought or wrote about moral education. In 1958, that stereotype was not far from the mark. It was not until 1971 that an academically serious journal on the topic was started, *The Journal of Moral Education*. In writings in the early 1960s, I speculated on some implications of moral stage development for education. In 1969, I was galvanized into deeper reflection when to my surprise a graduate student, Moshe Blatt, engaged intermediate and high school students in a semester of Socratic classroom dilemma discussions and found that a third of the students moved up a stage, in contrast to control students, who remained unchanged (Volume III, Chapter 13). My first response to this evidence of stage change as a result of Socratic teaching was a lecture (published as Chapter 2 in Volume I, on philosophy) reasserting the ideas of Socrates about teaching about the knowledge of the good. My second response was to write a systematic treatise called "Moral Stages as the Basis for Moral Education" (1971).

These early educational writings were done before I personally attempted to engage in moral education, first in the Niantic prison in Niantic, Connecticut, starting in 1971, and then in the Cluster School, the alternative public high school in Cambridge, Massachusetts, beginning in 1974. Both the preface to Volume III and the chapters themselves make clear how my ideas about moral education changed through my experience of educational practice.

Volume I, on philosophy presents essays written after my initial psychological and educational writing. The prod to writing was primarily educational. If an aim of education is stage growth, as I believe, then one must give a philosophic rationale for why a higher stage is a better stage. "Later" does not automatically mean "better," or senescence and death would be best of all. My answer focused on the idea of justice; later I became aware of moral philosophic issues not answered by the idea of rational justice but dealt with profoundly by literature and theology.

In summary, the volumes span a ten-year period of continual elaboration and revision of ideas. I have not attempted to present a single final statement, because my thinking and that of my colleagues are changing and growing.

Order in the Reading of the Three Volumes

Although my writings started first as psychology, psychology should not be our first concern as writers or readers about moral development. The key chapter in Volume I, Chapter 4, "From *Is* to *Ought*," clearly indicates why some hard philosophic reflection on moral development is required before beginning empirical psychological research on the topic.

For this reason, I have placed Volume I, on moral, political, and educational philosophy, before the volume on moral psychology and its applications to education. The reader is likely to start with Meno's psychological question to Socrates (in Plato's *Meno*): "Can you tell me, Socrates, is virtue something that can be taught? Or does it come by practice? Or is it neither teaching or practice but natural aptitude or instinct?" For the psychologist, it is wiser not instantly to respond with a favored theory of conditioning, instinct, or cognitive development but to recognize the prior philosophic question and to reply, like Socrates, "You must think I am singularly fortunate to know whether virtue can be taught or how it is acquired. The fact is that far from knowing whether it can be taught, I have no idea what virtue itself is."

Once the psychologist recognizes that the psychology of moral development and learning cannot be discussed without addressing the philosophic questions "What is virtue?" and "What is justice?" the only path to be taken is that taken by Plato and Dewey, which ends with the writing of a treatise describing moral development in a school and society that to the philosopher seems just.

Although I initially approached moral development and education as a research psychologist, I have attempted to avoid "the psychologist's fallacy": that what makes a theory good for assembling and organizing psychological research data is what makes it good for defining the aims and methods of education. An example of this fallacy, in my opinion, is the belief that, because Skinner's theory of operant conditioning—behavior modification—is good for accumulating and ordering psychological data on animal and sometimes human learning, it must therefore be a good theory for prescribing to teachers the methods and aims of classroom learning.

Skinner's theory commits the psychologist's fallacy in so far as it claims that because a psychologist can go "beyond freedom and dignity" in the ideas ordering and interpreting research data on children's learning, the ideas of freedom and dignity are therefore not necessary ideas for teachers and citizens engaged in moral education. This claim of Skinner's is examined in Chapter 3 of Volume I, "Development as the Aim of Education." In contrast, Rochelle Meyer and I claim that concepts of justice, or of the right of each child or adult to liberty and human dignity, are the starting point of psychological research and educational practice rather than psychological hypotheses emerging from quantitative research data.

In moral philosophy, the "psychologist's fallacy" is called the "naturalistic fallacy." It is the fallacy that the philosophic question "Why is some action really right or good?" can be directly answered by social scientific statements about the causation or motivation of the action. The central chapter in Volume I, "From *Is* to *Ought*: How to Commit the Naturalistic Fallacy and Get Away with It in the Study of Moral Development," is a discussion of the uses of moral stage psychology in answering philosophic questions while avoiding the psychologist's "naturalistic fallacy."

Order of the Contents of Volume I, on Philosophy

Volume I addresses the question posed by Socrates: "What is a virtuous man, and what is a virtuous school and society which educates virtuous men?" The answers given in Volume I are not new. They are the answers given by Socrates (Chapter 2); next by Kant, as interpreted by John Rawls's *A Theory of Justice* (Chapter 5); then by John Dewey, in *Democracy and Education* (Chapter 3); and most recently by Piaget, in *The Moral Judgment of the Child* (Chapter 4). Following Socrates, Kant, and Piaget, the answer I and my colleagues offer says that the first virtue of a person, school, or society is justice—interpreted in a democratic way as equity or equal respect for all people.

Democratic justice is an answer to the deontological question, "What are the rights of people, and what duties do these rights entail?" Given the democratic justice answer to the deontological question, we still need to answer the teleological question "What is the purpose of a person's life or of a school or society's existence?" Our answer is John Dewey's answer (and, in a sense, Aristotle's): the aim of education and of civic life is intellectual, moral, and personal development (Chapter 3).

What is new in our answers to these questions is the systematic stage framework with which we approach them. Basic to the cognitive developmental theory of moral psychology presented in these volumes is the framework of *structuralism* (the analysis of invariant systems of relations among ideas), which underlies any attempt to define stages. On the philosophic side, this framework of structuralism gives rise to a theory of virtue as *justice*. Although Plato, Dewey, and Piaget each meant different things by *justice*, each recognized justice as the first virtue of a person because it is the first virtue of a society. Each recognized justice as a *structure*, a pattern of equilibrium or harmony in a group or society. The interface between my psychological theory and structural theories of moral philosophy is the subject of the first volume.

Volume I is divided into four parts. Part One uses the moral stages to approach the problems of educational philosophy. Like Socrates and Dewey, I and my colleagues feel that the question of moral philosophy (the question "What is virtue?"), is both first and finally a question of education, which is the practice of philosophy.

Part II focuses directly on issues of moral philosophy. Thus, the heart of Volume I is this part, containing two chapters, "From *Is* to *Ought*" (Chapter 4) and "Justice as Reversibility" (Chapter 5). These chapters argue that there are stages of moral reasoning and judgment, that the core of each stage is an underlying conception of justice, and that each higher stage is better for resolving justice problems.

The two remaining parts of Volume I apply the stage theory developed in Parts One and Two to problems in the humanities. Part Three applies the moral stages and the ideal of justice they imply to questions of political philosophy and the philosophy of law. It focuses on two U.S. Supreme Court decisions.

The first Supreme Court decision, considered in Chapter 7, is the *Furman* decision, prohibiting many uses of capital punishment as a violation of the Eighth Amendment prohibiting "cruel and unusual punishment." Chapter 7 supports this decision on the grounds (1) that, very slowly, public and individual sentiment is moving toward viewing capital punishment as cruel and unusual, and (2) that capital punishment violates Rawlsian justice and other Stage 6 justice principles.

In Chapter 8, I consider a second decision, the *Schempp* decision, making religious observation and teaching in the school a violation of the First Amendment and of the separation of church and state. This decision has been interpreted as prohibiting moral education in the schools on the grounds that such education is the propagation of a creed of secular humanism. In the chapter, I argue that the teaching of justice in the schools is not a violation of the right of religious minorities or majorities but is, in fact, a part of the Founding Fathers' vision of the mission of the public schools. I offer a developmental conception of the teaching of justice.

Part Four reaches into areas of the humanities that deal with questions beyond justice, the humanities of theology and literature. Justice is the first virtue of law and of political and personal action, so it is the first virtue of a person. But life is not just, so what is one to think or feel when one's sense of justice does not fit one's actions or the actions of others? This is the central issue raised for the reader or writer of tragedies. It is the central issue theologians face when talking about religion or faith. Chapters 9 and 10 do not try to answer these deep questions; they only attempt to point to the justice element presupposed by these questions and by answers to them.

Volume I, then, includes the following chapters:

PART ONE. MORAL STAGES AND THE AIMS OF EDUCATION

Chapter 1. "Indoctrination Versus Relativity in Value Education" (1971)

Can moral educators escape indoctrinating students with their own arbitrary and relative values or do more than simply clarify the student's own arbitrary values? I propose moral education through stimulating moral development as a way out of this dilemma.

Chapter 2. "Education for Justice: A Modern Statement of the Socratic View" (1970)

Can "a bag of virtues" guide moral education? I use the moral stages as a basis for restating Socrates' claim that virtue is justice, that it rests on knowledge of the good, and that moral education is a drawing out from within through dialogue.

Chapter 3. "Development as the Aim of Education: the Dewey View" (1972), with Rochelle Mayer

We clarify the relation between psychological and philosophical ethical theories in formulating educational aims and present Dewey's progressive educational theory, which combines a cognitive developmental psychology with a philosophic ethic of liberalism.

PART TWO. MORAL STAGES AND THE PROBLEM OF JUSTICE

Chapter 4. "From Is to Ought: How to Commit the Naturalistic Fallacy and Get Away with It in the Study of Moral Development" (1971)

In this chapter, I present a culturally universal or nonrelative concept of morality and justice, outline the moral stages as justice structures, claim that a higher stage is a better stage, and give an account of the relation between psychology and philosophy in studying moral development.

Chapter 5. "Justice as Reversibility: The Claim to Adequacy of a Highest Moral Stage" (1978)

Here I give an elaboration of the principles and process of judgment at Stage 6 and discuss Rawls's theory as a justification of Stage 6 moral judgments.

PART THREE. MORAL STAGES AND LEGAL AND POLITICAL ISSUES

Chapter 6. "The Future of Liberalism as the Dominant Ideology of the Western World" (1977)

My introductory structural analysis of liberal or progressive political philosophies leads to a statement of moral evolution at the societal level and places Rawls's Stage 6 concept of justice in the context of contemporary problems.

Chapter 7. "Moral Judgments About Capital Punishment: A Developmental-Psychological View" (1975), with Donald Elfenbein

Here we work out in detail the philosophic and psychological aspects of one moral problem, capital punishment. Our explanations of why capital punishment is uniformly rejected at the highest stage but accepted at the lower stages indicate the relation between the content and structure of moral thought.

Chapter 8. "Moral and Religious Education in the Public Schools: A Developmental View" (1967)

In this chapter, I assert that the teaching of justice in the public schools is not a violation of children's religious liberties or of the separation of church and state.

PART FOUR. MORAL STAGES AND PROBLEMS BEYOND JUSTICE

Chapter 9. "Moral Development, Religious Thinking, and the Question of a Seventh Stage" (1979), with Clark Power

We explore the relation between the moral stages and religious thinking. In this chapter, we postulate a stage of religious orientation to deal with issues unresolved by the highest stage of moral judgment (Stage 6).

Chapter 10. "Moral Development and the Theory of Tragedy" (1973)

As in the chapter on religion, in this chapter I use stages of justice to illuminate the form and experience of tragedy, a "postrational" experience that involves the limits of Stage 6 rational human morality.

Epilogue. "Education for Justice: The Vocation of Janusz Korczak"

The life of a martyred Polish educator illuminates the centrality of education for justice in a "Stage 7" commitment to serving children.

Order of the Contents of Volume II, on Psychology

Volume II is divided into three parts. Part One traces the psychological theory of moral stages from earlier formulations to the present.

Part Two presents the longitudinal data, and the method of scoring it, that justify the theory. Part Three, which is less technical, uses the stages to illuminate different eras in the life cycle.

Although the oldest chapter in Volume II, Chapter 1, was published in 1968, it was preceded by ten years of research and writing on the psychology of moral development, commencing with my doctoral dissertation (Kohlberg, 1958). I started the dissertation as an effort to replicate Piaget's (1948) description of moral judgment stages, to extend them to adolescence, and to examine the relation of stage growth to opportunities to take the role of others in the social environment. These goals led to my revision and elaboration of Piaget's two-stage model into six stages of moral judgment, at first cautiously labeled as "developmental ideal types." One thread running through Volume II is the progressive refining of my stage definitions and assessing of them through a twenty-year longitudinal study designed to clarify whether my ideal types were "really" stages; that is, whether they formed an invariant sequence through which all human beings move although at varying rates and endpoints of development. This longitudinal work is presented in Part Two of Volume II, with chapters ordered by date of writing.

Without waiting for clear longitudinal results on this invariant sequence assumption of the stage hypothesis, I began to sketch its theoretical implications for the process of moral development and its relation to moral behavior. These implications define a cognitive-developmental theory or paradigm for the study of the child's moralization that is basically different from that offered by behavioristic learning theories or psychoanalytic accounts of superego formation. I explicated these differences in the first two chapters of Part One by comparing some of the research findings from each paradigm. The third theoretical chapter presents a more recent statement of the nature of the moral judgment stages and their implications for the moralization process. The complex issues and findings relating moral judgment to action are dealt with in the last chapters on theory.

Part Three of Volume II, "Moral Stages and the Life Cycle," provides the easiest introduction to the idea of stages. It uses cognitive and moral stages to characterize the "whole person" in three eras: early childhood, adolescence, and late adulthood. These are eras of transition when the growing person as philosopher speaks out most clearly. The data base is wide-ranging interview material interpreted mainly from an intuitive perspective. Part Three is placed last, although it is

the least technical, because it builds on and clarifies the earlier material on structural stages, which are distinct from life cycle eras, such as
adolescence, but which illuminate the particular characteristics and
issues of life's eras; for instance, the understanding gained about adolescence through knowledge of the transition from Stage 4 to 5—
"Stage 4½."

Volume II, then, includes the following essays:

PART ONE. BASIC THEORY

*Chapter 1. "Psychological Approaches to the Study of Moral Develop-
ment" (1968)*

In this chapter, I place my cognitive-developmental approach to studying moral development in a historical survey of the basic schools of
moral psychology and sociology and the theoretical assumptions of
each school, and review the basic empirical findings of each
approach.

*Chapter 2. "Stage and Sequence: The Cognitive-Developmental Ap-
proach to Socialization" (1969)*

Here I clearly distinguish the cognitive-developmental research paradigm grounded in stages from other approaches to socialization and
social learning. I extend the paradigm from moral stage growth to
processes of imitation, identification, and sex-role development.

*Chapter 3. "Moral Stages and Moralization: The Cognitive Develop-
mental Approach" (1976)*

This chapter presents a recent summary of my cognitive-developmental theory of moralization, of the nature of each of the six stages,
and of methods for assessing stages.

*Chapter 4. "The Relations between Moral Judgment and Moral Ac-
tion" (1980), with Daniel Candee*

In a review of studies relating moral judgment stage to actual moral
behavior, we posit that a stage of judgments of justice is a necessary
but not a sufficient condition for moral action, which also requires a
second phase judgment of responsibility and "ego strength" or
"will."

*Chapter 5. "Justice, Responsibility, and Practical Moral Judgment"
(1980), with Ann Higgins and Clark Power*

Following Carol Gilligan's lead, our research on "real-life" dilemma
interviews suggests levels of judgments of responsibility somewhat
distinguishable from stage of judgments of justice, and tied to relationships of interpersonal caring and community.

Chapter 6. "Exploring the Moral Atmosphere of Institutions: A Bridge between Moral Judgment and Moral Action" (1980), with Clark Power and Ann Higgins

Here we discuss research relating moral conduct to interviews about real rather than hypothetical situations and emphasize the importance of studying group and institutional moral expectations or norms.

Chapter 7. "A Response to Critics of the Theory" (1981), with Charles Levine and Ros Hewer

This chapter summarizes and responds to often-made criticisms of the theory as represented by the writings of Elizabeth Leone Simpson, Edmund Sullivan, Carol Gilligan, and John Gibbs. (Criticisms of the research method as distinct from the theory are summarized and responded to in Chapter 8.)

PART TWO. METHOD AND MEASUREMENT

Chapter 8. "The Meaning and Measurement of Moral Development: The History of Stage Scoring and the Longitudinal Results" (1980), with Anne Colby

We report the actual longitudinal findings of sequence in moral judgment with standard issue scoring and deal with methodological issues in the reality of moral stages.

Chapter 9. "Continuities and Discontinuities in Moral Development" (1969), with Richard Kramer

Focus on "sophomoritis," apparent retrogression in the college years, leads us to posit that Eriksonian ego identity questioning in a "moratorium" period leads to such apparent or temporary retrogression.

Chapter 10. "Continuities and Discontinuities in Moral Development Revisited" (1973)

In another look at college "retrogression," I view it as a "Stage 4½," an "outside of society perspective" in transition from a conventional "member of society" to a principled "prior to society" perspective. I speculate on whether stage growth can occur in adulthood as opposed to childhood and adolescence.

Chapter 11. "An Introduction to Standard Issue Scoring" (1980), with Anne Colby and Kelsey Kauffman

Here we present the logic of the stage scoring manual and of its basic unit, the criterion judgment, defined by issue, norm, element, and stage.

Chapter 12. "Cultural Universality of the Stages: A Longitudinal

Study in Turkey" (1980), with Mordecai Nisan
In this chapter, we discuss the results of ten-year longitudinal data analyzed using the Standard Issue Scoring System.

PART THREE. MORAL STAGES AND THE LIFE CYCLE
Chapter 13. "The Young Child as a Philosopher" (1979)
The meaning of cognitive and moral stages for understanding the young child (ages 3–8) and for communication between teacher and child are considered in this chapter.

Chapter 14. "The Adolescent as a Philosopher" (1973), with Carol Gilligan
Here we discuss the meaning of cognitive and moral stages for understanding the adolescent (ages 12–18), and the educational implications.

Chapter 15. "The Aging Person as a Philosopher" (1980), with Richard Shulik
A discussion of the meaning of cognitive and moral stages in understanding adult development and aging provides the foundation for a description of the two highest moral stages as phenomena of early adult development, and of a hypothetical stage of moral and metaphysical-religious integration as the focus of development in the aging.

Order of the Contents in Volume III, on Education

As noted earlier, the prod to my thinking and writing about moral education was Blatt's (1969) finding of upward stage change through classroom discussion of hypothetical dilemmas (reported in Chapter 13 of Volume III). My reaction to the finding was mixed. On the one hand, such an approach to moral education seemed almost like "teaching to the test" in order to raise scores on verbal interviews about hypothetical dilemmas. On the other hand, it seemed a modern reaffirmation of the Socratic vision of moral education as dialogue about knowledge of the good (Chapter 2 in Volume I).

My first paper for teachers, written with Elliot Turiel in 1971, tried to justify and explain Socratic moral discussion as a method for dealing with both hypothetical dilemmas and real classroom conflicts (Chapter 2 in Volume III).

My next paper for teachers elaborated the broader implications of John Dewey's view of development as the aim of moral education

(Chapter 3 in Volume III). The first practical result of this line of thought was to bring dilemma discussion into the curriculum. I first accomplished this in collaboration with Edwin Fenton, an outstanding "new social studies" curriculum writer. I elaborated the justification of this marriage of dilemma discussion with social studies objectives in Chapter 5 of Volume III, "Moral Development and the New Social Studies."

By 1970, while continuing work on strategies for combining moral dilemma discussion with the academic curriculum of the school, I had become aware of the fact that moral education needed to deal with the "hidden curriculum" or the "moral atmosphere" of the school (Chapter 7 in Volume III). The most melodramatic statement of the need to attend to the moral atmosphere or hidden curriculum of an institution came out of work on moral reeducation in the prison (Chapter 9 in Volume III). This chapter notes that reformatory inmates seriously engaged in Socratic discussion of hypothetical moral dilemmas but lived in a prison environment of real moral dilemmas punctuated by inmates, and occasionally also guards, beating inmates. This conflict led us to attempt to create in one prison unit the moral atmosphere of a just community. The just community would be the heart of an enterprise that would also engage in dilemma discussion (Chapter 10 in Volume III). At the time when I was struggling hardest for an approach to explicate the concept of moral atmosphere, I paid a research visit to Kibbutz Sassa in Israel (Chapter 8, Volume III). In addition to operating as a direct democracy in most areas of decision, the kibbutz enlisted the authority of the group in the name of community. Although I as well as the kibbutz teachers worried about the implications of conformity to the group, the teachers, and some of the older students, clearly were principled people, not conformists. The visit led to serious effort by myself and my colleagues to clarify the idea of community we were trying to implement and add to the democratic justice practices in the prison unit. The result was a growing and changing theory of a just community, first developed in the prison setting (Chapters 9 and 10 in Volume III), and then in the Cambridge Cluster alternative public high school (Chapters 11, 12, and 15 in Volume III). Both the theory and the school and prison experiments are changing, in flux. Both, however, have sufficient viability to make writing about them worthwhile.

The chapters in Volume III, then, are as follows:

of the stage of moral atmosphere implicitly generated by teachers and administrators by modeling and by methods of creating and enforcing rules.

Chapter 8. "Cognitive-Developmental Theory and the Practice of Collective Moral Education" (1971)

This chapter is my report on the effects of kibbutz moral atmosphere and practices of moral education, stressing community and collective responsibility in moral stage development. Together with Chapter 7, on the moral atmosphere of the American school, this analysis laid the groundwork for my own experimental work.

Chapter 9. "The Justice Structure of the Prison—A Theory and an Intervention" (1972), with Peter Scharf and Joseph Hickey

Analyzing and trying to improve the moral atmosphere of the prison were the beginnings of the "just community interventions."

PART THREE. THE THEORY OF THE JUST COMMUNITY

Chapter 10. "The Just Community Approach to Correction: A Theory" (1975), with Kelsey Kaufmann, Peter Scharf, and Joseph Hickey

Our first (and continuing) intensive experiment in moral education was the creation of a participatory democracy stressing moral discussion in a woman's prison. We here present the theory behind that intervention.

Chapter 11. "High School Democracy and Educating for a Just Society" (1979)

In this chapter, I trace my thinking about education from (1) an initial focus on Socratic dialogue ultimately leading to Stage 6 to (2) a focus on helping create imperfect high school just communities leading to Stage 4 civic responsibility.

Chapter 12. "The Just Community Approach to Alternative High Schools: A Theory" (1981), with Clark Power and Ann Higgins

Here we elaborate and integrate Lewin's concepts of group dynamics and Durkheim's concept of group morality with our moral stage theory for promoting moral value change in the school group.

PART FOUR. REPORTS OF EXPERIMENTAL MORAL
EDUCATION PRACTICE

Chapter 13. "The Effects of Classroom Moral Discussion Upon Children's Level of Moral Judgment" (written 1969, published 1975), with Moshe Blatt

This report of the first systematic experiments in moral education demonstrates that developmental moral discussion of hypothetical dilemmas leads to stage change. We give examples of such discussions.

Chapter 14. "The Effects of Secondary School Moral Discussion on Development of Moral Reasoning" (1976), with Anne Colby, Edwin Fenton, and Betsy Speicher-Dubin

A Stone Foundation–sponsored project incorporated moral dilemma discussion into Fenton's high school "new social studies" curriculum in twenty classrooms in Boston and Pittsburgh. The 1975 Blatt and Kohlberg findings were replicated when discussions were led by "average" high school teachers within the context of social studies curriculum goals and content. Methods of leading discussions are illustrated with transcripts from some typical classes.

Chapter 15. "A Just Community Alternative in a Large Public High School: A Report on Four Years of the Cluster School" (1981), with Ann Higgins and Clark Power

In this chapter, we report the structure of the Cluster alternative school and document with interviews and community meeting records the evolution over four years of its moral atmosphere.

Chapter 16. "The Just Community Approach in Practice at the Scarsdale Alternative School: A Student's View" (1979), by Edward Zalaznick

The other chapters in this volume reflect the perspective of the theorist and researcher. It seems important to include, in this volume on practice, a participating high school student's perception of the theory and its meaning to himself and his peers. He discusses both the value of the just community approach and some of the unresolved complications the theory presents to students.

Volume III, on education, most explicitly represents a stance that also characterizes the earlier volumes. The chapters represent, not a fixed system attempting to be invulnerable to criticism, but an open "approach" that recognizes that the phenomena of a field such as moral education cannot be fully encompassed by any single theory. At the same time, conceptual growth requires pushing a theory to its limits and then revising it, rather than bland eclecticism. In Volume III, I moved to thinking through the philosophic issues of Volume I and then expanded and revised the theory in light of continuing experience in classrooms and community meetings in a "just community school."

Of the three volumes, Volume III (on education) is the most unfinished, but its publication at this point seems warranted as a means for suggesting the practical import of the first two volumes.

The central practice to which psychology is relevant is education. Following Dewey, I believe that theory and research in psychology that do not directly address issues of practice are more than sterile—they are misleading or vague in their real meaning. The "operations" of a psychology dedicated to constructs with operational meaning are eventually the operations of an ongoing practice. I follow Dewey in making a similar claim about philosophy. Modern philosophy is primarily the logical analysis and criticism of underlying concepts and methods of thought in such basic areas as morality. The concepts and methods to be ultimately analyzed by philosophy are basically not those of other professional philosophers but of those engaged in the everyday practice of philosophy. The everyday practice of philosophy is primarily education, because teachers (and students) necessarily undertake to understand, evaluate, and transmit the core concepts of world culture, philosophy, and science, including the concepts of morality and justice. In this sense, the importance of moral education for scholars is not so much that it is a field of application of theory to enlighten ignorant teachers as that it is the arena of practice in which moral theory should be worked out.

It is gratifying, therefore, to see a revival of scholarly interest in moral education in the last five years. Some reasons for this revival are discussed in Volume III, reasons deeper than reactions to such contemporary events as Watergate or Vietnam. This revival is primarily due to the weakening of the American faith in conventional morality (discussed in Volumes II and III), a weakening of faith that leads parents and educators to seek guidance from scholars rather than from tradition. This is not the first time in which the weakening of traditional morality has led to serious dialogue about moral education. The first time was the Athens of Socrates, Plato, and Aristotle. I hope that these volumes serve some purpose in reviving the dialogue in contemporary North America and Great Britain.

Introduction

THE FOLLOWING general introduction reviews the threads that run through all four parts of Volume I and provides an overview of the six moral stages in relation to philosophy. This first volume is divided into four parts, each preceded by an introduction:

Part One. Moral Stages and the Aims of Education
Part Two. Moral Stages and the Idea of Justice
Part Three. Moral Stages and Legal and Political Issues
Part Four. Moral Stages and Problems Beyond Justice

The threads running through this volume are fundamental philosophic themes that are restated in each chapter in light of a new topic. I believe that complex and difficult philosophic issues are best clarified by addressing them in the variety of ways they touch on the topical problems. The relativity of values is the fundamental underlying issue I have struggled with in this volume. I claim that the problems that arise from this philosophic issue are in part answered by my conception of culturally universal stages of moral development and the idea of justice that the stages embody.

Questions and problems raised by the value relativity issue and answers to them are discussed in the four parts of this volume. Part One poses the question of value relativity in the context of educational philosophy, culminating in an argument for human development as the universal aim of education. Part Two begins with the question of value relativity as central to moral philosophy issues and ends with the argument of the greater philosophic adequacy of a highest stage of moral judgment. Part Three applies the moral principles of the highest stages to issues of political and legal philosophy. The major chapter in this part addresses the issue of capital punishment and argues for its abolition on grounds both of moral philosophy and of constitutional jurisprudence. The fourth and final part deals with meta-physical questions that the idea of justice cannot answer. Part Four culminates with an analysis of the experience of tragedy, which both requires a sense of justice and moves beyond it.

I have placed Part One, on education, first because the value relativity question and the developmental answer to it can be presented more easily by using the concrete dilemma that faces teachers: how to think about values when deciding what and how to teach.

Chapter 1, "Indoctrination Versus Relativity in Value Education," discusses the value relativity problem as it faces practicing teachers or educators. As teachers, as well as human beings, people must orient themselves to a set of values. The problem arises: "What if my values are different from the values of my students or of other human beings who are affected by my actions? What right do I have to impose my values on others by my actions or by my teaching?" The chapter outlines a set of easy answers or "cop-outs" to this dilemma and shows why these do not really answer the problem. One such answer is to postulate a "bag of virtues" that sounds like something everyone can agree on. Yet a closer inspection of the bag of virtues shows that "everyone has his own bag." This chapter then shifts to a second answer, which describes a teaching strategy of helping students clarify their own values. However, a problem still arises: once students have clarified their values, they may endorse American Nazism, for example. Ultimately, we must ask ourselves, "Are our values universal? Is there a hierarchy of values that everyone does or should accept?"

This first chapter does not answer these questions but it does point a way toward answering them through considering the following six moral stages:

Stage 1. Punishment and obedience
Stage 2. Instrumental exchange
Stage 3. Interpersonal conformity
Stage 4. Social system and conscience maintenance
Stage 5. Prior rights and social contract
Stage 6. Universal ethical principles

Cross-cultural studies discussed in Volume II indicate that universal values and even some hierarchy of values do exist. Research shows there is an order of development in moral reasoning, and Socratic discussion stimulates the advance of students through that order; that is, in a direction in which they are naturally going under normal environmental conditions. Accordingly, the teacher can engage students not only in clarifying their own values but also in sorting out claims as to which answers or reasons are better. Thus, without indoctrinating students with their own or their society's arbitrary values, teachers can move beyond the relativistic view that everyone has his or her own "bag of virtues."

Chapter 2, "Education for Justice: A Modern Statement of the Socratic View," recapitulates some points of Chapter 1 and further considers the implications of Socratic dialogue as an approach to moral education. Socrates was not impelled only by an "inquiry learning" approach to values. For him, Socratic dialogues rested on a sense of some personal virtue in himself that was displayed not by preaching but by implicit convictions of belief and action. These convictions were

- *First,* virtue is ultimately one, not many, and it is always the same ideal form regardless of climate or culture.
- *Second,* the name of this ideal form is justice.
- *Third,* not only is the good one, but virtue is knowledge of the good. He who knows the good chooses the good.
- *Fourth,* the kind of knowledge of the good that is virtue is philosophical knowledge or intuition of the ideal form of the good, not correct opinion or acceptance of conventional beliefs.
- *Fifth,* the good can then be taught, but its teachers must in a certain sense be philosopher-kings.
- *Sixth,* the reason the good can be taught is because we know it all along dimly or at a low level and its teaching is more a calling out than an instruction.
- *Seventh,* the reason we think the good cannot be taught is because the same good is known differently at different levels and direct instruction cannot take place across levels.
- *Eighth,* then the teaching of virtue is the asking of questions and the pointing of the way, not the giving of answers. Moral education is the leading of people upward, not the putting into the mind of knowledge that was not there before.

Chapter 2 claims that moral development research provides some empirical credence to these assumptions of Socrates.

Chapter 3, "Development as the Aim of Education: The Dewey View," returns to the problem of the relativity of values in education by asking a fundamental question: "How are the aims of education justified, whether intellectual or moral?" My Socratic approach to moral education assumes that the main aim of education is development. To support this assumption, I look to John Dewey, the foremost modern educational psychologist-philosopher.

An overview of three fundamental approaches to education and its aims begins the chapter. Because each approach combines a psychological theory with a philosophy or a set of value premises, I call the approaches *ideologies*. A first *cultural transmission* ideology has a psychology of learning through direct teaching and a set of value premises making the aim of education the transmission of the skills and values prized by the culture or the society.

The "cultural transmission" ideology, probably the most popular view, is directly opposed by the *romantic* ideology. From Rousseau onward, romantics have espoused the psychology that intellectual and moral growth comes naturally from within like a plant unfolding. Philosophically, the romantic educator is a libertarian stressing the child's liberty and meeting his or her needs. The polarity between imposition and libertarianism is transcended, we claim, by a third educational ideology—Dewey's *progressivism*. This ideology holds a cognitive-developmental psychology: developmental because it is a psychology of stages, cognitive because the stages involve forms of thinking. This psychology is *interactional:* it holds that stages do not mature biologically but develop through interaction between the child's structuring capacities and the intellectual and social stimulation of the environment. On the philosophic side, the progressive view is *liberal:* it defines the child's liberty by principles of justice that emphasize not only the child's rights but also the child's recognition of the like rights of others. It stresses democracy as the key protection from indoctrination and a key stimulus to intellectual and moral growth.

In Chapter 3, I argue not only that the progressive view embodies a psychology most adequate to the facts of development but also that it alone offers a democratic or nonelitist idea of education. In Skinner's *Walden Two* utopia of cultural transmission, the culture transmitted is defined by the behavioral engineer—Skinner's notion of the philosopher-king. Neill's romantic Summerhill leaves the future philosopher free to become a philosopher and the future garbage man free to become a garbage man, with nothing common to both. Only a school whose aim is stimulating development and whose means are democratic is fully compatible with a democratic society.

The first three chapters of this volume (Part One) center on the issue of value relativity in education and the kind of answer that a moral stage theory gives to this and related philosophic issues. Part Two lays out the philosophic assumptions and implications of the six moral stages.

Chapter 4, "From *Is* to *Ought:* How to Commit the Naturalistic Fallacy and Get Away with It in the Study of Moral Development," again addresses the issue of value relativity and the answers given to the relativist by research on moral stages. Here my posing of the issue and my statement of moral stage theory is in the more "technical" language of professional philosophy and professional psychology. Here I elaborate my view of the relations between moral philosophy and moral psychology. Before fruitful empirical psychological work on moral development can be undertaken, there must be a moral philosophic clarification and justification of the terms *moral* and *development.* Philosophy, then, must be present before starting adequate empirical work in psychology. I also claim, however, that moral philosophy needs the work of the empirical moral psychologist. Findings on moral stages can support or refute initial philosophic assumptions about moral development and so can help revise and correct them when they fly in the face of empirical results. Thus moral philosophy comes at the end as well as at the beginning of empirical work on moral development. Philosophers tell psychologists they cannot go "from *is* to *ought"* by erecting a philosophy of the good and the right simply from a study of what people do value as good and right. To do so, they claim, is to commit "the naturalistic fallacy." My colleagues and I agree with them. Psychologists can, and should, however, move back and forth between philosophic assumptions and empirical findings.

A case of the naturalistic fallacy I treated at length in this chapter is the issue of cultural relativity of values. The relativist usually starts by saying moral values are relative to culture, as a statement of social science fact. When facts about universal values developing through a universal stage sequence are brought out, many cultural relativists shift to philosophic or ethical relativism, which claims that the factual search for ethical development implies a more adequate standard toward which development is moving and thereby is "value biased" and "unscientific." I argue that neither science nor ethics can progress without the postulation of moral methods or standards. In fact, most relativists do hold at least one principle as desirable for *all* to hold, the principle of tolerance. I agree with them and define this principle as the heart of Stage 5's social contract for equal protection of basic rights.

In Chapter 4, then, I attempt to refute both cultural and ethical relativism, as has been done many times before in moral philosophy. It is easier, however, to "disprove" relativism than it is to "prove" certain ethical principles and their adequacy. In Chapter 5, "Justice as Reversibility," I discuss John Rawls's *A Theory of Justice* (1971), which is probably the most rigorous effort to define and prove a set of moral principles in the history of philosophy. I identify Rawls's set of moral principles with the sixth or highest stage of justice. Judging by the critical response to Rawls, he proves his principles only to the audience, which already shares them. I interpret Rawls's efforts at proof as effective for people who hold Stage 5 principles of prior rights and social contract. They can see the need to endorse the clearer and more universalizable justice principles that Rawls presents and that help define Stage 6. Rawls's arguments are not convincing, however, for an ethical relativist or cultural relativist who equates morality with the existing standards of society.

Accordingly, in neither Chapter 4 nor in Chapter 5 do I formally attempt to prove any special set of principles. Instead, I attempt something that I hope is easier: to give good reasons why each later stage of justice reasoning is a better method of reasoning than its predecessor. I try two strategies for doing this in Chapter 4. The first is an appeal to formal properties any moral judgment should meet. Judgments to be moral should rest on certain principles, on those principles that are universalizable. Each higher moral stage comes closer to this principled form. The second strategy is a demand that each higher stage should be able to answer questions or problems unsolved at the next lower stage. Particularly, a person using Stage 5 reasoning is left with the problem of ethical relativity. The Stage 5 position cannot clearly go beyond a social and legal contract for tolerance and preservation of certain rights in answering moral questions. Stage 5 reasoning, for instance, cannot say whether a person is obligated or not to steal if necessary to save the life of a friend or acquaintance. Stage 6 attempts to construct answers to such questons that all rational moral agents could follow.

Chapter 5, "Justice as Reversibility," begins where "From *Is* to *Ought*" ends. It claims that there is one moral principle at the heart of ethics, the Golden Rule. Another name for the Golden Rule is *reversibility:* "Put yourself in everyone else's place." Still another name is "moral musical chairs": "Let everyone trade places before choosing and be willing to be in the worst-off chair." As stated by Rawls, the rational principles for a society are the principles of justice as fairness, those we would choose or contract into under the "veil of ignorance" as to who in the society we would be. The equilibrium of justice as reversibility in ethics is the "moving equilibrium" Piaget attributes to a highest stage of logical or moral reasoning.

In Chapter 5, I appeal to the reader's intuitions by discussing dilemmas in which there is a conflict between the principle of utility as the greatest good of the greatest number and the principle of justice as respect for individual human dignity. I claim that justice as reversibility (moral musical chairs) resolves these dilemmas by recognizing utility within the framework of respect for individual dignity expressed as the willingness to trade places with others; that is, the Golden rule.

Both Chapter 4 and Chapter 5 advocate ideas of justice that are supported by professional moral philosophers but that also correspond to the natural intuitions of adults reasoning at Stages 5 and 6. Part Three of this volume accepts the fact that these ideas of justice are different from the majority opinion. Most adults in American society reason mainly not at the principled but at the conventional stages, Stages 3 and 4. In spite of the fact that Stage 5 or 6 reasoning is displayed by only a minority of Americans, in Chapter 6, "The Future of Liberalism as the Dominant Ideology of the Western World," I claim that the dominant ideology of the United States and other Western countries has been a liberal social contract view corresponding to Stage 5. Although currently this liberal view is doubted and questioned everywhere, in this Chapter I trace a thread of sociomoral progress in Western societies compatible with the liberal faith. I also suggest that the liberal faith is and should be evolving toward the ideas of justice embodied in a sixth stage.

Chapters 6 and 7 apply the moral psychology and philosophy developed in earlier parts to two U.S. Supreme Court decisions. As noted, the adult majority in American society reason at the conventional stages. This poses some problems for legal philosophers and Supreme Court justices, whose reasoning is often at Stage 5 or 6. In the United States, legislators are usually responsive to public opinion, but the Supreme Court should be responsive to "evolving standards of justice" rather than to common opinion when interpreting the Constitution. Supreme Court justices have the right to be Platonic philosopher-kings or guardians on topics touching on individual or civil rights. The Warren Court took the role of guardians seriously, and I here look in depth at two of its decisions as material for applying the theory expounded in Chapters 4 and 5.

In Chapter 7, I take up the difficult Supreme Court decision in *Furman* v. *Georgia,* which prohibited capital punishment, at least under certain conditions. The major rationale for the decision came from Stage 5 reasoning concerned with violation of procedural justice in capital punishment sentencing. Beyond this, however, were Stage 6 Supreme Court voices saying that capital punishment was inherently a violation of the right to human dignity, a right retained even by convicted murderers, and was therefore "cruel and unusual punishment." These voices spoke not for public opinion but for "evolving standards of justice" in our society. In Chapter 7, I use both empirical data on evolving views of capital punishment and Rawls's idea of justice as the Golden Rule to support these Supreme Court voices.

The post mortem analysis of Chapter 7 shows that only a minority in the Court used the type of reasoning I use to claim that the death penalty is "cruel and unusual punishment." When various states attempted to correct the procedural justice of capital punishment by making it mandatory for some offenses, the Court majority decreed it to be not a violation of the Bill of Rights.

The *Schempp* decision, discussed in Chapter 8, touches fundamentally on the whole enterprise of moral education central to all three volumes. In restricting prayer in the school, it potentially can be interpreted as prohibiting moral as well as religious teaching in the school. Chapter 8 clarifies the Stage 5 idea of justice that underlies both the First Amendment and the Founding Fathers' conception of the public school as a preparation for citizenship in a democratic society. I support this conception with research evidence of the separability of moral development from religious training.

Chapter 8 is an argument for the legal separation of church and state in public school moral education, not an argument for secular humanism as a religious or world view. The relation of moral development to religion and faith is taken up as a deeper problem in Chapter 9, "Moral Development, Religious Thinking, and the Question of a Seventh Stage." In this chapter, I restate the autonomy of ethics, the claim that stages of justice and the highest-stage formulation of principles of justice stand on philosophic and psychological grounds independent of religious thinking or religious faith. However, I also point to stages of religious and metaphysical orientation parallel to the moral stages. I acknowledge the fact that each moral stage poses and leaves unanswered such questions as "Why be just or moral in a world that often appears to be unjust?" Finally, I consider as a hypothetical "seventh stage" kinds of religious thought and experience that can offer answers to the questions left unanswered by Stage 6 rational justice.

The notion of a metaphoric seventh stage underlies my interpretation of tragedy in Chapter 10. Acknowledging the contribution of other psychologies to explaining our responses to tragedy, I stress the element of growth of stagelike moral wisdom occurring in and through tragedy. I also imply, however, that the endpoint of tragedy is not a reaffirmation of Stage 6 principles of justice. "The tragic wisdom is rather religious; it is the resignation of the demand for justice in order to accept life in a cosmos that is just in no humanly understandable sense."

An epilogue discusses the life of Janusz Korczak, a moral educator who was able to make a "Stage 7" affirmation of life even en route to a Nazi death camp. Thus we conclude by returning to the first theme of the volume, education for justice, in light of perspectives beyond justice.

ESSAYS ON MORAL DEVELOPMENT

VOLUME I

The Philosophy of Moral Development

PART ONE

Moral Stages and the
Aims of Education

⊱⊰

THIS VOLUME on philosophy begins with education because I think that philosophic issues are best approached first as educational issues." This was also the assumption of the two philosophers, Plato and Dewey, on whom I draw in Part One. Both explicitly equated education with the practice of philosophy, and both were practicing educators. Philosophic theory is the reflective analysis of, and justification for, fundamental normative ideas such as the ideas of truth and justice. Considering how these ideas should enter into the education of the young is the best path to the philosophic theory of the ideas themselves.

The chapters in Part One portray the child and adolescent as natural philosophers, concerned with such fundamental categories of experience as the idea of justice. Therefore, I argue, teachers too must be concerned with the idea of justice. Relativity of values is another philosophic issue that must also be an educational concern for teachers, because their implicit stance on this issue determines their response to value problems arising in the classroom.

My first chapter starts out by noting that, like it or not, teachers are moral educators (or miseducators) as creators of the "hidden curriculum" of the moral climate of the classroom. Insofar as educators do not critically examine the values that govern life and discipline in the classroom or simply opt for enforcing existing conventions, they "cop out" from really dealing with the values issue, and they engage in subtle or blatant forms of indoctrination. Therefore, teachers must face Socrates' question "What is virtue?"

A first strategy for dealing with values in education has usually been called "character education." A traditional answer to the question "What is virtue?" is to enumerate a list or "bag" of virtues. I criticize such a conception of virtue in different ways in all three chapters in Part One. The problem with the "bag of virtues" approach is that it equates the teaching of virtue with indoctrination of conventional or social consensus morality. This is a theory of virtue that commends itself to the "common sense" of those whose view of morality is conventional. In more elaborated form, a theory of the virtues usually rests on social relativism, the doctrine that, given the relativity of values, the only objective framework for studying values is relative to the majority values of the group or society in question, an assumption I criticize.

In a sense, the view of moral education as *character education for a set of virtues* never gets a complete fair hearing in this volume. To do so would mean a full restatement of a psychological and philosophic tradition that runs from Aristotle to such modern philosopher-psychologists as Richard S. Peters. Volume II has a more explicated statement and critique of the psychological research effort to study moral character as a set of virtues, a critique going back in detail to the assumptions and findings of Hartshorne and May in the 1920s. It is a fair statement of the history of psychological research in the field to say that the study of character as a set of virtues has not been a flourishing or successful research paradigm.

My philosophical critique of the "bag of virtues" approach is mainly a critique of "cultural transmission" or indoctrination strategies of education. In these chapters, I do not present or critique the view of writers such as Peters, who would say that moral education is a two-phase process. According to that view, parents and educators of young children must necessarily first rely on cultural transmission, inculcating a set of virtues before (or at the same time as) stimulating reflective moral development under conditions of free moral discussion. This mixture of indoctrination and reason is the solution of Plato's *Republic,* although it is not part of the original Socratic viewpoint elaborated in Chapter 2. Plato recognized, however, that indoctrinative moral education presupposed a just society, which he conceived to be a utopian community guided by philosopher-kings. In Volume III, on education, I report on a "just community" school, governed by participatory democracy instead of philosopher-kings. The teachers in this school go beyond Socratic moral dialogue to advocate the virtues of justice and community intended to guide the school. Because the school is governed by a democratic process rather than by a hidden process based on authority, the danger of indoctrination through advocacy can be checked.

A second strategy that I rule out as a response to the question "What is virtue?" is that provided by values clarification. Although the clarification of student values is an essential part of moral education, values clarification neither clarifies nor resolves questions of the nature of virtue, about which students and teachers alike must be concerned. In some sense, it is the modern equivalent of the practice of relativistic Greek Sophists such as Protagoras, a practice developing better articulation of the student's values without concern for the intrinsic worth of these values.

Chapter 1 suggests a way out from the Scylla of indoctrination and the Charybdis of "laid-back" relativism or values clarification—Socratic dialogue to stimulate stage development. I introduce in a brief and relatively superficial way some of the psychological findings that make Socratic dialogue for development a viable solution to the dilemma of indoctrination versus relativism.

Chapter 2 starts with the limitations of psychology for answering the Socratic philosophical question "What is virtue?" It assumes the importance of asking this prior question before giving psychological answers to Meno's question as to whether virtue can be taught. My procedure in this chapter on "Education for Justice" is not to derive a theory of virtue and its teaching from our psychological studies but to report some psychological findings that support the assumptions of Socrates about justice. I offer a rhetorical invitation to consider the moral theories that guided Socrates and Martin Luther King as moral educators, on the grounds that, if the practice of Socrates cannot be lightly dismissed, neither can the theory that inspired it. The lecture on which this chapter is based was given shortly after the death of Martin Luther King and was an effort to reaffirm the meaning of his life.

Chapter 3, "Development as the Aim of Education," is one of the few pieces I have written that I believe stands without the need of revision from the perspective of a later time. This is perhaps because it is "warmed-over" Dewey, a restatement for the current generation of a viewpoint that Dewey elaborated in writing from the turn of the century until 1938, when he wrote *Experience and Education*. The

chapter shifts attention from "What is virtue?" to "What is development?" a question presupposed by my efforts to deal with indoctrination and relativity in education in the first two chapters.

Chapter 3 develops in a more general and complete form points
made in the first two chapters that argue against indoctrinative and
relativistic approaches to education. The fundamental philosophical
and psychological assumptions of the two major educational approaches or ideologies—cultural transmission and romanticism—are
clarified and critiqued. The cultural transmission ideology maintains
that values are determined by each particular society. Teaching is a
process of imparting such values to children, who are viewed as passive learners. The romantic ideology turns to the individual as the
source of values rather than the society. In opposition to the cultural
transmission ideology, the ideology of romanticism sees the educational
process as one that should free the individual for natural inner-direct-
ed growth. Romanticism is based on the psychological theory of ma-
turationism, which conceptualizes the individual as possessing in an
embryonic form all the important elements necessary for growth.

I argue that only a third ideology can resolve the conflict between
the society and the individual as the determinant of values. That ideology is *progressive interactionism,* which escapes the trap of either
indoctrination or relativism. Such an ideology is philosophically sound
because it first rationally attempts to define and justify what should be
the ends of education. Moreover, it is psychologically sound because it
is supported empirically by cognitive developmental research. In discussing the relationship of psychology to education, I offer a notion
that is developed further in Part Two of this volume and throughout
Volume III, on education—"the psychologist's fallacy." From the educational point of view, the "psychologist's fallacy" is the fallacy that
the laws and generalizations that order psychological research data are
necessarily the foundations of a valid educational practice. The mistake made by psychologists who commit this fallacy is that they attempt to derive prescriptions about desirable educational aims and
practices from descriptions about psychological functioning. I elaborate a critique of the "psychologist's fallacy" contained in the social
relativism of, for instance, the theory of Skinner. He may dispense
with ideas of freedom and dignity to arrive at a theory valid for explaining studies of rewards in children and animals, but a theory "be-

yond freedom and dignity" must have serious flaws as a guide to teacher behavior.

Chapters 1 and 2 introduce the reader to the six moral stages. These descriptions are outdated where they refer to young adolescent data as examples of Stage 6, which later work (reported in Volume II) treats as a rare stage of adult development rather than something found and scored among young adolescents. This confusion is embodied in our use of an appeal to conscience or guilt and an appeal to the sacredness of human life as criteria of Stage 6. These appeals are already often present at Stage 4 in our current scoring system. With the exception of Stage 6, current cross-cultural studies reported in Volume II do support my statement in Chapter 1 of the cultural universality of the stages.

1. Indoctrination Versus Relativity in Value Education

THE FIRST point I want to make is that the problem raised by my title, "Indoctrination Versus Relativity in Value Education," requires coming to grips with morality and moral education. I hope I will be able to make moral education a somewhat less forbidding term by presenting my own approach to it. My basic task, however, is not to convince you of my approach to moral education but to convince you that the only way to solve the problems of relativity and indoctrination in value education is to formulate a notion of *moral development* that is justified philosophically and psychologically.

Although *moral education* has a forbidding sound to teachers, they constantly practice it. They tell children what to do, make evaluations of children's behavior, and direct children's relations in the classrooms. Sometimes teachers do these things without being aware that they are engaging in moral education, but the children are aware of it. For example, my second-grade son told me that he did not want to be one of the bad boys. Asked "Who were the bad boys?" he replied, "The ones who don't put their books back where they belong and get yelled at." His teacher would have been surprised to know that her concerns with classroom management defined for her children what she and her school thought were basic moral values or that she was engaged in value indoctrination.

Most teachers are aware that they are teaching values, like it or not, and are very concerned as to whether this teaching is unjustified indoctrination. In particular, they are uncertain as to whether their own moral opinions should be presented as "moral truths," whether they should be expressed merely as personal opinion or should be omitted

Lawrence Kohlberg presented this paper at the eighteenth summer conference of the Institute on Religion in an Age of Science, Star Island, New Hampshire, July 31–August 6, 1971.

This chapter, "Indoctrination Versus Relativity in Value Education," first appeared in *Zygon 6* (1971): 285–310. Copyright © 1971 Joint publication board of *Zygon* and the University of Chicago.

from classroom discussion entirely. As an example, an experienced junior high school teacher told us,

My class deals with morality and right and wrong quite a bit. I don't expect all of them to agree with me; each has to satisfy himself according to his own convictions, as long as he is sincere and thinks he is pursuing what is right. I often discuss cheating this way but I always get *defeated*, because they still argue cheating is all right. After you accept the idea that kids have the right to build a position with logical arguments, you have to accept what they come out with, even though you drive at it ten times a year and they still come out with the same conclusion.

This teacher's confusion is apparent. She believes everyone should "have his own ideas," and yet she is most unhappy if this leads to a point where some of these ideas include the notion that "it's all right to cheat." In other words, she is smack up against the problem of relativity of values in moral education. Using this teacher as an example, I will attempt to demonstrate that moral education can be free from the charge of cultural relativity and arbitrary indoctrination that inhibits her when she talks about cheating.

Cop-Out Solutions to the Relativity Problem

To begin with, I want to reject a few cop-outs or false solutions sometimes suggested as solving the relativity problem. One is to call moral education *socialization*. Sociologists have sometimes claimed that moralization in the interests of classroom management and maintenance of the school as a social system is a hidden curriculum; that it performs hidden services in helping children adapt to society (Jackson, 1968). They have argued that, since praise and blame on the part of teachers is a necessary aspect of the socialization process, the teacher does not have to consider the psychological and philosophic issues of moral education. In learning to conform to the teacher's expectations and the school rules, children are becoming socialized, they are internalizing the norms and standards of society. I argue in Chapter 2 why this approach is a cop-out. In practice, it means that we call the teacher's yelling at her students for not putting their books away *socialization*. To label it *socialization* does not legitimate it as valid education, nor does it remove the charge of arbitrary indoctrination from it. Basically, this sociological argument implies that respect for social authority is a moral good in itself. Stated in different terms, the notion that it is valid for the teacher to have an unreflective hidden curriculum is based on the notion that the teacher is the agent of the state, the church, or the social system, rather than being a free moral agent dealing with children who are free moral agents. The notion that the teacher is the agent of the state is taken for granted in some educational systems, such as that of the Soviets. However, the moral curriculum is not hidden in Soviet education; it is done explicitly and well as straight indoctrination (Bronfenbrenner, 1968). For the moment, I will not argue what is wrong with indoctrination but will assume that it is incompatible with the conceptions of civil liberties that are central not only to American democracy but to any just social system.

Let us turn now to the second cop-out. This is to rely on vaguely positive and honorific-sounding terms such as "moral values" or "moral and spiritual values." We can see in the following statements how a program called "Teaching Children Values in the Upper Elementary School" (Carr and Wellenberg, 1966) relies on a vague usage of "moral and spiritual values":

Many of our national leaders have expressed anxiety about an increasing lack of concern for personal moral and spiritual values. Throughout history, nations have sought value systems to help people live congenially. The Golden Rule and the Ten Commandments are examples of such value systems. Each pupil needs to acquire a foundation of sound values to help him act correctly and make proper choices between right and wrong, truth and untruth. The teacher can develop a sound value system in the following ways:

1. Be a good example.
2. Help young people to assess conflict situations and to gain insight into the development of constructive values and attitudes. Situations arise daily in which pupils can receive praise that will reinforce behavior that exemplified desired values.
3. Show young people how to make generalizations concerning experience through evaluation and expression of desirable values.
4. Help students acquire an understanding of the importance of values that society considers worthwhile.
5. Aid children to uphold and use positive values when confronted by adverse pressure from peers. [p. 11]

The problem, however, is to define these "positive values." We may agree that "positive values" are desirable, but the term conceals the fact that teachers, children, and societies have different ideas as to

what constitutes "positive values." Although Carr and Wellenberg cite
the Ten Commandments and the Golden Rule as "value systems
sought by nations," they also could have used the code of the Hitler or
of the communist youth as examples of "value systems sought by
nations."

I raise the issue of the "relativity of values" in this context because
the words *moral, positive,* and *values* are interpreted by each teacher
in a different way, depending on the teacher's own values and
standards.

This becomes clear when we consider our third cop-out. This is the
cop-out of defining moral values in terms of what I call a "bag of
virtues." By a "bag of virtues," I mean a set of personality traits generally considered to be positive. Defining the aims of moral education
in terms of a set of "virtues" is as old as Aristotle, who said, "Virtue . . .
[is] of two kinds, intellectual and moral. . . . [The moral] virtues we get
by first exercising them . . . we become just by doing just acts, temperate by doing temperate acts, brave by doing brave acts."

The attraction of such an approach is evident. Although it is true
that people often cannot agree on details of right and wrong or even
on fundamental moral principles, we all think such "traits" as honesty
and responsibility are good things. By adding enough traits to the virtue bag, we eventually get a list that contains something to suit
everyone.

This approach to moral education was widely prevalent in the public schools in the 1920s and 1930s and was called "character education." The educators and psychologists, such as Havighurst and Taba
(1949), who developed these approaches defined character as the sum
total of a set of "those traits of personality which are subject to the
moral sanctions of society."

One difficulty with this approach to moral character is that everyone has his own bag. However, the problem runs deeper than the
composition of a given list of virtues and vices. Although it may be
true that the notion of teaching virtues, such as honesty or integrity,
arouses little controversy, it is also true that a vague consensus on the
goodness of these virtues conceals a great deal of actual disagreement
over their definitions. What is one person's "integrity" is another person's "stubbornness," what is one person's honesty in "expressing
your true feelings" is another person's insensitivity to the feelings of
others. This is evident in controversial fields of adult behavior. Student

protesters view their behavior as reflecting the virtues of altruism, idealism, awareness, and courage. Those in opposition regard the same behavior as reflecting the vices of irresponsibility and disrespect for "law and order." Although this difficulty can be recognized clearly in college education, it is easier for teachers of younger children to think that their judgments in terms of the bag of virtues are objective and independent of their own value biases. However, a parent will not agree that a child's specific failure to obey an "unreasonable" request by the teacher was wrong, even if the teacher calls the act "uncooperative," as some teachers are prone to do.

I have summarized three cop-outs from the relativity problem and rejected them. Socialization, teaching positive values, and developing a bag of virtues all leave the teacher where she was—stuck with her own personal value standards and biases to be imposed on her students. There is one last cop-out to the relativity problem. That is to lie back and enjoy it or encourage it. In the new social studies, this is called *value clarification*.

As summarized by Engel (in Simon, 1971, p. 902), this position holds that

In the consideration of values, there is no single correct answer, but value clarification is supremely important. One must contrast value clarification and value inculcation. Inculcation suggests that the learner has limited control and hence limited responsibility in the development of his own values. He needs to be told what values are or what he should value.

This is not to suggest, however, that nothing is ever inculcated. As a matter of fact, in order to clarify values, at least one principle needs to be adopted by all concerned. Perhaps the only way the principle can be adopted is through some procedure which might best be termed *inculcation*. That principle might be stated as follows: in the consideration of values there is no single correct answer. More specifically it might be said that the adequate posture both for students and teachers in clarifying values is openness.

Although the basic premise of this value clarification approach is that "everyone has his own values," it is further advocated that children can and should learn (1) to be more aware of their own values and how they relate to their decisions, (2) to make their values consistent and to order them in hierarchies for decisions, (3) to be more aware of the divergencies between their value hierarchies and those of others, and (4) to learn to tolerate these divergencies. In other words, although values are regarded as arbitrary and relative, there may be universal, rational strategies for making decisions that maximize these values. Part of this rational strategy is to recognize that values are relative. Within this set of premises, it is quite logical to teach that values are relative as part of the overall program.

An elaboration of this approach can be found in *Decision Making: A Guide for Teachers Who Would Help Preadolescent Children Become Imaginative and Responsible Decision Makers* (Dodder and Dodder, 1968). In a portion of this book, modern social scientific perspectives are used to develop a curriculum unit entitled "Why Don't We All Make the Same Decisions?" A set of classroom materials and activities are then presented to demonstrate to children the following propositions: (1) we don't all make the same decisions because our values are different; (2) our values tend to originate outside ourselves; (3) our values are different because each of us has been influenced by different important others; and (4) our values are different because each of us has been influenced by a different cultural environment.

The teacher is told to have the children discuss moral dilemmas in such a way as to reveal those different values. As an example, one child might make a moral decision in terms of avoiding punishment, another in terms of the welfare of other people, another in terms of certain rules, another in terms of getting the most for himself. The children are then to be encouraged to discuss their values with each other and to recognize that everyone has different values. Whether or not "the welfare of others" is a more adequate value than "avoiding punishment" is not an issue to be raised by the teacher. Rather, the teacher is instructed to teach only that "our values are different."

Indeed, acceptance of the idea that *all* values are relative does, logically, lead to the conclusion that the teacher should not attempt to teach *any* particular moral values. This leaves the teacher in the quandary of our teacher who could not successfully argue against cheating. The students of a teacher who has been successful in communicating moral relativism will believe, like the teacher, that "everyone has his own bag" and that "everyone should keep doing his thing." If one of these students has learned his relativity lesson, when he is caught cheating he will argue that he did nothing wrong. The basis of his argument will be that his own hierarchy of values, which may be different from that of the teacher, made it right for him to cheat. Although recognizing that other people believe that cheating is wrong, he himself holds the "value" that one should cheat when the opportunity presents itself. If teachers want to be consistent and retain their relativistic beliefs, they would have to concede.

Now I am not criticizing the value clarification approach itself. It is a basic and valuable component of the new social studies curricula, as I have discussed (1973). My point is, rather, that value clarification is not a sufficient solution to the relativity problem. Furthermore, the actual teaching of relativism is itself an indoctrination or teaching of a fixed belief, a belief that we are going to show is not true scientifically or philosophically (see Chapter 4).

A Typological Scheme on the Stages of Moral Thought

In other words, I am happy to report that I can propose a solution to the relativity problem that has plagued philosophers for three thousand years. I can say this with due modesty because it did not depend on being smart. It only happened that my colleagues and I were the first people in history to do detailed cross-cultural studies on the development of moral thinking.

The following dilemma should clarify the issue:

The Heinz Dilemma

In Europe, a woman was near death from a very bad disease, a special kind of cancer. There was one drug that the doctors thought might save her. It was a form of radium that a druggist in the same town had recently discovered. The drug was expensive to make, but the druggist was charging ten times what the drug cost him to make. He paid $200 for the radium and charged $2,000 for a small dose of the drug. The sick woman's husband, Heinz, went to everyone he knew to borrow the money, but he could get together only about $1,000, which was half of what it cost. He told the druggist that his wife was dying and asked him to sell it cheaper or let him pay later. But the druggist said, "No, I discovered the drug and I'm going to make money from it." Heinz got desperate and broke into the man's store to steal the drug for his wife.

Should the husband have done that? Was it right or wrong? Is your decision that it is right (or wrong) objectively right, is it morally universal, or is it your personal opinion? If you think it is morally right to steal the drug, you must face the fact that it is legally wrong. What is the basis of your view that it is morally right, then, more than your

personal opinion? Is it anything that can be agreed on? If you think
so, let me report the results of a National Opinion Research Survey on
the question, asked of a representative sample of adult Americans.
Seventy-five percent said it was wrong to steal, though most said they
might do it.

Can one take anything but a relativist position on the question? By
a relativist position, I mean a position like that of Bob, a high school
senior. He said, "There's a million ways to look at it. Heinz had a
moral decision to make. Was it worse to steal or let his wife die? In
my mind, I can either condemn him or condone him. In this case, I
think it was fine. But possibly the druggist was working on a capitalist
morality of supply and demand."

I went on to ask Bob, "Would it be wrong if he didn't steal it?"

Bob replied, "It depends on how he is oriented morally. If he thinks
it's worse to steal than to let his wife die, then it would be wrong what
he did. It's all relative; what I would do is steal the drug. I can't say
that's right or wrong or that it's what everyone should do."

But even if you agree with Bob's relativism you may not want to go
as far as he did. He started the interview by wondering if he could
answer because he "questioned the whole terminology, the whole moral bag." He continued, "But then I'm also an incredible moralist, a
real puritan in some sense and moods. My moral judgment and the
way I perceive things morally changes very much when my mood
changes. When I'm in a cynical mood, I take a cynical view of morals,
but still, whether I like it or not, I'm terribly moral in the way I look
at things. But I'm not too comfortable with it." Bob's moral perspective was well expressed in the late Joe Gould's poem called "My Religion." Brief and to the point, the poem said, "In winter I'm a
Buddhist, in the summer I'm a nudist."

Now, Bob's relativism rests on a confusion. The confusion is that
between relativity as the social science fact that different people *do*
have different moral values and relativity as the philosophic claim that
people *ought* to have different moral values, that no moral values are
justified for all people.

To illustrate, I quote a not atypical response of one of my graduate
students to the same moral dilemma. She said, "I think he should steal
it because if there is any such thing as a universal human value, it is
the value of life, and that would justify it."

I then asked her, "Is there any such thing as a universal human value?" and she answered, "No, all values are relative to your culture."

She began by claiming that one ought to act in terms of the universal value of human life, implying that human life is a universal value in the sense that it is logical and desirable for all people to respect all human life, that one can demonstrate to other people that it is logical and desirable to act in this way. If she were clear in her thinking, she would see that the fact that all people do not always act in terms of this value does not contradict the claim that all people ought to always act in accordance with it. Because she made this confusion, she ended in total confusion.

What I am going to claim is that if we distinguish the issues of universality as fact and the possibility of universal moral ideals we get a positive answer to both questions. As far as facts go, I claim just the opposite of what Dodder and Dodder (1968) claimed to be basic social science truths. I claim that

1. We often make different decisions and yet have the same basic moral values.
2. Our values tend to originate inside ourselves as we process our social experience.
3. In every culture and subculture of the world, both the same basic moral values and the same steps toward moral maturity are found. Although social environments directly produce different specific beliefs (for example, smoking is wrong, eating pork is wrong), they do not engender different basic moral principles (for example, "consider the welfare of others," "treat other people equally," and so on).
4. Basic values are different largely because we are at different levels of maturity in thinking about basic moral and social issues and concepts. Exposure to others more mature than ourselves helps stimulate maturity in our own value process.

All parents know that the basic values of their children do not come from the outside, from the parents, although many wish they did. For example, at the age of four my son joined the pacifist and vegetarian movement and refused to eat meat because, he said, it is bad to kill animals. In spite of his parents' attempts to dissuade him by arguing about the difference between justified and unjustified killing, he remained a vegetarian for six months. However, he did recognize that some forms of killing were "legitimate." One night I read to him from a book about Eskimo life that included a description of a seal-killing expedition. While listening to the story, he became very angry and said, "You know, there is one kind of meat I would eat, Eskimo meat. It's bad to kill animals so it's all right to eat Eskimos."

This episode illustrates (1) that children often generate their own moral values and maintain them in the face of cultural training, and (2) that these values have universal roots. Every child believes it is bad to kill because regard for the lives of others or pain at death is a natural empathic response, although it is not necessarily universally and consistently maintained. In this example, the value of life led both to vegetarianism and to the desire to kill Eskimos. This latter desire comes also from a universal value tendency: a belief in justice or reciprocity here expressed in terms of revenge or punishment (at higher levels, the belief that those who infringe on the rights of others cannot expect their own rights to be respected).

I quoted my son's response because it is shockingly different from the way you think and yet it has universal elements you will recognize. What is the shocking difference between my son's way of thinking and your own? If you are a psychoanalyst, you will start thinking about oral cannibalistic fantasies and defenses against them and all that. However, that is not really what the difference is at all. You do not have to be cannibalistic to wonder why it is right for humans to kill and eat animals but it is not right for animals or humans to kill and eat humans. The response really shows that my son was a philosopher, like every young child: he wondered about things that most grown-ups take for granted. If you want to study children, however, you have to be a bit of a philosopher yourself and ask the moral philosopher's question: "Why is it all right to kill and eat animals but not humans?" I wonder how many of you can give a good answer. In any case, Piaget started the modern study of child development by recognizing that the child, like the adult philosopher, was puzzled by the basic questions of life: by the meaning of space, time, causality, life, death, right and wrong, and so on. What he found was that the child asked all the great philosophic questions but answered them in a very different way from the adults. This way was so different that Piaget called the difference a difference in stage or quality of thinking, rather than a difference in amount of knowledge or accuracy of thinking.

The difference in thinking between you and my son, then, is basically a difference in stage.

My own work on morality started from Piaget's notions of stages and Piaget's notion that the child was a philosopher. Inspired by Jean Piaget's (1948) pioneering effort to apply a structural approach to moral development, I have gradually elaborated over the years a typological scheme describing general stages of moral thought that can be defined independently of the specific content of particular moral decisions or actions. We studied seventy-five American boys from early adolescence on. These youths were continually presented with hypothetical moral dilemmas, all deliberately philosophical, some found in medieval works of casuistry. On the basis of their reasoning about these dilemmas at a given age, we constructed the typology of definite and universal levels of development in moral thought.

The typology contains three distinct levels of moral thinking, and within each of these levels are two related stages. These levels and stages may be considered separate moral philosophies, distinct views of the social-moral world.

We can speak of the children as having their own morality or series of moralities. Adults seldom listen to children's moralizing. If children throw back a few adult chichés and behave themselves, most parents—and many anthropologists and psychologists as well—think that the children have adopted or internalized the appropriate parental standards.

Actually, as soon as we talk with children about morality we find that they have many ways of making judgments that are not "internalized" from the outside and that do not come in any direct and obvious way from parents, teachers, or even peers.

The preconventional level is the first of three levels of moral thinking; the second level is conventional; and the third is postconventional or autonomous. Although preconventional children are often "well behaved" and responsive to cultural labels of good and bad, they interpret these labels in terms of their physical consequences (punishment, reward, exchange of favors) or in terms of the physical power of those who enunciate the rules and labels of good and bad.

This level is usually occupied by children aged four to ten, a fact well known to sensitive observers of children. The capacity of "properly behaved" children of this age to engage in cruel behavior when there are holes in the power structure is sometimes noted as tragic

(*Lord of the Flies* and *High Wind in Jamaica*), sometimes as comic (Lucy in *Peanuts*).

The second or conventional level also can be described as *conformist*—but that is perhaps too smug a term. Maintaining the expectations and rules of the individual's family, group, or nation is perceived as valuable in its own right. There is a concern not only with conforming to the individual's social order but in maintaining, supporting, and justifying this order.

The postconventional level is characterized by a major thrust toward autonomous moral principles that have validity and application apart from authority of the groups or people who hold them and apart from the individual's identification with those people or groups.

Within each of these three levels, there are two discernible stages. The following paragraphs explain the dual moral stages of each level just described.

Definition of Moral Stages

Preconventional Level

At this level, the child is responsive to cultural rules and labels of good and bad, right or wrong, but interprets these labels in terms of either the physical or the hedonistic consequences of action (punishment, reward, exchange of favors) or in terms of the physical power of those who enunciate the rules and labels. The level is divided into the following two stages:

Stage 1. The Punishment and Obedience Orientation

The physical consequences of action determine its goodness or badness regardless of the human meaning or value of these consequences. Avoidance of punishment and unquestioning deference to power are valued in their own right.

Stage 2. The Instrumental Relativist Orientation

Right action consists of that which instrumentally satisfies one's needs and occasionally the needs of others. Human relations are viewed in terms like those of the marketplace. Elements of fairness, reciprocity, and equal sharing are present, but they are always interpreted in a physical, pragmatic way. Reciprocity is a matter of "You scratch my back and I'll scratch yours."

Conventional Level

At this level, maintaining the expectations of the individual's family, group, or nation is perceived as valuable in its own right, regardless of immediate and obvious consequences. The attitude is not only one of conformity to personal expectations and social order, but of loyalty to it, of actively maintaining, supporting, and justifying the order and of identifying with the people or group involved in it. At this level, there are the following two stages:

Stage 3. The Interpersonal Concordance or "Good Boy–Nice Girl" Orientation

Good behavior is that which pleases or helps others and is approved by them. There is much conformity to stereotypical images of what is majority or "natural" behavior. Behavior is frequently judged by intention—the judgment "he means well" becomes important for the first time. One earns approval by being "nice."

Stage 4. Society Maintaining Orientation

There is an orientation toward authority, fixed rules, and the maintenance of the social order. Right behavior consists of doing one's duty, showing respect for authority, and maintaining the given social order for its own sake.

Postconventional, Autonomous, or Principled Level

At this level, there is a clear effort to define moral values and principles that have validity and application apart from the authority of the groups or people holding these principles and apart from the individual's own identification with these groups. This level again has two stages:

Stage 5. The Social Contract Orientation

Right action tends to be defined in terms of general individual rights and in terms of standards that have been critically examined and agreed on by the whole society. There is a clear awareness of the relativism of personal values and opinions and a corresponding emphasis on procedural rules for reaching consensus. Aside from what is constitutionally and democratically agreed on, the right is a matter of personal "values" and "opinion." The result is an emphasis on the

"legal point of view," but with an emphasis on the possibility of changing law in terms of rational considerations of social utility (rather than freezing it in terms of Stage 4 "law and order"). Outside the legal realm, free agreement and contract are the binding elements of obligation. This is the "official" morality of the American government and Constitution.

Stage 6. The Universal Ethical Principle Orientation

Right is defined by the decision of conscience in accord with self-chosen ethical principles appealing to logical comprehensiveness, universality, and consistency. These principles are abstract and ethical (the Golden Rule, the categorical imperative); they are not concrete moral rules such as the Ten Commandments. At heart, these are universal principles of justice, of the reciprocity and equality of human rights, and of respect for the dignity of human beings as individuals.

To understand what these stages mean concretely, let us look at them with regard to two of twenty-five basic moral concepts or aspects used to form the dilemmas we used in our research. One such aspect, for instance, is "motive given for rule obedience or moral action." In this instance, the six stages look like this:

1. Obey rules to avoid punishment.
2. Conform to obtain rewards, have favors returned, and so on.
3. Conform to avoid disapproval and dislike by others.
4. Conform to avoid censure by legitimate authorities and resultant guilt.
5. Conform to maintain the respect of the impartial spectator judging in terms of community welfare.
6. Conform to avoid self-condemnation.

In another of these twenty-five moral aspects, the value of human life, the six stages can be defined thus:

1. The value of human life is confused with the value of physical objects and is based on the social status or physical attributes of the possessor.
2. The value of human life is seen as instrumental to the satisfaction of the needs of its possessor or of other people.

3. The value of human life is based on the empathy and affection of family members and others toward its possessor.
4. Life is conceived as sacred in terms of its place in a categorical moral or religious order of rights and duties.
5. Life is valued both in terms of its relation to community welfare and in terms of life being a universal human right.
6. Human life is sacred—a universal human value of respect for the individual.

I have called this scheme a *typology*. This is because about 67 percent of most people's thinking is at a single stage, regardless of the moral dilemma involved. We call our types *stages* because they seem to represent an invariant developmental sequence. "True" stages come one at a time and always in the same order.

In our stages, all movement is forward in sequence and does not skip steps. Children may move through these stages at varying speeds, of course, and may be found half in and half out of a particular stage. Individuals may stop at any given stage and at any age, but if they continue to move, they must move in accord with these steps. Moral reasoning of the conventional kind or Stages 3–4, never occurs before the preconventional Stage 1 and Stage 2 thought has taken place. No adult in Stage 4 has gone through Stage 5, but all Stage 5 adults have gone through Stage 4.

Although the evidence is not complete, my study strongly suggests that moral change fits the stage pattern just described.

As a single example of our findings of stage sequence, take the progress of two boys on the aspect "the value of human life." The first boy, Tommy, who had suggested that one should perhaps steal for an important person, is asked, "Is it better to save the life of one important person or a lot of unimportant people?" At age ten, he answers, "All the people that aren't important because one man just has one house, maybe a lot of furniture, but a whole bunch of people have an awful lot of furniture, and some of these poor people might have a lot of money and it doesn't look it."

Clearly Tommy is Stage 1: he confuses the value of a human being with the value of the property he possesses. Three years later (age thirteen), Tommy's conceptions of life's values are most clearly elicited by the question "Should the doctor 'mercy kill' a fatally ill woman requesting death because of her pain?" He answers, "Maybe it would

be good to put her out of pain, she'd be better off that way. But the husband wouldn't want it, it's not like an animal. If a pet dies you can get along without it—it isn't something you really need. Well, you can get a new wife, but it's not really the same."

Here his answer is Stage 2: the value of the woman's life is partly contingent on its instrumental value to her husband, who cannot replace her as easily as he can a pet.

Three years later still (age sixteen), Tommy's conception of life's value is elicited by the same question, to which he replies, "It might be best for her, but her husband—it's human life—not like an animal; it just doesn't have the same relationship that a human being does to a family. You can become attached to a dog, but nothing like a human, you know."

Now Tommy has moved from a Stage 2 instrumental view of the woman's value to a Stage 3 view based on the husband's distinctively human emphathy and love for someone in his family. Equally clearly, it lacks any basis for a universal human value of the woman's life, which would hold if she had no husband or if her husband did not love her. Tommy, then, has moved step by step through three stages during the age ten to sixteen. Although bright (IQ 120), he is a slow developer in moral judgment.

Let us take another boy, Richard, to show us sequential movement through the remaining three steps. At age thirteen, Richard said about the mercy killing, "If she requests it, it's really up to her. She is in such terrible pain, just the same as people are always putting animals out of their pain," and in general showed a mixture of Stage 2 and Stage 3 responses concerning the value of life. At sixteen, he said, "I don't know. In one way, it's murder, it's not right or privilege of man to decide who shall live and who should die. God put life into everybody on earth and you're taking away something from that person that came directly from God, and you're destroying something that is very sacred, it's in a way part of God and it's almost destroying a part of God when you kill a person. There's something of God in everyone."

Here Richard clearly displays a Stage 4 concept of life as sacred in terms of its place in a categorical moral or religious order. The value of human life is universal; it is true for all humans. It still, however, depends on something else—on respect for God and God's authority; it is not an autonomous human value. Presumably if God told Richard to murder, as God commanded Abraham to murder Isaac, he would do so.

At age twenty, Richard said to the same question, "There are more and more people in the medical profession who think it is a hardship on everyone, the person, the family, when you know they are going to die. When a person is kept alive by an artificial lung or kidney, it's more like being a vegetable than being a human. If it's her own choice, I think there are certain rights and privileges that go along with being a human being. I am a human being, and I have certain desires for life, and I think everybody else does too. You have a world of which you are the center, and everybody else does too, and in that sense we're all equal."

Richard's response is clearly Stage 5, in that the value of life is defined in terms of equal and universal human rights in a context of relativity ("You have a world of which you are the center, and in that sense we're all equal") and of concern for utility or welfare consequences.

At twenty-four, Richard says, "A human life, whoever it is, takes precedence over any other moral or legal value. A human life has inherent value whether or not it is valued by a particular individual. The worth of the individual human being is central where the principles of justice and love are normative for all human relationships."

This young man is at Stage 6 in seeing the value of human life as absolute in representing a universal and equal respect for the human as an individual. He has moved step by step through a sequence culminating in a definition of human life as centrally valuable rather than derived from or dependent on social or divine authority.

In a genuine and culturally universal sense, these steps lead toward an increased morality of value judgment, where morality is considered as a form of judging, as it has been in a philosophic tradition running from the analyses of Kant to those of the modern analytic or "ordinary language" philosophers. At Stage 6 people have disentangled judgments of—or language about—human life from status and property values (Stage 1); from its uses to others (Stage 2); from interpersonal affection (Stage 3); and so on; they have a means of moral judgment that is universal and impersonal. Stage 6 people answer in moral words such as *duty* or *morally right* and use them in a way implying universality, ideals and impersonality. They think and speak in phrases such as "regardless of who it was" or "I would do it in spite of punishment."

Universal Invariant Sequence of Moral Development

When I first decided to explore moral development in other cultures, I was told by anthropologist friends that I would have to throw away my culture-bound moral concepts and stories and start from scratch learning a whole new set of values for each new culture. My first try consisted of a brace of villages, one Atayal (Malaysian aboriginal) and the other Taiwanese.

My guide was a young Chinese ethnographer who had written an account of the moral and religious patterns of the Atayal and Taiwanese villages. Taiwanese boys in the ten to thirteen age group were asked about a story involving theft of food: A man's wife is starving to death but the store owner would not give the man any food unless he could pay, and he cannot. Should he break in and steal some food? Why? Many of the boys said, "He should steal the food for his wife because if she dies he'll have to pay for her funeral, and that costs a lot."

My guide was amused by these responses, but I was relieved: they were, of course, "classic" Stage 2 responses. In the Atayal village, funerals were not such a big thing, so the Stage 2 boys said, "He should steal the food because he needs his wife to cook for him."

This means that we have to consult our anthropologists to know what content Stage 2 children will include in instrumental exchange calculations, or what Stage 4 adults will identify as the proper social order. But one certainly does not have to start from scratch. What made my guide laugh was the difference in form between the children's Stage 2 thought and his own, a difference definable independently of particular cultures.

Figures 1.1 and 1.2 indicate the cultural universality of the sequence of stages we have found. Figure 1.1 presents the age trends for middle-class urban boys in the United States, Taiwan, and Mexico. At age ten in each country, the order of use of each stage is the same as the order of its difficulty or maturity.

In the United States, by age sixteen the order is the reverse, from the highest to the lowest, except that Stage 6 is still little used. At age thirteen, the good-boy middle stage (Stage 3) is most used.

The results in Mexico and Taiwan are the same, except that development is a little slower. The most conspicuous feature is that, at the age of sixteen, Stage 5 thinking is much more salient in the United States than in Mexico or Taiwan. Nevertheless, it is present in the

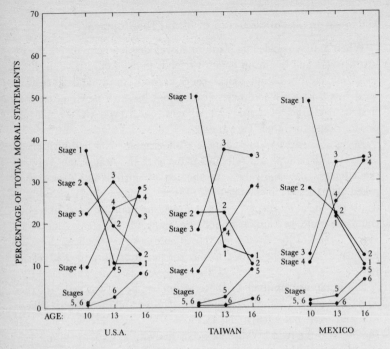

Figure 1.1. Moral development of middle-class urban boys in the United States, Taiwan, and Mexico. At age ten, the stages are used according to difficulty. At age thirteen, Stage 3 is most used by all three groups. At age sixteen, U.S. boys have reversed the order of age ten stages (with the exception of 6). In Taiwan and Mexico, conventional (3–4) stages prevail at age sixteen, with Stage 5 also little used (Kohlberg, 1968a).

other countries, so we know that this is not purely an American democratic construct.

Figure 1.2 shows strikingly similar results from two isolated villages, one in Yucatan, one in Turkey. Although conventional moral thought increases steadily from ages ten to sixteen, it still has not achieved a clear ascendancy over preconventional thought.

Trends for lower-class urban groups are intermediate in the rate of development between those for the middle-class and for the village boys. In the three divergent cultures that I studied, middle-class children were found to be more advanced in moral judgment than matched lower-class children. This was not due to the fact that the

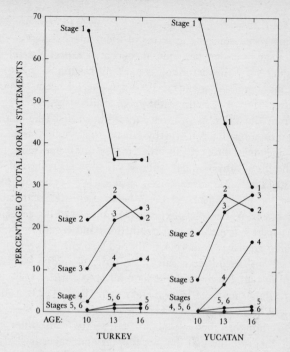

Figure 1.2. Two isolated villages, one in Turkey, the other in Yucatan, show similar patterns in moral thinking. There is no reversal of order, and conventional (stages 3–4) thought does not gain a clear ascendancy over pre-conventional stages at age sixteen (Kohlberg, 1968a).

middle-class children heavily favored some one type of thought that could be seen as corresponding to the prevailing middle-class pattern. Instead, middle-class and working-class children move through the same sequences, but the middle-class children move faster and farther.

This sequence is not dependent on a particular religion or on any religion at all in the usual sense. I found no important differences in the development of moral thinking among Catholics, Protestants, Jews, Buddhists, Moslems, and atheists.

In summary, the nature of our sequence is not significantly affected by widely varying social, cultural, or religious conditions. The only thing that is affected is the rate at which individuals progress through this sequence.

Why should there be such a universal invariant sequence of development? In answering this question, we need first to analyze these developing social concepts in terms of their internal logical structure. At each stage, the same basic moral concept or aspect is defined, but at each higher stage this definition is more differentiated, more integrated, and more general or universal. When one's concept of human life moves from Stage 1 to Stage 2, the value of life becomes more differentiated from the value of property, more integrated (the value of life enters an organizational hierarchy where it is "higher" than property so that one steals property in order to save life), and more universalized (the life of any sentient being is valuable regardless of status or property). The same advance is true at each stage in the hierarchy. Each step of development, then, is a better cognitive organization than the one before it, one that takes account of everything present in the previous stage but making new distinctions and organizes them into a more comprehensive or more equilibrated structure. The fact that this is the case has been demonstrated by a series of studies indicating that children and adolescents comprehend all stages up to their own, but not more than one stage beyond their own (Rest, 1973) And, importantly, they prefer this next stage.

Moral thought, then, seems to behave like all other kinds of thought. Progress through the moral levels and stages is characterized by increasing differentiation and increasing integration, and hence is the same kind of progress that scientific theory represents. Like acceptable scientific theory—or like any theory or structure of knowledge—moral thought may be considered partially to generate its own data as it goes along, or at least to expand so as to contain in a balanced, self-consistent way a wider and wider experiential field. The raw data in the case of our ethical philosophies may be considered as conflicts between roles, or values, or as the social order in which people live.

The social worlds of all people seem to contain the same basic structures. All the societies we have studied have the same basic institutions—family, economy, law, government. In addition, however, all societies are alike because they are societies—systems of defined complementary roles. In order to play a social role in the family, school, or society, children must implicitly take the role of others toward themselves and toward others in the group. These role-taking tendencies form the basis of all social institutions. They represent various patternings of shared or complementary expectations.

In the preconventional and conventional levels (Stages 1-4), moral content or value is largely accidental or culture bound. Anything from "honesty" to "courage in battle" can be the central value. But in the higher postconventional levels, Socrates, Lincoln. Thoreau, and Martin Luther King tend to speak without confusion of tongues, as it were. This is because the ideal principles of any social structure are basically alike, if only because there simply are not that many principles that are articulate, comprehensive, and integrated enough to be satisfying to the human intellect. And most of these principles have gone by the name of justice.

I have discussed at some length the culturally universal sequences of stages of moral judgment. I have not entirely clarified how such a sequence helps to resolve relativistic questioning of moral principles, a task taken up in our Chapter 4, "From *Is* to *Ought*." It is easier to clarify how such a sequence helps resolve the dilemma of relativity versus indoctrination in values education. The sequence provides us with a concept of moral development that can be stimulated by education without indocrination and yet that helps to move student judgment toward more adequate principles.

The way to stimulate stage growth is to pose real or hypothetical dilemmas to students in such a way as to arouse disagreement and uncertainty as to what is right. The teacher's primary role is to present such dilemmas and to ask Socratic questions that arouse student reasoning and focus student listening on one another's reasons.

I noted research by Rest (1973) showing that students prefer the highest stage of reasoning they comprehend but that they do not comprehend more than one stage above their own. As a result, assimilation of reasoning occurs primarily when it is the next stage up from the student's level. Developmental moral discussion thus arouses cognitive-moral conflict and exposes students to reasoning by other students at the next stage above their own.

Using this approach, Blatt and Kohlberg (1975) were able to stimulate one-third of experimental classes of students to advance one stage in a time period in which control classes remained unchanged in moral stage. One year later, the experimental classes retained their relative advance over the control classes.

The developmental approach, first experimentally elaborated by Blatt, is one that any thoughtful classroom teacher may practice. Unlike values clarification, its assumptions are not relativistic but, rather, are based on universal goals and principles. It asks the student for reasons, on the assumption that some reasons are more adequate than others.

The approach differs from indoctrinative approaches because it tries to move student's thinking in a direction that is natural for the student rather than moving the student in the direction of accepting the teacher's moral assumptions. It avoids preaching or didacticism linked to the teacher's authority.

As I have characterized developmental moral education, it is neither an indoctinative or relativistic classroom discussion process. When we shift from a curriculum of moral discussion to the "hidden curriculum" of the classroom, a further set of philosophic and educational issues are raised. In my opinion, the resolution, of these problems rests on creating a democratic classroom in which issues of fairness are settled by discussion and a democratic vote. These issues are discussed in Volume III and presuppose the concepts of justice developed in this volume.

2. Education for Justice: A Modern Statement of the Socratic View

I⊤ IS surely a paradox that a modern psychologist should claim as his most relevant source not Freud, Skinner, or Piaget but the ancient believer in the ideal form of the good. Yet as I have tried to trace the stages of development of morality and to use these stages as the basis of a moral education program, I have realized more and more that its implication was the reassertion of the Socratic faith in the power of the rational good.

It is usually supposed that psychology contributes to moral education by telling us appropriate *methods* of moral teaching and learning. A Skinnerian will speak of proper schedules of reinforcement in moral learning, a Freudian will speak of the importance of the balance of parental love and firmness that will promote superego identification, and so on. When Skinnerians or Freudians speak on the topic of moral education, then, they start by answering yes to Meno's question "Is virtue something that can be taught?" and go on to tell us how. In *Walden Two*, Skinner not only tells us that virtue comes by practice and reinforcement but also designs an ideal republic that educates all its children to be virtuous in this way.

My own response to these questions was more modest. When confronted by a group of parents who asked me, "How can we help make our children virtuous?" I had to answer, as did Socrates, "You must think I am very fortunate to know how virtue is acquired. The fact is that, far from knowing whether it can be taught, I have no idea what

---

This chapter was originally entitled "Education for Justice: A Modern Statement of the Platonic View." I have rephrased it the "Socratic View" to indicate that it draws on Socrates' views as portrayed in Plato's earlier *Dialogues*. These *Dialogues* present a view of moral education as democratic and based on dialogue. In later writings of Plato, such as the *Republic* and the *Laws,* a more indoctrinative and hierarchical view of moral education is advanced.

"Education for Justice: A Modern Statement of the Platonic [Socratic] View" is reprinted by permission of the publishers from *Moral Education: Five Lectures,* Cambridge, Mass.: Harvard University Press, copyright © 1970 by the President and Fellows of Harvard College.

virtue really is." Like most psychologists, I knew that science could teach me nothing as to what virtue is. Science could speak about causal relations, about the relations of means to ends, but it could not speak about ends or values themselves. If I could not define virtue or the ends of moral education, could I really offer advice as to the means by which virtue should be taught? Could it really be argued that the means for teaching obedience to authority are the same as the means for teaching freedom of moral opinion, that the means for teaching altruism are the same as the means for teaching competitive striving, that the making of a good storm trooper involves the same procedures as the making of a philosopher-king?

It appears, then, that we must either be totally silent about moral education or speak to the nature of virtue. In this chapter I shall throw away my graduate school wisdom about the distinction of fact and value and elaborate a view of the nature of virtue like that of Socrates and Plato. Let me summarize some of the elements of this Platonic view (already noted in the introduction to this volume).

- *First,* virtue is ultimately one, not many, and it is always the same ideal form regardless of climate or culture.
- *Second,* the name of this ideal form is justice.
- *Third,* not only is the good one, but virtue is knowledge of the good. He who knows the good chooses the good.
- *Fourth,* the kind of knowledge of the good that is virtue is philosophical knowledge or intuition of the ideal form of the good, not correct opinion or acceptance of conventional beliefs.
- *Fifth,* the good can then be taught, but its teachers must in a certain sense be philosopher-kings.
- *Sixth,* the reason the good can be taught is because we know it all along dimly or at a low level and its teaching is more a calling out than an instruction.
- *Seventh,* the reason we think the good cannot be taught is because the same good is known differently at different levels and direct instruction cannot take place across levels.
- *Eighth,* then the teaching of virtue is the asking of questions and the pointing of the way, not the giving of answers. Moral education is the leading of people upward, not the putting into the mind of knowledge that was not there before.

I will spend little time on my disagreements with Plato except to point out that I conceive of justice as equality instead of Plato's hierarchy. I should note, however, that I have also discussed my views within John Dewey's framework (see Chapter 3). In speaking of a Platonic view, I am not discarding my basic Deweyism, but I am challenging a brand of common sense first enunciated by Aristotle, with which Dewey partly agrees. According to Aristotle's *Ethics,* "Virtue is of two kinds, intellectual and moral. While intellectual virtue owes its birth and growth to teaching, moral virtue comes about as a result of habit. The moral virtues we get by first exercising them; we become just by doing just acts, temperate by doing temperate acts, brave by doing brave acts."

Aristotle then is claiming that there are two spheres, the moral and the intellectual, and that learning by doing is the only real method in the moral sphere. Dewey, of course, does not distinguish the intellectual from the moral and objects to lists of virtues and vices in either area. Nevertheless, Deweyite thinking has lent itself to the Boy Scout approach to moral education, which has dominated American practices in this field and which has its most direct affinities with Aristotle's views.

American educational psychology, like Aristotle, divides the personality up into cognitive abilities, passions or motives, and traits of character. Moral character, then, consists of a "bag of virtues and vices." One of the earliest major American studies of moral character, that done by Hartshorne and May (1928–1930), was conducted in the late 1920s. Their bag of virtues included honesty, service, and self-control. A more recent major study by Havighurst and Taba (1949) added responsibility, friendliness, and moral courage to the Hartshorne and May bag. Aristotle's original bag included temperance, liberality, pride, good temper, truthfulness, and justice. The Boy Scout bag is well known: a Scout shoud be honest, loyal, reverent, clean, and brave.

Given a bag of virtues, it is evident how we build character. Children should be exhorted to practice these virtues, should be told that happiness, fortune, and good repute will follow in their wake; adults around them should be living examples of these virtues; and children should be given daily opportunities to practice them. Daily chores will build responsibility; the opportunity to give to the Red Cross will build service or altruism, and so on.

Let me quote a concrete program of moral education from Jonathan Kozol's book *Death at an Early Age: The Destruction of the Hearts and Minds of Negro Children in the Boston Public School* (1967, pp. 174–176).

There is a booklet published by the Boston Public Schools bearing the title, "A Curriculum Guide in Character Education." This is the list of character traits which the teacher is encouraged to develop in a child: Obedience to duly constituted authority, self-control, responsibility, kindness, perseverance, loyalty, fair play. . . .

The section on obedience begins with the following "selected memory gems." "We must do the thing we must before the thing we may. . . . We are unfit for any trust til we can and do obey—Honor thy father and mother—True obedience is true liberty—The first law that ever God gave to man was a law of obedience."

The section on self-control begins with the necessity for self-discipline by all people. The teacher is then advised to give examples of self-disciplined people: Abraham Lincoln, Charles Lindbergh, Robinson Crusoe, Florence Nightingale, Dwight D. Eisenhower.

It is hardly surprising that this approach to moral education doesn't work. Hartshorne and May found that participation in character education classes of this sort, in the Boy Scouts, and in Sunday school did not lead to any improvement in moral character as measured by experimental tests of honesty, service, and self-control, and more recent research does not provide any more positive evidence as to the effects of character-building programs.

Let me point out, too, that although Kozol's example sounds both particularly systematic and particularly old fashioned, it is in principle quite typical of enlightened public schools throughout the country. As long as teachers direct classroom groups, they must inevitably moralize about rules. They may choose to try to be value neutral and treat all rules as traffic rules; that is, to asssume that definition and maintenance of the rules is a matter of administrative convenience.

Let me cite an example from my observation of an enlightened and effective young fourth-grade teacher. The teacher was in the back of the room working with a project group, the rest of the class engaged with their workbooks. In the front row, a boy said something to his neighbor, who retaliated by quietly spitting in his face. The first boy equally quietly slugged the other, without leaving his seat, by which time the teacher noted the disturbance. She said calmly, "Stop that and get back to your workbooks." The boy who had done the slugging said, "Teacher, I hit him because he spit in my face." The teacher replied, "That wasn't polite; it was rude. Now get back to work, you're supposed to be doing your workbooks." As they went back to work, the boy who had done the spitting said to his opponent with a grin, "I will grant you that; it was rude."

However, even teachers who prefer to keep moralizing oriented to traffic rules have to specify some moral goals. The teacher just mentioned had put together suggestions of the class. The code had the following commandments:

1. Be a good citizen.
2. Be generous by helping our friends.
3. Mind your own business.
4. Work quietly.
5. No fighting.
6. Play nicely and fairly.
7. Be neat and clean.
8. Be prepared.
9. Raise your hand.
10. Be polite.

Although this code lacks a little in depth and completeness, a little more system and we would come up with one of the bags of virtues we have mentioned.

Let me try to systematize my objections to the bag of virtues, because it will start us on the road to a more Platonic view. Your reaction to the Boston program is likely to be similar to that of Kozol. He says,

You look in vain through this list for anything to do with an original child or an independent style; there is an emphasis on obedience characteristics. The whole concept of respect for unearned authority is bitter to children within these kinds of schools. I wonder whether anyone really thinks that you are going to teach character, or anything else by rattling off a list of all the people in America who have struggled to make good. [p. 179]

These comments don't themselves carry us very far, positively. They suggest a new bag of virtues centering on creativity instead of on obedience. They suggest substituting newer and more liberal models (read the name *Langston Hughes* for *Robinson Crusoe* or *Dwight Eisenhower*).

Beyond a greater sympathy for the minds and hearts of black children, Kozol suggests no real solution. He does appear to suggest a solution in another setting, the Newton Junior High School, described by him in a *New York Times Magazine* article (October 29, 1967). There a modern moral education course is called "Man Alone" and is, according to Kozol, "a whirlwind tour of alienation, loneliness, dying, and narcotics with writings from John Donne to Bruno Bettelheim." According to Kozol, in this class a picture of one of the Hell's Angels was projected on the wall in gory, swastika-painted vividness.

"Cool, man, great," a voice shouted.

"That's sick," said another.

"He's honest, anyway," chimed in another. "He's living out his own feelings."

"He's not faking."

Kozol goes on to say, "The teacher then ventured the idea that an alienated person might not be able to be truly creative. A creative person is really alive and noncompulsive; alienation means the opposite."

In this seminar, the class has turned the virtues around 180 degrees so that the Hell's Angels are truly honest and creative, while the teacher uses psychological jargon about compulsivity and alienation to rotate the virtues back partway toward moral conformity. Clearly, this jazzing up of the bag of virtues has no more rational base than the program of the Boston public schools. There is no substitute for a good hard look at what virtue is.

Let us start at the beginning, then. The objection of the psychologist to the bag of virtues is that there are no such things. Virtues and vices are labels by which people award praise or blame to others, but the ways people use praise and blame toward others are not the ways in which they think when making moral decisions themselves. You or I may not find a Hell's Angel truly honest, but he may find himself so. Hartshorne and May (1928–1930) found this out to their dismay forty years ago by their monumental experimental studies of children's cheating and stealing. In brief, they and others since have found that

1. You can't divide the world into honest and dishonest people. Almost everyone cheats some of the time; cheating is distributed in bell-curve fashion around a level of moderate cheating.

2. If a person cheats in one situation, it doesn't mean he or she will or won't in another. There is very little correlation between situational cheating tests. In other words, it is not a character trait of dishonesty that makes children cheat in a given

situation. If it were, you could predict they would cheat in a second situation if they did in the first.

3. People's verbal moral values about honesty have nothing to do with how they act. People who cheat express as much or more moral disapproval of cheating as those who don't cheat.

The fact that there are no traits of character corresponding to the virtues and vices of conventional language should comfort us. Those who try to achieve the bag of virtues prescribed by the culture find themselves in the plight described by the theme song of the show *You're a Good Man, Charlie Brown.*

You're a good man, Charlie Brown. You have humility, nobility and a sense of honor that is very rare indeed. You are kind to all the animals and every little bird. With a heart of gold, you believe what you're told, every single solitary word. You bravely face adversity; you're cheerful through the day; you're thoughtful, brave and courteous. You're a good man, Charlie Brown. You're a prince, and a prince could be a king. With a heart such as yours you could open any door—if only you weren't so wishy-washy.*

If we, like Charlie Brown, define our moral aims in terms of virtues and vices, we are defining them in terms of the praise and blame of others and are caught in the pull of being all things to all people and end up being wishy-washy. The attraction of the bag of virtues approach to moral education is that it encourages the assumption that everyone can be a moral educator. It assumes that any adult of middle-class respectability or virtue knows what virtue is and is qualified to teach it by dint of being adult and respectable. We must all make these assumptions as parents, but perhaps they are not sound. Socrates asked "whether good men have known how to hand on to someone else the goodness that was in themselves" and went on to cite one virtuous Greek leader after another who had nonvirtuous sons. Shortly, I will describe what I believe to be a valid measure of moral maturity. When this measure was given to a group of middle-class men in their twenties and also to their fathers, we found almost no correlation between the two. The morally mature father was no more likely to

*Lyrics from the title song "You're a Good Man, Charlie Brown," from the musical play *You're a Good Man, Charlie Brown,* words and music by Clark Gesner © 1965 and 1967 by Jeremy Music Inc. and reprinted by permission.

have a morally mature son than was a father low on moral development. So numbers now support Socrates' bitter observation that good fathers don't have good sons or don't qualify as teachers of virtue.

In the context of the school, the foolishness of assuming that any teacher is qualified to be a moral educator becomes evident if we ask, "Would this assumption make sense if we were to think of moral education as something carried on between one adult and another?" A good third-grade teacher of the new math and a good math teacher of graduate students operate under much the same set of assumptions. How many moralizing schoolteachers, however, would wish to make the claim that Protagoras made to young graduate students, that "I am rather better than anyone else at helping a man to acquire a good and noble character, worthy of the fee I charge"?

If we think of moral education as something carried on at the adult level, we recognize that the effective moral educator is something of a revolutionary rather than an instiller of virtues. Protagoras could safely collect his fees for improving character because by moral education he meant the teaching of the rhetorical skills for getting ahead. When Socrates really did engage in adult moral education, however, he was brought up on trial for corrupting the Athenian youth. Perhaps there is still nothing more dangerous than the serious teaching of virtue. Socrates was condemned to death, because, as he said in the *Apology,*

I do nothing but go about persuading you all, old and young alike, not to take thought for your person or property, but for the improvement of the soul. I tell you virtue is not given by money, but that from virtue comes money, and every other good of man, public as well as private. This is my teaching, and if this is the doctrine which corrupts the youth, my doctrines are mischievous indeed. Therefore, Men of Athens, either acquit me or not; but whichever you do, understand that I shall never alter my ways not even if I have to die many times.

I stress the revolutionary nature of moral education partly because at this time it is comforting to reach back into history and recall that it is not only America that kills its moral educators. Martin Luther King joins a long list of people who had the arrogance not only to teach justice but to live it in such a way that other people felt uncomfortable about their own goodness, their own justice. I have frequently heard the question, "Why King, not Carmichael or Brown?" It is not the people who preach power and hate who get assassinated. They are not a threat; they are like the worst in others. It is the people who are too good for other people to take, who question the basis on which people erect their paltry sense of goodness, who die.

Martin Luther King and Socrates as examples of moral educators suggest that, although the bag of virtues encapsulated the need for moral improvement in the child, a genuine concern about the growth of justice in the child implies a similar concern for the growth of justice in the society. This is the implicit basis of Kozol's challenging the moral authority of a passive teacher in a ghetto school. I do not mean to imply by this that true moral education is a matter of political indoctrination of the young in the name of reform. Rather, I am arguing that the only constitutionally legitimate form of moral education in the schools is the teaching of justice and that the teaching of justice in the schools requires just schools. Ball (1967) has argued that the Supreme Court's *Schempp* decision calls for the restraint of public school efforts at moral education, because such education is equivalent to the state propagation of religion, conceived as any articulated value system.

The problems as to the legitimacy of moral education in the public schools disappear, however, if the proper content of moral education is recognized to be the values of justice that themselves prohibit the imposition of beliefs of one group on another. The requirement implied by the Bill of Rights that the schools recognize the equal rights of individuals in matters of belief or values does not mean that the schools are not to be "value oriented." Recognition of equal rights does not imply value neutrality; that is, the view that all value systems are equally sound. Because we respect the individual rights of members of particular groups in our society, it is sometimes believed that we must consider their values as valid as our own. Because we must respect the rights of an Eichmann, however, we need not treat his values as equal to that of the values of liberty and justice.

Public education is committed not only to maintenance of the rights of individuals but also to the transmission of the values of respect for individual rights. The school is no more committed to value neutrality than is the government or the law. The school, like the government, is an institution with a basic function of maintaining and transmitting some, but not all, of the consensual values of society. The most fundamental values of a society are termed *moral,* and the major moral values in our society are the values of justice. According to any interpretation of the U.S. Constitution, the rationale for government is the preservation of the rights of individuals; that is, of justice. The public school is as much committed to the maintenance of justice as is the court. Desegregation of the schools is not only a passive recognition of the equal rights of citizens to access to a public facility, like a swimming pool, but an active recognition of the responsibility of the school for "moral education"; that is, for transmission of the values of justice on which our society is founded. From my point of view, then, moral education may legitimately involve certain elements of social reform if they bear directly on the central values of justice on which the public schools are based.

The delicate balance between social reform and moral education is clarified by the example of Martin Luther King. King was a moral leader, a moral educator of adults, not because he was a spokesperson for the welfare of blacks, not because he was against violence, not because he was a minister of religion, but because, as he himself said, he was a drum major for justice. His words and deeds were primarily designed to induce America to respond to racial problems in terms of a sense of justice, and any particular action he took had value for this reason, not just because of the concrete political end it might achieve.

I have used King as an example of a moral educator to indicate that the difference between the political reformer and the moral educator is not a difference in the content of their concern. Civil rights is as much a matter of morality as is honesty in financial matters. The distinctive feature of moral education as against ordinary political action is in the relation of means and ends. Black power politicians using unjust means in the name of civil rights are clearly not in the enterprise of teaching justice, any more than are policemen in the enterprise of teaching honesty when they shoot down rioters. King's acts of civil disobedience, however, flowed directly from a sense of principles of justice and thus were moral leadership, not just propaganda or protest.

Let me recapitulate my argument so far. I have criticized the "bag of virtues" concept of moral education on the grounds, first, that there are no such things and, second, if there were, they couldn't be taught or at least I don't know how or who could teach them. Like Socrates, I have claimed that ordinary people certainly don't know how to do it, and yet there are no expert teachers of virtue as there are for the other arts. Rather than turning to nihilism, I have pointed to an example of an effective moral educator at the adult social level, Martin Luther King. Since I cannot define moral virtue at the individual level, I tried it at the social level and found it to be justice, and claimed that the central moral value of the school, like that of the society, was justice. Justice, in turn, is a matter of equal and universal human rights. I pointed to the cloud of virtue labels attributed to King and pointed out that only one meant anything. Justice was not just one more fine-sounding word in a eulogy; it was the essence of King's moral leadership.

My hope is to have stirred some feelings about the seriousness and the reality of that big word, that Platonic form, *justice*, because people like King were willing to die for it. I suppose there may have been people willing to die for honesty, responsibility, and the rest of the bag of virtues, but, if so, I have no empathy with them. I am going to argue now, like Plato, that virtue is not many, but one, and its name is *justice*. Let me point out first that justice is not a character trait in the usual sense. You cannot make up behavior tests of justice, as Hartshorne and May (1928–1930) did for honesty, service, and self-control. One cannot conceive of a little set of behavior tests that would indicate that Martin Luther King and Socrates were high on a trait of justice. The reason for this is that justice is not a concrete rule of action such as lies behind virtues like honesty.

To be honest means "Don't cheat, don't steal, don't lie." But justice is not a rule or a set of rules, it is a moral principle. By a moral principle, I mean a mode of choosing that is universal, a rule of choosing that we want all people to adopt always in all situations. We know it is all right to be dishonest and steal to save a life because it is just, because one person's right to life comes before another person's right to property. We know it is sometimes right to kill, because it is sometimes just. The Germans who tried to kill Hitler were doing right because respect for the equal values of lives demands that we kill someone who is murdering others, in order to save lives. There are exceptions to rules, then, but no exception to principles. A moral obligation is an obligation to respect the right or claim of another person. A moral principle is a principle for resolving competing claims: you versus me, you versus a third person. There is only one principled basis for resolving claims: justice or equality. Treat every person's claim impartially regardless of the person. A moral principle is not only a rule of action but a reason for action. As a reason for action, justice is called *respect for* people.

Because morally mature people are governed by the principle of justice rather than by a set of rules, there are not many moral virtues, but one. Let me restate the argument in Plato's terms. Plato's argument is that what makes a virtuous action virtuous is that it is guided by knowledge of the good. A courageous action based on ignorance of danger is not courageous; a just act based on ignorance of justice is not just; and so on. If virtuous action is action based on knowledge of the good, then virtue is one, because knowledge of the good is one. I have already claimed that knowledge of the good is one because the good is justice. Let me briefly document these lofty claims by some lowly research findings. Using hypothetical moral situations, I and my colleagues have interviewed children and adults about right and wrong in the United States, Britain, Turkey, Taiwan, and Yucatan. In all cultures, we find the same forms of moral thinking. There are six forms of moral thought, and they constitute an invariant sequence of stages in each culture. These stages are summarized in the Appendix.

Why do I say that existence of culturally universal stages means that knowledge of the good is one? First, because it implies that concepts of the good are culturally universal. Second, because people at a given level are pretty much the same in their thinking regardless of the situation they are presented with and regardless of the particular aspect of morality being tapped. There is a general factor of maturity of moral judgment much like the general factor of intelligence in cognitive tasks. If they know one aspect of the good at a certain level, they know other aspects of the good at that level. Third, because at each stage there is a single principle of the good, which only approaches a moral principle at the higher levels. At all levels, for instance, there is some reason for regard for law and some reason for regard for rights. Only at the highest stage, however, is regard for law a regard for universal moral law and regard for rights a regard for universal human rights. At this point, both regard for law and regard for human rights are grounded on a clear criterion of justice that was present in confused and obscure form at earlier stages.

Let me describe the stages in terms of the civil disobedience issue in a way that may clarify the argument I have just made. Before the Civil War, we had laws that allowed slavery. According to the law, escaped slaves had to be returned to owners like runaway horses.

Some people who didn't believe in slavery disobeyed the law, hid the runaway slaves, and helped them to escape. Were they doing right or wrong?

A bright, middle-class boy, Johnny, answers the question this way when he is ten: "They were doing wrong because the slave ran away himself. They're being just like slaves themselves trying to keep'em away." Asked, "Is slavery right or wrong?" he answers, "Some wrong, but servants aren't so bad because they don't do all that heavy work."

Johnny's response is Stage 1, *punishment and obedience orientation.* Breaking the law makes it wrong; indeed, the badness of being slaves washes off on their rescuers.

Three years later, Johnny is asked the same question. His answer is mainly Stage 2 *instrumental relativism.* He says, "They would help them escape because they were all against slavery. The South was for slavery because they had big plantations and the North was against it because they had big factories and they needed people to work and they'd pay. So the Northerners would think it was right but the Southerners wouldn't."

So early comes Marxist relativism. He goes on: "If a person is against slavery and maybe likes the slave or maybe dislikes the owner, it's OK for him to break the law if he likes, provided he doesn't get caught. If the slaves were in misery and one was a friend he'd do it. It would probably be right if it was someone you really loved."

At the end, his orientation to sympathy and love indicates the same Stage 3, *orientation to approval, affection, and helpfulness,* better suggested by Charlie Brown.

At age nineteen, in college, Johnny is Stage 4, *orientation to maintaining a social order of rules and rights.* He says, "They were right, in my point of view. I hate the actual aspect of slavery, the imprisonment of one man ruling over another. They drive them too hard and they don't get anything in return. It's not right to disobey the law, no. Laws are made by the people. But you might do it because you feel it's wrong. If 50,000 people break the law, can you put them all in jail? Can 50,000 people be wrong?"

Johnny here is oriented to the rightness and wrongness of slavery itself and of obedience to law. He doesn't see the wrongness of slavery in terms of equal human rights but in terms of an unfair economic relation, working hard and getting nothing in return. The same view of rights in terms of getting what you worked for leads Johnny to say about school integration, "A lot of colored people are now just living off of civil rights. You only get education as far as you want to learn, as far as you work for it, not being placed with someone else, you don't get it from someone else."

Johnny illustrates for us the distinction between virtue as the development of principles of justice and virtue as being unprejudiced. In one sense, Johnny's development has involved increased recognition to the fellow-humanness of the slaves. From thinking of slaves as inferior and bad at age ten, he thinks of them as having some sort of rights at age nineteen. He is still not just, however, because his only notions of right are that you should get what you earn, a conception easily used to justify a segregated society. In spite of a high school and college education, he has no real grasp of the conceptions of rights underlying the Constitution or the Supreme Court decisions involved. Johnny's lack of virtue is not that he doesn't want to associate with blacks, it is that he is not capable of being a participating citizen of our society because he does not understand the principles on which our society is based. His failure to understand these principles cuts both ways. Not only does he fail to ground the rights of blacks on principles, but he also fails to ground respect for law on this base. Respect for law is respect for the majority. But if 50,000 people break the law, can 50,000 be wrong? Whether the 50,000 people are breaking the law in the name of rights or of the Ku Klux Klan makes no difference in this line of thought.

It is to be hoped that Johnny may reach our next stage, Stage 5, *social contract orientation,* by his mid-twenties, because some of our subjects continue to develop up until this time. Instead of taking one of our research subjects, however, let us take some statements by Socrates as an example of Stage 5. Socrates is explaining to Crito why he refuses to save his life by taking advantage of the escape arrangements Crito has made:

"Ought one to fulfill all one's agreements?" Socrates asks. "Then consider the consequences. Suppose the laws and constitution of Athens were to confront us and ask, 'Socrates, can you deny that by this act you intend, so far as you have power, to destroy us. Do you imagine that a city can continue to exist if the legal judgments which are pronounced by it are nullified and destroyed by private persons? At an earlier time, you made a noble show of indifference to the possibility of dying. Now you show no respect for your earlier professions and no regard for us, the laws, trying to run away in spite of the contracts by which you agreed to live as a member of our state. Are we not speaking the truth when we say that you have undertaken in deed, if not in word, to live your life as a citizen in obedience to us? It is a fact, then, that you are breaking covenants made with us under no compulsion or misunderstanding. You had seventy years in which you could have left the country if you were not satisfied with us or felt that the agreements were unfair.'"

As an example of Stage 6, *orientation to universal moral principles,* let me cite Martin Luther King's "Letter from a Birmingham Jail" (1965):

There is a type of constructive nonviolent tension which is necessary for growth. Just as Socrates felt it was necessary to create a tension in the mind so that individuals could rise from the bondage of half-truths, so must we see the need for nonviolent gadflies to create the kind of tension in society that will help men rise from the dark depths of prejudice and racism.

One may well ask, "How can you advocate breaking some laws and obeying others?" The answer lies in the fact that there are two types of laws, just and unjust. One has not only a legal but a moral responsibility to obey just laws. One has a moral responsibility to disobey unjust laws. An unjust law is a human law that is not rooted in eternal law and natural law. Any law that uplifts human personality is just, any law that degrades human personality is unjust. An unjust law is a code that a numerical or power majority group compels a minority group to obey but does not make binding on itself. This is difference made legal.

I do not advocate evading or defying the law, as would the rabid segregationist. That would lead to anarchy. One who breaks an unjust law must do so openly, lovingly, and with a willingness to accept the penalty. An individual who breaks a law that conscience tells him is unjust, and willingly accepts the penalty of imprisonment in order to arouse the conscience of the community over its injustice, is in reality expressing the highest respect for law.

King makes it clear that moral disobedience of the law must spring from the same root as moral obedience to law, out of respect for justice. We respect the law because it is based on rights both in the sense that the law is designed to protect the rights of all and because the law is made by the principle of equal political rights. If civil disobedience is to be Stage 6, it must recognize the contractual respect for law of Stage 5, even to accepting imprisonment. That is why Stage 5 is a way of thinking about the laws that are imposed on all, while a morality of justice that claims to judge the law can never be anything but a free, personal ideal. It must accept the idea of being put in jail by its enemies, not of putting its enemies in jail. Although I classified Socrates' statements to Crito as Stage 5, his statement of his civilly disobedient role as a moral educator, quoted earlier, was Stage 6, at least in spirit.

Both logic and empirical study indicate there is no shortcut to autonomous morality, no Stage 6 without a previous Stage 5.

I have claimed that knowledge of the moral good is one. I now will try to show that virtue in action is knowledge of the good, as Plato claimed. I have already said that knowledge of the good in terms of what Plato calls opinion or conventional belief is not virtue. An individual may believe that cheating is very bad but that does not predict that he or she will resist cheating in real life. Espousal of unprejudiced attitudes toward blacks does not predict action to assure civil rights in an atmosphere where others have some prejudice; however, true knowledge, knowledge of principles of justice, does predict virtuous action. With regard to cheating, the essential elements of justice are understood by both Stage 5 and Stage 6 subjects. In cheating, the critical issue is recognition of the element of contract and agreement implicit in the situation, and the recognition that, although it doesn't seem so bad if one person cheats, what holds for all must hold for one. In a recent study (Krebs, 1967), 100 sixth-grade children were given experimental cheating tests and our moral judgment interview. The majority of the children were below the principled level in moral judgment; they were at our first four moral stages. Seventy-five percent of these children cheated. In contrast, only 20 percent of the principled subjects—that is, Stage 5 or 6—cheated. In another study conducted at the college level, only 11 percent of the principled subjects cheated, in contrast to 42 percent of the students at lower levels of moral judgment. In the case of cheating, justice and the expectations of conventional authority both dictate the same behavior.

What happens when justice and authority are opposed? An experimental study by Stanley Milgram (1963) involved such an opposition. Under the guise of a learning experiment, undergraduate subjects were ordered by an experimenter to administer what they thought were increasingly more severe electric shocks as punishment to a stooge victim. In this case, the principles of justice involved in the Stage 5 social contract orientation do not clearly prescribe a decision. The victim had voluntarily agreed to participate in the experiment, and the subjects had contractually committed themselves to perform the experiment. Only Stage 6 thinking clearly defined the situation as one in which the experimenter did not have the moral right to ask subjects to inflict pain on another person. Accordingly, 75 percent of those at Stage 6 quit or refused to shock the victim, as compared to only 13 percent of all the subjects at lower stages.

A study of Berkeley students carries the issue into political civil disobedience. Berkeley students were faced with a decision to sit in the administration building in the name of political freedom of communication. Haan, Smith, and Block (1968) administered moral judgment interviews to over 200 of these students. The situation was like that in Milgram's study. A Stage 5 social contract interpretation of justice, which was that held by the university administration, could take the position that students who came to Berkeley came with foreknowledge of the rules and could go elsewhere if they did not like them. About 50 percent of the Stage 5 subjects sat in. For Stage 6 students, the issue was clear-cut, and 80 percent of them sat in. For students at the conventional levels, Stages 3 and 4, the issue was also clear-cut, and only 10 percent of them sat in. These results will sound very heartwarming to those who have engaged in protest activities. Protesting is a sure sign of being at the most mature moral level; however, there was another group who was almost as disposed to sit in as the Stage 6 students. These were Stage 2 instrumental relativists, of whom about 60 percent sat in. From longitudinal studies, we know that most Stage 2 college students are in a state of confusion. In high school, most were at the conventional level, and in college they kick conventional morality, searching for their thing, for self-chosen values, but cannot tell an autonomous morality of justice from one of egoistic relativism, exchange, and revenge. Our longitudinal studies indicate that all of our middle-class Stage 2 college students grow out of it to become principled adults (Kohlberg and Kramer, 1969). If the pressures are greater and you are a Stokely Carmichael, things may take a different course.

I make the point to indicate that protest activities, like other acts, are neither virtuous nor vicious; it is only the knowledge of the good that lies behind them that can give them virtue. As an example, I would take it that a Stage 6 sense of justice would have been rather unlikely to find virtue in the sit-in at Harvard University to prevent Dow Chemical from recruiting employees. The rules being disobeyed by the protesters were not unjust rules, and the sit-in was depriving individuals of rights, not trying to protect individual rights. Principled civil disobedience is not illegitimate propaganda for worthy political causes, it is the just questioning of injustice.

I hope these two last examples indicate the complexity of the behaviors by which knowledge of justice may be manifested and that no trait of virtue in the ordinary sense describes the behavior of the principled or just person. Having, I hope, shown the validity of the Socratic view of virtue, I will take the little time left to consider the sense in which it may be taught. The Socratic view implies that, in a sense, knowledge of the good is always within but needs to be drawn out like geometric knowledge in Meno's slave.* In a series of experimental studies, we have found that children and adolescents rank as "best" the highest level of moral reasoning they can comprehend. Children comprehend all lower stages than their own, and often comprehend the stage one higher than their own and occasionally two stages higher, although they cannot actively express these higher stages of thought. If they comprehend the stage one higher than their own, they tend to prefer it to their own. This fact is basic to moral leadership in our society. Although the majority of adults in American society are at conventional Stages 3 and 4, leadership in our society has usually been expressed at Stages 5 and 6, as the example of Martin Luther King suggests. While it may be felt as dangerous, the moral leadership of the Platonic philosopher-ruler is nonetheless naturally felt.

Returning to the teaching of virtue as a drawing out, the child's preference for the next level of thought shows that it is greeted as already familiar, that it is felt to be a more adequate expression of that already within, of that latent in the child's own thought. If the child were responding to fine words and external prestige, he would not pick the next stage continuous with his own, but something else.

Let me now suggest an example used in Chapter 1 to indicate another sense in which moral teaching must be a drawing out of that already within. At the age of four, my son joined the pacifist and vegetarian movement and refused to eat meat, because, as he said, "It's bad to kill animals." In spite of lengthy Hawk argumentation by his parents about the difference between justified and unjustified killing, he remained a vegetarian for six months. Like most Doves, however, his principles recognized occasions of just or legitimate killing. One night I read him a book of Eskimo life involving a seal-killing expedition. He got angry during the story and said, "You know, there is one kind of meat I would eat, Eskimo meat. It's bad to kill animals so it's all right to eat Eskimos."

For reasons I won't detail, this eye-for-an-eye, tooth-for-a-tooth

---

* By simply asking questions, Socrates led Meno's slave to understand the relationship between the area of a square and the area of the square of its diagonal.

concept of justice is Stage 1. You will recognize, however, that it is a very genuine although four-year-old sense of justice and that it contains within it the Stage 6 sense of justice in shadowy form. The problem is to draw the child's perceptions of justice from the shadows of the cave step by step toward the light of justice as an ideal form. This last example indicates another Platonic truth, which is that children who turn from the dark images of the cave toward the light are at first still convinced that the dark images best represent the truth. Like Meno's slave, children are initially quite confident of their moral knowledge, of the rationality and efficacy of their moral principles. The notion that children feel ignorant and are eager to absorb the wisdom of adult authority in the moral domain is one that teacher or parent will know is nonsense.

Let me give another example. Following a developmental timetable, my son moved to an expedient Stage 2 orientation when he was six. He told me at that time, "You know, the reason people don't steal is because they're afraid of the police. If there were no police around, everyone would steal." Of course, I told him that I and most people didn't steal because we thought it wrong, because we wouldn't want other people to take things from us, and so on. My son's reply was "I just don't see it, it's sort of crazy not to steal if there are no police."

The story indicates that, like most ordinary fathers, I had no great skill in teaching true virtue. My son, of course, has always been virtuous in the conventional sense. Even when he saw no rational reason for being honest, he received the highest marks on his report card on the basis of the bag of virtues of obedience, responsibility, and respect for property. Contrary to what we usually think, it is quite easy to teach conventionally virtuous behavior but very difficult to teach true knowledge of the good.

The first step in teaching virtue, then, is the Socratic step of creating dissatisfaction in students about their knowledge of the good. This we do experimentally by exposing the students to moral conflict situations for which their principles have no ready solution. Second, we expose them to disagreement and argument about these situations with their peers. Our Platonic view holds that if we inspire cognitive conflict in students and point the way to the next step up the divided line, they will tend to see things previously invisible.

In practice, then, our experimental efforts at moral education have involved getting students at one level, say Stage 2, to argue with those at the next level, say Stage 3. The teacher would support and clarify the Stage 3 arguments. Then he or she would pit the Stage 3 students against the Stage 4 students on a new dilemma. Initial results with this method with a junior high school group indicated that 50 percent of the students moved up one stage and 10 percent moved up two stages. In comparison, only 10 percent of a control group moved up one stage in the four-month period involved (Blatt and Kohlberg, 1975).

Obviously, the small procedures I have described are only a way station to genuine moral education. As my earlier comments suggested, a more complete approach implies full student participation in a school in which justice is a living matter. Let me sketch out one Platonic republic with this aim, a boarding school I recently visited. The heart of this school is described in its brochure somewhat as follows:

The sense of community is most strongly felt in the weekly Meeting, consisting of faculty, their families, and students. Decisions are made by consensus rather than by majority rule. This places responsibility on each member to struggle to see through his own desires to the higher needs of others and the community, while witnessing the deepest concerns of his conscience. The results of these decisions are not rules in the traditional sense, but agreements entered into by everyone and recorded as minutes.

The brochure goes on to quote a letter by one of its graduating students:

The School is an entity surrounded by the rest of the world in which each individual struggles against that which restrains him—himself. It has been said that the School gives too much freedom to its young, often rebellious students. But a film will darken to a useless mass of chemical if it's not developed in time. People change early, too. If they meet a loving atmosphere, they are affected by it profoundly. Growing up is a lonely thing to be doing, but at the Meeting School it is also a beautiful thing.

All schools need not and cannot be self-contained little Republics in which knowledge of the good is to be brought out through love and community as well as through participation in a just institution. Such schools do stand as a challenge to an educational establishment that makes a pious bow to the bag of virtues while teaching that true goodness is tested on the College Boards. The Platonic view I've been espousing suggests something still revolutionary and frightening to me if not to you, that the schools would be radically different places if they took seriously the teaching of real knowledge of the good.

3. Development as the Aim of Education: The Dewey View

with ROCHELLE MAYER

THE MOST important issue confronting educators and educational theorists is the choice of ends for the educational process. Without clear and rational educational goals, it becomes impossible to decide which educational programs achieve objectives of general import and which teach incidental facts and attitudes of dubious worth. Although there has been a vast amount of research comparing the effects of various educational methods and programs on various outcome measures, there has been very little empirical research designed to clarify the worth of these outcome measures themselves. After a deluge of studies in the 1960s examining the effects of programs on IQ and achievement tests and on drawing policy conclusions, researchers finally began to ask the question "What is the justification for using IQ tests or achievement tests to evaluate programs in the first place?"

The present chapter examines such fundamental issues and considers the strategies by which research facts can help generate and substantiate educational objectives and measures of educational outcomes. Three prevalent strategies for defining objectives and relating them to research facts are considered: the desirable trait or "bag of virtues" strategy, the prediction of success or "industrial psychology" strategy, and the "developmental-philosophic" strategy. We will claim in this chapter that the first two strategies: (1) lack a clear theoretical rationale for defining objectives that can withstand logical and philosophic criticism, and (2) that as currently applied they rest on assumptions that conflict with research findings. In contrast, we claim that the developmental-philosophic strategy for defining educational objectives, which emerges from the work of Dewey and Piaget, is a theoretical rationale that withstands logical criticism and is consistent with, if not "proved" by, current research findings.

This chapter is reprinted by permission of the publishers from *Harvard Educational Review 42*, no. 4:449–496. Copyright © 1972 by the President and Fellows of Harvard College.

This presentation begins by making explicit how a cognitive-developmental *psychological* theory can be translated into a rational and viable progressive *educational ideology*; that is, a set of concepts defining desirable aims, content, and methods of education. We contrast the progressive ideology with the "romantic" and the "cultural transmission" schools of thought, with respect to underlying psychological, epistemological, and ethical assumptions. In doing so, we focus on two related problems of value theory. The first is the issue of *value relativity*, the problem of defining some general ends of education whose validity is not relative to the values and needs of each individual child or to the values of each subculture or society. The second is the problem of relating psychological statements about the actual characteristics of children and their development to philosophic statements about desirable characteristics, the problem of relating the natural *is* to the ethical *ought*. We claim that the cognitive-developmental or progressive approach can satisfactorily handle these issues because it combines a psychological theory of development with a rational ethical philosophy of development. In contrast, we claim that other educational ideologies do not stem from psychological theories which can be translated into educational aims free of the philosophic charge that they are arbitrary and relative to the values of the particular educator or school.

Then, we look at the ways in which these ideologies form the basis for contemporary educational policy. We evaluate longitudinal evidence relevant to the "bag of virtues" definition of education objectives favored in maturationist models of education, and the academic achievement definition of objectives favored in environmental learning models. We conclude that the available research lends little support for either of these alternative educational strategies. More specifically,

1. The current prevalent definition of the aims of education, in terms of academic achievement supplemented by a concern for mental health, cannot be justified empirically or logically.
2. The overwhelming emphasis of educational psychology on methods of instruction and tests and measurements that presuppose a "value-neutral" psychology is misplaced.
3. An alternative notion that the aim of the schools should be the stimulation of human development is a scientifically, ethically, and practically viable conception that provides the framework for a new kind of educational psychology.

Three Streams of Educational Ideology

There have been three broad streams in the development of Western educational ideology. Although their detailed statements vary from generation to generation, each stream exhibits a continuity based on particular assumptions of psychological development.

Romanticism

The first stream of thought, the "romantic," commences with Rousseau and is currently represented by Freud's and Gesell's followers. A. S. Neill's Summerhill is an example of a school based on these principles. Romantics hold that what comes from within the child is the most important aspect of development; therefore, the pedagogical environment should be permissive enough to allow the inner "good" (abilities and social virtues) to unfold and the inner "bad" to come under control. Thus, teaching the child the ideas and attitudes of others through rote or drill would result in meaningless learning and the suppression of inner spontaneous tendencies of positive value.

Romantics stress the biological metaphors of "health" and "growth" in equating optimal physical development with bodily health and optimal mental development with mental health. Accordingly, early education should allow the child to work through aspects of emotional development not allowed expression at home, such as the formation of social relations with peers and adults other than parents. It should also allow the expression of intellectual questioning and curiosity. To label this ideology "romantic" is not to accuse it of being unscientific; rather, it is to recognize that the nineteenth-century discovery of the natural development of the child was part of a larger romantic philosophy, an ethic and epistemology involving a discovery of the natural and the inner self.

With regard to childhood, this philosophy involved not only an awareness that the child possessed an inner self but also a valuing of childhood, to which the origins of the self could be traced. The adult, by taking the child's point of view, could experience otherwise inaccessible elements of truth, goodness, and reality.

As stated by G. H. Mead (1936, p. 61), "The romantic comes back to the existence of the self as the primary fact. That is what gives the standard to values. What the Romantic period revealed was not simply a past but a past as the point of view from which to come back at the self. . . . It is this self-conscious setting-up of the past again that constitutes the origin of romanticism."

The work of G. Stanley Hall, the founder of American child psychology, contains the core ideas of modern romantic educational thought, including "deschooling":

The guardians of the young should strive first to keep out of nature's way and to prevent harm and should merit the proud title of the defenders of the happiness and rights of children. They should feel profoundly that childhood, as it comes from the hand of God, is not corrupt but illustrates the survival of the most consummate thing in the world; they should be convinced that there is nothing else so worthy of love, reverence, and service as the body and soul of the growing child.

Before we let the pedagogue loose upon childhood, we must overcome the fetishes of the alphabet, of the multiplication tables, and must reflect that but a few generations ago the ancestors of all of us were illiterate. There are many who ought not to be educated and who would be better in mind, body, and morals if they knew no school. What shall it profit a child to gain the world of knowledge and lose his own health? [1901, p. 24]

Cultural Transmission

The origins of the cultural transmission ideology are rooted in the classical academic tradition of Western education. Traditional educators believe that their primary task is the transmission to the present generation of bodies of information and of rules or values collected in the past; they believe that the educator's job is the direct instruction of such information and rules. The important emphasis, however, is not on the sanctity of the past, but on the view that educating consists of transmitting knowledge, skills, and social and moral rules of the culture. Knowledge and rules of the culture may be rapidly changing, or they may be static. In either case, however, it is assumed that education is the transmission of the culturally given.

More modern or innovative variations of the cultural transmission view are represented by educational technology and behavior modification.[1] As in traditional education, these approaches assume that knowledge and values—first located in the culture—are afterward internalized by children through the imitation of adult behavior models

---

[1] The romantic-maturationist position also has conservative and radical wings. Emphasizing "adaptation to reality," psychoanalytic educators such as A. Freud (1937) and Bettelheim (1970) stress mental health as ego control, while radicals stress spontaneity, creativity, and so on.

or through explicit instruction and reward and punishment. Accordingly, the educational technologist evaluates the individual's success in terms of ability to incorporate the responses he or she has been taught and to respond favorably to the demands of the system. Although technologists stress the child as an individual learner, learning at his or her own pace, they, like traditionalists, assume that what is learned and what is valued in education is a culturally given body of knowledge and rules.

There are, of course, a number of contrasts between the traditional academic and the educational technology variations of the cultural transmission ideology. The traditional academic school has been humanistic in the sense that it has emphasized the transmission of knowledge considered central to Western culture. The educational technology school, in contrast, has emphasized the transmission of skills and habits deemed necessary for adjustment to a technological society. With regard to early education, however, the two variations of the cultural transmission school find an easy rapprochement in stressing such goals as literacy and mathematical skills. The traditionalist sees literacy as the central avenue to Western culture, the technologist sees it as a means to vocational adaptation to a society depending on impersonal information codes. Both approaches, however, emphasize definition of educational goals in terms of fixed knowledge or skills assessed by standards of cultural correctness. Both also stress internalization of basic moral rules of the culture. The clearest and most thoughtful contemporary elaboration of this view in relation to preschool education is to be found in the writing of Bereiter and Engelmann (1966).

In contrast to the child-centered romantic school, the cultural transmission school is society centered. It defines educational ends as the internalization of the values and knowledge of the culture. The cultural transmission school focuses on the child's need to learn the discipline of the social order, while the romantic stresses the child's freedom. The cultural transmission view emphasizes the common and the established; the romantic view stresses the unique, the novel, and the personal.

Progressivism

The third stream of educational ideology, which is still best termed *progressive,* following Dewey (1938), developed as part of the pragmatic functional-genetic philosophies of the late nineteenth and early twentieth centuries. As an educational ideology, progressivism holds that education should nourish the child's natural interaction with a developing society or environment. Unlike the romantics, the progressives do not assume that development is the unfolding of an innate pattern or that the primary aim of education is to create an unconflicted environment able to foster healthy development. Instead, they define development as a progression through invariant, ordered sequential stages. The educational goal is the eventual attainment of a higher level or stage of development in adulthood, not merely the healthy functioning of the child at a present level.

In 1895, Dewey and McLellan (1964, p. 207) suggested the following notion of education for attainment of a higher stage: "Only knowledge of the order and connection of the stages in the development of the psychical functions can insure the full maturing of the psychical powers. Education is the work of supplying the conditions which will enable the psychical functions, as they successively arise, to mature and pass into higher functions in the freest and fullest manner." In the progressive view, this aim requires an educational environment that actively stimulates development through the presentation of resolvable but genuine problems or conflicts. For progressives, the organizing and developing force in the child's experience is the child's active thinking, and thinking is stimulated by the problematic, by cognitive conflict. Educative experience makes the child think—think in ways that organize both cognition and emotion. Although both the cultural transmission and the progressive views emphasize "knowledge," only the latter sees the acquisition of "knowledge" as *an active change in patterns of thinking* brought about by experiential problem-solving situations. Similarly, both views emphasize "morality," but the progressive sees the acquisition of morality as an active change in patterns of response to problematic social situations rather than the learning of culturally accepted rules.

Progressive educators stress the essential links between cognitive and moral development; they assume that moral development is not purely affective and that cognitive development is a necessary although not sufficient condition for moral development. The development of logical and critical thought, central to cognitive education, finds its larger meaning in a broad set of moral values. Progressives also point out that moral development arises from social interaction in situations of social conflict. Morality is neither the internalization of established cultural values nor the unfolding of spontaneous impulses and emotions; it is justice, the reciprocity between the individual and others in the social environment.

Psychological Theories Underlying Educational Ideologies

We have described three schools of thought describing the general ends and means of education. Central to each of these educational ideologies is a distinctive educational psychology, a distinctive psychological theory of development (Kohlberg, 1968b). Underlying the romantic ideology is a maturationist theory of development; underlying the cultural transmission ideology is an associationistic learning or environmental contingency theory of development; and underlying the progressive ideology is a cognitive-developmental or interactionist theory of development.

The three psychological theories described represent three basic metaphors of development (Langer, 1969). The romantic model views the development of the mind through the metaphor of organic growth, the physical growth of a plant or animal. In this metaphor, the environment affects development by providing necessary nourishment for the naturally growing organism. Maturationist psychologists elaborating the romantic metaphor conceive of cognitive development as unfolding through prepatterned stages. They have usually assumed not only that cognitive development unfolds but also that individual variations in rate of cognitive development are largely inborn. Emotional development is also believed to unfold through hereditary stages, such as the Freudian psychosexual stages, but is thought to be vulnerable to fixation and frustration by the environment. For the maturationist, although both cognitive and social-emotional development unfold, they are two different things. Because social-emotional development is an unfolding of something biologically given and is not based on knowledge of the social world, it does not depend on cognitive growth.

The cultural transmission model views the development of the mind through the metaphor of the machine. The machine may be the wax on which the environment transcribes its markings, it may be the telephone switchboard through which environmental stimulus energies are transmitted, or it may be the computer in which bits of information from the environment are stored, retrieved, and recombined. In any case, the environment is seen as "input," as information or energy more or less directly transmitted to, and accumulated in, the organism. The organism in turn emits "output" behavior. Underlying the mechanistic metaphor is the associationistic, stimulus-response, or environmentalist psychological theory, which can be traced from John Locke to Thorndike to B. F. Skinner. This psychology views both specific concepts and general cognitive structures as reflections of structures that exist outside the child in the physical and social world. The structure of the child's concepts or behavior is viewed as the result of the association of discrete stimuli with one another, with the child's responses, and with experiences of pleasure and pain. Cognitive development is the result of guided learning and teaching. Consequently, cognitive education requires a careful statement of desirable behavior patterns described in terms of specific responses. Implied here is the idea that the child's behavior can, be shaped by immediate repetition and elaboration of the correct response and by association with feedback or reward.

The cognitive-developmental metaphor is not material, it is dialectical; it is a model of the progression of ideas in discourse and conversation. The dialectical metaphor was first elaborated by Plato, given new meaning by Hegel, and finally stripped of its metaphysical claims by John Dewey and Jean Piaget, to form a psychological method. In the dialectical metaphor, a core of universal ideas are redefined and reorganized as their implications are played out in experience and as they are confronted by their opposites in argument and discourse. These reorganizations define qualitative levels of thought, levels of increased epistemic adequacy. The child is not a plant or a machine; he or she is a philosopher or a scientist-poet. The dialectical metaphor of progressive education is supported by a cognitive-developmental or interactional psychological theory. Discarding the dichotomy between maturation and environmentally determined learning, Piaget and Dewey claim that mature thought emerges through a process of development that is neither direct biological maturation nor direct learning, but rather a reorganization of psychological structures resulting from organism-environment interactions. Basic mental structure is the product of the patterning of interaction between the organism and the environment, rather than a direct reflection of either innate neurological patterns or external environmental patterns.

To understand this Piaget-Dewey concept of the development of mental pattern, we must first understand its conception of cognition.

Cognitions are assumed to be structures, internally organized wholes or systems of internal relations. These structures are *rules* for the processing of information or the connecting of events. Events in the child's experience are organized actively, through these cognitive connecting processes—not passively, through external association and repetition. Cognitive development, which is defined as change in cognitive structures, is assumed to depend on experience. But the effects of experience are not regarded as learning in the ordinary sense (training, instruction, modeling, or specific response practices). If two events that follow one another in time are cognitively connected in a child's mind, this implies that he relates them by means of a category such as causality; he perceives his operant behavior as causing the reinforcer to occur. A program of reinforcement, then, cannot directly change the child's causal structures, because it is assimilated by the child in terms of his present mode of thinking. When a program of reinforcement cannot be assimilated to the child's causal structure, however, the child's structure may be reorganized to obtain a better fit between the two. Cognitive development is a dialogue between the child's cognitive structures and the structures of the environment. Further, the theory emphasizes that the core of development is not the unfolding of instincts, emotions, or sensorimotor patterns but instead is cognitive change in distinctively human, general patterns of thinking about the self and the world. The child's relation to his social environment is cognitive; it involves thought and symbolic interaction.

Because of its emphasis on ways of perceiving and responding to experience, cognitive-developmental theory discards the traditional dichotomy of social *versus* intellectual development. Rather, cognitive and affective development are parallel aspects of the structural transformations that take place in development. At the core of this interactional or cognitive-developmental theory is the doctrine of cognitive stages. Stages have the following general characteristics:

1. Stages imply distinct or qualitative differences in children's modes of thinking or of solving the same problem.
2. These different modes of thought form an invariant sequence, order, or succession in individual development. While cultural factors may speed up, slow down, or stop development, they do not change its sequence.
3. Each of these different and sequential modes of thought forms a

"structural whole." A given stage response on a task does not just represent a specific response determined by knowledge and familiarity with that task or tasks similar to it; rather, it represents an underlying thought organization.

4. Cognitive stages are hierarchical integrations. Stages form an order of increasingly differentiated and integrated *structures* to fulfill a common function. [Piaget, 1960, pp. 13-15]

In other words, a series of stages form an invariant developmental sequence; the sequence is invariant because each stage stems from the previous one and prepares the way for the subsequent stage. Of course, children may move through these stages at varying speeds, and they may be found to be half in and half out of a particular stage. Individuals may stop at any given stage and at any age, but if they continue to progress they must move in accord with these steps.

The cognitive-developmental conception of stage has a number of features in common with maturational theory conceptions of stage. The maturational conception of stage, however, is "embryological," while the interactional conception is "structural-hierarchical." For maturational theory, a stage represents the total state of the organism at a given period of time; for example, Gesell's embryological concept of stage equates it with the typical behavior pattern of an age period, such as a stage of "five-year-olds." Although in the theories of Freud and Erikson stages are less directly equated with ages, psychoanalytic stages are still embryological in the sense that age leads to a new stage regardless of experience and regardless of reorganizations at previous stages. As a result, education and experience become valuable not for movement to a new stage but for healthy or successful integration of the concerns of the present stage. Onset of the next stage occurs regardless of experience; only healthy integration of a stage is contingent on experience.

By contrast, in cognitive-developmental theory a stage is a delimited structure of thought, fixed in a sequence of structures but theoretically independent of time and total organismic state (Kohlberg, 1969; Loevinger, Wessler, and Redmore, 1970). Such stages are hierarchical reorganizations; attainment of a higher stage presupposes attainment of the prior stage and represents a reorganization or transformation of it. Accordingly, attainment of the next stage is a valid aim of educational experience.

For the interactionist, experience is essential to stage progression, and more or richer stimulation leads to faster advance through the series of stages. The maturational theory assumes that extreme deprivation will retard or fixate development but that enrichment will not necessarily accelerate it. To understand the effects of experience in stimulating stage development, cognitive-developmental theory holds that one must analyze the relation of the structure of a child's specific experience to behavior structures. The analysis focuses on discrepancies between the child's action system or expectancies and the events experienced. The hypothesis is that some moderate or optimal degree of conflict or discrepancy constitutes the most effective experience for structural change.

As applied to educational intervention, the theory holds that facilitating the child's movement to the next step of development involves exposure to the next higher level of thought and conflict requiring the active application of the current level of thought to problematic situation. This implies (1) attention to the child's mode or styles of thought; that is, stage; (2) match of stimulation to that stage; for example, exposure to modes of reasoning one stage above the child's own; (3) arousal, among children, of genuine cognitive and social conflict and disagreement about problematic situations (in contrast to traditional education, which has stressed adult "right answers" and has reinforced "behaving well"); and (4) exposure to stimuli toward which the child can be active, in which assimilatory response to the stimulus situation is associated with "natural" feedback.

In summary, the maturationist theory assumes that basic mental structure results from an innate patterning. The environmentalist learning theory assumes that basic mental structure results from the patterning or association of events in the outside world. The cognitive-developmental theory assumes that basic mental structure results from an interaction between organismic structuring tendencies and the structure of the outside world, not reflecting either one directly. This interaction leads to cognitive stages that represent the transformations of early cognitive structures as they are applied to the external world and as they accommodate to it.

Epistemological Components of Educational Ideologies

We have considered the various psychological theories as parts of educational ideologies. Associated with these theories are differing epistemologies or philosophies of science, specifying what knowledge is; that is, what are observable facts, and how can these facts be interpreted? Differences in epistemology, like differences in actual theory, generate different strategies for defining objectives.

Romantic educational ideology springs not only from a maturational psychology but also from an existentialist or phenomenological epistemology, defining knowledge and reality as referring to the immediate inner experience of the self. Knowledge or truth in the romantic epistemology is self-awareness or self-insight, a form of truth with emotional as well as intellectual components. As this form of truth extends beyond the self, it is through sympathetic understanding of humans and natural beings as other "selves."

In contrast, cultural transmission ideologies of education tend to involve epistemologies that stress knowledge as that which is repetitive and "objective," that which can be pointed to in sense experience and measurement and which can be culturally shared and tested.

The progressive ideology, in turn, derives from a functional or pragmatic epistemology that equates knowledge with neither inner experience nor outer sense reality but with an equilibrated or resolved relationship between an inquiring human actor and a problematic situation. For the progressive epistemology, the immediate or introspective experience of the child does not have ultimate truth or reality. The meaning and truth of a child's experience depends on its relationship to the situations in which he or she is acting. At the same time, the progressive epistemology does not attempt to reduce psychological experience to observable responses in reaction to observable stimuli or situations. Rather, it attempts to functionally coordinate the external meaning of the child's experiences as *behavior* with its internal meaning as it appears to the observer.

With regard to educational objectives, these differences in epistemology generate differences with respect to three issues. The first issue concerns whether to focus objectives on internal states or external behavior. In this respect, cultural transmission and romantic ideologies represent opposite poles. The cultural transmission view evaluates educational change from children's performances, not from their feelings or thoughts. Social growth is defined by the conformity of behavior to particular cultural standards such as honesty and industriousness. These skill and trait terms are found in both commonsense evaluations of school grades and report cards and in "objective" educational psychological measurement. Behaviorist ideologies systematize this focus by rigorously eliminating references to internal or subjective experience as "nonscientific." Skinner (1971, p. 15), says "We can follow the path taken by physics and biology by turning directly to the relation between behavior and the environment and neglecting . . . states of mind. . . . We do not need to try to discover what personalities, states of mind, feelings . . . intentions—or other prerequisites of autonomous man really are in order to get on with a scientific analysis of behavior."

In contrast, the romantic view emphasizes inner feelings and states. Supported by the field of psychotherapy, romantics maintain that skills, achievements, and performances are not satisfying in themselves but are only a means to inner awareness, happiness, or mental health. They hold that educators or therapists who ignore the child's inner states in the name of science do so at their peril, because these states are most real to the child.

The progressive or cognitive-developmental view attempts to integrate both behavior and internal states in a functional epistemology of mind. It takes inner experience seriously by attempting to observe thought process rather than language behavior and by observing valuing processes rather than reinforced behavior. In doing so, however, it combines interviews, behavioral tests, and naturalistic observation methods in mental assessment. The cognitive-developmental approach stresses the need to examine mental competence or mental structure as opposed to examining only performance, but it employs a functional rather than an introspective approach to the observation of mental structure. An example is Piaget's systematic and reproducible observations of the preverbal infant's thought structure of space, time, and causality. In short, the cognitive-developmental approach does not select a focus on inner experience or on outer behavior objectives by epistemological fiat, but uses a functional methodology to coordinate the two through empirical study.

A second issue in the definition of educational objectives involves whether to emphasize immediate experience and behavior or long-term consequences in the child's development. The progressive ideology centers on education as it relates to the child's experience but attempts to observe or assess experience in functional terms rather than by immediate self-projection into the child's place. As a result, the progressive distinguishes between *humanitarian* criteria of the quality of the child's experience and *educative* criteria of quality of experience, in terms of long-term developmental consequences. According to Dewey (1963, pp. 25–28):

Some experiences are miseducative. Any experience is miseducative that has the effect of arresting or distorting the growth of further experience. . . . An experience may be immediately enjoyable and yet promote the formation of a slack and careless attitude . . . [which] operates to modify the quality of subsequent experiences so as to prevent a person from getting out of them what they have to give. . . . Just as no man lives or dies to himself, so no experience lives or dies to itself. Wholly independent of desire or intent, every experience lives on in further experiences. Hence the central problem of an education based on experience is to select the kind of present experiences that live fruitfully and creatively in subsequent experience.

Dewey maintains that an educational experience that stimulates development is one that arouses interest, enjoyment, and challenge in the immediate experience of the student. The reverse is not necessarily the case; immediate interest and enjoyment do not always indicate that an educational experience stimulates long-range development. Interest and involvement is a necessary but not sufficient condition for education as development. For romantics, especially of the "humanistic psychology" variety, having a novel, intense, and complex experience is *self-development* or self-actualization. For progressives, a more objective test of the effects of the experience on later behavior is required before deciding that the experience was developmental. The progressive views the child's enjoyment and interest as a basic and legitimate criterion of education but views it as a humanitarian rather than an educational criterion. The progressive holds that education must meet humanitarian criteria but argues that a concern for the enjoyment and liberty of children is not in itself equivalent to a concern for their development.

Psychologically, the distinction between humanitarian and developmental criteria is the distinction between the short-term value of the child's immediate experience and the long-term value of that experience as it relates to development. According to the progressive view, this question of the relation of the immediate to the long term is an empirical rather than a philosophic question. As an example, a characteristic behaviorist strategy is to demonstrate the reversibility of learning by performing an experiment in which a preschooler is reinforced for interacting with other children rather than withdrawing in a corner. This is followed by a reversal of the experiment, demonstrating that when the reinforcement is removed the child again becomes withdrawn. From the progressive or cognitive-developmental perspective, if behavior changes are of this reversible character they cannot define genuine educational objectives. The progressive approach maintains that the worth of an educational effect is decided by its effects on later behavior and development. Thus, in the progressive view, the basic problems of choosing and validating educational ends can only be solved by longitudinal studies of the effects of educational experience.

The third basic issue is whether the aims of education should be universal as opposed to unique or individual. This issue has an epistemological aspect because romantics have often defined educational goals in terms of the expression or development of a unique self or identity; "objectivist" epistemologies deny that such concepts are accessible to clear observation and definition. In contrast, cultural transmission approaches characteristically focus on measures of individual differences in general dimensions of achievement or in social behavior dimensions on which any individual can be ranked. The progressive, like the romantic, questions the significance of defining behavior relative to some population norm external to the individual. Searching for the "objective" in human experience, the progressive seeks universal qualitative states or sequences in development. Movement from one stage to the next is significant because it is a sequence in the individual's own development, not just a population average or norm. At the same time, insofar as the sequence is a universally observed development it is not unique to the individual in question.

In summary, the cognitive-developmental approach derives from a functional or pragmatic epistemology that attempts to integrate the dichotomies of the inner versus the outer, the immediate versus the remote in time, the unique versus the general. The cognitive-developmental approach focuses on an empirical search for continuities between inner states and outer behavior and between immediate reaction and remote outcome. Although focusing on the child's experience, the progressive ideology defines such experience in terms of universal and empirically observable sequences of development.

Ethical Value Positions Underlying Educational Ideologies

When psychologists such as Dewey, Skinner, Neill, and Montessori actually engage in innovative education, they develop a theory that is not a mere statement of psychological principle, but an ideology. This is not because of the dogmatic, nonscientific attitude they have as psychologists but because prescription of educational practice cannot be derived from psychological theory or science alone. In addition to theoretical assumptions about how children learn or develop (the psychological theory component), educational ideologies include value assumptions about what is educationally good or worthwhile. To call a pattern of educational thought an *ideology* is to indicate that it is a fairly systematic combination of a theory about psychological and social fact with a set of value principles.

The Fallacy of Value Neutrality

A "value-neutral" position, based only on facts about child development or about methods of education, cannot in itself directly contribute to educational practice. Factual statements about what the processes of learning and development *are* cannot be directly translated into statements about what children's learning and development *ought to be* without introducing some value principles.

In "value-neutral" research, learning does not necessarily imply movement to a stage of greater cognitive or ethical adequacy. As an example, acquisition of a cognitively arbitrary concept is considered learning in the same general sense as is acquisition of a capacity for logical inference. Such studies do not relate learning to some justifiable notion of knowledge, truth, or cognitive adequacy. Values are defined relative to a particular culture. Thus, morality is equivalent to conformity to, or internalization of, the particular standards of the child's group or culture. As an example, Berkowitz (1964, p. 44) writes, "Moral values are evaluations of actions generally believed by the members of a given society to be either 'right' or 'wrong.'"

Such "value-free" research cannot be translated into prescriptions for practice without importing a set of value-assumptions having no relation to psychology itself. The effort to remain "value-free" or "non-ideological" and yet prescribe educational goals usually has followed the basic model of counseling or consulting. In the *value-free consulting model,* the client (whether student or school) defines educational ends, and the psychologist can then advise about means of education without losing value neutrality or imposing values. Outside education, the value-free consulting model not only provides the basic model for counseling and psychotherapy, where the client is an individual, but also for industrial psychology, where the client is a social system. In both therapy and industrial psychology, the consultant is paid by the client, and the financial contract defines whose values are to be chosen. The educator or educational psychologist, however, has more than one client. What the child wants, what parents want, and what the larger community wants are often at odds with one another.

An even more fundamental problem for the "value-free" consulting model is the logical impossibility of making a dichotomy between value-free means and value-loaded ends. Skinner (1971, p. 17) claims that "a behavior technology is ethically neutral. Both the villain and the saint can use it. There is nothing in a methodology that determines the values governing its use." But consider the use of torture on the rack as a behavior technology for learning that could be used by saint and villain alike. On technological grounds, Skinner advises against punishment, but this does not solve the ethical issue.

Dewey's logical analysis and our present historical awareness of the value consequences of adopting new technologies have made us realize that choices of means, in the last analysis, also imply choices of end results. Advice about means and methods involves value considerations and cannot be made purely on a basis of "facts." Concrete, positive reinforcement is not an ethically neutral means. To advise the use of concrete reinforcement is to advise that a certain kind of character, motivated by concrete reinforcement, is the end goal of education. Not only can advice about means not be separated from choice of ends, but there is no way for educational consultants to avoid harboring their own criteria for choosing ends. The "value-neutral" consulting model equates value neutrality with acceptance of value relativity; that is, acceptance of whatever the values of the client are. But the educator or educational psychologist cannot be neutral in this sense either.

Values and the Cultural Transmission Ideology

In an effort to cope with the dilemmas inherent in the prescription of value neutrality, many psychologists tend to move to a cultural transmission ideology based on the value premise of *social relativity*. Social relativity assumes some consistent set of values characteristic of the culture, nation, or system as a whole. Although these values may be arbitrary and may vary from one social system to another, there is at least some consensus about them. This approach says, "Since values are relative and arbitrary, we might as well take the given values of the society as our starting point and advocate 'adjustment' to the culture or achievement in it as the educational end." For example, Bereiter and Engelmann (1966, p. 24) state the social relativist basis of the system as follows: "In order to use the term *cultural deprivation,* it is necessary to assume some point of reference. . . . The standards of the American public schools represent one such point of reference. . . . There are standards of knowledge and ability which are consistently held to be valuable in the schools, and any child in the schools who falls short of these standards by reason of his particular cultural background may be said to be culturally deprived."

The Bereiter-Engelmann preschool model takes as its standard of value "the standard of the American public schools." It recognizes that this standard is arbitrary and that the kinds of learning prized by the American public schools may not be the most worthy, but it accepts this arbitrariness because it assumes that "all values are relative"' that there is no ultimate standard of worth for learning and development.

Unlike Bereiter and Engelmann, many social relativist educators do not simply accept the standards of the school and culture and attempt to maximize conformity to them. Rather, they are likely to elaborate or create standards for a school or society based on value premises derived from what we shall call "the psychologist's fallacy." According to many philosophical analysts, the effort to derive statements of *ought* (or value) directly from statements of *is* (or fact) is a logical fallacy termed the "naturalistic fallacy" (Kohlberg, 1971a). The psychologist's fallacy is a form of the naturalistic fallacy. As practiced by psychologists, the naturalistic fallacy is the direct derivation of statements about what human nature, human values, and human desires *ought to be* from psychological statements about what they *are*. Typically, this derivation slides over the distinction between what is desired and what is desirable.

The following statement from B. F. Skinner (1971, p. 104) offers a good example of the psychologist's fallacy:

Good things are positive reinforcers. Physics and biology study things without reference to their values, but the reinforcing effects of things are the province of behavioral science, which, to the extent that it concerns itself with operant reinforcement, is a science of values. Things are good (positively reinforcing) presumably because of the contingencies of survival under which the species evolved. It is part of the genetic endowment called "human nature" to be reinforced in particular ways by particular things. . . . The effective reinforcers are matters of observation and no one can dispute them.

In this statement, Skinner equates or derives a value word (*good*) from a fact word (*positive reinforcement*). This equation is questionable; we wonder whether obtaining positive reinforcement really is good. The psychologist's fallacy or the naturalistic fallacy is a fallacy because we can always ask the further question "Why is that good?" or "By what standard is that good?" Skinner does not attempt to deal with this further question, called the "open question" by philosophers. He also defines good as "cultural survival." The postulation of cultural survival as an ultimate value raises the open question too. We may ask, "Why should the Nazi culture (or the American culture) survive?" The reason Skinner is not concerned with answering the open question about survival is because he is a cultural relativist, believing that any nonfactual reasoning about what is good or about the validity of moral principles is meaningless. He says, "What a given group of people calls good is a fact, it is what members of the group find reinforcing as a result of their genetic endowment and the natural and social contingencies to which they have been exposed. Each culture has its own set of goods, and what is good in one culture may not be good in another" (p. 128).

The Fallacy of Value Relativism

Behind Skinner's value relativism, then, lie the related notions that (1) all valid inferences of principles are factual or scientific, (2) valid statements about values must be statements about facts of valuing, and (3) what people actually value differs. The fact that people do value different things only becomes an argument for the notion that values are relative if one accepts the first two assumptions listed. Many philosophers believe both assumptions to be mistaken because they represent forms of the fact-value confusion already described as the naturalistic fallacy. Confusing discourse about fact with discourse about values, the relativist believes that when ethical judgment is not empirical science it is not rational. This equation of science with rationality arises because the relativist does not correctly understand philosophical modes of inquiry. In modern conceptions, philosophy is the clarification of concepts for the purpose of critically evaluating beliefs and standards. The kinds of beliefs that primarily concern philosophy are normative beliefs or standards, beliefs about what ought to be rather than about what is. These include standards of the right or good (ethics), of the true (epistemology), and of the beautiful (esthetics). In science, the critical evaluation of factual beliefs is limited to criteria of causal explanation and prediction; a "scientific" critical evaluation of normative beliefs is limited to treating them as a class of facts. Philosophy, by contrast, seeks rational justification and criticism of normative beliefs, based on considerations additional to their predictive or causal explanatory power. There is fairly widespread agreement among philosophers that criteria for the validity of ethical judgments can be established independent of "scientific" or predictive criteria. Because patterns for the rational statement and justification of normative beliefs, or "oughts," are not identical with patterns of scientific statement and justification, philosophers can reject both Skinner's notion of a strictly "scientific" ethics and Skinner's notion that whatever is not "scientific" is relative. The open question "Why is reinforcement or cultural survival good?" is meaningful because there are patterns of ethical justification that are ignored by Skinner's relativistic science.

Distinguishing criteria of moral judgment from criteria of scientific judgment, most philosophers accept the "methodological nonrelativism" of moral judgment just as they accept the methodological nonrelativism of scientific judgment (Brandt, 1959). This ethical nonrelativism is based on appeal to principles for making moral judgments, just as scientific nonrelativism is based on appeal to principles of scientific method or of scientific judgment.

In summary, cultural transmission ideologies rest on the value premise of social relativism—the doctrine that values are relative to, and based on, the standards of the particular culture and cannot be questioned or further justified. Cultural transmission ideologies of the "scientific" variety, such as Skinner's, do not recognize moral principles, because they equate what is desirable with what is observable by science, or with what is desired. Philosophers do not agree on the exact formulation of valid moral principles, although they agree that such formulations center around such notions as "the greatest welfare" or "justice as equity." They also do not agree on choice of priorities between principles such as "justice" and "the greatest welfare." Most philosophers do agree, however, that moral evaluations must be rooted in, or justified by, reference to such a realm of principles. Most also maintain that certain values or principles ought to be universal and that these principles are distinct from the rules of any given culture. A principle is a universalizable, impartial mode of deciding or judging, not a concrete cultural rule. "Thou shalt not commit adultery" is a rule for specific behavior in specific situations in a monogamous society. By contrast, Kant's categorical imperative—"Act only as you would be willing that everyone should act in 'the same situation"—is a principle. It is a guide for choosing among behaviors, not a prescription for behavior. As such, it is free from culturally defined content; it both transcends and subsumes particular social laws. Hence it has universal applicability.

In regard to values, Skinner's cultural transmission ideology is little different from other, older ideologies based on social relativism and on subjective forms of hedonism, such as social Darwinism and Benthamite utilitarianism. As an educational ideology, however, Skinner's relativistic behavior technology has one feature that distinguishes it from older forms of social utilitarianism. This is its denial that rational concern for social utility is itself a matter of moral character or moral principle to be transmitted to the young. In Skinner's view, moral character concepts that go beyond responsiveness to social reinforcement and control rely on "prescientific" concepts of free will. Stated in different terms, the concept of moral education is irrelevant to Skinner; he is not concerned with teaching to the children of his society the value principles that he himself adopts. Culture designers are *psychologist*-king, value relativists, who somehow make a free, rational decision to devote themselves to controlling individual behavior more effectively in the service of cultural survival. In Skinner's scheme, there is no plan to make the controlled controllers or to educate psychologist-kings.

Values and the Romantic Ideology

At first sight, the value premises of the romantic ideology appear to be the polar opposites of Skinner's cultural transmission ideology. Opposed to social control and survival is individual freedom, freedom for children to be themselves. For example, A. S. Neill (1960, p. 297) says, "How can happiness be bestowed? My own answer is: Abolish authority. Let the child be himself. Don't push him around. Don't teach him. Don't lecture him. Don't elevate him. Don't force him to do anything."

As we have pointed out, the romantic ideology rests on a psychology that conceives of the child as having a spontaneously growing mind. In addition, however, it rests on the ethical postulate that "the guardians of the young should merit the proud title of the defenders of the hap-

piness and rights of children" (Hall, 1901, p. 24). The current popu-
larity of the romantic ideology in "free school," "deschool," and "open
school" movements is related to increased adult respect for the rights
of children. Bereiter (1972, pp. 26–27) carries this orientation to an
extreme conclusion:

Teachers are looking for a way to get out of playing God.... The same
humanistic ethos that tells them what qualities the next generation should
have also tells them that they have no right to manipulate other people or
impose their goals upon them. The fact is that there are no morally safe goals
for teachers any more. Only processes are safe. When it comes to goals, everything is in doubt.... A common expression, often thrown at me when I have
argued for what I believed children should be taught, is "Who are we to say
what this child should learn?" The basic moral problem ... is inherent in
education itself. If you are engaged in education, you are engaged in an effort
to influence the course of the child's development ... it is to determine what
kinds of people they turn out to be. It is to create human beings; it is, therefore, to play God.

This line of thought leads Bereiter to conclude (p. 25), "The God-
like role of teachers in setting goals for the development of children is
no longer morally tenable. A shift to informal modes of education does
not remove the difficulty. This paper, then, questions the assumption
that education itself is a good undertaking and considers the possibilities of a world in which values other than educational ones, come to
the fore."

According to Bereiter, then, a humanistic ethical concern for the
child's rights must go beyond romantic free schools, beyond deschooling, to the abandonment of an explicit concern for education. Bereiter
contrasts the modern "humanistic ethic" and its concern for the child's
rights with the earlier "liberal" concern for human rights, which held
education and the common school to be the foundation of a free society. This earlier concern Bereiter sees expressed most cogently in
Dewey's progressivism.

The historical shift in the conception of children's rights and human
rights that leads Bereiter to reject Dewey's position is essentially a
shift from the liberal grounding of children's rights in ethical principles to the modern humanistic grounding of their rights in the doctrine
of ethical relativity.

Bereiter is led to question the moral legitimacy of education because
he equates a regard for the child's liberty with a belief in ethical rela-

tivity and does not recognize that liberty and justice are universal ethical principles. "The teacher may try to play it safe by sticking to the middle of the road and only aiming to teach what is generally approved, but there are not enough universally endorsed values (if, indeed, there are any) to form the basis of an education" (Bereiter, 1972, p. 27). Here he confuses an ethical position of tolerance or respect for the child's freedom with a belief in ethical relativity, not recognizing that respect for the child's liberty derives from a principle of justice rather than from a belief that all moral values are arbitrary. Respect for children's liberty means awarding them the maximum liberty compatible with the liberty of others (and of themselves when older), not refusal to deal with their values and behavior. The assumption of individual relativity of values underlying modern romantic statements of children's liberty is also reflected in the following quote from Neill (1960, p. 4): "Well, we set out to make a school in which we should allow children freedom to be themselves. In order to do this, we had to renounce all discipline, all direction, all suggestion, all moral training, all religious instruction. We have been called brave, but it did not require courage. All it required was what we had—a complete belief in the child as a good, not an evil, being. For almost forty years, this belief in the goodness of the child has never wavered; it rather has become a final faith."

For Neill, as for many free school advocates, value relativity does not involve what it did for Bereiter—a questioning of all conceptions of what is good in children and good for them. Neill's statement that the child is "good" is a completely nonrelativist conception. It does not, however, refer to an ethical or moral principle or standard used to direct the child's education. Instead, just as in Skinner's cultural transmission ideology, the conception of the good is derived from what we have termed the "psychologist's fallacy." Neill's faith in the "goodness of the child" is the belief that what children *do* want, when left to themselves, can be equated with what they *should* want from an ethical standpoint. In one way, this faith is a belief that children are wired so as to act and develop compatibly with ethical norms. In another sense, however, it is an ethical postulation that decisions about what is right for children should be derived from what children do desire— that whatever children do is right.

This position begs the open questions "Why is freedom to be oneself good—by what standard is it a good thing?"

The question is raised by Dewey as follows (1963, p. 75): "The objection made [to identifying the educative process with growing or developing] is that growth might take many different directions: a man, for example, who starts out on a career of burglary may grow in that direction . . . into a highly expert burglar. Hence it is argued that 'growth' is not enough; we must also specify the direction in which growth takes place, the end toward which it tends."

In Neill's view, it is not clear whether there is a standard of development—that is, some standard of goodness that children who grow up freely all meet—or whether children who grow up freely are good only by their own standards, even if they are thieves or villains by some other ethical standards. To the extent that there is a nonrelativist criterion employed by Neill, it does not derive from, nor is it justified by, the ethical principles of philosophy. Rather, it is derived from matters of psychological fact about "mental health" and "happiness." For example, "The merits of Summerhill are the merits of healthy free children whose lives are unspoiled by fear and hate" (Neill, 1960, p. 4). And "The aim of education, in fact, the aim of life is to work joyfully and to find happiness" (p. 297).

Freedom, then, is not justified as an ethical principle but as a matter of psychological fact, leading to "mental health and happiness." These are ultimate terms, as are the terms "maximizing reinforcement" and "cultural survival" for Skinner. For other romantic educators, the ultimate value terms are also psychological; for example, "self-realization," "self-actualization," and "spontaneity." These are defined as "basic human tendencies" and are taken as good in themselves, rather than being subject to the scrutiny of moral philosophy.

We have attempted to show that romantic libertarian ideologies are grounded on value relativism and reliance on the psychologist's fallacy, just as are cultural transmission ideologies, which see education as behavior control in the service of cultural survival. As a result of these shared premises, both romantic and cultural transmission ideologies tend to generate a kind of elitism. In the case of Skinner, this elitism is reflected in the vision of the psychologist as a culture designer, who "educates others" to conform to culture and maintain it but not to develop the values and knowledge that would be required for culture designing. In the case of the romantic, the elitism is reflected in a refusal to impose intellectual and ethical values of libertarianism, equal justice, intellectual inquiry, and social reconstructionism on the child, even though these values are held to be the most important ones: "Summerhill is a place in which people who have the innate ability and wish to be scholars will be scholars; while those who are only fit to sweep the streets will sweep the streets. But we have not produced a street cleaner so far. Nor do I write this snobbishly, for I would rather see a school produce a happy street cleaner than a neurotic scholar" (Neill, 1960, pp. 4–5).

In summary, in spite of their libertarian and nonindoctrinative emphases, romantic ideologies also have a tendency to be elitist or patronizing. Recalling the role of Dostoevsky's Grand Inquisitor, they see education as a process that only intends the child to be happy and adjusted rather than one that confronts the child with the ethical and intellectual problems and principles that educators themselves confront. Skinner and Neill agree it is better for the child to be a happy pig than an unhappy Socrates. We may question, however, whether they have the right to withhold that choice.

Value Postulates of Progressivism

Progressive ideology, in turn, rests on the value postulates of ethical liberalism.* This position rejects traditional standards and value relativism in favor of ethical universals. Further, it recognizes that value universals are ethical principles formulated and justified by the method of philosophy, not simply by the method of psychology. The ethical liberal position favors the active stimulation of the development of these principles in children. These principles are presented through a process of critical questioning that creates an awareness of the ground and limits of rational assent; they also are seen as relevant to universal trends in the child's own social and moral development. The liberal recognition of principles as *principles* clears them from confusion with psychological facts. To be concerned about children's happiness is an ethical imperative for the educator without regard to "mental health," "positive reinforcement," or other psychological terms used by educators who commit the psychologist's fallacy. Rational ethical principles, not the values of parents or culture, are the final value arbiters in

---

*There are two main schools of ethical liberalism. The more naturalistic or utilitarian one is represented in the works of Mill, Sidgewick, Dewey, and Tufts. The other is represented in the works of Locke, Kant, and Rawls. A modern statement of the liberal ethical tradition in relation to education is provided by Peters (1968).

defining educational aims. Such principles may call for consultation with parents, community, and children in formulating aims, but they do not warrant making them final judges of aims.

The liberal school recognizes that ethical principles determine the ends as well as the means of education. There is great concern not only to make schools more just—that is, to provide equality of educational opportunity and to allow freedom of belief—but also to educate so that free and just people emerge from the schools. Accordingly, liberals also conscientiously engage in moral education. It is here that the progressive and romantic diverge, in spite of a common concern for the liberty and rights of the child. For the romantic, liberty means noninterference. For the liberal, the principle of respect for liberty is itself defined as a moral aim of education. Not only are the rights of children to be respected by the teacher, but the children's development is to be stimulated so that they may come to respect and defend their own rights and the rights of others.

Recognition of concern for liberty as a principle leads to an explicit, libertarian conception of moral education. According to Dewey and McLellan ([1895] 1964, p. 207),

"Summing up, we may say that every teacher requires a sound knowledge of ethical and psychological principles. . . . Only psychology and ethics can take education out of the rule-of-thumb stage and elevate the school to a vital, effective institution in *the greatest of all constructions—the building of a free and powerful character.*"

In the liberal view, educational concern for the development of a "free character" is rooted in the principle of liberty. For the romantic or relativist libertarian, this means that "everyone has their own bag," which may or may not include liberty, and to actively stimulate the development of regard for liberty or a free character in the child is as much an imposition on the child as any other educational intervention. The progressive libertarians differ on this point. They advocate a strong rather than a weak application of liberal principles to education. Consistent application of ethical principles to education means that education *should* stimulate the development of ethical principles in students.

In regard to ethical values, the progressive ideology adds the postulates of *development* and *democracy* to the postulates of liberalism. The notion of educational democracy is one in which justice between teacher and child means joining in a community in which value decisions are made on a shared and equitable basis, rather than noninterference with the child's value decisions. Because ethical principles function as principles, the progressive ideology is "democratic" in a sense that romantic and cultural transmission ideologies are not.

In discussing Skinner, we pointed to a fundamental problem in the relation between the ideology of the relativist educator and that of the student. Traditional education did not find it a problem to reconcile the role of teacher and the role of student. Both were members of a common culture and the task of the teacher was to transmit that culture and its values to the student. In contrast, modern psychologists advocating cultural transmission ideologies do not hold this position. As social relativists, they do not really believe in a common culture; instead, they are in the position of transmitting values that are different both from those they believe in and those believed in by the student. At the extreme, as we mentioned earlier, Skinner proposes an ideology for ethically relative psychologist-kings or culture designers who control others. Clearly there is a contradiction between the ideology for the psychologist-king and the ideology for the child.

Romantic or radical ideologies are also unable to solve this problem. Romantics adopt what they assume are the child's values or take as their value premise what is "natural" in the child rather than endorsing the culture's values. But, while the adult believes in the child's freedom and creativity and wants a free, more natural society, the child neither fully comprehends nor necessarily adheres to the adult's beliefs. In addition, the romantic must strive to give the child freedom to grow even though such freedom may lead the child to become a reactionary. Like the behavior modifier, then, the romantic has an ideology, but it is different from the one that the student is supposed to develop.

Progressives are nonelitist because they attempt to get all children to develop in the direction of recognizing the principles they themselves hold. But is this not indoctrinative? Here we need to clarify the postulates of development and democracy as they guide education.

For the progressive, the problem of offering a nonindoctrinative education that is based on ethical and epistemological principles is partially resolved by a conception that these principles represent developmentally advanced or mature stages of reasoning, judgment, and action. Because there are culturally universal stages or sequences of moral development (Kohlberg and Turiel, 1971), stimulation of the child's development to the next step in a natural direction is equivalent to a long-range goal of teaching ethical principles.

Because the development of these principles is natural, they are not imposed on the children—they choose principles themselves. A similar developmental approach is taken toward intellectual values. Intellectual education in the progressive view is not merely a transmission of information and intellectual skills, it is the communication of patterns and methods of "scientific" reflection and inquiry. These patterns correspond to higher stages of logical reasoning, to Piaget's formal operations. According to the progressive, there is an important analogy between scientific and ethical patterns of judgment or problem solving, and there are overlapping rationales for intellectual and ethical education. In exposing the child to opportunities for reflective scientific inquiry, teachers are guided by the principles of scientific method that the teachers themselves accept as the basis of rational reflection. Reference to such principles is nonindoctrinative if these principles are not presented as formulas to be learned ready-made or as rote patterns grounded in authority. Rather, they are part of a process of reflection by students and teachers. A similar approach guides the process of reflection on ethical or value problems.

The problem of indoctrination is also resolved for the progressive by the concept of democracy. A concern for the child's freedom from indoctrination is part of a concern for the child's freedom to make decisions and act meaningfully. Freedom, in this context, means democracy; that is, power and participation in a social system that recognizes basic equal rights. It is impossible for teachers not to engage in value judgments and decisions. A concern for the liberty of the child does not create a school in which the teacher is value neutral, and any pretense of such neutrality creates "the hidden curriculum" (Kohlberg, 1970a). But it can create a school in which the teacher's value judgments and decisions involve the students democratically.

We turn, now, to the nature and justification of these universal and intrinsically worthy aims and principles. In the next sections, we attempt to indicate the way in which the concept of development, rooted in psychological study, can aid in prescribing aims of education without commission of the psychologist's fallacy. We call this "the developmental-philosophic strategy for defining educational aims."

Strategies for Defining Educational Objectives and Evaluating Educational Experience

We have considered the core psychological and philosophical assumptions of the three major streams of educational ideology. Now we consider these assumptions as they have been used to define objectives in early education.

There appear to be three fundamental strategies for defining educational objectives, which we call "the bag of virtues" or "desirable trait" strategy, the "industrial psychology" or "prediction of success" strategy, and the "developmental-philosophic" strategy. These strategies tend to be linked, respectively, with the romantic, the cultural transmission, and the progressive educational ideologies.

The romantic tends to define educational objectives in terms of a "bag of virtues"—a set of traits characterizing an ideal healthy or fully functioning personality. Such definitions of objectives are justified by a psychiatric theory of a spontaneous, creative, or self-confident personality. This standard of value springs from the romantic form of the psychologist's fallacy. Statements of value (desirability of a character trait) are derived from psychological propositions of fact; for example a given trait may be believed to represent psychological "illness" or "health."

The cultural transmission ideology defines immediate objectives in terms of standards of knowledge and behavior learned in school. It defines the long-range objective as eventual power and status in the social system (such as income or success). In Skinner's terms, the objective is to maximize the reinforcement each individual receives from the system, while maintaining the system. In defining objectives, this focus on prediction of later success is common to those whose interest lies in maintaining the system in its present form and those whose interest lies in equalizing opportunity for success in the system.

Within the cultural transmission school, there is a second strategy for elaborating objectives that we have called the "industrial psychology" approach (Kohlberg, 1973d). Psychologically, this strategy is more explicitly atheoretical than the "bag of virtues" approach; with regard to values, it is more socially relativistic. Adopting the stance of the value-free consultant, it evaluates a behavior in terms of its usefulness as a means to the student's or the system's ends and focuses on the empirical prediction of later successes. In practice, this approach has focused heavily on tests and measurements of achievement as they predict or relate to later success in the educational or social system.

The third strategy, the developmental-philosophic, is linked to the progressive ideology. The progressive believes that a liberal conception of education pursuing intrinsically worthy aims or states is the best one for everyone. Such a conception of objectives must have a psychological component. The progressive defines the psychologically valuable in developmental terms. Implied in the term *development* is the notion that a more developed psychological state is more valuable or adequate than a less developed state.

The developmental-philosophic strategy attempts to clarify, specify, and justify the concept of adequacy implicit in the concept of development. It does so through (1) elaborating a formal psychological theory of development (the cognitive-developmental theory), (2) elaborating a formal ethical and epistemological theory of truth and worth linked to the psychological theory, (3) relating both of these to the facts of development in a specific area, and (4) describing empirical sequences of development worth cultivating.

Now we need to critically examine the three strategies. Our task is both logical and empirical. Logically, the chief question is "Does the strategy define objectives that are intrinsically valuable or universally desirable? Can it deal with the charge that its value is relative or arbitrary?" Empirically, the major question is "Does the strategy define objectives predicting to something of long-term value in later life?"

The Bag of Virtues Strategy

The "bag of virtues" strategy for choosing objectives is the approach that comes most naturally to educators. An example is the formulation of a Head Start list of objectives, as cited in Edith Grotberg's review (1969), offered by a panel of authorities on child development. One goal is "helping the emotional and social development of the child by encouraging self-confidence, spontaneity, curiosity, and self-discipline." We may note that development is defined here in terms of trait words. From the point of view of the philosophic developmentalist, the qualification of the term *social development* by such trait words is superfluous and misleading. The developmentalist would chart universals in preschool social development empirically and theoretically with implications for later development and would indicate the conditions that stimulate such development. Such a charting of development would make trait words such as *spontaneity* and *self-confidence* unnecessary.

The justification for using trait words to qualify development as an educational end has usually been that *development* is too vague a term. We consider this question later. Here we need only note the arbitrariness and vagueness that underlies all efforts to use the positive connotations of ordinary trait terms of personality or character to define educational standards and values. This arbitrariness and vagueness exists in lists of mental health traits such as the Head Start list and also in lists of moral virtues composing moral character, such as the Hartshorne and May (1928–1930) objectives of "honesty, service, and self-control." Arbitrariness exists first in composing the list or "bag" of virtues itself. One member of the committee likes *self-discipline*," another *spontaneity*; the committee includes both. Although both words sound nice, one wonders whether cultivating self-discipline and cultivating spontaneity are consistent with one another. Second, we may note that the observable meaning of a virtue word is relative to a conventional cultural standard that is both psychologically vague and ethically relative. The behavior that one person labels "self-discipline" another calls "lack of spontaneity." Because the observable meaning of a virtue word is relative to a conventional cultural standard, its meaning is psychologically vague, a fact first demonstrated by Hartshorne and May for the virtue word *honesty*. Hartshorne and May were dismayed to discover that they could locate no such stable personality trait as honesty in schoolchildren. A child who cheated on one occasion might or might not cheat on another: cheating was for the most part situationally determined. In a factor analysis, there was no clearly identifiable factor or correlation pattern that could be called *honesty*. Furthermore, "honesty" measurements did not predict to later behavior. This contradicts the commonsense notion underlying the bag of virtues approach. It turns out that dictionary terms for personality do not describe situationally general personality dispositions that are stable or predictive over development.

Related to the problem of psychological definition and measurement is the problem of the relativity of the standard of value defining "honesty" or any other virtue. Labeling a set of behaviors displayed by a child with positive or negative trait terms does not signify that they are of adaptive or ethical importance. It represents an appeal to particular community conventions.

We have criticized the "bag of virtues" approach on the grounds of *logical* questions raised by a procedure of sorting through the dictionary for trait terms with positive meaning. We need next to question two "scientific" or *psychological* assumptions, the concept of the personality trait and the concept of mental health, as they relate to the development of children. With regard to the trait assumption, longitudinal research findings lead us to question whether there are positive or adaptive childhood personality traits that are stable or predictive over time and development, even if such traits are defined by psychological rather than lexical methods. The relatively general and longitudinally stable personality traits that have been identified in earlier childhood are traits of temperament—introversion-extroversion, passivity-activity—that have been shown to be in large part hereditary temperamental traits without adaptive significance (research reviewed in Ausubel and Sullivan, 1970; Kohlberg, 1969; Kohlberg, La Crosse, and Ricks, 1971). The longitudinal research indicates that the notions of "mental health" or "mental illness" are even more questionable as concepts defining the meaning and value of personality traits. Unlike *development*, the term *mental health* has no clear psychological meaning when applied to children and their education. When clinicians examine a child with reference to mental health, they record the child's lags (and advances) in cognitive, social, and psychomotor development. Occasionally such lags are indicative of "illness," for example, of an organic brain condition. But, in general, if "illness" means anything beyond retarded development it means a prognosis of continued failure to develop. Considering the child's development as an aim of education, the metaphors of health and illness add little to detailed and adequate conceptions of cognitive and social development. This also is indicated by empirical longitudinal findings (Kohlberg, La-Crosse, and Ricks, 1971). We are led to ask whether early childhood traits with apparent negative mental health implications such as dependency, aggression, or anxiety, have predictive value as indicators of adult difficulties in "life adjustment" or "mental health." The answer at present is no: the mental health traits listed among the Head Start objectives, as well as those commonly included among the goals of other early education programs, have failed to show their predictive value for positive or negative adult life adjustment. Even if the behavior changes sought in such programs were achieved, the child would be no more likely than before to become a well-adjusted adult.

Secondly, from the philosophic point of view, those who espouse the mental health bag of virtues commit the psychologist's fallacy and a related fallacy, that a panel of psychiatrists or child psychiatrists such as the one defining Head Start objectives are "experts" on ethical principles or values.

In educational practice, a concern for mental health has at least meant an ethical concern for the happiness of the child; this was neglected by the cultural transmission school. But ethical principles based on a concern for the child's liberty and happiness can stand on their own without a mental health bag of virtues to rationalize them.

The Industrial Psychology Rationale

Translating educational objectives into a "bag of virtues" (skills) in the intellectual domain does not run into all the difficulties it has encountered in the social-emotional domain. This is because reasonable precision has been attained in defining and measuring intellectual skills and achievements, because there is some degree of predictability over time in these skills, and because the questions of value relativity raised by concepts of "moral character" and "mental health" as educational objectives are not as obvious when school aims are defined in terms of intellectual skills. But concepts of intellectual skills have only appeared satisfactory because of the high empirical overlap or correlation of these skills with cognitive development (in the developmental-philosophic sense) and because of the overlap with noneducational or "biological" constant of general intelligence. Once cognitive skills are defined and measured by educational *achievement* measures, they have little clear use in defining educational objectives.

The "achievement skills" conception is a joint product of the "bag of virtues" and "industrial psychology" approach to educational aims. We have noted that the industrial psychology approach rests on identifying and measuring relative individual success in meeting the task demands of a current job or work position, and on identifying characteristics predicting to later success or mobility in the job system. Its application in education has been the development of achievement tests. Although not originally developed to define operational educational goals, achievement tests have frequently been used for this purpose. The massive Coleman Report (Coleman and others, 1966) rested its entire analysis of the quality and effects of schooling on variations in achievement test scores. A number of academic early education programs, including the Bereiter and Engelmann program (1966) previously quoted, essentially define their objective as the improvement of later achievement scores.

From the ethical or philosophic point of view, the use of achievement tests to measure educational objectives rests on a compounding of one type of relativism on another. The items composing an achievement test do not derive from any epistemological principles of adequate patterns of thought and knowledge but, rather, represent samples of items taught in the schools. The information taught in the schools is relative and arbitrary: Latin and Greek for one hour, computer programming for another. There is no internal logical or epistemological analysis of these items to justify their worth. Another relativistic aspect of achievement tests is "marking on the curve." This leads to what Edward Zigler has called "defining compensatory education objectives as raising the entire country above the 50th percentile in achievement tests" (unpublished comment, Washington, D.C., 1970).

Finally, and most basically, the relativism underlying achievement tests involves predicting to success in a system without asking whether the system awards success in an ethically justifiable manner or whether success itself is an ethically justifiable goal. The original ethical impulse in constructing the achievement test was to equalize educational opportunity by a more impartial selection system than is offered by teachers' grades, recommendations, and the quality of schools the child has previously attended. This was done with relativistic acceptance that the content and demands of the school serve as social status gating mechanisms. It is hardly surprising that the whole desire to equalize opportunity, or increase educational and occupational justice through raising educational achievement scores, has failed in every possible sense of the word *failure* (Jencks and others, 1972).

On the psychological and factual side, there have been two basic and related flaws in the assumption that achievement tests represent something of educational value. The first is the notion that correlation or prediction can be substituted for causation. The second, related, notion is that success within an arbitrary system, the schools, implies success in other aspects of life. With regard to the first assumption, advocates of the industrial psychology strategy and achievement tests based on it feel that the relation between causation and prediction is unimportant. We can efficiently select those who will do well in college, become successful salespeople, or become juvenile delinquents without facing the causation issue. But if we shift from using a test or a measure of behavior as a selector to using it as the criterion for an educational objective, the problem is quite different. Unless a predictor of later achievement or adjustment is also a causal determinant of it, it cannot be used to define educational objectives.

As an example of the confusion between correlation and causation, we know that grades and achievement scores in elementary school predict to comparable scores in high school, which in turn predict to comparable scores in college. The assumption is then made that the *cause* of particular achievement scores is the earlier achievement. It is assumed that children who do not attain a second-grade level of performance on reading achievement will not attain an adequate level of reading later because they are low in reading achievement at second grade.

In fact, the prediction of early to later achievement is mainly due to factors extraneous to achievement itself. Longitudinal studies show that the stability or predictive power of school achievement tests is largely due, first, to a factor of general intelligence and, second, to social class. Achievement scores correlate with IQ scores and both measures predict to later school achievement; early elementary achievement does not predict to later achievement any better than does IQ alone. In other words, bright children learn what they're taught in school faster, but learning what they're taught in school does not make them brighter nor does it necessarily mean that they will learn later material faster.

Achievement tests also fail to predict to success in later life; in fact, longitudinal studies indicate that school achievement predicts to nothing of value other than itself.

For example, in terms of future job success, high school dropouts do as well as graduates who do not attend college; high school graduates with poor achievement scores and grades do as well as those with good scores; and college graduates with poor grades do as well as those with good grades (see Kohlberg, LaCrosse, and Ricks, 1971; Jencks and others, 1972).

In summary, academic achievement tests have no theoretical rationale. Their practical rationale is primarily an individual psychology "prediction for selection." But even by industrial psychology standards the tests do not do well, because they fail to predict later life achievement.

The criticisms do not imply that schools should be unconcerned with academic learning. They do suggest (1) a heavy element of arbitrariness in current school objectives in academic learning, (2) the inability of educational testing methods endorsed by the industrial psychology school to make these objectives less arbitrary, and (3) the invalidity of assuming that, if academic achievement is good, early achievement is best. Schools should teach reading, writing, and arithmetic, but their goals and success in teaching these subjects should not be judged by skill or achievement tests.

The Developmental-Philosophic Strategy

The developmental-philosophic strategy, as opposed to the other two, can deal with the ethical question of having a standard of nonrelative or universal value and with factual questions of prediction. The concept of development, as elaborated by cognitive-developmental theory, implies a standard of adequacy *internal* to, and governing, the developmental process itself. It is obvious that the notion of development must do more than merely define what comes later in time. It is not clear that what comes later must be better. As an example, if anal interests mature later in time than oral interests, this in itself is no reason for claiming that the anal interests are better than the oral interests.

Cognitive-developmental theory, however, postulates a formal internal standard of adequacy that is not merely an order of events in time. In doing so, it elaborates the ordinary-language meaning of the term *development*. Webster's Dictionary tells us that *to develop* means "to make active, to move from the original position to one providing more opportunity for effective use, to cause to grow and differentiate along lines natural of its kind; to go through a process of natural growth, differentiation, or evolution by successive changes." This suggests an internal standard of adequacy governing development; it implies that development is not just any behavior change but is a change toward greater differentiation, integration, and adaptation. Cognitive-developmental psychological theory postulates that movement through a sequential progression represents movement from a less adequate psychological state to a more adequate psychological state. The existence of this "internal standard of adequacy" is suggested by studies that show that children prefer thinking at the next higher moral or logical stage to thinking at their own stage (or at lower stages) (Rest, 1973) and that they move in that direction under normal conditions of stimulation.

The concept of development also implies that such an internal standard of adequacy is different from notions of adaptation based on culturally relative success or survival. As a case, we may take stages of morality. Being at the highest moral stage led Socrates and Martin Luther King to be put to death by members of their culture. Obviously, then, moral development cannot be justified as adaptive by standards of survival or of conformity to cultural standards. In terms of developmental psychological theory, however, King's morality was more adequate than the morality of most people who survive longer. Formally, King's morality was more differentiated and integrated than that of most people, because it would resolve for everyone moral problems and conflicts unresolved by lower-stage moralities.

As the example of King suggests, the formal standard of cognitive-developmental psychological theory is not itself ultimate but must be elaborated as a set of ethical and epistemological principles and justified by the method of philosophy and of ethics. The distinctive feature of the developmental-philosophic approach is that a philosophic conception of adequate principles is coordinated with a psychological theory of development and with the fact of development.

In contrast to "value-free" approaches, the approach suggested by Dewey and Piaget considers questions of value or adequacy at the very start. Piaget begins by establishing epistemological and logical criteria for deciding which thought structures are most adaptive and adequate for coping with complexity. Similarly, our work on ethical stages has taken a philosophic notion of adequate principles of justice (represented especially in the work of Kant and Rawls) to guide us in defining the direction of development. Epistemological and ethical principles guide psychological inquiry from the start. Thus, the strategy attempts to avoid the naturalistic fallacy of directly deriving judgments of value from judgments about the facts of development, although it assumes that the two may be systematically related. It takes as an hypothesis for empirical confirmation or refutation that development is a movement toward greater epistemological or ethical adequacy as defined by philosophic principles of adequacy.

The progressives' philosophical method differs from the approaches of philosophers of other persuasions in that the progressive or developmental method is partly empirical rather than purely analytic. It combines a prior conception of development with a prior notion of an ethical standard of adequacy, but these notions can be revised in light of the facts, including the facts of development. If the facts of development do not indicate that individuals move toward philosophically desired principles of justice, then the initial philosophic definition of the direction of development is in error and must be revised. The analytic and normative "ought" of the developmental philosopher must take into account the facts of development but is not simply a translation of these facts.

This method of "empirical" or "experimental" philosophy is especially central for an educational philosophy prescribing educational aims. Philosophical principles cannot be stated as ends of education until they can be stated psychologically. This means translating them into statements about a more adequate stage of development. Otherwise the rationally accepted principles of the philosopher will only be arbitrary concepts and doctrines for the child. Accordingly, to make a genuine statement of an educational end, the educational philosopher must coordinate notions of principles with understanding of the facts of development.

Development as the Aim of Education

We have attempted to clarify and justify the basic claim that developmental criteria are the best ones for defining educationally important behavior changes. We need now to clarify how the psychological study of development can concretely define educational goals. A common criticism is that the concept of development is too vague to genuinely clarify the choice of the curricular content and aims of education. A second, related, criticism is that the concept of development, with its connotation of the "natural," is unsuited to determine actual educational policy.

With regard to the issue of vagueness, if the concept of development is to aid in selecting educational aims and content, this assumes that only some behavior changes out of many can be labeled *developmental*. We need to justify this assumption and to clarify the conditions for developmental change.

Our position has been challenged by Bereiter (1970), who claims that determining whether or not a behavior change is development is a matter of theory, not an empirical issue. For example, Piagetian research shows that fundamental arithmetical reasoning (awareness of one-to-one correspondence, of inclusion of a larger class in a subclass, of addition and subtraction as inverse operations), usually develops naturally, without formal instruction or schooling; that is, it constitutes development. Such reasoning can also be explicitly taught, however, following various nondevelopmental learning theories. Accordingly, says Bereiter, to call fundamental arithmetical reasoning *developmental* does not define it as a developmental educational objective distinct from nondevelopmental objectives such as rote knowledge of the multiplication tables.

In answer, the cognitive-developmental position claims that developmental behavior change is irreversible, general over a field of responses, sequential, and hierarchical (Kohlberg, 1970b). When a set of behavior changes meets all these criteria, changes are termed *stages* or *structural reorganizations*. A specific area of behavioral change such as fundamental arithmetical reasoning may or may not meet these criteria. Engelmann claims to have artificially taught children the "naturally developing" operation of conservation, but Kamii (1971) found that the children so taught met Engelmann's criteria of conservation without meeting the criteria of development; for example, the response could be later forgotten or unlearned, and it was not generalized.

When a set of responses taught artificially do not meet the criteria of natural development, this is not because educational intervention is generally incompatible with developmental change. It is because the particular intervention is found to mimic development rather than to stimulate it. The issue of whether an educational change warrants the honorific label *development* is a question for empirical examination, not simply a matter of theory.

We have claimed that development can occur either naturally or as the result of a planned educational program. As discussed earlier, development depends on experience. It is true, however, that the way in which experience stimulates development (through discrepancy and match between experienced events and information-processing structures) is not the way experience is programmed in many forms of instructions and educational intervention. It is also true that the kinds of experience leading to development must be viewed in terms of a stimulation that is general rather than highly specific in its content or meaning.

Because the experiences necessary for structural development are believed to be *universal*, it is possible for the child to develop the behavior naturally, without planned instruction. But the facts that only about half of the adult American population fully reach Piaget's stage of formal operational reasoning and that only 5 percent reach the highest moral stage demonstrate that natural or universal forms of development are not inevitable but depend on experience (Kuhn, Langer, Kohlberg, and Haan, 1977).

If this argument is accepted, it not only answers the charge that development is a vague concept but also helps answer the charge that there are kinds of development (such as growth in skill at burglary) that are not valuable.

Such questionable types of "development" do not constitute development in the sense of a universal sequence or in the sense of growth of some general aspect of personality. As stated by Dewey (1963, p. 75): "That a man may grow in efficiency as a burglar . . . cannot be doubted. But from the standpoint of growth as education and education as growth the question is whether such growth promotes or retards growth in general.

Although a coherent argument has been made for why universal developmental sequences define something of educational value, we need to consider why such sequences comprise the ultimate criteria of educational value. We also need to consider how they relate to competing educational values. How does universal structural development as an educational aim relate to ordinary definitions of information and skills central to the educational curriculum? It seems obvious that many changes or forms of learning are of value that are not universals in development. As an example, while many unschooled people have learned to read, the capacity and motivation to read does not define a developmental universal; nonetheless, it seems to us a basic educational objective. We cannot dispose of "growth in reading" as an educational objective, as we could "growth in burglary," simply because it is not a universal in development. But we argue that the ultimate importance of learning to read can only be understood in the context of more universal forms of development. Increased capacity to read is not itself a development, although it is an attainment reflecting various aspects of development. The value or importance of reading lies in its potential contribution to further cognitive, social, and esthetic development. As stated by Dewey (1898, p. 29):

No one can estimate the benumbing and hardening effect of continued drill in reading as mere form. It should be obvious that what I have in mind is not a Philistine attack upon books and reading. The question is not how to get rid of them, but how to get their value—how to use them to their capacity as servants of the intellectual and moral life. To answer this question, we must consider what is the effect of growth in a special direction upon the attitudes and habits which alone open up avenues for development in other lines.

A developmental definition of educational objectives must cope not only with competing objectives usually defined nondevelopmentally, but also with the fact that the universal aspects of development are multiple. Here, as in the case of evaluating nondevelopmental objectives, the progressive educator must consider the relation of a particular development to development in general. As an example, Kamii (1971) has defined a program of preschool intervention related to each of the chapter headings of Piaget's books: space, time, causality, number, classification, and so on. Kamii's intent in making use of all the areas of cognitive development discussed by Piaget is not to imply that each constitutes a separate, intrinsic educational objective. Rather, her interest is to make use of all aspects of the child's experience relevant to *general* Piagetian cognitive development. Such a concept of generalized cognitive-stage development is meaningful because DeVries and Kohlberg (1977) and others have shown that there is a general Piagetian cognitive-level factor distinct from psychometric general intelligence.

In contrast to the psychometric concept of intelligence, the developmental-level concept of intelligence does provide a standard or a set of aims for preschool education. It does not assume a concept of fixed capacity or "intelligence quotient" constant over development. In this sense, developmental level is more like "achievement" than like "capacity," but developmental level tests differ from achievement tests in several ways. Although the developmental-level concept does not distinguish between achievement and capacity, it does distinguish between cognitive achievement (performance) and cognitive process (or competence). Developmental tests measure level of thought process, not the difficulty or correctness of thought product. They measure not cognitive performance but cognitive competence; the basic possession of a core concept, not the speed and agility with which the concept is expressed or used under rigid test conditions.

Psychometric and developmental level concepts of intelligence are quite different. In practice, however, the two kinds of measures are highly correlated with one another, explaining why clear theoretical and operational distinctions between the two concepts of intelligence have not been made until recently. Factor-analytic findings now can provide an empirical basis for this distinction (DeVries and Kohlberg, 1977). Although psychometric measures of general intelligence and of "primary mental abilities" at mental age six correlate with Piagetian measures of cognitive level, there is also a common factor to all developmental level tests. This factor is independent of general intelligence or of any special psychometric ability. In other words, it is possible to distinguish between psychometric capacity and developmental-level concepts or measures of intelligence. Given the empirical distinction, cognitive stage measures provide a rational standard for educational intervention where psychometric intelligence tests do not. This is true for the following reasons:

1. The core structure defined by stage tests is in theory and experiment more amenable to educational intervention—Piagetian theory is a theory of stage movement occurring through *experience* of structural disequilibrium.

2. Piagetian performance predicts later development independent of a fixed biological rate or capacity factor, as demonstrated by evidence for longitudinal stability or prediction independent of IQ. Because Piaget items define invariant sequences, development to one stage facilitates development to the next.

3. Piagetian test content has cognitive value in its own right. If children are able to think causally instead of magically about phenomena, for instance, their ability has a cognitive value apart from arbitrary cultural demands—it is not a mere indicator of brightness, like knowing the word *envelope* or *amanuensis*. This is reflected in the fact that Piaget test scores are qualitative; they are not arbitrary points on a curve. The capacity to engage in concrete logical reasoning is a definite attainment, being at mental age six is not. We can ask that all children reason in terms of logical operations; we cannot ask that all children have high IQs.

4.   This cognitive value is culturally universal, the sequence of development occurs in every culture and subculture.

The existence of a general level factor in cognitive development allows us to put particular universal sequences of cognitive development into perspective as educational aims. The worth of a development in any particular cognitive sequence is determined by its contribution to the whole of cognitive development.

We must now consider the relation of developmental aims of education to the notion of developmental acceleration as an educational objective. We indicated that a concept of stages as "natural" does not mean that they are inevitable; many individuals fail to attain the higher stages of logical and moral reasoning. Accordingly, the aim of the developmental educator is not the acceleration of development but the eventual adult attainment of the highest stage. In this sense, the developmentalist is not interested in *stage acceleration,* but in avoiding *stage retardation.* Moral development research reviewed elsewhere suggests that there is what approaches an optimal period for movement from one stage to the next (Turiel, 1969). When children have just attained a given stage, they are unlikely to respond to stimulation toward movement to the next stage. In addition, after a long period of use of a given stage of thought, children tend to "stabilize" at that stage and develop screening mechanisms for contradictory stimulation. Accordingly, it has been found that both very young and older children at a given stage (compared to the age norm for that stage) are less responsive or less able to assimilate stimulation at the next higher stage than children at the age norm for that stage. The notion of an "open period" is not age specific, it is individual. A child late in reaching Stage 2 may be "open" to Stage 3 at an age beyond that of another child who reached Stage 2 earlier. Nevertheless, gross age periods may be defined that are "open periods" for movement from one stage to the next. Avoidance of retardation as an educational aim means presenting stimulation in these periods where the possibility for development is still open.

We need to consider a related distinction between *acceleration* and *decalage* as an aim of education. Piaget distinguishes between the appearance of stage and its "horizontal decalage," its spread or generalization across the range of basic physical and social actions, concepts, and objects to which the stage potentially applies. As a simple example, concrete logic or conservation is first noted in the concept of mass and only later in weight and volume. Accordingly, acceleration of the stage of concrete operations is one educational enterprise and the encouragement of decalage of concrete reasoning to a new concept or phenomenon is another. It is the latter that is most relevant to education. Education is concerned not so much with age of onset of children's capacity for concrete logical thought as with the possession of a logical mind—the degree to which they have organized experience or the world in a logical fashion.

It is likely that the occurrence of such horizontal decalage, rather than age of first appearance of concrete operations, predicts to later formal operational thought. Formal reasoning develops because concrete reasoning represents a poor, although partially successful, strategy for solving many problems. The child who has never explored the limits of concrete logical reasoning and lives in a world determined by arbitrary unexplained events and forces will see the limits of the partial solutions of concrete logic as set by intangible forces rather than looking for a more adequate logic to deal with unexplained problems.

We have so far discussed development only as general cognitive development. According to cognitive-developmental theory, there is always a cognitive component to development, even in social, moral, and esthetic areas. Development, however, is broader than cognitive-logical development. One central area is moral development, as defined by invariant stages of moral reasoning. On the one hand, these stages have a cognitive component; attainment of a given Piaget cognitive stage is a necessary, although not sufficient, condition for the parallel moral stage. On the other hand, moral reasoning stages relate to action, principled moral reasoning has been found to be a precondition for principled moral action (see Chapter 4, Volume II). For reasons elaborated throughout this chapter, the stimulation of moral development through the stages represents a rational and ethical focus of education related to, but broadening, an educational focus on cognitive development as such (Kohlberg and Turiel, 1971). Programs effective in stimulating moral development have been successfully demonstrated (Blatt and Kohlberg, 1975).

Although developmental moral education widens the focus of cognitive-developmental education beyond the purely cognitive, there is a still broader unity, called *ego development,* of which both cognitive and moral development are part (Loevinger, Wessler, and Redmore, 1970). Particularly in the earlier childhood years, it is difficult to distinguish moral development from ego development. Cognitive development, in the Piagetian sense, is also related to ego development, because both concern the child's core beliefs about the physical and social world. Much recent research demonstrates that the development of the ego, as attitudes and beliefs about the self, involves step-by-step parallel development of attitudes and beliefs about the physical and social world. Further, it indicates definite stages of ego development, defined by Loevinger and her colleagues (1970). Van den Daele (1970), and others, that imply step-by-step parallels to Piaget's cognitive stages, although they include more social emotional content. In general, attainment of a Piagetian cognitive stage is a necessary but not sufficient condition for attainment of the parallel ego stage. All children at a given ego stage must have attained the parallel cognitive stage, but not all children at a cognitive stage will have organized their self-concept and social experience at the corresponding ego stage. Thus, a general concept of ego development as a universal sequential phenomenon is becoming an empirically meaningful guide to defining broad educational objectives. Furthermore, experimental educational programs to stimulate ego development have been piloted with some definite success as both the preschool and the high school levels (Van den Daele,1970; Sprinthall and Mosher, 1970).

Thus, education for general cognitive development, and perhaps even education for moral development, must be judged by its contribution to a more general concept of ego development. In saying this, we must remember that *ego development* is the psychologist's term for a sequence that also must have a philosophic rationale. One pole of ego development is self-awareness; the parallel pole is awareness of the world. Increasing awareness is not only "cognitive," it is moral, esthetic, and metaphysical; it is the awareness of new meanings in life.

Finally, we need to note that in the realm of ego development, a focus on "horizontal decalage" rather than acceleration is especially salient. The distinction reflects in a more precise and viable fashion the concern of maturational or romantic stage-theorists for an educational focus on "healthy" passage through stages, rather than their acceleration. In maturational theories of personality stages, age leads to a new stage regardless of experience and reorganizations at previous stages. As a result, education and experience become valuable not for movement to a new stage, but for healthy or *successful integration* of the concerns of a stage. Onset of the next stage occurs regardless of experience; only healthy integration of the stages is contingent on experience and that should be the focus for education. Without accepting this contention, cognitive-developmental theory would agree that premature development to a higher ego stage without a corresponding *decalage* throughout the child's world and life presents problems. In psychoanalytic maturational terms, the dangers of uneven or premature ego development are expressed as defects in ego strength with consequent vulnerability to regression. In cognitive-developmental terms, inadequate *"horizontal decalage"* represents a somewhat similar phenomenon. Although the relation of "ego strength" to logical and moral *decalage* is not well understood, there are many reasons to believe they are related. A child who continues to think in magical or egocentric terms in some areas of cognition and morality is likely to be vulnerable to "regression" under stress later in life.

In conclusion, if a broad concept of development, conceived in stage-sequential terms, is still vague as a definer of educational ends, that is not due to the inherent narrowness or vagueness of the concept. Rather, it is due to the fact that researchers have only recently begun the kind of longitudinal and educational research needed to make the concept precise and usable. When Dewey advocated education as development at the turn of the century, most American educational psychologists turned instead to industrial psychology or to.the mental health bag of virtues. Although the results of the cognitive-developmental research of the last decades are still limited, they indicate real promise for finally translating Dewey's vision into a precise reality.

Summary and Conclusions

This chapter essentially recapitulates the progressive position first formulated by John Dewey. Our position has been clarified psychologically by the work of Piaget and his followers; its philosophic premises have been advanced by the work of such modern analytic philosophers as Hare, Rawls, and Peters. The progressive view of education makes the following claims:

1. That the aims of education may be identified with development, both intellectual and moral.
2. That education so conceived supplies the conditions for passing through an order of connected stages.
3. That such a developmental definition of educational aims and

processes requires both the method of philosophy or ethics and the method of psychology or science. The justification of education as development requires a philosophic statement explaining why a higher stage is a better or a more adequate stage. In addition, before one can define a set of educational goals based on a philosophical statement of ethical, scientific, or logical principles one must be able to translate it into a statement about psychological stages of development.

4. This, in turn, implies that the understanding of logical and ethical principles is a central aim of education. This understanding is the philosophic counterpart of the psychological statement that the aim of education is the development of the individual through cognitive and moral stages. It is characteristic of higher cognitive and moral stages that children themselves construct logical and ethical principles; these, in turn, are elaborated by science and philosophy.

5. A notion of education as attainment of higher stages of development, involving an understanding of principles, was central to "aristocratic" Platonic doctrines of liberal education. This conception is also central to Dewey's notion of a democratic education. The democratic educational end for all humans must be "the development of a free and powerful character." Nothing less than democratic education will prepare free people for factual and moral choices that they will inevitably confront in society. Democratic educators must be guided by a set of psychological and ethical principles that they openly present to their students, inviting criticism as well as understanding. The alternative is "educator-kings," such as the behavior modifiers with an ideology of controlling behavior, or the teacher-psychiatrists with an ideology of "improving" students' mental health. Neither types expose their ideology to the students, allowing them to evaluate its merit for themselves.

6. A notion of education for development and education for principles is liberal, democratic, and nonindoctrinative. It relies on open methods of stimulation through a sequence of stages, in a direction of movement that is universal for all children. In this sense, it is natural.

The progressive position appears idealistic rather than pragmatic, industrial-vocational or adjustment-oriented, as is often charged by critics of progressivism who view it as ignoring "excellence." But Dewey's idealism is supported by Piagetian psychological findings, which indicate that all children, not only well-born college students, are "philosophers" intent on organizing their lives into universal patterns of meaning. It is supported by findings that most students seem to move forward in developmentally oriented educational programs. Furthermore, the idealism of the developmental position is compatible with the notion that the child is involved in a process of both academic and vocational education. Dewey denied that educational experience stimulating intellectual and moral development could be equated with academic schooling. He claimed that practical or vocational education as well as academic education could contribute to cognitive and moral development; it should be for all children, not only for the poor or the "slow." Our educational system currently faces a choice between two forms of injustice, the first an imposition of an arbitrary academic education on all, the second a division into a superior academic track and an inferior vocational track. The developmental conception remains the only rationale for solving these injustices and for providing the basis for a truly democratic educational process.

PART TWO

Moral Stages and the
Idea of Justice

෨෪

In Chapter 3, I rejected "the psychologist's fallacy" in defining the aims of education and recommended instead the "developmental-philosophic" strategy, which, I said, integrated philosophic principles with empirical psychological findings. A statement of aims useful to education must be translatable into psychological observations of educational gains by students. If it is to escape the psychologist's fallacy, however, this psychological statement of development as an intrinsic educational goal must be independently grounded in philosophic reasoning on why a higher stage is a better stage.

Although in Chapter 3 I recommended the developmental-philosophic strategy, I did not elaborate the philosophic assumptions underlying this strategy. This task is left for Chapter 4, "From *Is* to *Ought,*" which is the key chapter of the entire volume because it elaborates the concept of justice inherent in the moral stages.

The title of the chapter is a little misleading, because it suggests that it derives a moral *ought,* a set of valid moral principles, from the *is* of psychological theory and research without committing the psychologist's fallacy or the naturalistic fallacy. Alston (1971) says this is pulling out a full-fledged moral philosophy rabbit from a moral psychology hat. In fact, my own process of reasoning starts with philosophic assumptions as guides in the search for facts about moral development. Because philosophy enters into the endeavor at the start of empirical inquiry, it is not surprising that it emerges again in the form of conclusions from the empirical findings. In my view, progress in moral philosophy and in moral psychology occurs through a spiral or bootstrapping process in which the insights of philosophy serve to suggest insights and findings in psychology that in turn suggest new insights and conclusions in philosophy.

In Chapter 4, I begin by spelling out the moral philosophic assumptions that I believe must guide the search for facts about moral development. My central assumption is that there is no philosophically neutral starting point for the psychological study of morality. Cultural relativism, which claims to be a philosophically neutral starting point, is itself a moral philosophy of ethical relativism, which I claim is philosophically incorrect, not philosophically neutral. Certainly the study of facts about moral beliefs and practices requires a degree of objectivity. I argue, however, that the objective study of the history and development of moral ideas must be guided not by cultural and ethical relativism but by reflective rational standards and principles of morality, just as the objective study of the development of scientific ideas must be guided by reflective conceptions of scientific method and principles.

Critics of my claim of universal moral stages, such as Simpson (1974) and Sullivan (1977), do not dispute the facts reported from our cross-cultural studies but, rather, charge that the structural-developmental theory, in terms of which I interpret the facts, is "culturally biased" and is a Western liberal theory. I do not claim that the structural-developmental theory is culturally universal in the sense of being grounded in, and acceptable to, all cultures. Like the enterprise of moral philosophy itself, the theory springs from Western liberal thought. Therefore, my claim is not that the theory is culturally universal but that basic moral principles are universal.

I claim that those who attain stage 5 (or 6) in any culture attempt to formulate universalizable principles and that the principles they formulate are recognizably similar from one culture to the next. Any social science theory, whether this one or some other theory that rejects stages, must still acknowledge this universality. In this regard, my theory is like many other philosophic theories that argue for "methodological nonrelativism." Methodological nonrelativism is the doctrine that certain criteria (importantly, reversibility or universalizability) of moral reasoning or principles are universally relevant. It means that, even if there are observed cultural divergences of moral standards, there are rational principles and methods that can reconcile these divergences or lead to agreement.

My colleagues and I must distinguish our particular moral theory from (1) the more general assumptions of methodological nonrelativism, which we share with much moral philosophy; and (2) from the observations we have made about moral judgments in various cultures.

Our theoretical delineation of principles of justice and their growth is not a final dogmatic conclusion; it is reshaped by continuing advances in social science research and in moral philosophy. Here again, we must keep separate the claim of universality and adequacy of moral principles from the unviersality and adequacy of our own moral theory, which is open to revision.

Perhaps the most important theoretical statement in Chapter 4 is the statement of the section entitled "Moral Stages as a Hierarchy of Forms of Moral Integration." This section proposes *structural isomorphism* between the psychological explanation of development from stage to stage and the philosophic justification of each higher stage. From the viewpoint of structural theories in both psychology and philosophy, moral judgment and reasoning may be characterized by formal features that have differing degrees of adequacy. The formal features of a moral stage may be stated in terms of the kind of balance or equilibrium it attains. Each higher stage achieves a higher degree of equilibrium than its predecessor. Equilibrium is central to justice, as metaphors of justice as balance suggest. In structural theory, progressive equilibration is basic to both psychological explanations of moral change and to philosophic treatment of the adequacy of a moral principle or lines of argument for a set of moral principles.

Chapter 4, "From *Is* to *Ought*," sets out the general approach to moral stages as successive structural forms of moral equilibration. Chapter 5, "Justice as Reversibility," takes up the argument as it leads to an understanding of one philosophic theory, Rawls's theory of justice, and as it leads through Rawls to an argument for the principles we believe to be formulated at Stage 6, the highest stage of moral reasoning.

For Rawls, principles of justice represent an equilibrium among competing claims. Justice, however, represents equilibrium only under certain assumptions, in particular the assumptions that each player is choosing from an "original position" before the establishment of a society or a practice and is choosing under a "veil of ignorance," so that no one knows his or her position in the society. Specifically, this decision process leads to the "difference principle"—no inequalities are justified unless they are acceptable to the person if he or she were in the most disadvantaged position. Behind Rawls's theory lies a principle recognized as the core of morality in almost every culture and religion—the Golden Rule. Rawls's procedure, I argue, is equivalent to a "moral musical chairs" mode of decision making that is the ultimate extension of the Golden Rule. This procedure for choice leads in many situations to a utilitarian solution. In Chapter 4, however, I present an example of a dilemma, the captain's dilemma, in which a utilitarian solution seems counterintuitive or unjust. This kind of dilemma is not resolvable by rejecting the utilitarian principle altogether and accepting a fixed rule that would lead everyone in the lifeboat to go down if no one volunteered. Instead, an equitable distribution of risk seems intuitively to be the best solution, as well as the one recommended by Rawls's decision procedure or by "moral musical chairs."

Rawls claims that moral principles are best formulated through an interactive process of "reflective equilibrium." Principles codify existing moral intuitions, but in new cases our intuitions may clash with our principles. As a result, there is a to-and-fro process of revising our principles and of reconsidering our intuitions until the two correspond. In addition to being a statement of theory, Chapter 4 attempts to engage readers in the process of reflective equilibration by presenting a set of dilemmas to which they must apply their principles.

My discussion of the claims to adequacy of the highest stage, Stage 6, is philosophical and theoretical. At this point, our empirical findings do not clearly delineate a sixth stage. My colleagues and I believe Stage 5 is firmly established by longitudinal studies carried out in the United States, Turkey, and Israel. None of our longitudinal subjects, however, have reached the highest stage. Our examples of Stage 6 come either from historical figures or from interviews with people who have extensive philosophic training. We are continuing to collect longitudinal data on adults to clarify empirically the existence and description of Stage 6. In the meantime, Stage 6 is perhaps less a statement of an attained psychological reality than the specification of a direction in which, our theory claims, ethical development is moving.

4. From *Is* to *Ought:* How to Commit the Naturalistic Fallacy and Get Away with It in the Study of Moral Development

Genetic Epistemology and Moral Psychology

The general questions discussed in this chapter are (1) "What can the psychological study of the development of moral concepts tell us about their epistemological or moral philosophic status?" and (2) "What does the psychological study of the development of moral concepts require in the way of epistemological or moral philosophic assumptions about moral reasoning?"

I think psychologists are clear as to why child psychology needs epistemology. Many of us feel that the study of cognition by American child psychology failed to progress for two generations because of an inadequate epistemology, sometimes called *logical positivism* or *behaviorism.* The critical defect of this epistemology for child psychology was that it did not allow the psychologist to think about cognitive processes as involving knowledge. The critical category of the stimulus-response (S-R) approach was "learning," not "knowing," where the concept of "learning" did not imply "knowing." Accordingly, S-R

"From *Is* to *Ought:* How to Commit the Naturalistic Fallacy and Get Away with It in the Study of Moral Development" is reprinted by permission of the publishers from T. Mischel, ed., *Cognitive Development and Epistemology* (New York, Academic Press, copyright © 1971 Academic Press). In revising this chapter, I have attempted to deal with some of the issues raised by Peters's and Alston's comments. Although I cannot thank them for accepting my presumptuous contentions, I can thank them for taking my contentions seriously enough to make sympathetic, penetrating, and helpful comments. The empirical psychological side of the work discussed here is more fully documented in Kohlberg (1969). The philosophic contentions in their application to education have been discussed in Kohlberg (1970b, 1971b). The research discussed has been supported by NICHD Grant 0246903.

theory assumes that the process of learning truths is the same as the process of learning lies or illusions. It explains the learning of logical operations or "truths" in terms of the same processes as those involved in learning a social dance step (which is cognitively neutral) or in "learning" a psychosis or a pattern of maze errors (which are cognitively erroneous).

To study cognition, one must have some sort of concept of knowledge in terms of which children's development is observed. Piaget's fundamental contribution to developmental psychology has been to observe children's development in terms of the categories (space, time, causality, and so on) that philosophers have deemed central to knowing. The fact that the cognitive categories of the philosopher are central for understanding the behavior development of the child is so apparent, once pointed out, that one recognizes that it is only the peculiar epistemology of the positivistic behaviorist that could have obscured it.

In my own area, moral development, the epistemological blinders psychologists have worn have hidden from them the fact that the concept of morality is itself a philosophical (ethical) rather than a behavioral concept. When I started my research on the psychology of moral development, I was aware of the necessity for orienting to philosophic concepts of morality (Kohlberg, 1958), and I believe it is mainly for that reason that I have uncovered some quite important facts not previously noted. I was not aware, however, that empirical developmental study might contribute to the solution of distinctively philosophic problems in both normative ethics and metaethics. The focus of this chapter is on the implications I now believe my genetic studies have for philosophic ethics; hence the title "From *Is* [the facts of moral development] to *Ought* [the ideal content and epistemological status of moral ideas]." My assumption that one needs to orient developmental research to philosophic concepts of morality will not be very controversial to philosophers. One can be pluralistic as to philosophic concepts and arrive at the same research conclusions: Piaget need not have an ultimately correct concept of causality, as a philosophic category, to conduct valid research on the empirical development of causal concepts. Similarly, whether one starts from Kant, Mill, Hare, Ross, or Rawls in defining morality, one gets similar research results. Although philosophic concepts of morality differ from one another, their differences are minor compared with the differences between almost any philosophic concept of morality and such psychological concepts of morality as "Conscience is a conditioned avoidance reaction to certain classes of acts or situations" (Eysenck, 1961) or "Moral values are evaluations of action believed by members of a given society to be 'right' " (Berkowitz, 1964).

However, when one turns from using philosophy to orient empirical research to claiming that empirical research results help clarify and define an ultimately adequate, universal, and mature conception of morality, one enters much more controversial ground. As Alston (1971, pp. 276–277) puts it,

Unless Kohlberg can do more than he has done to show that his choice of a definition of "moral" is based on something more than a personal preference among the variety of definitions that have been proposed, the fact that his later stages conform more exactly to his conception of moral judgment has no objective significance. . . . If Kohlberg wants to investigate the development of moral reasoning according to some arbitrarily selected criterion of "moral," well and good; he may come up with something interesting. But if he wants to use the developmental approximations to the purely moral in his sense as a basis for pronouncements as to how people *ought* to reason in their action-guiding deliberations, that is another matter. If these pronouncements are to carry any weight, he will have to show that his sense of "moral" which is functioning as his standard has itself some recommendation other than congeniality to his predilections.

Now, obviously a developmental psychologist must be a fool to enter the den of philosophical wolves (even if they were all as tolerant and gentlemanly as Alston, 1971, and Peters, 1971) with a set of *"is* to *ought"* claims unless he has to. It is my belief that the developmental psychologist must eventually do so for two reasons. First, it is necessary for any ethically justifiable educational or other practical application of his research findings. It is almost self-evident that no psychologist would engage in moral research with the notion that the use of such research is the creation of instrumentalities of manipulation and control to be made available to adult "socializing agents." By any philosophic definition, it is not moral to subject a child to such manipulation. It was because of this practical concern, the concern to develop my research implications into an active program of moral education (Kohlberg, 1971b; Blatt and Kohlberg, 1975; see also Chapter 2), that I first began to worry seriously about the implication of my moral research for a definite ethical position. Earlier, my major philosophic claim was that the stimulation of development is the only ethically acceptable form of moral education. I believe this claim can be upheld regardless of my more controversial claim (in this chapter) that I have successfully defined the ethically optimal end point of moral development. Ultimately, however, a complete approach to moral education requires consideration of this more controversial claim.

The second reason I have entered the philosophic arena is more theoretical. My article may be read as a partial answer to the issue raised by Peters (1971, p. 264) when he says,

[Kohlberg's] findings are of unquestionable importance, but there is a grave danger that they may become exalted into a general theory of moral development. Any such general theory presupposes a general ethical theory, and Kohlberg himself surely would be the first to admit that he had done little to develop the details of such a general ethical theory.

I agree with the position implied by Peters's comment, the position that *a psychological theory of ethics (or of cognition) is incomplete, even as a psychological theory, if its philosophic implications are not spelled out.* I claim, persuaded by some of my philosopher friends, that an ultimately adequate *psychological* theory as to why a child does move from stage to stage, and ultimately adequate *philosophical* explanation as to why a higher stage is more adequate than a lower stage are one and the same theory extended in different directions.

As I understand Piaget, he takes the same position; that is, he takes his theory of cognitive stages to be a *theory of genetic epistemology,* rather than to be a purely psychological theory. Put in other terms, an adequate psychological explanation of cognition or of morality must include an explanation of the universality of these concepts throughout humanity, an explanation that cannot be purely psychological in the usual sense. Hence, I would claim not only that the cognitive psychologist needs the epistemologist, but also that part of the measure of the psychologist's success is his or her contribution to a solution of epistemological problems.

The psychologist cannot study cognition or morality in an epistemologically neutral way, and I argue that it is not epistemologically (metaethically) *neutral* to say, as Berkowitz has, that "moral values are evaluations of action believed by members of a given society to be 'right' "—it is metaethically *wrong.* If the psychological study of concepts presupposes an epistemological position, must not the results of psychological inquiry lead to both partial validation and partial correction of its initial epistemology? That insight into the "is" (the development of knowledge and morality) and insight into the "ought" (epistemological and moral norms and criteria) must have some relationship seemed obvious to philosophers and psychologists of fifty years ago such as Dewey, Mead, and Baldwin. One wonders whether it was anything but the desperate desire of behaviorists, logical positivists, and analytic philosophers to set up "independent disciplines" (or "games") of psychology and philosophy that made them think the psychologist-philosophers of fifty years ago were wrong.

In ethics, the start of the fifty-year separation was Moore's attack on the "naturalistic fallacy," the fallacy of deriving *ought* statements from *is* statements. My chapter weaves uneasily through many forms of the naturalistic fallacy, treating some as genuine fallacies, and others not. The one form of the "naturalistic fallacy" that this chapter presupposes, however, is the "fallacy" that the *ought* statements of philosophers of knowledge and morality, and the *is* statements of psychologists of knowledge and morality, should be based on mutual awareness.

Universals and Relativity in Moral Development

I have already noted that I started my studies of moral development fifteen years ago with the notion (1) that there were universal ontogenetic trends toward the development of morality as it has been conceived by Western moral philosophers, and (2) that the development of such "rational" or "mature morality" is a process different from the learning of various "irrational" or "arbitrary" cultural rules and values. My first step in this chapter is to show that the common assumption of the cultural relativity of ethics, on which almost all contemporary social scientific theorizing about morality is based, is in error. Although there are major theoretical differences among sociological role theorists, psycho-analytic theorists, and learning theorists, they all view moral development and other forms of socialization as "the process by which an individual, born with behavior potentialities of an enormously wide range, is led to develop actual behavior confined within the much narrower range of what is customary and acceptable for him according to the standards of his group" (Child, 1954). Thus, moral and social development is defined as the direct internalization of external norms of a given culture.

A second process assumption, closely linked to the assumptions of ethical relativity, is that morality and moral learning are fundamentally emotional and irrational *processes* based on mechanisms of habit, reward and punishment, identification, and defense. If common social science theories are in error in assuming value relativity, then their further notions as to the processes of moral development and functioning are also likely to be in error or at least to yield only partial insights into morality.

In the next section, I consider the evidence for a nonrelativist "cognitive-developmental" theory of the developmental *process*. My account is based on a rejection of the relativity assumption and an acceptance of the contrasting view that "ethical principles" are the end point of sequential "natural" development in social functioning and thinking; correspondingly, the stimulation of their development is a different matter from the inculcation of arbitrary cultural beliefs. Before considering my theory of process, however, I must consider relativism as a doctrine that can be evaluated regardless of preference for one psychological process theory or another. Here, then, I consider whether the empirical propositions derivable from the relativity postulation are factually correct statements about variations in human moral behavior and judgment.

Although my discussion focuses on relativism as a doctrine about "is," about the facts of individual and cultural variability of morals, I also need to come to grips with relativism as a doctrine of "ought"; that is, of the possibility of rational ethics, of people coming to agreement about issues of right or wrong through guidance by rational standards.

Relativism, Tolerance, and Scientific Neutrality: Some Confusions of Social Science

Brandt (1961, p. 433) has pointed out that ethical relativism, as understood by contemporary social scientists, usually consists of three beliefs: (1) that moral principles are culturally variable in a fundamental way; (2) that such divergence is logically unavoidable—that is, that there are no rational principles and methods that could reconcile observed divergencies of moral beliefs; and (3) that people ought to live according to the moral principles they themselves hold. Brandt adds (p. 433),

It is important to see that the first two principles are distinct. Failure to see this distinction has been one of the confusions which have beset discussions of the subject. . . . We shall call a person who accepts the first principle a *cultural relativist*. In contrast, we shall reserve the term *ethical relativism* for the view that *both* the first and second principles are true. According to our terminology, then, a man is not an ethical relativist unless he is also a cultural relativist; but he may well be a cultural relativist without being an ethical relativist.

As held by many social scientists, however, value relativism is often a confusion between the idea that "everyone has their own values" and the idea that "everyone ought to have their own values." In other words, the value-relativity position often rests on logical confusion between matters of fact (there are no standards accepted by all people), and matters of value (there are no standards that all people ought to accept); that is, it represents the naturalistic fallacy.

To illustrate, I quote again the response of one of my psychology graduate students to the moral dilemma about stealing a drug to save one's wife from death by cancer. Part of her reply, as noted in Chapter 1, was as follows: "I think he should steal it because if there is any such thing as a universal human value, it is the value of life, and that would justify stealing it." I then asked her, "Is there any such thing as a universal human value?" and she answered, "No, all values are relative to your culture." This response illustrates a typical confusion of the relativist. She started out by claiming that one ought to act in terms of the universal value of human life, that it is logical and desirable for all people to respect all human life; but she failed to see that this does not conflict with the *fact* that all people do not always act in terms of this value and so ended by denying the possibility of making a value judgment going beyond herself.

This young woman's confusion is only one of a number of "fallacies" frequently found in social-scientific arguments for relativism. Philosophers who are aware of these logical confusions do not generally accept ethical relativity and assume that there is a rational enterprise termed "normative ethics." But ethical and cultural relativism has a very powerful hold on social scientists that is not explicable in terms of the facts of cultural relativity. In essence, this is because social scientists think relativism is required by attitudes of (1) questioning the arbitrary or conventional nature of the morality of their own culture, (2) fairness to other cultures and to minority groups, and (3) scientific value neutrality or objectivity in studying values. Accordingly, I shall briefly try to show (making use of some of Brandt's, 1959, logical distinctions) that *cultural relativism* neither gives nor receives logical support from these *ethical relativist* postulates, which most of us think of as central to a social science orientation.

I have already mentioned the first, most general, fallacy behind relativism, namely, the confusion between ethical relativity and cultural relativity. This naturalistic fallacy is exemplified by the following argument in Feuer's *Psychoanalysis and Ethics* (1955, pp. 5–11):

Statements as to "ultimate values" are testable. . . . Nietzsche's "ultimate value," the satisfaction of the will to power, presupposes a testable theory of human nature. Nietzsche assumes that the drive for power is basic and ineradicable in every human being. If this theory of human nature is confuted, the ethical doctrine, which is its expression, collapses with it. For statements about "ultimate values" are psychological assertions, and all the methods which are employed in psychological science can be used for their verification.

An assertion that a value is ultimate is, in effect, an affirmation that there is a corresponding unconditioned and irreducible drive in the human organism. . . . Rational values are those which diminish frustration and repression. . . .

When Nietzsche says that "power" is an ultimate value, his assertion is not validated by the psychological facts of man. Powerseeking is not a primitive motivation . . . [but the result of] gnawing anxieties far within one's unconscious. . . . The distinction between authentic values and inauthentic ones is one between values which are expressive of the primal drives of the organism and those which are anxiety induced.

Feuer's argument is that ethical statements about the "rationality" or "authenticity" of values (for example, of sex as opposed to power) can be directly derived from establishing empirical truths about their origins. This commits the naturalistic fallacy by identifying a value judgment with a factual judgment. We may accept the factual truth of the statements "Sexuality is an unconditioned drive" and "Expressing sexuality diminishes frustration and repression" and still question the ethical statement "Sexual expressions are authentic values," or "Sexual expression is right and good." To ignore this "open question" is to commit the naturalistic fallacy. As Frankena (1963, p. 82) puts it, "The 'open question' argument is that we may agree that something has P, and yet ask significantly, "But is it good?" or "Is it right?"

ethical terms do not lend themselves to analisis, scientif. really

That is, we can sensibly say, "This has *P* but is it good (or right)?"
... Likewise, one can say "This has *P* but it is not good (or right),"
"without contradicting oneself."

Feuer, like Flugel (1955) and many other psychoanalytic ethicists,
denies that it is really possible to ask the open question when he says,
"We cannot say that we can define or analyze the meaning of "good."
For in a strict sense, we might say that ethical terms cannot be logically analyzed, they can only be psychoanalyzed. Ethical language differs, in this respect, from scientific language." (1955, p. 23.)

Let us imagine Feuer to be an actual analyst talking to a patient.
Feuer tells the patient, "Your striving for power is irrational and inauthentic and bad." The patient asks, "But why is it bad? Why
should I give it up?" Feuer replies, "Because it is based on anxiety."
The patient then asks "the open question"; that is, "But why does that
make it bad?" And Feuer says, "That is a meaningless question:
words like *good* and *bad* have no true meaning, only scientific description has true meaning." The patient at this time either replies plain-
tively, "What did you mean, then, telling me my power striving was
bad?" or else starts climbing the walls. The patient is left climbing the
walls because Feuer is taking a position similar to that of the graduate
student cited earlier. He starts out by absolutistically defining "authentic," "rational" values and ends up with the relativistic statement
"Ethical terms cannot be logically analyzed, they can only be psychoanalyzed."

A negative rather than assertive form of the same confusion is the
move from "There are no universal human values" to "There ought
not to be any universal human values; every person or culture ought to
do its thing." An extreme relativist might say, "Some people strive for
power, some do not, therefore one cannot say, 'One ought not to strive
for power.'" Brandt gives examples of such "official" social scientific
confusions (1959, p. 288):

An executive committee of the American Anthropological Association, in a
published statement on human rights, included the remark that *"respect* for
differences between cultures is *validated* by the scientific fact that no tech-
nique of qualitatively evaluating cultures has been discovered...." Melville
Herskovitz writes ... "The relativist point of view brings into relief the *validity* of every set of norms *for* the people whose lives are guided by them."

But Herskowitz's remark is a fallacy, because

It is one thing for a person to have a certain ethical opinion or ethical conviction, and another thing for that ethical opinion to be correct. . . . It does not follow directly from the fact that the Romans approved of infanticide and we do not, that infanticide was really right for them and really wrong for us or that it is neither right nor wrong for everybody. [Brandt, 1959, p. 84]

Very often the confusion of "is" and "ought" also operates in the reverse direction. Instead of the facts of cultural diversity leading to confusion about ideal morality, relativistic ideas of tolerance (ethical relativism) lead to confusions about the facts (cultural relativism). Confusions about (1) the facts of cultural relativism in turn rest on confusion between (2) "ethical relativity," and (3) "ethical tolerance" as moral doctrines. An illustration of this confusion of (2) and (3), as well as of (1) and (2), is provided by the American Anthropological Association. American anthropology developed a passionate moral conviction that the nineteenth-century assumption of the cultural superiority of "white civilization" was both intellectually blind and socially destructive to people in other cultures. Quite correctly, the anthropologists felt that these "white cultural supremacy" doctrines violated fundamental moral principles of justice, respect for human personality, and tolerance for diversity of belief and values. Instead of recognizing that their concern for tolerance was based on "white civilization's" universalizable principles of justice, anthropologists attempted to support their pleas for tolerance on the grounds that no principles were universalizable.

The second basic fallacy, then, is the confusion between (2), the relativistic ethical proposition "no moral beliefs or principles are absolutely valid" and (3), the nonrelativistic liberal's proposition "It is a valid moral principle to grant liberty and respect to any human being regardless of his moral beliefs or principles." We shall argue that (3) is valid but does not depend for support on (2). Indeed, if the principle of tolerance, (3), is ethically valid, the principle of ethical relativity, (2), cannot be, because the principle of tolerance, if valid, is not itself "relative," "arbitrary," and so on.

Stated in a different way, the confusion is between (2), the relativity of moral principles, and (3), the relativity of blaming or punishing people or groups who do not act in accordance with those principles. I argue later that valid (Stage 6) universal moral principles of obligation do not generate any obligation to blame or punish people who deviate from those principles. One may question the justice of punishing or

even blaming a ghetto adolescent who steals without questioning principles of justice that make it an obligation for that adolescent not to
steal. *One may then deny that there are any precise, justifiable rules
for blame and punishment without being a relativist in the sense of
denying that there are basic moral principles.* A related confusion of
the relativist is the notion that the function of moral principles is to
judge cultures or societies as wholes, and, because one cannot legitimately make absolute moral evaluations of one culture as worth more
or less than another, there are no nonrelative moral principles. Moral
principles, however, prescribe universal human obligations; they are
not scales for evaluating collective entities.

The import of these confusions for the handling of facts may be
illustrated by social-scientific opinion about "class differences in moral
values." Reviews of the many studies of class differences in Piaget or
Kohlberg measures of moral judgment in many cultures (Kohlberg,
1963b) all show the same thing: the direction of age change is the
same for lower-class and middle-class children in all cultures on all
measures, showing regular age trends in either class group, but middle-class children advance faster and further on these measures in all
cultures. It is a simple matter of fact that middle-class children are
advanced on measures of moral age development. The fact, however,
has been interpreted by relativistic social scientists (for example, Bronfenbrenner, 1962a) as indicating that Piaget's (or Kohlberg's) measures of moral development are based on culturally biased "middle-
class standards." They deny the facts on the (confused) ground that
the developmental measure is "unjust to" or "biased against" lower-
class children and that it is relative to middle-class standards.

A related example comes from repeated research results indicating
that lower-class and ghetto children cheat and steal more than middle-
class white children. Fearing prejudice, social scientists have argued
that honesty is a "middle-class value" in terms of which lower-class
children should not be judged. In fact, however, the research studies
repeatedly indicate that honesty is verbally ranked just as high (or
higher) by lower-class black children and adults as by middle-class
whites (studies summarized in Kohlberg, 1963b). Although it is much
more difficult for a ghetto child or parent to act "honestly" than for a
middle-class child (because of differences in social perspective and
situational opportunities), it is just as much of a value to the ghetto
child.

The ethically "rational" position for the social scientist to take is that awarding blame to groups with higher crime or dishonesty rates is itself morally ungrounded, because moral principles require treating each child as an individual of equal fundamental moral worth. Anyone would recognize that rounding up a group of ghetto dwellers and imprisoning them all because some are criminals would be unjust collective punishment. Collective blame of groups with a high crime rate is equally unjust. To combat this injustice does not require an effort to prove that there is no valid conception of justice; for example, that acts of injustice (including theft) are all "culturally relative."

I have cited examples in which social scientists reject both fact and the natural intuition that there is something universally "rational," "ethical," or "mature" in principles of justice that prohibit stealing. I have suggested that this is because a belief in ethical relativity (2) is illogically derived from a concern for ethical tolerance (3) toward minority groups or cultures, and then confused with facts about cultural relativism (1).

A third, related fallacy behind much social-scientific thinking is *the confusion of ethical relativism (2) with "value neutrality" or "scientific impartiality."* I have already noted that Berkowitz thinks it "neutral" to define moral values as "evaluations of actions generally believed by the members of a given society to be either 'right' or 'wrong'" (Berkowitz, 1964, p. 4). In fact, this doctrine is not scientifically neutral or impartial, because it prejudges the facts. It assumes that there are *no* culturally universal criteria that might aid in defining the field of the moral and that variations in cultural evaluations may not themselves be assessed as more or less adequate or moral in terms of some universal criterion. We may gather the import of the definition by imagining a similar strategy for defining scientific beliefs; for example, that they are "beliefs about the world generally believed by members of a given society to be true or false." This implies that there are no universal characteristics that distinguish scientific beliefs from other beliefs: that is, that arrival at beliefs through some culturally universal conception of scientific method or reasoning is irrelevant to their definition as "scientific" and that the adequacy of the belief may not be judged independent of its conformity to group opinion. As a social scientist, I reject such a definition of science. Recognizing it as epistemologically faulty, I also recognize that it cannot be a useful basis for social-scientific explanation. A psychologist or social historian who explained the development of Darwin's belief in evolution in the same terms as he explained the development of an Anglican bishop's belief in divine creation would simply be a poor social scientist. We must at least consider that the same possibility exists in the moral sphere.

Berkowitz's definition of moral values reflects a special form of the relativist's third confusion; that is, the confusion between an *a priori* definition of morality in terms of cultural relativity and the conclusion that morality is culturally relative. Because most people or cultures do not agree that morality is defined by the values of the majority, why is Berkowitz's definition less arbitrary than that of a Catholic priest who defines morality as belief in the catechisms? Concealed behind Berkowitz's definition of morality lies a normative ethical theory and a social science theory. The ethical theory is that morality derives from social contract and is justified by its contribution to the welfare of society (Stage 5). The social science theory is the Durkheim theory that the social psychological origins of morality are to be found in the collective beliefs of the group, as these form a system above the beliefs of individuals. These theories might be acceptable, but this requires justification and cannot be assumed antecedent to inquiry.

The confusion of "scientific neutrality" with relativism involved in Berkowitz's definition does not derive from a confusion of "is" and "ought," but from the view of people such as Weber (1949) who distinguish between a rational sphere of social science methods and findings ("is"), and a sphere of values ("ought"), toward which a rational person or a scientist must take a stance of "value neutrality"; that is, recognize that his or her position is personal, arbitrary, and historically conditioned.

This brings us to the fourth confusion, *the confusion between the "rational" as "the scientific or factual" and the "rational" as the "value neutral."* The concept of the "value neutrality" (4) of the social scientist assumes ethical relativity rather than justifies it. To assume ethical relativity is to rule out the possibility of rational methods of coming to ethical agreement without considering the validity of such methods in actual detail. Weber himself argues that one moral idea cannot be said to be more adequate than another and that there is no moral progress. But his argument is legislative, not based on careful analysis of empirical trends. He says, "The use of the term *progress* is legitimate in our disciplines when it refers to 'technical' problems; that is, to the 'means' of attaining an unambiguously given end. It can never elevate itself into the sphere of 'ultimate' evaluations" (1949, p. 38). But Weber cannot legislate that "moral progress" is an illegitimate concept for a social scientist, nor can he legislate that rational agreement is impossible for philosophers: these issues are subjects for inquiry.

The point is that when Weber takes a value stand (including the stand of value neutrality) he attempts to support it by a very careful rational argument. Moreover, as Brandt (1959) points out, moral philosophers can define methodological criteria of moral judgment and argument with about as much agreement and clarity as philosophers of science can define methodological criteria of scientific judgment and argument. Thus, although Weber denies the possibility of a "neutral" attitude to matters of ethical adequacy, philosophers engage in discussions of the adequacy of moral principles with a set of methodological rules for impartial argument analogous to those of scientists dicusssing matters of fact. Indeed, Weber's own arguments about value neutrality seek to conform to roughly those criteria of value discussions.

Weber properly postulates the need for scientific neutrality in inquiry; that is, the need to examine factual-causal connections in behavior regardless of the desirability of these connections. In this he is quite correct. However, he then confuses the scientists' use of some criterion of adequacy of the value systems studied with "bias." But factual investigation need not, and cannot, be based on ignoring the criteria of adequacy of the behavior investigated. To establish "objective" scientific-historical connections in the growth of Darwin's beliefs about evolution presupposes some justifiable standpoint about the cognitive-scientific adequacy of these beliefs. The same is true with regard to the growth of moral beliefs.

In summary, I have listed a number of confusions and *a priori* assumptions that have severely biased social scientists in favor of both cultural relativity and ethical relativity in advance of considering the facts about cultural variability and the philosophic arguments about the possibilities of rational and moral agreement. These confusions have led social scientists to argue that the scientist cannot find moral development or evolution and that moral philosophers cannot come to agreement. I have tried to demonstrate a truism: it is illogical to claim that something is impossible in advance of inquiry. I may now go on to the results of empirical inquiry.

Empirical Studies of Moral Development and Their Implications

For fifteen years, I have been studying the development of moral judgment and character, primarily by following the same group of seventy-five boys at three-year intervals from early adolescence (at the beginning, the boys were aged 10–16) through young manhood (they are now aged 22–28), supplemented by a series of studies of development in other cultures.

These studies have led me to define the stages described in the Appendix. The methods by which I have defined these stages are responses to hypothetical moral dilemmas, deliberately "philosophical," some found in medieval works of casuistry. (A complete treatment of the dilemmas and their scoring can be found in Colby and Kohlberg, 1982). When I first decided to explore development in other cultures by this method, my first try was a study of two villages—one Atayal (Malaysian aboriginal), one Taiwanese. When my guide, a young Chinese ethnographer, started to translate the children's responses, he would start to laugh. There are cultural differences, but they are not what made him laugh. To illustrate, let me quote for you a dilemma, similar to the Heinz dilemma on stealing, adapted for the villages investigated: A man and wife had just migrated from the high mountains. They started to farm, but there was no rain, and no crops grew. No one had enough food. The wife got sick, and finally she was close to dying from having no food. There was only one grocery store in the village, and the storekeeper charged a very high price for the food. The husband asked the storekeeper for some food for his wife, and said he would pay for it later. The storekeeper said, "No, I won't give you any food unless you pay first." The husband went to all the people in the village to ask for food, but no one had food to spare. So he got desperate, and broke into the store to steal food for his wife. Should the husband have done that? Why?

Our Stage 2 types in the Taiwanese village would reply to this story as follows: "He should steal the food for his wife, because if she dies he'll have to pay for her funeral and that costs a lot." In the Atayal village, funerals were not such a big thing, and the Stage 2 boys would say, "He should steal the food because he needs his wife to cook for him." In other words, we have to consult our ethnographer to know what content a Stage 2 child will include in his instrumental exchange calculations, but what made our anthropologist laugh was the difference in form between the child's thought and his own, a difference definable independently of the particular culture.

It is this emphasis on the distinctive form (as opposed to the content) of the child's moral thought that allows us to call moral development *universal*. In all cultures, we find the same aspects or categories of moral judgment and valuing; these aspects are listed in Table 4.1.

Our notions of moral categories come from both the Piagetian psychological tradition and from traditional ethical analysis. Piaget's structural analysis of cognitive development is based on dividing cognition into basic categories such as logic, space, time, causality, and number. These categories define basic kinds of judgments, or relationships, in terms of which any physical experience must be construed— that is, it must be located in spatial and temporal coordinates, considered as the effect of a cause, and so on. Piaget's cognitive categories derive from Kant's analysis of the categories of pure reason, and for Kant there is an analogous set of categories of pure practical reason or of action under the mode of freedom.

Kant's categories of moral judgment are not as useful for my purposes as is Dewey's (1903) treatment of moral categories, which echoes Kant's distinctions in a way closer to my own use. Dewey says (1903, p. 22),

The distinctively intellectual judgment construes one object in terms of other similar objects and has necessarily its own inherent structure which supplies the ultimate categories of all physical science. Units of space, time, mass, energy define to us the limiting conditions under which judgments of this type do their work. The limiting terms of moral judgment (of the judgment construing an activity and content in terms of each other) constitute the characteristic features, or *categories*, of the object of ethical science, just as the limiting terms of the judgment which construes one object in terms of another object constitute the categories of physical science. A discussion of moral judgment from this point of view may be termed the "Logic of Conduct." Ethical discussion is full of such terms; the sensuous and the ideal, the *standard* and the right, *obligation* and duty, freedom and *responsibility* are samples.

The particular terms listed by Dewey we term *modes*, that is, terms defining *functional kinds* of moral judgment. Equally basic are *elements* or principles of judgment such as welfare, respect, and justice. As Table 4.1 indicates, we also find universal moral *norms*, or values (the application of the categories to content area of institutions), rang-

Table 4.1. Universal Categories of Moral Judgment

ELEMENTS

MODAL ELEMENTS

1. *Obeying (consulting)* persons or deity. Should obey, get consent (should consult, persuade).
2. *Blaming (approving)*. Should be blamed for, disapproved (should be approved).
3. *Retributing (exonerating)*. Should retribute against (should exonerate).
4. *Having a right (having no right)*.
5. *Having a duty (having no duty)*.

VALUE ELEMENTS

1. Egoistic consequences:
   a. *Good reputation (bad reputation)*
   b. *Seeking reward (avoiding punishment)*
2. Utilitarian consequences:
   a. *Good individual consequences (bad individual consequences)*
   b. *Good group consequences (bad group consequences)*
3. Ideal or harmony-serving consequences:
   a. *Upholding character*
   b. *Upholding self-respect*
   c. *Serving social ideal or harmony*
   d. *Serving human dignity and autonomy*
4. Fairness
   a. *Balancing perspectives or role taking*
   b. *Reciprocity or positive desert*
   c. *Maintaining equity*
   d. *Maintaining social contract or freely agreeing*

NORMS

1. Life	6. Authority
a. Preservation	7. Law
b. Quality and quantity	8. Contract
2. Property	9. Civil rights
3. Truth	10. Religion
4. Affiliation	11. Conscience
5. Erotic love and sex	12. Punishment

ing from law to authority to life. Any given moral judgment may be simultaneously assigned to a modal element, to a value element, and to a norm in our scheme. Each mode, element, and issue is defined at each of the stages of development. As an example, Table 4.2 defines the orientation of each stage to the issue "Value of Human Life" and gives concrete examples of the way this value is defined at each of the stages.

Table 4.2. Six Stages in Conceptions of the Moral Worth of Human Life

STAGE 1
Definition:

There is no differentiation between the moral value of life and its physical or social status value.

Example:

Q.: Why should the druggist give the drug to the dying woman when her husband couldn't pay for it?

TOMMY (age ten): If someone important is in a plane and is allergic to heights and the stewardess won't give him medicine because she's only got enough for one and she's got a sick ... friend in back, they'd probably put the stewardess in a lady's jail because she didn't help the important one.

Q.: Is it better to save the life of one important person or a lot of unimportant people?

TOMMY (age ten): All the people aren't that important because one man just has one house, maybe a lot of furniture, but a whole bunch of people have an awful lot of furniture and some of these poor people might have a lot of money and it doesn't look it.

STAGE 2
Definition:

Value of a human life is seen as instrumental to satisfaction of the needs of its possessor or others. Decision to save life is relative to, or to be made by, its possessor. (There is differentiation of physical and interest value of life, of its value to self and to others.)

Example:

Q.: Should the doctor "mercy-kill" a dying woman requesting death because of her pain?

TOMMY (age thirteen): Maybe it would be good to put her out of her pain, she'd be better off that way. But the husband wouldn't want it, it's not like an animal. If a pet dies you can get along without it—it isn't something you really need. Well, you can get a new wife, but it's not really the same.

RICHARD (age thirteen): If she requests it, it's really up to her. She is in such terrible pain, just the same as people are always putting animals out of their pain.

STAGE 3
Definition:

Value of a human life is based on empathy and affection of family and others toward its possessor. (Value is based on social sharing, community, love; differentiated from instrumental and hedonistic value applicable also to animals.)

Example:

Q.: Should the doctor "mercy-kill" the woman?

TOMMY (age sixteen): It might be best for her, but her husband—it's a human life—not like an animal, it just doesn't have the same relationship that a human being does to a family. You can become attached to a dog, but nothing like a human, you know.

STAGE 4

Definition:

Life is conceived as sacred in terms of its place in a categorical moral or religious order of rights and duties. (Value is in relation to a moral order, differentiated from value to specific others in family, and so on. Value still partly depends, however, on serving the group, the state, God, and so on.)

Example:

Q.: Should the doctor "mercy-kill" the woman?

RICHARD (age sixteen): I don't know. In one way, it's murder, it's not a right or privilege of man to decide who shall live and who should die. God put life into everybody on earth, and you're taking away something from that person that came directly from God, and you're destroying something that is very sacred, it's in a way part of God, and it's almost destroying a part of God when you kill a person. There's something of God in everyone.

STAGE 5

Definition:

Life valued both in terms of its relation to community welfare and in terms of being a universal human right. (Obligation to respect the basic right to life is differentiated from generalized respect for the sociomoral order. General value of the independent human life is a primary autonomous value, not dependent on other values.)

Example:

Q.: Should the doctor "mercy-kill" the woman?

RICHARD (age twenty-two): Given the ethics of the doctor, who has taken on responsibility to save human life—from that point of view he probably shouldn't, but there is another side, there are more and more people in the medical profession who are thinking it is a hardship on everyone, the person, the family, when you know they are going to die. When a person is kept alive by an artificial lung or kidney, it's more like being a vegetable than being a human who is alive. If it's her own choice, I think there are certain rights and privileges that go along with being a human being. I am a human being and have certain desires for life, and I think everybody else does, too. You have a world of which you are the center, and everybody else does, too, and in that sense we're all equal.

STAGE 6

Definition:
Human life is sacred because of the universal principle of respect for the individual. (Moral value of a human being, as an object of moral principle, is differentiated from a formal recognition of his or her rights.

Example:
Q.: Should the husband steal the drug to save his wife? How about for someone he just knows?

RICHARD (age twenty-five): Yes. A human life takes precedence over any other moral or legal value, whoever it is. A human life has inherent value whether or not it is valued by a particular individual.

Q.: Why is that?

RICHARD (age twenty-five): The inherent worth of the individual human being is the central value in a set of values where the principles of justice and love are normative for all human relationships.

The concept of stages just described implies something more than age trends. First, stages imply invariant sequence. Each child must go step by step through each of the kinds of moral judgment outlined. It is, of course, possible for a child to move at varying speeds and to stop (become "fixated") at any level of development; but if he continues to move upward, he must move in accord with these steps. The longitudinal study of American boys at ages ten, thirteen, sixteen, nineteen, and twenty-three suggests that this is the case. Examples of such stepwise movement were cited in Chapter 1 and are given here in Table 4.2. Tommy is Stage 1 at age ten, Stage 2 at age thirteen, and Stage 3 at age sixteen. Richard is Stage 4 at age sixteen, Stage 5 at age twenty, and Stage 6 at age twenty-four. (See Kohlberg, 1963a, 1969, for a more detailed discussion of empirical findings.)

Second, stages define "structured wholes," total ways of thinking, not attitudes toward particular situations. As can be seen in Table 4.3, which illustrates prepared arguments ("motives") for and against stealing the drug, a stage is a way of thinking that may be used to support either side of an action choice; that is, it illustrates the distinction between moral form and moral content (action choice). Our correlational studies indicate a general factor of moral level that cross-cuts aspect. An individual at Stage 6 on a "cognitive" aspect (universalized value of life) is also likely to be Stage 6 on a "motive" aspect (motive

Table 4.3. Motives for Engaging in Moral Action

STAGE 1. Action is motivated by avoidance of punishment, and "conscience" is irrational fear of punishment.

> PRO: If you let your wife die, you will get in trouble. You'll be blamed for not spending the money to save her, and there'll be an investigation of you and the druggist for your wife's death.
>
> CON: You shouldn't steal the drug because you'll be caught and sent to jail if you do. If you do get away, your conscience would bother you thinking how the police would catch up with you at any minute.

STAGE 2. Action is motivated by desire for reward or benefit. Possible guilt reactions are ignored and punishment viewed in a pragmatic manner. (Differentiates own fear, pleasure, or pain from punishment consequences.)

> PRO: If you do happen to get caught, you could give the drug back and you wouldn't get much of a sentence. It wouldn't bother you much to serve a little jail term, if you have your wife when you get out.
>
> CON: He may not get much of a jail term if he steals the drug, but his wife will probably die before he gets out, so it won't do him much good. If his wife dies, he shouldn't blame himself, it wasn't his fault she has cancer.

STAGE 3. Action is motivated by anticipation of disapproval of others, actual or imagined hypothetical (for example, guilt). Differentiates disapproval from punishment, fear, and pain.)

> PRO: No one will think you're bad if you steal the drug, but your family will think you're an inhuman husband if you don't. If you let your wife die, you'll never be able to look anybody in the face again.
>
> CON: It isn't just the druggist who will think you're a criminal, everyone else will too. After you steal it, you'll feel bad thinking how you've brought dishonor on your family and yourself; you won't be able to face anyone again.

STAGE 4. Action is motivated by anticipation of dishonor; that is, institutionalized blame for failures of duty, and by guilt over concrete harm done to others. (Differentiates formal dishonor from informal disapproval. Differentiates guilt for bad consequences from disapproval.)

> PRO: If you have any sense of honor, you won't let your wife die because you're afraid to do the only thing that will save her. You'll always feel guilty that you caused her death if you don't do your duty to her.
>
> CON: You're desperate and you may not know you're doing wrong when you steal the drug. But you'll know you did wrong after you're punished and sent to jail. You'll always feel guilty for your dishonesty and lawbreaking.

STAGE 5. There is concern about maintaining respect of equals and of the community (assuming their respect is based on reason rather than emotions). There is also concern about own self-respect; that is, to avoid judging self as irrational, inconsistent, nonpurposive. (Discriminates between institutionalized blame and community disrespect or self-disrespect.)

PRO: You'd lose other people's respect, not gain it, if you don't steal. If you let your wife die, it would be out of fear, not out of reasoning it out. So you'd just lost self-respect and probably the respect of others too.

CON: You would lose your standing and respect in the community and violate the law. You'd lose respect for yourself if you're carried away by emotion and forget the long-range point of view.

STAGE 6. There is concern about self-condemnation for violating one's own principles. (Differentiates between community respect and self-respect. Differentiates between self-respect for general achieving rationality and self-respect for maintaining moral principles.)

PRO: If you don't steal the drug and let your wife die, you'd always condemn yourself for it afterward. You wouldn't be blamed and you would have lived up to the outside rule of the law but you wouldn't have lived up to your own standards of conscience.

CON: If you stole the drug, you wouldn't be blamed by other people but you'd condemn yourself because you wouldn't have lived up to your own conscience and standards of honesty.

Note: By current stage definitions, the motives described would not necessarily represent the fifth or sixth stages but could represent the fourth stage (see Colby and Kohlberg, and others, 1982).
SOURCE: Rest, 1968.

---

for difficult moral action in terms of internal self-condemnations). An individual at Stage 6 on a situation of stealing a drug for a wife is likely to be at Stage 6 on a story involving civil disobedience (helping slaves escape before the Civil War). It should be noted that any individual is usually not entirely at one stage. Typically, as children develop they are partly in their major stage (about 50 percent of their ideas), partly in the stage into which they are moving, and partly in the stage they have just left behind. Seldom, however, do they use stages at developmental removes from one another.

Third, a stage concept implies universality of sequence under varying cultural conditions. It implies that moral development is not merely a matter of learning the verbal values or rules of the child's culture but reflects somethimg more universal in development, something that would occur in any culture.

Figures 1.1 and 1.2 in Chapter 1 (see pp. 24 and 25) indicate the cultural universality of the sequence of stages that we have found. Figure 1.1 presents the age trends for middle-class urban boys in the United States, Taiwan, and Mexico. At age ten in each country, the greater number of moral statements are scored at the lower stages. In the United States, by age sixteen, the order is reversed, so that the greater proportion use higher stages, with the exception of Stage 6, which is rarely used. The results in Mexico and Taiwan are the same, except that development is a little slower. The most conspicuous feature is that Stage 5 thinking is much more salient in the United States than in Mexico or Taiwan at age sixteen. Nevertheless, it is present in the other countries, so we know that it is not purely an American democratic construct. Figure 1.2 indicates results from two isolated villages, one in Yucatan, one in Turkey. The similarity of the pattern in the two villages is striking. Although conventional moral thought (Stages 3 and 4) increases steadily from age ten to sixteen, at sixteen it still has not achieved a clear ascendency over premoral thought (Stages 1 and 2). Stages 5 and 6 are totally absent in this group. Our studies then suggest that the same basic ways of moral valuing are found in every culture and develop in the same order.

It should also be noted that we have found no important differences in development of moral thinking between Catholics, Protestants, Jews, Buddhists, Moslems, and atheists. Children's moral values in the religious area seem to go through the same stages as their general moral values, so that a Stage 2 child is likely to say, "Be good to God and he'll be good to you." Both cultural values and religion are important factors in selectively elaborating certain themes in the moral life, but they are not unique causes of the development of basic moral values.

If basic moral values or principles are universal, the relativist's next defense is to say that the ordering or hierarchy of these values is idiosyncratic and relative. For instance, one might agree that everyone would value both life and property rights but that what is valued most depends on a culturally relative hierarchy of values. In fact, however, basic hierarchies of moral values are primarily reflections of developmental stages in moral thought. Anyone who understands the values of life and property recognizes that life is morally more valuable than property. Even at Stage 2, boys know that the druggist in the story would rather save his own life than his property, so that the druggist's property is less valuable than the woman's life. Table 4.2, defining the

six stages in the development of the basic moral category, the value of
life, suggests these are steps not only in conceptions of life's value, but
also in the differentiation of life from other values and in the hierarchical dominance of life over such values as that of property. (Another
example of such hierarchies of value is the current problem of law and
order versus justice; see Chapter 2).

Let me make explicit the implications of my studies for doctrines of
cultural relativity. Extreme relativism denies that there is a culturally
universal meaning to moral terms and implies that (1) differences in
value standards between individuals or groups cannot be *explained* by
a theory of morality but must be explained by a theory of psychological need, or of culture and subculture. Thus, sociologists have pointed
out that delinquent actions may be motivated by the need to "do right"
or conform to standards, both the standards of the delinquent gang
and the great American standard of fast success. A psychiatrist has
suggested that "While from the standpoint of society, behavior is either 'good' or 'bad,' from the standpoint of the individual it always has
some positive value. It represents the best solution for his conflicting
drives that he has been able to formulate" (Josselyn, 1948). From
either view, moral character terms are external value judgments useless for understanding the child. Extreme relativists would thus deny
the usefulness of defining individual differences in moral terms at all,
holding that to label individual differences as more or less moral is
simply judging them by arbitrary standards that have no scientific value or meaning.

A more popular view among social scientists is moderate sociological relativism. Moderate relativism starts with the notion that, although the content of moral rules and beliefs varies from group to
group, all groups have something called *morality* that has common
formal and functional properties. As stated by Brandt (1959, p. 87),

Anthropologists tell us that everywhere language enables one to distinguish
between the desired and the desirable, the wanted and the good or right. So
we can infer first that everywhere there is some sort of distinction between
momentary impulse or personal desire, and what is good, desirable, right, or
justifiable in some sense or other. Second, the great utility of rules regulating
what is to be done in types of recurrent situation is obvious. The importance
of such rules for social living will lead us to expect that surviving societies will
have some kind of authoritative rules of this sort, and hence some concept like
"it is legally obligatory to" or, for more informal rules, "it is morally obligatory to," or both.

Brandt is saying that there are culturally universal meanings to moral terms. All cultures use moral terms, all have those categories I call the modes of moral judgment ("obligation," "moral evaluation," "punishment and reward"). But, although all cultures use the moral modes, the content that is judged moral, or to which the modes apply, varies from culture to culture.

I call this moderate relativism "sociological" because this doctrine has been used to justify the notion that morality is a sociocultural product, that it originates at the social system level, not the individual level. Although all groups or societies require rules (ethical form), the content of these rules is determined by the requirements of the particular society. The implication of the sociological doctrine is that both the culturally universal and the culturally arbitrary components of morality develop in the individual through internalization of the external culture; that is, the "universal functional requirements of society" are learned by the individual in the same way as are the arbitrary standards of a particular culture.

Examples of such sociological theories are those of Sumner (1906) and Durkheim (1961), which make a sharp distinction between a culturally universal moral form and culturally variable content. Durkheim admits that, in spite of the culturally variable content of rules and principles, there is a culturally universal moral attitude of obligation (Kant), but he argues that it arises from the culturally universal sense of the group's authority rather than from the validity of any moral principles as such. Sumner's (1906) variation of the argument is that all societies have moral terms, but these terms refer to the standards of the specific society; that is, "X is right" basically means "X is in accord with the mores of my society."

Sociological relativists treat variations in moral beliefs and actions within a culture as radically distinct from moral variations between culture. Durkheim holds that an individual's attitude to the norms of his group is more or less moral depending on the extent to which he displays respect for, and attachment to, cultural moral content. One cannot, however, characterize the differences in norms from one society to another as being more or less moral, because the essence of morality is the form of respect for the norms of the group; differences in the content of these norms is irrelevant to the fact that they involve the moral form (respect). As a doctrine about the empirical nature of morality, Durkheim's doctrine assumes that theories explaining differences in norms from culture to culture are not theories as to why some individuals are more or less moral (feel more or less respect) than others. As a normative doctrine, it holds that children within a culture may be judged as more or less moral and that the less moral child should be made more moral, but that cultural differences cannot as such be morally evaluated and that moral education should be one thing in one culture, another in another.

In contrast to both extreme and sociological relativism, I have first pointed out that there are universal moral concepts, values, or principles, that there is less variation between individuals and cultures than has been usually maintained in the sense that (1) almost all individuals in all cultures use the same twenty-nine basic moral categories, concepts, or principles (see Table 4.1); and (2) all individuals in all cultures go through the same order or sequences of gross stages of development, though varying in rate and terminal point of development.

Second, I have pointed out that the marked differences between individuals and cultures that exist are differences in stage or developmental status. There are marked individual and cultural differences in the definition, use, and hierarchical ordering of these universal value concepts, but the major source of this variation, both within and between cultures, is developmental. Insofar as these individual differences are developmental, they are not morally neutral or arbitrary. This means empirically that the theory that explains cultural and individual differences in values is also the same general theory as to why children become capable of moral judgment and action at all. It means normatively that there is a sense in which we can characterize moral differences between groups and individuals as being more or less adequate morally. I am arguing, then, that even moderate or sociological relativism is misleading in its interpretation of the facts: not only is there a universal moral form, but the basic content principles of morality are also universal.

I do not quite mean by this that moral principles are shared by all people. This has been suggested, for example, by Asch (1952) when he says that differences in values "are frequently not the consequence of diversity in ethical principles but of differences in the comprehension of a situation." But although this is true, the vast differences that Asch interprets as due to "differences in level of knowledge" are something more: they are fundamental differences in principles or modes of moral evaluation. My positive definition of a "moral principle" is a moral mode, element, or value defined at a certain developmental level. Moral stages constitute "principles" in the sense that they represent the major consistencies of moral evaluation within the individual not directly due to factual beliefs. (My evidence for this is that factor analysis indicates a single "stage" factor cutting across all moral situations, and all aspects of morality on which the individual is assessed.) In this perspective, my findings lead me to conclude that there are differences in fundamental moral principles between individuals or between groups, differences in stage. However, these stages or "fundamental ethical principles" on which people differ (1) are culturally universal, (2) occur in an invariant order of development, and (3) are interpretations of categories that are universal.

These findings are not compatible with moderate or sociological relativism. Such relativism has some plausibility at the conventional level, where there is some truth to the Durkheim-Sumner argument that the basic meaning of "X is wrong" is "X violates the rules of my group." But this is not true for moral judgment at either the preconventional or the postconventional levels. It is also true that the conventional level has a vast amount of "stretch" to absorb arbitrary but socially authoritative content. However, this does not indicate the absence of universal content to conventional morality. Stage 3 Southern conservative racists may "stretch" what is "nice" or "loving" to absorb a great deal of racist behavior, as they may stretch "maintaining social order" or "giving people their just due." Nevertheless, the basic content of the "principles" appealed to by the conventional person is not arbitrary.

As an example, we say that killing innocent civilians in war is considered morally right in some cultures (Japanese, Vietnamese, Nazi) but not in others (American). What the My Lai massacre and the public opinion polls about it prove, however, is that American conventional morality finds such a massacre right under many circumstances, just as does the Vietnamese. The one enlisted man who clearly resisted engaging in the massacre was at the principled level, rather than adhering strongly to conventional American values. The somewhat greater stretch of conventional Vietnamese morality does not indicate a cultural difference in moral principle. This is an accommodation to cultural givens, or to what "most people do" and does not mean that the core moral concepts of the conventional morality are merely culturally variable internalizations.

In sum, my evidence supports the following conclusions: There is a universal set of moral principles held by people in various cultures,

Stage 6. (These principles, I argue, could logically and consistently be held by all people in all societies; they would in fact be universal to all humankind if the conditions for sociomoral development were optimal for all individuals in all cultures.) At lower levels than Stage 5 or 6, morality is not held in a fully principled form. Accordingly, it is more subject to specific content influence by group definition of the situation than is principled morality. Nevertheless, the more generalized and consistently held content "principles" of conventional morality are also universal. Even Stage 6 principles are somewhat accommodated to cultural content, for example, Lincoln and Jefferson were able to partially accommodate their principles to slavery in response to social pressure. Accommodations at the conventional stage are much more marked, but this does not mean that conventional principles, any more than Stage 6 principles, are direct reflections of cultural content.

My finding that our two highest stages are absent in preliterate or semiliterate village culture, and other evidence, also suggests a mild doctrine of social evolutionism, such as was elaborated in the classic work of Hobhouse (1906). He worked out the stages of moral evolution of cultures given in Table 4.4, which parallel our own stages in many ways.

Table 4.4. Comparison of Kohlberg and Hobhouse Systems

	Kohlberg		Hobhouse
STAGE 1	Obedience and punishment orientation	STAGE 1	Taboo and private or group vengeance
STAGE 2	Instrumental hedonism and exchange		
STAGE 3	Orientation to approval and stereotypes of virtue	STAGE 2	Ideals of character
STAGE 4	Law and order orientation	STAGE 3	Social rules and maintenance of a social order of unequal statuses
STAGES 5–6	Orientation to principles of justice and welfare	STAGE 4	General ethical principles of justice based on equal rights

My data indicate that, although cultures differ in most frequent or modal stage, a culture cannot be located at a single stage, and the individual's moral stage cannot be derived directly from his or her culture's stage. There are, however, differences in the frequencies of the higher stages in various cultural groups, related to the cognitive and social complexity of the group. It is easier to develop to Stage 6 in modern America than in fifth-century Athens or first-century Jerusalem, even though Americans such as Lincoln and King still get killed for being Stage 6. Furthermore, there is historical "horizontal decalage" or an easier extension of principles of Stage 6 thought; Socrates was more accepting of slavery than was Lincoln, who was more accepting of it than King.

It is very interesting to note that cultural relativists have never attempted to refute the basic facts convincingly organized by Hobhouse. Indeed, Westermarck, a leading critic of moral evolutionism, essentially concedes the facts in *Ethical Relativity* (1960) when, after noting the fundamental similarity of the content of values or moral rules in savage and civilized societies, he recognizes certain major differences in form between the meaning of these rules. He says,

When we pass from the lower races to people more advanced in civilization, we find that the social unit has grown larger, that the nation has taken the place of the tribe, and that the circle within which the infliction of injuries is prohibited has been extended accordingly. And if we pass to the rules laid down by moralists and professedly accepted by a large portion of civilized humanity, the change from the savage attitude has been enormous. [p. 203]

Westermarck, then, accepts what other writers have claimed were trends toward moral evolution, but he argues against calling those trends *evolution*, not on scientific grounds but because he believes that what is meant by a "higher" or more "developed consciousness" can be "nothing else than agreement with the speaker's own moral convictions." Although Westermarck assumed that one cannot define the more advanced without an arbitrary value standard, Hobhouse and our own group define a "developed consciousness" by objective measures of ontogenetic or historical sequence, measures quite independent of "agreement with the speaker's conviction."

Our developmental research also suggests that the confusion of ethical and cultural relativity is part of *an extreme ethical relativism* characteristic of a transitional phase in the movement from conventional to principled morality (Kohlberg and Kramer, 1969). In about 20 percent of college youths, the transition from conventional to principled thought is marked by extreme relativism accompanied by an apparent retrogression to Stage 2 instrumental hedonism. As example of such adolescent relativism, in response to our Heinz dilemma, a college student, age twenty, said,

He was a victim of circumstances and can only be judged by other men whose varying value and interest frameworks produce subjective decisions which are neither permanent nor absolute. The same is true of the druggist. I'd do it. A husband's duty is up to the husband to decide. If he values her life over the consequences of theft, he should do it.

A high school student, age eighteen, said,

There's a million ways to look at it. Heinz had a moral decision to make. Was it worse to steal or to let his wife die? In my mind I can either condemn him or condone him. In this case I think it was fine. But possibly the druggist was working on a capitalist morality of supply and demand.

But our longitudinal study shows that our extreme relativists eventually moved on to principled stages (Kohlberg and Kramer, 1969). Usually they moved to Stage 5, and became methodological nonrelativists, representatives of the view that there is a rational way of coming to moral agreement although the content of moral principles may be arbitrary. Occasionally, however, they moved on to Stage 6, to the recognition of universal substantive principles behind the moral point of view.

This suggests that relativism, like much philosophy, is the disease of which it is the cure; the very questioning of the arbitrariness of conventional morality presupposes a dim intuition of nonarbitrary moral principles. Purely conventional people can accept the relativity of the rules of their group because they seek nothing more. Intense awareness of relativity, however, implies a search for, or a dim awareness of, universal principles in terms of which conventional morality seems arbitrary. Royce pointed this out long ago, and termed "the moral insight" the recognition that the sense of relativity itself presupposes an implicit valid universal principle (1885, pp. 132–141).

The Cognitive-Developmental Theory of Moralization

In the previous section, I presented evidence that there is a culturally universal invariant sequence of stages in moral judgment. In this section, I present a psychological theory explaining (1) *why* there are culturally universal elements to morality at every stage, and (2) *why* movement is always upward and occurs in an invariant sequence. My psychological theory as to why moral development is upward and sequential is broadly the same as my *philosophical* justification for claiming that a higher stage is more adequate or more moral than a lower stage.

I argue that I am not committing the naturalistic fallacy by simply postulating that the later in time is the better. Rather, I am proposing a psychological theory to explain why the moral ideas that are later in time come later and supplant earlier ideas, based on the thesis that the cognitively and ethically higher or more adequate must come later than the less adequate and supplant the earlier because it is more adequate. In other words, I explain the ontogenesis, or time order, of idea systems in terms of their philosophic adequacy rather than inferring from order in time to philosophic adequacy. As Alston (1971) correctly says, there is nothing surprising about our claim that the scientific theory as to why people move upward from stage to stage coincides with a moral theory as to why they *should* prefer a higher stage to a lower "just because the 'scientific' theory has built into it claims about the relative worth of the various stages."

Evidence for an Order of Psychological Adequacy in Our Stages

Insofar as assumptions about philosophical adequacy function as explanatory constructs in my psychological theory, they have been empirically tested. The most direct test of these assumptions are the studies of Rest (Rest, Turiel, and Kohlberg, 1969; Rest, 1973), studies that form the core data that link our psychological explanations to issues of philosophic adequacy. In these studies, adolescents were first pretested with standard moral dilemmas, then asked to put in their own words, prepared arguments at each stage pro and con a choice for each of two newly presented dilemmas (for example, stealing the drug in the Heinz dilemma). An example of these arguments was presented in Table 4.3. (Similar statements were also used for the aspects of law, life, and rights.) Typically, adolescents distorted arguments higher than their own moral stage into ideas at their own stage or one below. An extreme example is a bright seventeen-year-old, Stage 2 boy, interpreting the Stage 6 conscience statement (that is, not to steal and to let your wife die is not living up to your own standards of conscience; see

Table 4.3), saying, "Yes, that's right, it's a matter of personal conscience, if he cares enough for her to steal for her, he should steal it. If
not he should let her die. It's up to him." Here the boy translates the
Stage 6 conception of conscience into a Stage 2 conception that "everyone has his bag, he should do what is instrumental to his desires."

In contrast to such distortion downward of stages *above* their own,
adolescents had no difficulty comprehending arguments *below* their
own modal stage. All subjects understood all arguments at or below
their own level. Some subjects understood thinking one and occasionally two stages above their dominant or modal stage. In such cases, however, they showed some (20 percent) use of the higher stages that they
comprehended. In other words, where subjects comprehended stages
higher than their own major stage, (1) it was usually only the next
stage above their own, and (2) they were already in transition to the
higher stage. One major implication of these findings is that our stages
constitute a hierarchy of cognitive difficulty with lower stages available to, but not used by those at higher stages. (The detailed nature of
this cognitive hierarchy is discussed in the next section.)

The fact that our stages constitute an order of *cognitive difficulty*
and *inclusiveness*, however, does not indicate that the stages constitute
an order of *moral adequacy*. The fact that Kant's moral theory is more
difficult to understand than that of Mill does not mean that it is a
more adequate theory. Rest, however, also found that his adolescent
subjects did perceive the statements for each stage as representing a
hierarchical order of *perceived moral adequacy*. This was most clearly
the case for the stages that they comprehended. The order of perceived
"goodness of thinking" corresponds to the order of stages comprehended by the subjects. There was also a tendency to rank Stage 5 and 6
statements high, even when they were not comprehended, but it was
much less clear-cut. From this, one would predict that, eliminating the
stage at which they are, the subjects should most assimilate moral
judgments one stage above their own, and assimilate much less those
which are two or more stages above, or one or more stages below, their
own. These predictions have been clearly and consistently verified in
four different experimental studies (Turiel, 1966; Rest, 1973; Rest,
Turiel, and Kohlberg, 1969; Blatt and Kohlberg, 1975).

In this sense, a psychological theory that has "built-in claims about
the relative worth of the various stages" receives strong empirical support. But this empirical support does not philosophically prove the

greater moral adequacy of the higher stages. A distinguished moral philosopher who took the moral judgment questionnaire wrote an accompanying note saying, "I am not sure whether you will score my responses as Stage 5 or Stage 6. They may sound Stage 5 in content, but I believe they have an underlying Stage 6 rationale. However, if I am mistaken, will you please follow the Rest and Turiel procedures and send me some Stage 6 responses so that I may move one stage up and be saved." Indeed, by our scoring manual the philosopher was judged as a mixture of Stages 5 and 6, so we sent him some pure Stage 6 responses. Needless to say, this philosopher was not "saved" as easily as were Rest's subjects and continues to elaborate his mixture of Stage 5 and 6 ethics.

A Freudian psychologist faced with such resistance would dismiss it as defensive, saying that one cannot expect a man who has invested years in publishing Stage 5 philosophy to abandon it, as do Rest's uncommitted adolescents. It is possible, however, that Rest's adolescents are philosophically wrong in judging Stage 6 as better than Stage 5, perhaps responding merely to its nobler ring. Still, it is clear that there are some ways in which Stage 6 is more adequate, and these determine the nonphilosopher's preference. Whether they should determine an ultimate philosophic judgment of (moral) adequacy I discuss later.

Stage Order and Stage Movement in a Cognitive-Developmental Theory

I must now clarify the sense in which a logical normative analysis of the adequacy of moral ideas can lay claim to being a psychological theory or explanation of their development. Such analysis explains within the total context of a general theory or approach termed "cognitive-developmental" (Kohlberg, 1969). A cognitive-developmental theory of moralization holds that there is a sequence of moral stages for the same basic reasons that there are cognitive or logicomathematical stages; that is, because cognitive-structural reorganizations toward the more equilibrated occur in the course of interaction between the organism and the environment. In the area of logic, Piaget holds that a psychological theory of development is closely linked to a theory of normative logic. Following Piaget, I claim the same is true in the area of moral judgment.

A cognitive-developmental theory of moralization is broader than

Piaget's own theory, however. By "cognitive-developmental," I refer to a set of assumptions common to the moral theories of Dewey and Tufts (1932), Mead (1934), Baldwin (1906), Piaget (1948), and myself. All have postulated (1) *stages* of moral development representing (2) *cognitive-structural transformations* in conception of self and society. All have assumed (3) that these stages represent successive modes of *taking the role of others* in social situations, and hence that (4) the social-environmental determinants of development are its *opportunities for role taking*. More generally, all have assumed (5) an *active* child who structures his or her perceived environment, and hence, have assumed (6) that moral stages and their development represent the *interaction* of the child's structuring tendencies and the structural features of the environment, leading to (7) successive forms of equilibrium in interaction. This equilibrium is conceived as (8) a level of *justice*, with (9) change being caused by disequilibrium, where (10) some optimal level of match or discrepancy between the child and the environment is necessary for change.

These assumptions of my *psychological theory* correspond to parallel metaethical assumptions of a *moral theory;* that is, to assumptions as to the basic nature and validity of moral judgment. Surely, metaethical assumptions must be compatible with, if not derived from, acceptable psychological theory and findings on moral judgment. If there is irrefutable evidence that forms of moral judgment clearly reflect forms of cognitive-logical capacity, the emotivist notion that moral judgments are merely the expressions of sentiments is wrong. Again, the existence of six qualitatively different systems of moral apprehension and judgment arising in invariant order is clear evidence that moral principles are not the intuitions of an inborn conscience or faculty of reason of the sort conceived by Butler or Kant. And if stages of moral judgment develop through conflict and reorganization, this is incompatible with the notion that moral judgment is a direct apprehension of natural or nonnatural facts. My interactional theory claims that moral judgments and norms are to be ultimately understood as universal constructions of human actors that regulate their social interaction, rather than as passive reflections of either external facts (including psychological states of other humans), or of internal emotions.

Both psychological and philosophical analyses suggest that the more mature stage of moral thought is the more structurally adequate. This greater adequacy of more mature moral judgment rests on structural criteria more general than those of truth value or efficiency. These general criteria are the *formal* criteria that developmental theory holds as defining all mature structures, the criteria of increased differentiation and integration. Now, these formal criteria (differentiation and integration) of development map into the formal criteria that philosophers of the formalist school have held to characterize genuine or adequate moral judgments.

From Kant to Hare, formalists have stressed the distinctively *universal* and *prescriptive* nature of adequate moral judgments. The increasingly prescriptive nature of more mature moral judgments is reflected in the series of differentiations we have described, which is a series of increased differentiations of "is" and "ought" (or of morality as internal principles from external events and expectations). As I elaborate later, this series of differentiations of the morally autonomous or categorical "ought" from the morally heteronomous "is" also represents a differentiation of the moral from the general sphere of value judgments.

Corresponding to the criterion of integration is the moral criterion of universality, which is closely linked to the criterion of consistency, as formalists since Kant have stressed. The claim of principled morality is that it defines the right for anyone in any situation. In contrast, conventional morality defines good behavior for a Democrat but not for a Republican, for an American but not for a Vietnamese, for a father but not for a son.

The way in which these criteria are embodied in our stages is indicated by Table 4.2, the moral worth of human life. The series is a series toward increased prescriptivity, because the moral imperative to value life becomes increasingly independent of the factual properties of the life in question. First, people's furniture becomes irrelevant to their value; next, whether they have loving families; and so on. (It is correspondingly a series of differentiation of moral considerations from other value considerations.) In parallel fashion, it is movement toward increased universality of moral valuing of human life. At Stage 1, only important people's lives are valued; at Stage 3, only family members; at Stage 6, all life is to be morally valued equally.

These combined criteria, differentiation and integration, are considered by developmental theory to entail a better equilibrium of the structure in question. A more differentiated and integrated moral structure handles more moral problems, conflicts, or points of view in a more stable or self-consistent way. Because conventional morality is not fully universal and prescriptive, it leads to continual self-contradictions, to different definitions of right for Republicans and Democrats, for Americans and Vietnamese, for fathers and sons. In contrast, principled morality is directed to resolving these conflicts in a stable self-consistent fashion.

The Cognitive Components and Antecedents of Moral Development

The psychological assumption that moral judgment development centrally involves cognitive development is not the assumption that this is an increased "knowledge" of rules found outside the child, in his or her culture and its socialization agents. Studies of "moral knowledge" and belief (Hartshorne and May, 1928–1930) at younger ages indicate that most children know the basic moral rules and conventions of our society by the first grade. Studies and tests of moral knowledge at older ages have not been especially enlightening. By insisting on the cognitive core of moral development, I mean rather that the distinctive characteristics of the moral is that it involves active *judgment*, as Alston (1968) seems to me to have clearly demonstrated from a philosophic point of view. Judgment is neither the expression of, nor the description of, emotional or volitional states, it is a different kind of function with a definite cognitive structure. We have studied this structure of judgment as children's use and interpretation of rules in conflict situations and their reasons for moral action, rather than as correct knowledge of rules or conventional belief in them.

My cognitive hypothesis is, basically, that moral judgment has a characteristic form at a given stage and that this form is parallel to the form of intellectual judgment at a corresponding stage. This implies a *parallelism* or *isomorphism* between the development of the forms of logical and ethical judgment. By this I mean that each new stage of moral judgment entails a new set of logical operations not present at the prior stage. The sequence of logical operations involved is defined by Piaget's stages of logico-mathematical thinking.

I said in the last section that our empirical data were consistent with the hypothesis that our moral stages are "true stages" meeting the following criteria:

1. Stages imply invariant order or sequence under varying environmental conditions.

2. Stages imply a "structured whole," a deep structure or organization uniting a variety of superficially different types of response; they imply qualitative differences in mode of response rather than quantitative increase in information or in strength of response.

3. Another criterion is that stages are *hierarchical integrations*. This implies that higher stages include lower stages as components reintegrated at a higher level. Lower stages, then, are in a sense available to, or comprehended by, people at a higher stage. There is, however, a hierarchical order of preference for higher over lower stages. This condition is also met by our stages, as I discussed in considering the Rest studies (Rest, 1968; Rest, Turiel, and Kohlberg, 1969).

Because Piaget's logical or cognitive stages also meet these criteria (Kohlberg, 1966b, 1968c), it is logically necessary that the two sets of stages be isomorphic. Moral stages must have a logical organization or explication if they are "true" stages. In a given stage, each aspect of the stage *must logically imply* each other aspect, so that there is a logical structure underlying each moral stage. Furthermore, an invariant sequence of stages implies a *logical order* among the stages. Stage 3 must imply Stage 2 and must not imply Stage 4, and so on. Such a logical order within a stage and between stages implies that the stages themselves involve logical operations or relations. In other words, a higher moral stage at least partly entails a lower moral stage, because it involves a higher logical structure entailing a lower logical structure.

This provides an explanation for the fact that movement in moral thought is usually irreversibly forward in direction, an explanation that does not require the assumption that moral progression is wired into the nervous system or is directly caused by physical natural forces. It also helps explain why the step-by-step sequence of stages is invariant. The sequence represents a universal inner logical order of moral concepts, not a universal order found in the educational practices of all cultures or an order wired into the nervous system. This inner logical order is suggested by the statements in parentheses in Tables 4.2 and 4.3. These indicate each new basic differentiation made by each stage logically depends on the differentiation before it; the order of differentiations could not logically be other than it is.

But the isomorphism of cognitive and moral stages does not mean that moral judgment is simply the *application* of a level of intelligence to moral problems. I believe moral development is its own sequential process rather than the reflection of cognitive development in a slightly different content area. A child deprived of all moral social stimulation until adolescence might perhaps develop "principled" or formal operational, logical thought in adolescence but would still have to go through all the stages of morality before developing moral principles rather than automatically reflecting cognitive principles in a morally principled form of thought. Although moral stages are not simply special applications of logical stages, logical stages must be *prior* to moral stages, because they are more general. In other words, one can be at a given logical stage and not at the parallel moral stage, but the reverse is not possible.

To summarize, there is a one-to-one *parallelism* or *isomorphism* between cognitive and moral stages, but this correspondence does not mean high or perfect empirical correlation between the two. This is because a person at a given cognitive stage may be one or more stages lower in morality. Our theory predicts that all children at a given moral stage will pass the equivalent-stage cognitive task, but not all children at the given cognitive stage will pass the equivalent moral task. The results of three relevant studies conform to the prediction. It was found that

1. Almost all (93 percent) children aged five to seven who passed a moral reasoning task at Stage 2 passed a corresponding task of logical reciprocity or reversibility. However, many (52 percent) children who passed the logical task did not pass the moral task (DeVries and Kohlberg, 1977).

2. Few (16 percent) children aged nine to eleven at the conventional stages (Stages 3 and 4) of morality failed a corresponding task involving the inversion of reciprocity in a cognitive role-taking task. Some (25 percent) children who passed the role-taking task did not achieve conventional moral judgment (Selman, 1971).

3. All adolescents and adults using Stage 5 or 6 reasoning are capable of formal reasoning on the Inhelder and Piaget pendulum and correlation problems. Many adolescents and adults capable of the latter show no Stage 5 or 6 moral reasoning (Kuhn, Langer, Kohlberg, and Haan, 1977).

These findings support what we all know: you have to be cognitively mature to reason morally, but you can be smart and never reason morally. The findings are also supported by findings relating moral judgment to IQ or mental age. Although mental age on standard intelligence tests is not a direct indication of Piaget cognitive stage, the two kinds of tests correlate quite well ($r = 70$–80, DeVries and Kohlberg, 1977). Accordingly, IQ tests correlate with moral maturity, but not as well as do Piaget tests (De Vries and Kohlberg, 1977).

The Affective-Volitional Components and Antecedents of Moral Judgment Development

One reason for the asymmetry between cognitive level and level of moral judgment might be that cognitive potential is not actualized in moral judgment because of a will, or desire, factor. It is obviously to one's self-interest to reason at one's highest level in the cognitive realm, less clearly so in the moral realm. Stage 6 may be the cognitively most advanced morality, but perhaps those *capable* of reasoning that way do not wish to be martyrs like Socrates, Lincoln, or King, and *prefer* to reason at a lower level.

Put in a slightly different way, we all know it is easier to think reasonably about physical matters than about moral matters, and this may be due to disruption by will, desire, and emotion in the moral realm. This is an extension of the issue raised by Alston (1971) when he distinguishes between having and using a concept, and points out that a person "might conceivably possess the concepts of Stage 4, 5, or 6, even though he does not habitually employ them in his moral thinking" (p. 270). But this explanation of the discrepancy between logical-intellectual level and moral level is not adequate, because there is not that much discrepancy between comprehension and usage of moral thought. The Rest studies indicate that subjects very seldom understand higher modes of thinking that they do not use spontaneously. Although the explanation is not adequate, it does explain some of the slippage involved in the relatively low correlation between intelligence and moral judgment measures (see Rest, 1973).

Discussions of cognition and affect usually founder on the assumption that cognitions and affects are different mental states, leading to the question "Which is quantitatively more influential in moral judgment, states of cognition or states of affect?" In contrast to irrational emotive theories of moral development such as those of Durkheim and Freud, the cognitive-developmental view holds that "cognition" and "affect" are different aspects, or perspectives, on the same mental events, that all mental events have both cognitive and affective aspects, and that the development of mental dispositions reflects structural changes recognizable in both cognitive and affective perspectives. It is

evident that moral judgments often involve strong emotional components, but this in no way reduces the cognitive components of moral
judgment, although it may imply a somewhat different functioning of
the cognitive component than is implied in more neutral areas. An
astronomer's calculation that a comet will hit the earth will be accompanied by strong emotion, but this does not make his or her calculation less cognitive than the calculation of a comet's orbit that had no
earthly consequences. Just as the quantitative strength of the emotional component is irrelevant to the theoretical importance of cognitive
structure for understanding the development of scientific judgment, so
the quantitative role of affect is relatively irrelevant for understanding
the structure and development of moral judgment.

The astronomer example is misleading, however, in that affective
aspects of mental functioning enter into moral judgment in a different
way than in scientific judgments. Moral judgments are largely about
sentiments and intuitions of persons, and to a large extent they express
and are justified by reference to the judger's sentiments. The development of sentiment, as it enters into moral judgment is, however, a
development of structures with a heavy cognitive component. As an
example, I presented in Table 4.3 six stages in the development of
sentiments of fear, shame, and guilt as they enter into moral judgment.
The emergence of self-condemnation as a distinctive sentiment in moral judgment is a higher step in a series of differentiations that, like all
differentiations in development, are cognitive in nature. This series of
differentiations is related to those (presented in Table 4.2) involved in
the development of human life, on the face of it not an "affective"
concept. Both spring from the central differentiations involved in the
stages as a whole (see Appendix). This is shown by the fact that there
is a good empirical correlation between a child's stage on the life concept and on the guilt concept. Further, the slip between logical and
moral development is not particularly large in the area involving concepts of sentiments. Thus, a child's stage on the aspect "concepts of
moral sentiments" correlates well with his or her stage on nonaffective
concepts and correlates about as well with IQ as do the nonaffective
concepts.

In general, then, the quality (as opposed to the quantity) of affects
involved in moral judgment is determined by its cognitive-structural
development and is part and parcel of the general development of the
child's conceptions of a moral order. Two adolescents, thinking of

stealing, may have the same feeling of anxiety in the pit of their stomachs. One adolescent (Stage 2) interprets the feeling as "being chicken" and ignores it. The other (Stage 4) interprets the feeling as "the warning of my conscience" and decides accordingly. The difference in reaction is one in cognitive-structural aspects of moral judgment, not in emotional "dynamics" as such.

Social Role-Taking Component and Antecedent of Moral Judgment Development

A more adequate explanation of the slip between intelligence and moral judgment contrasts the physical-intellectual not with the affective but with the social. As I will document, moral concepts are essentially concepts of social relationships as manifested in social institutions. Common to all social institutions or interactions are conceptions of complementary roles defined by rules or shared expectations. Ever since the brilliant analyses of Mead (1934) and Baldwin (1906), sociologists and social psychologists have clearly recognized that social cognition and judgment differs from cognition of physical objects because it involves "role taking." The primary meaning of the word *social* is the distinctively human structuring of action and thought by role taking, by the tendency to react to others as like the self and to react to the self's behavior from the other's point of view. The centrality of role taking for moral judgment is recognized in the notion that moral judgment is based on sympathy for others, as well as in the notion that the moral judge must adopt the perspective of the "impartial spectator" or the "generalized other," a notion central to moral philosophy from Adam Smith to Roderick Firth.

A great deal of variance in level of moral judgment remaining after the intellectual variance is removed is accounted for by social environmental factors that may be called "amount of opportunities for role taking." Piaget's theory (1948) has stressed peer-group participation as a source of moral role taking, while other theories (Mead, 1934) stress participation in the larger secondary institutions or in the family itself (Baldwin, 1897). Research results suggest that all these opportunities for role taking are important and that all operate in a similar direction by stimulating moral development rather than producing a particular value system. In four different cultures, middle-class children were found to be more advanced in moral judgment than matched lower-class children. This was not because the middle-class children heavily favored a certain type of thought that corresponded to the prevailing middle-class pattern. Instead, middle-class and working-class children seemed to move through the same sequences, but the middle-class children seemed to move faster and farther. Similar but even more striking differences were found between peer-group participators (popular children) and nonparticipators (unchosen children) in the American sample. Studies also suggest that moral judgment differences partly arise from, and partly add to, prior differences in opportunities for role taking in the child's family (family participation, communication, emotional warmth, sharing in decisions, awarding responsibility to the child, pointing out consequences of action to others). In particular, Holstein (1969) found that amount of parental encouragement of the child's participation in discussion (in a taped "revealed differences" mother-father-child discussion of moral conflict situations) was a powerful correlate of moral advance in the child.

An explanation of differential moral advance in terms of role taking is an explanation in terms of social cognition that differs from an emotional interpretation of differential moral advance. The environment that provides role-taking opportunities is not necessarily a warm, loving, identification-inducing environment, and an environment deprived of role-taking opportunities is not necessarily cold or rejecting. A certain minimum amount of warmth in face-to-face groups or institutions is required if a child or adolescent is to feel a sense of participation and membership in the group. However, the conditions for a child's maximal participation and role taking in a group is not that he or she receive maximal affection from the group, or that the group be organized on communal affiliation lines. At the extreme negative end, impersonal, cold environments are also deficient in role-taking opportunities. In traditional orphanages, a large majority of children are still at the preconventional level (Stages 1 and 2) at age sixteen (Thrower, 1970). At the more positive end (as environments promoting moral development) are both certain types of middle-class families and the kibbutz, not an especially warm or emotionally responsive or personal environment (Bar-Yam, Reimer, and Kohlberg, 1972).

Justice Components and Antecedents of Moral Judgment Development

One obvious implication of claiming that moral judgment rests on role taking is that moral judgment entails a concern for welfare consequences. This is true even at Stage 1. At every stage, children perceive basic values such as the value of human life and are able to empathize and take the roles of other people and other living things. In Chapter 1, I gave an example of such spontaneous sympathetic valuing in terms of my son's first moral action, which occurred at age four. At that time, he joined the pacifist and vegetarian movement and refused to eat meat. We can easily recognize that my son not only had a sense of empathy, but a sense of justice, although a Stage 1 "eye for an eye, tooth for a tooth" sense of justice. Justice, or reciprocity and equality, then, is also part of the primary experience of role taking in social interaction (Erikson, 1950; Mead, 1934; Homans, 1950; Malinowski, 1929; Piaget, 1948), and I believe this component of justice is central to the cognitive-structural transformation of role taking involved in movement from stage to stage.

The psychological unity of role taking and justice at mature stages of moral consciousness is easily recognized. For example, Tillich (1966) says that "the idea of justice, the various forms of equality and liberty, are applications of the imperative to acknowledge every potential person as a person." But this psychological unity of empathy and justice in moral role taking is also apparent at the very start of moral experience in my son's Stage 1 response. My son "took the role of the seal" in the sense of empathically experiencing its predicament. This in turn implied a Stage 1 sense of justice as equality, as the equal treatment of people and seals, and a Stage 1 sense of justice or reciprocity in the demand for an eye-for-an-eye retribution on its Eskimo hunter. Such Stage 1 concepts of justice become differentiated, integrated, and universalized with development until they eventually become Tillich's Stage 6 moral sense.

When we move from role taking to the resolution of conflicting roles, we arrive at the "principle" of justice. A moral conflict is a conflict between competing claims of people: "You versus me"; "You versus a third person." The precondition for a moral conflict is the human capacity for role taking. Most social situations are not moral, because there is no conflict between the role-taking expectations of one person and another. Where such conflicts arise, the principles we use to resolve them are principles of justice. Usually expectations or claims are integrated by customary rules and roles. The principles for making rules and distributing roles (rights and duties) in any institution, from the family to the government, are principles of justice or of fairness. At advanced stages, the most basic principle of justice is equality; treat every person's claim equally, regardless of the person. Equality is the principle of distributive justice; but there is another form of justice, commutative justice or reciprocity. Punishment for something bad, reward for something good, and contractual exchange, are all forms of reciprocity, which is equality in exchange. Arguments about what is just are either arguments about the relative claims of equality (everyone deserves a decent minimum income) versus reciprocity (only those who work hard should get the rewards of hard work), or arguments about equal liberty or opportunity versus equal benefit.

I have claimed that "role-taking tendencies" and the "sense of justice" are interlocked. Although role taking in the form of sympathy often extends more broadly than the sense of justice, organized or "principled" forms of role taking are defined by justice structures. In order for roles and rules to represent a sociomoral order, they must be experienced as representing *shared expectations or shared values,* and the general *sharability* of rules and role expectations in an institution rests centrally on a *justice structure* underlying specific rule and role definitions. As stated by Rawls (1971), "The primary subject of the principles of social justice is the basic structure of society, the arrangement of major institutions into one scheme of cooperation. These principles govern the assignment of rights and duties and they determine the appropriate benefits and burdens of social life." Because the central mechanisms of role taking are justice structures of reciprocity and equality, institutions better organized in terms of justice provide greater opportunities for role taking and a sense of sharedness than do unjust institutions.

Social environments or institutions not only facilitate moral development by providing role-taking opportunities, but their justice structure is also an important determinant of role-taking opportunities and consequent moral development. The formation of a mature sense of justice requires participation in just instituions. We are currently engaged in analyzing the perceived justice level of certain institutions for adolescents—for example, high school and reform school—as these influence the moral development of their inmates. Impressionistic observation suggests that many reform schools have an official level of justice that is a Stage 1 obedience and punishment orientation, while the inmate peer culture has a Stage 2 instrumental exchange orientation. An inmate high in participation in either of these structures is not likely to advance in moral judgment, even though in another sense he or she may be provided with "role-taking opportunities." (These data are partially discussed in Volume II and Volume III.)

Cognitive Conflict, Equilibrium, and Match in the Development of Moral Judgment

I have said that moral principles are cognitive structural forms of role taking, centrally organized around justice as equality and reciprocity. The concepts of role taking and justice, then, provide concrete meaning to the cognitive-developmental assumption that moral principles are neither external rules taken inward, nor natural ego tendencies of a biological organism but, rather, the interactional emergents of social interaction. As expressed by Piaget (1948, p. 196), "In contrast to a given rule, which from the first has been imposed upon the child from outside . . . the rule of justice is a sort of imminent condition of social relationships or a law governing their equilibrium."

Piaget argues that, just as logic represents an ideal equilibrium of thought operations, justice represents an ideal equilibrium of social interaction, with reciprocity or reversibility being core conditions for both logical and moral equilibrium. Although the sense of justice would not develop without the experience of social interaction, it is not simply an inward mirror of sociologically prescribed forms of these relations, any more than logic is an internalization of the linguistic forms of the culture.

In Piaget's theory, which I follow, the notion that logical and moral stages are interactional is united to the notion that they are forms of equilibrium, forms of integrating discrepancies or conflicts between the child's schemata of action and the actions of others. Opportunities to role take are opportunities to experience conflict or discrepancy between one's own actions and evaluations and the action and evaluations of others. To role take in a moral situation is to experience moral conflict; for example, the conflict of my wishes and claims and yours, or yours and a third party's. The integration is provided by the basic principles of justice of a stage. Social environment, then, stimulates development by providing opportunities for role taking or for experiences of sociomoral conflict that may be integrated by justice forms at or above the child's own level.

In contrast to this, exposure to higher stages of thinking presented to the child by significant figures in his or her environment is probably neither a necessary nor a sufficient condition for upward movement. The amount of change occurring in the Turiel (1966, 1969) and Rest (1973) studies of passive exposure was extremely slight. One reason for this is that a child at a given stage does not necessarily comprehend messages at the next stage up. Rest (1973) found that the only children who comprehended messages one stage above their own already showed substantial (20 percent) spontaneous usage of that stage of thought, and these children accounted for all learning or assimilation of models at one stage up. Presumably, then, movement to the next stage involves internal cognitive reorganization rather than the mere addition of more difficult content from the outside. Following cognitive-developmental theory, Turiel (1969) postulates that cognitive conflict is the central "motor" for such reorganization or upward movement. To test this postulate, Turiel conducted a series of experiments presenting children with varying combinations of contradictory arguments flowing from the same stage structure, as illustrated by the examples in Table 4.3 Without going into the details, the studies should provide concrete evidence for the general notion that stage change depends on conflict-induced reorganization. What Turiel hoped to show is that exposure to the next stage up effects change not through the assimilation of specific messages but by providing awareness that there are other, better or more consistent solutions than the children's own, forcing them to rethink their own solution.

If Turiel's analysis is correct, exposure to the next higher stage will prove to be only the first of a variety of environmental events promoting cognitive conflict. Others are exposures to real or verbal moral conflict situations not readily resolvable at the child's own stage and to disagreement with and among significant others about such situations. All these sources of conflict have been combined in the moral discussion classes conducted by Blatt (Blatt, 1969; Blatt and Kohlberg, 1975). In some of these classes, the teacher would present dilemmas and focus arguments between adjacent stages (that is, Stage 2 versus Stage 3, and so on), and this led most of the children to move up one stage, an advance retained over the control groups one year later. In other classes, children simply discussed moral dilemmas without teacher direction. Arguments between adjacent stages often developed naturally, and there was considerable change, varying with the class ability and interest in free discussion. (In the leaderless groups with high interest in discussion, upward change was about as great as it was in the teacher-led groups.)

These findings of Blatt suggest that the effects of naturally occurring moral discussions on moral judgment can be understood in the theoretical terms we have outlined, those in inducing cognitive conflict in the child and of subsequent reorganization at the next level of thinking.

Moral Stages as a Hierarchy of Forms of Moral Integration

I may summarize the cognitive-development theory as claiming that (1) moral judgment is a role-taking process that (2) has a new logical structure at each stage paralleling Piaget's logical stages; this structure is best formulated as (3) a justice structure that (4) is progressively more comprehensive, differentiated, and equilibrated than the prior structure. To concretize these claims, we may trace the progression of the role taking or justice structure through the stages. This shows how each stage is able to do things that prior stages could not, how it is a more differentiated, comprehensive, and integrated (equilibrated) structure than its predecessor.

Although psychological study of the greater equilibration of successive stages cannot be used to directly construct criteria of ethical adequacy, it can help isolate these criteria, which then require philosophical defense. Normative ethical debate generally centers around evaluating normative theories that constitute various forms of Stages 5 and 6. However, it is fairly evident that Stage 4 is more adequate than Stage 3, and Stage 3 than Stage 2, and so on. My analysis of the exact sense in which this is the case gives some criteria for more controversial evaluations. If Stage 6 can be shown to have the same properties relative to Stage 5 that Stage 5 has to Stage 4, and if these properties are recognized as making Stage 5 better than Stage 4, then I have constructed an argument as to why Stage 6 is better than Stage 5. My procedure will be to show (1) the new logical operation present at each stage, (2) the way in which this operation creates a new and more integrative or equilibrated form of justice as (3) this notion of justice forms the core of a sociomoral order.

Stages 1 and 2

I reported earlier that all children at Stage 2 or higher were able to pass Piaget tests of logical reciprocity or reversibility. A child knew that he was his brother's brother, or that a person facing him would have a right hand counterposed to his own left hand. Stage 1 children who fail these tasks of logical reciprocity think that bad acts or people will and should be followed by bad events (punishment), but they do not define "justice" as reciprocal equal exchanges between distinct individuals. Stage 1 thus defines the "sociomoral order" in terms of differentials of power status and possessions, rather than in terms of equality or reciprocity. The "principles" maintaining the social order are obedience by the weak to the strong and punishment by the strong of those who deviate. As examples, a son should give his father money that the son has been promised and has earned, because "it's his father, he owns him; he has to do what he says"; or a "troublemaker" should be the one to be sent on a suicide mission in the army "because he's bad and he has to do what the captain says."

In contrast, Stage 2 has a clear sense of fairness as quantitative equality in exchange and distribution between individuals. Positively, it prescribes acts of reciprocity conceived as the equal exchanges of favors or blows, or acts of cooperation in terms of a goal of which each person gets an equal share; negatively, it deems right noninterference in the sphere of another; for example, "You shouldn't hurt or interfere with me, and I shouldn't hurt or interfere with you." Where social or moral action requires more than this, it becomes, for Stage 2, either a matter of selfish whim ("what he feels like doing") or else an "inappropriate" extension of individual exchange and equality concepts (for example, Stage 2 subjects frequently say one should steal a drug to save a friend's life "because you may need him to do the same for you someday").

Stage 3

The limits of stage 2 are revealed by its response to role-taking tasks at which Stage 3 succeeds. Selman (1971) used two role-taking tasks that distinguish children at (or above) Stage 3 from those below Stage 3. The first was a guessing game requiring the child to conceal either a nickel or a dime that another child would then pick. Passing the task entailed recognizing that the other child would anticipate that the hider would try to anticipate him and so might hide the nickel. An immature response would be to hide the dime "because the other boy would want the dime." A mature response would be "He might think that I'll try to fool him by hiding the dime so he may not pick the dime." Eighty-four percent of children at Stage 3 or above passed this task; that is, the cognitive prerequisite of Stage 3 is recognizing a simultaneous or mutually reciprocal orientation. This reversal or inversion of an originally reciprocal orientation is the logical operation central to moral role taking. This is illustrated by Selman's second task: comprehension of the Golden Rule. Almost all the children in the study were able to state the formula "Do unto others as you would have them do unto you." They were then asked, "Why is it a good rule?" and "What would it tell you to do if someone just came up and hit you on the street?" To the latter question, most of the ten-year-olds said "Hit him back, do unto others as they do unto you." They interpreted the Golden Rule as Stage 2 reciprocity of actual exchange or revenge, instead of in terms of Stage 3 *ideal* reciprocity involving considering what you would wish if you were in the other's place. Their justification of the Golden Rule was also Stage 2: "If you follow the Golden Rule, other people will be nice back to you." Children able to correctly interpret the Golden Rule were at Stage 3 or above on the moral judgment scale. The intellectual effort required for understanding the formula is indicated by a ten-year-old Stage 3 boy: "Well, the Golden Rule is the best rule, because like if you were rich, you might dream like that you were poor and how it felt, and then the dream would go back in your own head and you would remember and you would help make the laws that way." The difficulty in comprehending the Golden Rule is that of imagining oneself simultaneously in two different roles oriented to one another.

The Stage 3 sense of justice centers on the Golden Rule ideal of imaginitive reciprocity, rather than exchange. Related to this is Stage 3's conception of equity; that is, it is fair to give more to more helpless people, because you can take their role and make up for their helplessness. Both ideal reciprocity and equity orient obligation to initial unilateral helping followed by gratitude, rather than to strict equal exchange. They disallow vengeance, because it is neither Golden Rule reciprocity nor does it restore the relationship. As Piaget points out, what the child comes to regard as just is "primarily behavior that admits of indefinitely sustained reciprocity. . . . The child sets forgiveness above revenge, not out of weakness, but because 'there is no end to revenge' (quote by a boy of ten)" (Piaget, 1948, p. 323). Characteristically, then, a Stage 3 conception of justice is integrated with a conception of a good (positive and stable) interpersonal relationship. The sociomoral order is conceived of as primarily composed of dyadic relations of mutual role taking, mutual affection, gratitude, and concern for one another's approval.

But the ideal role taking of Stage 3 is limited because it is indeter-

minate. The person engaged in practicing the Golden Rule is not requiring the person whose role he is taking to himself abide by it. The
Golden Rule, as ideal dyadic role taking, does not arrive at a determinate, equilibrated, or just solution to moral conflicts, because it does
not tell us whose role to take. Should the husband put himself in the
druggist's or his wife's place in deciding whether to steal the drug?
Customarily, Stage 3 decides by taking the roles of those with whom
he has ties; he also has a stock of stereotypes of "nice" or "mean"
people that tend toward the same decision. One would personally take
the role of one's wife, not the druggist, and this is consistent with
community approval. The "impartial spectator" would "put himself
in Heinz's place and see how desperate he was and how he would
need the medicine too," says a Stage 3 boy. At Stage 3, role taking is
both guided by, and congealed in, a bag of virtues and role stereotypes.
Indeed, as Adam Smith in his excellent exposition of the Stage 3 elements of moral psychology (*Theory of Moral Sentiments,* 1948) shows,
there is a fit between our notions of the virtues and their natural
meaning as facilitating role taking or sympathy with the individual
agent and motive of an act.

In sum, Stage 3 notions fit best the institutions of family and friendship that can be grounded on concrete, positive interpersonal relationship. But its limits are clearly seen in the idealized Christian ethic that
says, "Act as if all people loved one another, and if you meet a person
who does not respond with love to love, then turn the other cheek." In
practice, most of those who think and live this ethic also render unto
Caesar that which is Caesar's. What is Caesar's is the Stage 4 morality of law, order, and government.*

Stage 4

We saw that a Stage 3 conception of role taking and justice could
not easily be extended outside of concrete dyadic interpersonal relationships. Stage 4 solves these problems by defining justice in terms of
a system, a social *order* of roles and rules that are shared and accepted
by the entire community and that constitute the community. In terms

---

* From the more adequate perspective on the idealized Christian ethic presented in
Chapter 9, "Moral Development, Religious Thinking, and the Question of a Seventh
Stage," the use of this ethic as an example of the third moral stage is misleading. There
is a failure here to distinguish between a broader ethical perspective of agape and the
Stage 3 notion of justice as mutual affectionate concern.

of role taking, this means that each actor must orient to the other's orientation as part of a larger shared system to which they both belong and to which all are oriented.

Accordingly, justice is no longer a matter of real or ideal reciprocity or equality between individuals, as dyads, but a matter of the relations between each individual and the system. Questions of positive reciprocity are questions of the relation of individual work and merit to the rewards of the system, "a good day's work for a good day's pay"; merit should be rewarded by the system and every individual must contribute to society. Accordingly, Stage 4 positive reciprocity is exchange or reward for effort or merit, not interpersonal exchange of goods or service. Negative reciprocity is even more clearly centered on the social system: vengeance is the right of society and is conceived not as vengeance but as "paying your debt to society." The equality element of justice appears primarily in terms of the uniform and regular administration of the law, and as equity in an order of merit. Social inequality is allowed where it is reciprocal to effort, moral conformity, and talent, but unequal favoring of the "idle" and "immoral," poor, students, and so on, is strongly rejected.

It is apparent, then, that Stage 4 justice is primarily a principle for societal order rather than for personal moral choice. Furthermore, it is not an ideal principle for arranging the social order but is the pattern of maintaining the distribution of reward and punishment in an already existing system. For Stage 4, justice and maintenance of the basic rules and structure of society are much the same.

I have stressed as the key definition of Stage 4 that it is a law- (or rule) and-order-maintaining perspective. Other moral psychologists (Freud, Piaget) have failed to distinguish between the Stage 4 rules-and-authority-*maintaining* perspective and the Stage 1 rules-and-authority-*obeying* perspective. Because of this confusion, Piaget and Freud have treated a Stage 4 orientation as a primitive stage of direct internalization of external commands. Sociologists of morality, such as Durkheim, more adequately describe the rule-maintaining side of Stage 4 morality and are correct in seeing it as the "normal" adult morality of any society. In every society studied, Stage 4 is the most frequent mode of moral judgment in adults. But our data, indicating that it is an advanced sequential emergent from prior-stages quite unlike it, suggest that it is neither a direct internalization of current adult collective rules and beliefs (Durkheim) nor a primitive internalization of parental taboos and authority (Freud, Piaget). Because Stage 4 reflects a late step in role taking, it has a more "rational" core than most social scientists have believed.

Stage 5

Some moral philosophers and social scientists have argued that we must be satisfied with Stage 4 normative ethics because (1) all norms and values are relative, so that there is no ground for morality better than our culture's, and (2) moral norms ungrounded in collective belief are unsatisfying to their propounders as well as others. In the view of such sociologists as Durkheim (1924) and Sumner (1906), or of organicist philosophers such as Hegel and Bradley (1962), a more ideal and abstract morality is a fictional construction, detached from social reality and incapable of securing social agreement or emotional support. Our research "disproves" these contentions by showing that, independent of the intellectual constructions of moral philosophers and intellectuals, there arise moralities beyond Stage 4 that represent a substantial body (25 percent) of society and that more adequately handle moral problems than does Stage 4.

The obvious limits of the Stage 4 perspective, oriented to *Maintaining rules and social order,* are (1) it defines no clear obligations to people outside the order (for example, the nation-state) or to people who do not recognize the rules of one's own order; and (2) it provides no rational guides to social change, to the creation of new norms or laws. The core development of Stage 5 is the elaboration of a "rational" approach for *making laws or rules,* a law-making perspective that is clearly distinguished from the law-maintaining perspective.

Stage 1 completely confuses these two perspectives; for example, a ten-year-old boy tells us, "We should have a law that children under ten have to be in bed by eight. Then kids wouldn't get into trouble." Stage 3, at its best, advises the lawmaker to take the perspective of the obeyer of the law, without a specification of what the lawmaker's perspective requires in addition to sympathy with the obeyer. At Stage 4, the lawmaker's perspective is confused with the law maintainer's perspective; it is not the perspective of a rational individual, it is the perspective of "society," which, if democratic, is the perspective of the "general will." This is expressed as "I don't think anyone should disobey the law. Most people must have thought it was good to pass it, a minority bad. . . . It's still the will of the people." Primarily, Stage 4 is law maintaining, and the legislator, like the citizen, has a perspective primarily determined by the given rules and values of society, which he or she must maintain.

In contrast, Stage 5 clearly has a perspective necessary for rationally creating laws *ex nihilo* rather than for maintaining and solidifying rules. One element of this perspective is rule utilitarianism. Now, even Stage 4 justifies rule obedience on the ground that "if one person starts breaking the law, everyone will, and chaos will result." But this form of "rule utilitarianism" justifies any rule once made; it does not help specify what rules are to be made. Thus, at Stage 4, "rule utilitarian-ism" is defined in terms of consequences for maintaining a given soci-ety, whose value is taken for granted. In contrast, at Stage 5, consequences are defined in terms of criteria for a blueprint of society, criteria by which one law or society may be said to be better than another. The Stage 4 confusion between a law-maintaining and a law-making perspective is the confusion between what Rawls (1963) terms "justifying an action falling under a practice" and "justifying the practice." The focus of Stage 4 is on "justifying an action falling un-der a practice"; the answer to "Why should the judge punish the criminal?" is "Because he broke the law and was found guilty." Stage 4 will also go on to "justify the practice" by reference to welfare con-sequences. The answer to "Why should we have trials and punish-ments?" is "To stop people from committing crimes and hurting good citizens." But this is only a justification of the institution to other citizens; it is not a justification of the particular form of the practice, nor a criterion for improving the practice.

The distinction between the *law-maintaining* and the *law-creating* perspectives is also expressed in two different attitudes of respect for law and society. At Stage 4, it is a matter of defending the order against its enemies. Hostility and punitiveness toward criminals, dissi-dents, and enemies abroad both feeds on, and feeds, a respect for law, nation, and God, which are attacked by these enemies. The purpose of law and order is to defend the individual citizen ("Good American") against the common enemy, and the enemy is defined as someone dis-respecting law and order. The law-maintaining attitude confuses the individual self-interest and welfare of the law defender with the main-tenance of the collective structure. It also confuses the core of the col-lective structure with that which enemies attack (for example, private property is conceived as the core of our society, rather than as an institutional arrangement for maximizing the welfare of the individuals who make up society).

When attention shifts from the defense of law and order to the legislation necessary to maximize the welfare of individuals, an entirely different attitude of respect for law is involved. The law's function then is seen as adjudicating between the property rights and interests of one group of individuals as opposed to another, rather than as protecting the property rights of all decent citizens. Such adjudication requires conceptions of justice or liberty and equality prior to property rights, as well as a rational mode of calculating economic welfare. And it must be based on procedural rules that are formally just or impartial. Of these procedural rules, constitutional democracy is paramount. Stage 4 elevates majority rule or the general will into a sacred entity, while the Stage 5 notion of democracy is one of procedural mechanisms ensuring representation of individuals or pluralistic minorities and making law or society attractive to all of its members.

The procedural arrangements called *constitutional democracy* can make law and society attractive to rational members because they rest on their consent, provide equal representation for their self-interest, and include a Bill of Rights protecting their individual liberties (natural rights prior to law and society). It is clear that these procedural arrangements are prior to, and more "sacred" than (1) the concrete rules they generate, and (2) the actual enforcement of these rules in particular cases. For Stage 5, it is more important to maintain procedures of due process for criminals, for Stage 4 to secure the conviction of a particular criminal.

When we turn to the Stage 5 procedural rules for lawmaking, we find that they all invoke one or another element of the contract notion. This social contract notion is a procedural legislative principle that presupposes that both the obeyer of the law and the lawmaker have the proper orientation and that the lawmaker has received the rational consent of the individuals who make up society. In general, all sacrifices of rational self-interest to maintain the expectation of others are contractually defined for Stage 5; for example, marriage and family obligations and work obligations. Furthermore, the Stage 5 conception of contract as a procedure for generating rules, contrasts with a Stage 4 conception of contract as commitment to preexisting rules and expectations. Although Stage 4 recognizes the importance of keeping your word, such a keeping your word is maintaining your commitment to role obligations defined by society (for example, keeping your marriage vows), not a definition of obligation by mutual agreement.

The social contract that is the basis of the Stage 5 sociomoral order is a justice conception that presupposes reciprocity of the partners to the agreement and equality between them prior to the agreement, although the form of agreement takes priority over substantive justice, once agreement has been reached. Contract and due process are fundamental, and, because contracts cannot be binding without the liberty of the contractees, liberty typically takes priority over the other elements of justice (reciprocity and equality) in the Stage 5 view. Accordingly, the typical Stage 5 conception of distributive justice is one of equality of opportunity; that is, equality of formal liberty to attain substantive equality. For Stage 4, social injustice is failing to reward work and to punish demerit; for Stage 5, it is failing to give equal opportunity to talent and interest.

I have stressed Stage 5 as a lawmaking perspective rather than as a moral perspective because in ontogenetic development the formation of a Stage 5 lawmaking perspective occurs before the formation of a Stage 5 moral rule-making perspective. Rule utilitarianism was first historically developed as a principle of legislation or legislative reform, designed to validate and qualify the claims of the law and the state, rather than to validate moral rules as such. But it is important to recognize that critical moral philosophy and constitutional democracy arose together in the Western world, first in Athens, then in European Reformation thought. To see why this might be the case, consider our finding that Stage 5 presupposes what Piaget terms *formal operational thought*. Formal operations are logical operations on operations, combining all possibilities and giving rise to hypothetico-deductive thinking. Regularities or "laws" are no longer simple inductions or empirical correlations but are seen as exemplifications of universal logical possibilities. One implication of the recognition of possibilities is a sense of the arbitrariness of the individual's own role and rule system and with this sense the dawn of critical or metaethical thinking. The formal operational capacity to think about thought is, in the moral realm, the capacity to think about moral judgment, rather than to think about people, events, and institutions. The development of formal operations, then, allows children a new level of reflectivity, in which they can view systems as self-contained arbitrary systems and can consider the critical "meta" questions distinctive of moral philosophy. Just as adolescents ask, "What is it to be logical or scientific?" "What is a valid basis of logic or science?" and so on, so they ask, "What is it to be moral?" "What is a valid basis for ethics?" Unlike Stage 2 egotistic relativists, who equate "should" with their interests and wishes, adolescent relativists discard the category of "should" on metaethical grounds of relativity.

Further, the question "Why should I be moral?" is raised for the first time at the formal operational level. A Stage 2 instrumental egoistic child could never raise the question, because "to be moral" means nothing more than to serve the self in a context of social exchange. Stage 3 and 4 children do not raise the question, because for them it would mean "Why should I be the kind of self I am?" or "Why should I be part of society?" For the conventional, "Why be moral?" means "Why not be a criminal, inhuman being?" But adolescents in a skeptical metaethical phase can imagine themselves "outside society," or stripped of their Stage 3 and 4 ideas and attitudes, as Stage 2 instrumentally egoistic people. Accordingly, an increased orientation to instrumental egoistic consideration is found even in those adolescents who move from Stage 4 to Stage 5 without disruptive ethical relativism. It is understandable, then, that many of the classical arguments for Stage 5 moralities are social contract arguments designed to show that commitment to social law is the best strategy for Stage 2 instrumentally egoistic people.

The metaethical questioning that appears typically as a transitional phase in the movement from Stage 4 to Stage 5 does not always lead directly to Stage 5 thinking. Instead, it may generate a number of ideologies whose common feature is an exaltation of the self or of an ideological group as the supreme end from which all "moral" directives should be derived. Although our work suggests that such college student ideologies are usually short-lived transitional phases (Kohlberg and Kramer, 1969), there is no doubt that under some social conditions such ideologies become stabilized orientations. At their moral worst, these ideologies declare themselves "beyond good and evil," and the examples of Hitler and Stalin force us to take this amorality seriously; at their best, they celebrate a moral conscience little distinguishable in its principles from the Stage 3 or 4 moral sense but held as the sacred possession of an inner self whose moral integrity comes before both community welfare and rational discussion. I do not consider such ideologies as independent moral stages, however, because they come in many forms, are usually unstable and transitional and, most importantly, because they do not represent new modes of normative ethical reasoning. They employ Stage 2, 3 or 4 modes of ethical judgment, although they may give them unconventional content.

In summary, Stage 5 is the first of two and only two possible novel, consistent, systematic, and stable modes of moral judgment that provide answers to the skeptical and relativistic questioning that constitutes the dawn of moral philosophy (the other mode being Stage 6). Regardless of the diversities of metaethical positions of moral philosophers, there are only two broad structures of normative ethics (together with their mixtures) open to philosophical elaboration. To indicate why this is so, I have tried to show that social contract, rule utilitarianism, and the conception of law as the protection of individual interests and liberties are a set of interlocked conceptions "answering" the problems raised by a critical or skeptical orientation to morality and society. The social contract doctrine not only answers the critical awareness of the conflict between rational self-interest and social law, but also answers the problem of the relativity of laws and mores. Law is nonarbitrary when it accords with constitutional procedures that a rational person could accept without prior cultural values or conditioning. Particular laws are arbitrary, but still binding to a rational person in this context. But, as we shall see, there are a set of unsolved problems left by Stage 5, and these require a different conception of moral rationality, a conception we term *Stage 6*.

Stage 6

For Stage 5, laws should be made by constitutional contractual procedures in order to maximize the welfare of all, and laws should be obeyed as part of the contract of a citizen with society. But what should the actor do in situations where legal definitions do not exist or are questionable? Some situations are covered by Stage 5's sense of contract, or the requirement that one not violate the rights of others even where not legally protected, or by rational considerations of self-interest. For most Stage 5 subjects, however, there is a vast field of relativity or arbitrariness in individual moral choice outside the sphere of law, social contract, and agreement. Among the most compelling of such situations are those demanding civil disobedience of constitutionally legitimate laws because they prescribe unjust behavior. Here is

Jaye, a predominantly Stage 5 medical student, attempting to cope with the dilemma of whether it was right to break the law and aid slaves to escape before the Civil War:

JAYE: We have a law that says something must be done, and so in disobeying this law they are doing wrong. However, it would seem that the basic law itself is morally wrong and so *from a moral point of view*, the right thing to do is to disobey the law.

Q.: Why is the law morally wrong?

A.: Because it is treating human beings as animals.

Q.: Are you saying slavery is wrong or that in your opinion it is morally wrong?

A.: All I can say is that it is my opinion. I can't speak for anyone else. I think it was wrong, but I think you would have to take it back to the framework of the people of that time. Many people sincerely felt they were not dealing with human beings, maybe in that framework it was morally right from their point of view.

Q.: Then is it genuinely morally right to help the slave escape?

A.: Here we have a situation of an individual reaching in his mind the decision that something determined by the state is wrong. Now I think it is perfectly valid that an individual can have his own feeling and opinions. However, if he makes the decision that this law is wrong and decides to disobey it, he must do so with the full realization that it is the state's prerogative to do whatever it can to uphold this law. In breaking the laws the people were acting in a way they thought was morally right and what I would say is morally right, but nevertheless, the action was outside the bounds of society.

Clearly, this Stage 5 subject is in a bind, he is not in a stable state of equilibrium, he does not have an adequate ethic. He is not satisfied with viewing civil disobedience as morally relative, and yet he has no firm principles for defining something morally nonrelative or universal.

The first question we must ask is whether an extension of the Stage 5 legislative perspective to the making of moral rules and role norms outside the sphere of law can provide a systematic "moral point of view" that will solve such problems. The view that this can be done is, in one form, the notion that morality is embodied in "moral language," and that moral philosophy is an analysis of "ordinary moral language." In another form, it is the view that morality, like the law, consists of a system of specific rules or degrees that vary according to social conditions because they contain an arbitrary element based on the welfare needs of the particular society. As stated by Baier (1965, p. 114),

There is no *a priori* reason to assume that there is only one true morality. There are many moralities, and of these a large number may happen to pass the test which moralities must pass in order to be called true. For there will be many different moralities all of which are true, although each may contain moral convictions which would be out of place in one of the others. Thus, "Lending money for interest is wrong," "A man ought not to marry his brother's widow," "It is wrong to take more than one wife," and so on, may be true moral convictions in one set of social conditions, but false in another.

Clearly, such a modified or methodological nonrelativism is an improvement over Jaye's metaethical orientation. When the Stage 5 recognition of the formal properties of law (universality, impartiality) is extended to define criteria for moral rules and choice, it constitutes the neo-Kantian formalistic criterion of "moral principle" most recently and clearly elaborated by Hare (1963). In a somewhat broader formalistic way, the "moral point of view" may be equated with "qualified attitude" criteria of moral judgment, criteria including various checks or tests in making moral rules or moral judgment as elaborated by Brandt (1959) and Baier (1965). Such formal criteria are primarily "procedural" or "methodological," and rule utilitarianism, although more substantive than formalistic principles, also functions primarily as a methodological principle. Brandt (1968), who combines a "qualified attitude" and a "rule utilitarianism" approach, says rule utilitarianism can be viewed either as a "true principle of normative ethics or as a rule for valid inferences in ethics," but in actual use it is a methodological principle, "a rule of valid inference" to guide people making laws and social rules rather than a true substantive principle. "Rule utilitarianism" approaches to normative ethics qualify some claims of law and extend the legal perspective to extralegal role obligations but remain procedural principles for generating rules of a quasi-legal variety rather than representing substantive principles comprehensively defining individual moral obligation. Accordingly, the particular rules and obligations generated by "rule utilitarian" views, like those generated by formalistic "qualified attitude" views, are still arbitrary or culturally relative.

To document these points, I quote two moral philosophers who rely heavily on combinations of "qualified attitude" and "rule utilitarian" reasoning to resolve the "Heinz steals the drug" story.

PHILOSOPHER 1: What Heinz did was not wrong. The distribution of scarce drugs should be regulated by principles of fairness. In the absence of such regulations, the druggist was within his legal rights, but in the circumstances he has no moral complaint. He still was within his moral rights, however, unless it was within his society a strongly disapproved thing to do. While what Heinz did was not wrong, it was not his duty to do it. The crucial questions are (1) "Does a wife (or friend) have a right to the drug? (2) "Does the druggist have a right to withhold the drug?" (3) "Does Heinz have a duty to help his wife (or friend)?" In this case it is not wrong for Heinz to steal the drug but it goes beyond the call of duty, it is a deed of supererogation.

Q.: Should Heinz by punished by the judge, if caught?

A.: The judge's role is to apply the law. Unless there are very strong reasons for setting aside the law, he must do what the law prescribes. The circumstances are not so fully described that I would be confident in saying that they warrant the judge in setting aside the law, thereby creating a precedent entitling people in such conditions to steal.

PHILOSOPHER 2: Yes, he should steal the drug. It was right. Although there is a duty in general to obey the law and to form in oneself the habit of law abidingness (because it is nearly always harmful to disobey it), there obviously are cases (for example, protection of Jews in Nazi Germany) in which the law ought to be broken. These are, for the most part, cases in which one can prevent harm to other innocent people that is very much greater than the harm that comes of breaking the law. The present case appears to me to be one of these.

Q.: Did the druggist have the right to charge that much if it was not against the law?

A.: I think that in matters of life and death like this, common opinion is right to expect a degree of benevolence that is not expected in the ordinary line of business; more good than harm comes of the general observance of the principle that one should save others from grave harm at small cost to oneself if one can easily do so. It is a husband's duty to steal the drug. The principle that husbands should look after their wives to the best of their ability is one whose general observance does more good than harm. He should also steal it for a friend, if he were a very close friend (close enough for it to be understood that they would do this sort of thing for each other). The reasons are similar to those in the case of wives. If the person with cancer were a less close friend, or even a stranger, Heinz would be doing a good act if he stole the drug, but he has no duty to.

Q.: Should Heinz be punished by the judge, if caught?

A.: He should let him go free or give him a nominal sentence, if he has the discretion to do so. More good than harm comes of judges observing the principle of letting people off lightly who have broken the law for good moral reasons. A nominal sentence might be justified in order to maintain the principle that law breakers are to be punished.

Now, in these responses the claims and bases of law and social contract are left much as they were in non-philosophical Stage 5 subjects who have not elaborated a consistent moral point of view. Philosopher 1 says that, while the druggist has a legal and moral right to withhold the drug, he has no moral basis to complain of its theft. Heinz is not wrong for doing it, but he has no obligation to do it. There seems to be no clear basis *for obligation* here beyond law, although there is a clear distinction between legal violation and moral condemnation of the violator. There are fairly clear criteria of utility and justice in making laws ("distribution of scarce drugs should be regulated by principles of fairness"), but these principles have little effect in determining individual behavior. (They do not obligate the husband to steal, they do not exempt the judge from obligation to punish.)

For Philosopher 2, law obedience is itself a moral rule to be viewed by rule utilitarian criteria, but the criteria or circumstances under which the balance of harm over good would justify disobedience of law is not worked out in any clear or general way. The resolution of the conflict between legal and moral obligation is relatively vague. Rule utilitarianism does, however, define for Philosopher 2 a very definite set of moral "principles"; that is, those rules "whose general observance does more good than harm." But they are not universal across actors (they dictate that a husband has an obligation to steal, but not a friend or a stranger). "Principles" here seem to be behavior prescriptions similar to what sociologists call "role expectations"; that is, they refer to specific classes of people and prescribe general intentions and so are not suitable to be enacted as laws. (The way in which these principles are formulated, however, is similar to the way in which laws are formulated.)

This discussion and these case examples suggest that Stage 5 and its extensions cannot yield a universal morality on which all people could agree. They yield a set of procedural principles on which people could agree but do not yield substantive moral obligations or choices on which people will agree, any more than do the two philosophers quoted. A morality on which universal agreement could be based would require a different foundation. It would require that moral obligation be directly derived from a substantive moral principle that can define the choices of any person with out conflict or inconsistency. This, of course, was the original intent of Kant's categorical imperative as well as the intent of the earlier act utilitarianism. In practice, however, both the categorical imperative and act utilitarianism could not provide plausible weights to either institutionalized rules or substantive justice in their determinations. Accordingly, as embodied in current ethical thinking, they function as "Stage 5" procedural principles limiting concrete rules and laws.

There is, however, a more universalistic, moral orientation, which defines moral obligation in terms of what may alternately be conceived as (1) the principle of justice, (2) the principle of role taking, or (3) the principle of respect for personality. I call this orientation Stage 6. It is represented by the response of Philosopher 3 to the Heinz dilemma:

PHILOSOPHER 3: Yes. It was wrong legally, but right morally. I believe that one has at least a *prima facie* duty to save a life (when he is in a position to do so), and in this case the legal duty not to steal is clearly outweighed by the moral duty to save a life.

It is my belief that systems of law are valid only insofar as they reflect or embody the sort of moral law which most rational men recognize and all rational men can accept.

In the case of conflict between the imperative of a specific law and a moral imperative, one can often "see" or intuit that one "ought" to break a law in order to fulfill a moral duty. If this is not convincing, and it still is not clear why one ought to break the law against stealing in order to save a life, one can appeal to reason as well as to intuition. First of all, recognition of the moral duty to save a life whenever possible must be assumed. If someone claims not to recognize this duty, then one can only point out that he is failing to make his decision both reversible and universalizable; that is, that he is not viewing the situation from the role of the person whose life is being saved as well as the person who can save the life, or from the point of view of the possibility of anyone filling these two roles. Then one can point out that the value of property and thus the authority of the law protecting that property are subordinate to the value of a human life and the duty to preserve that life, respectively. Since all property has only relative value and only persons can have unconditional value, it would be irrational to act in such a manner as to make human life—or the loss of it—a means to the preservation of property rights.

One might deem it sufficient to weigh the amount of good produced by saving a life against the harm (pain) of stealing the drug. On the other hand, one might wish to refer solely to the results of everyone's acting on the rule, "Steal to save a life if necessary." Such things as the existence of an implicit social contract which allows men to act civilly to one another and the effect of a violation of the conditions of that contract would then be considered. But then if one went this far, *I think that one must take one more step and consider the personal justice involved in the situation—an even more basic root of the same social contract,* but hardly a utilitarian consideration. Not only can laws conflict but also laws can in some situations tend to contradict the ultimate ground of the purposive act of creating and maintaining a social institution. This ground is that of individual justice, the right of every person to an equal consideration of his claims in every situation—not just those which happen to be codified in law. It is a fact that all situations cannot be codified in law, and even if they could, it would not alter the fact that such laws would still be derivative from and express the "higher," "more basic," "absolute," and so on law of justice perhaps best formulated for the purpose here in Kant's "formula of autonomy," "treat each person as an end, not a means."

Q.: Did the druggist have the right to charge that much when there was no law actually setting a limit to the price? Why?

A.: As the legal system is set up in this country, the druggist had the legal right to charge that price. But I do not believe he had the moral right to do so. Because he is treating human life as a means rather than an end in itself—in this case, a means to making a profit.

Q.: If the husband does not feel very close or affectionate to his wife, should he still steal the drug?

A.: Yes. The value of her life is independent of any personal ties. The value of human life is based on the fact that it offers the only possible source of a categorical moral "ought" to a rational being acting in the role of a moral agent. All other possible ends of action and the value accorded to them must take only a subordinate, derivative position to that of human life for a rational, moral agent because they are hypothetical in the sense that they are contingent on either irrational interests and desires or heteronomous commands (for example, from God or human law.) The decision of what to do in such a situation must be a principled one; that is, must be made from a disinterested point of view that allows one to make a decision that can be justified and that is consistent with the decision of any rational agent in a similar situation.

Q.: Should the judge send Heinz to jail for stealing?

A.: The judge is put into the position of having both to uphold the laws of the state and to witness that the laws of the state are imperfect manifestations of a higher law. Given this position (and overlooking other, perhaps decisive factors), the judge should convict Heinz on the count of stealing and then suspend sentence for explicit, public reasons.

Philosopher 3 clearly spells out a Stage 6 position. He accepts Stage 5 rule utilitarian and social contract reasoning in its place but asserts two moral principles as defining a higher "moral law." These two "higher" principles, he holds, are ones from which the claims of civil law can be derived. The *first principle* is that *"people are of unconditional value,"* translatable into the Kantian principle "act so as to treat each person as an end, not as a means." The *second related principle* is individual *justice,* "the right of every person to an *equal* consideration of his *claims* in every situation, not just those codified into law." He treats the two principles as logically equivalent and claims that they are higher than "consider the amount of good and harm produced by stealing the drug" (act utilitarianism) or "consider the results of everyone's acting on the rule" (rule utilitarianism). He says that the utilitarian principle is not higher than law and social contract, it is at the same logical and moral level; hence, there is ambiguity when the two are played off against one another. In contrast, the principles of justice and respect for people as ends in themselves are *"higher than the law,"* because the claims of law and contract may be deduced from them. Finally, he says, from the two principles of justice and respect for persons, *an unconditional duty may be derived, the duty to save a life whenever possible.* To do otherwise is to irrationally treat a human life as a means (that is, not to view the situation from the role of the person whose life is being saved).

These substantive notions of "justice" and "respect for personality" are clarified by some additional features of the response. In marked contrast to the rule utilitarian, social contract philosophers, Philosopher 3 holds that the obligation of the husband is that of an ideal moral agent. It is an obligation to steal the drug for anyone whose life can only be saved in this way if no one else will, or can, act to save the person. For Philosopher 1, it is not a duty for the husband to steal; for Philosopher 2, it is a duty for the husband, but not for someone less close. For them, obligation is what may be "legislated" or expected for the natural person in a given role in a given society. Philosopher 2 thinks one can expect husbands to risk jail for their wives (not for less intimate friends); Philosopher 1 thinks one cannot even expect it of husbands. Their definitions of moral obligation depend on their different views of the psychology and sociology of roles in a particular society. In contrast, Philosopher 3 defines obligation in terms of a "rational being acting as a moral agent," deciding from "a disinterested point of view that allows one to make a decision consistent with the decision of any rational agent in a similar situation."

Philosopher 3's conception is *not only "ideal," it is universalistic.* The husband's act is to be determined by the fact that he is in a certain role, but this role only defines the situation within which he must act, not the values, rules, or considerations that should determine his choice. The considerations determining his choice are those which "any rational agent in a similar situation" should consider. Philosopher 3 uses universality as a positive "principle" of individual choice, making it a principle of role taking; that is, "consider what any human should do in the situation." This leads to a different notion of universality than the Kantian categorical imperative, "Act only on that maxim that you can at the same time will to become a universal law." Clearly, the maxim to be universalized is not a principle at the same level as the categorical imperative. When taken in isolation, the universality of the categorical imperative has a conservative, rule maintaining force, exemplified in Kant's conclusion that it is wrong to lie to save a life because to universalize lying for good causes is to negate the meaning of truth telling. The commonsense embodiment of this is Stage 4's "You can't make exceptions to rules—what if everyone started doing it?" For Stage 4, universalization is used in a rule-maintaining rather than a rule-creating perspective. As used by the rule utilitarian and the Kantian, universalization becomes a rule-creating perspective; for example, Philosopher 2's statement "the principle that husbands should look after their wives . . . is one whose general observance does more good than harm." In contrast to such rule universality in given roles, Philosopher 3 uses a more extensive notion of universality ("any moral agent in his place") and posits that such universality is to be a conscious guide to the actor in making a decision. (If it is something anyone should do in my place, it is an obligation for me, Philosopher 3 claims, so that a person who fails to recognize his or her duty to save a life "fails to make his decision reversible and universalizable.")

Philosopher 3's primary principles—Kant's "Treat each person as an end, not a means," and the principle of justice ("the right of every person to an equal consideration of his claims in every situation")—can be universalized in a different sense than a "maxim" or rule such as "Tell the truth" or "Help your wife." They are universal because they explicitly refer to "humanity in the person of yourself and every other"; they state what all of us always owe to every other human being. Such principles referring to all humanity are logically implied by the universalization of the actor's decision. To act in a way you want all humanity to act is to recognize the claims of all humanity. The requirement of reversibility implies that a universalizable moral act must have a universalizable object of action. The maxim "Tell the truth" need not be universalized in either sense, but the principles mentioned must be, they are *substantively universal.* One owes it even to the criminal seeking to murder "to treat him never simply as a means." One owes him "an equal consideration of his claims in every situation," but one does not owe him the truth about the whereabouts of his intended victim.

I (and Philosopher 3) claim that full universalization of moral judgment requires more than a formalistic claim—it requires substantive moral principles. These principles are themselves limited to those which are fully universalizable. Philosopher 3 restricts his use of the term *principled* to an orientation to moral decisions that is universalizable to all moral actors in all moral situations. The substantive principles meeting this claim are "justice" and "respect for personality." They are more or less equivalent: if everyone is to be treated as an end, then all people are to be treated equally. Although Kantian universality is identical to formal justice or impartiality, substantive principles (justice, equality, respect for person) add additional requirements and make the "ends in themselves" formulation workable. The principle of justice adds the specification that treatment of humans as "ends in themselves" is to be defined in terms of rights or claims. This implies that duties are correlative to rights (Raphael, 1955, p. 49), a notion that in turn implies that obligations are always to specific individuals or people. These two notions lie behind the general claim of deontological intuitionists such as Ross (1930) that there is a set of *prima facie* duties not reducible to utilitarian considerations, a "heap of unconnected obligations" that have something to do with the general notion of justice.

At all stages, the fundamental content of obligation, the fundamental norm of relationship between people is justice; that is, reciprocity and equality. At Stage 5, the core of justice is (1) liberty or civil rights, (2) equality of opportunity, and (3) contract. These three ideas are united by respect for the freedom of others, as this freedom is embodied in civil law and civil rights. At Stage 6, the sense of justice becomes clearly focused on the rights of humanity independent of civil society, and these rights are recognized as having a positive basis in respect for the equal worth of human beings as ends in themselves. This implies that (1) civil rights represent the basic ends of humans to be respected, (2) equality of opportunity means a fundamental treatment of all people as of equal basic worth, and (3) contractual relations are not just agreements, but the fundamental form of a community of ends in themselves as defined by trust.

Just how can these Stage 6 principles be used to achieve an integrated moral choice in concrete situations of conflict? The key to this is seen in Philosopher 3's equation of "universalizability" with "reversibility," which is the fundamental statement of equilibrated role taking. At Stage 3, Golden Rule ideal role taking does not achieve an equilibrated solution; that is, one that is completely reversible so that, in case of a dyad, both actors can switch places and get the same solution. (If a richer man gives all he has to the poor, he has followed the Golden Rule but he has not arrived at an equilibrated solution.) In contrast, equality or justice, is a reversible solution to problems of distribution, of when and how much one person gives to another. One element of such reversibility is contained in the notion that duties are correlative to, or reciprocal to, rights. One has no duty where a corresponding person has no right. Another element of reversibility is the recognition that a right implies the duty to recognize that right in others. Only claims that are reversible are valid. Stage 5 recognizes this in the notion that (1) the rights (liberty) of others limit the rights (liberty) of the individual, and (2) an individual who transgresses the rights of others can make no claim to have his or her own parallel rights respected. But at Stage 6 these notions are developed in a more positive sense. A just solution to a moral dilemma is a solution acceptable to all parties, considering each as free and equal and assuming none of them knew which role they would occupy in the situation (Rawls, 1971). As an example, in the Heinz dilemma the husband can take the role of the wife or of the druggist. But the druggist's claim to withhold property at the expense of a life is not reversible; he could not recognize this claim in the wife's role. The wife's claim to life at the expense of property rights, however, is a valid claim that could be recognized were she to switch roles with the husband or the druggist. In general, then, in situations of conflicting claims, the only valid claims are those consistent with recognition of the related claims of others. A claim is final only if one would uphold it as final no matter which role in the situation one were to play, and only such claims define duties.

In the sense just outlined, a universalizable decision is a decision acceptable to any person involved in the situation who must play one of the roles affected by the decision, but does not know which role he or she will play. This perspective is not that of the greatest good, nor is it that of an ideal spectator. Rather, it is a perspective sharable by all people, each of whom is concerned about the consequences to him or her under conditions of justice.

Our Stages Form an Order of Moral Adequacy: The Formalist Claim

Now to review: I have presented evidence of a culturally universal, invariant moral sequence, as well as evidence that this sequence represents a cumulative hierarchy of cognitive complexity perceived as successively more adequate by nonphilosopher subjects. I then outlined the logical structure of each stage, showing the way in which each higher stage (1) had new logical features, (2) incorporated the logical features of lower stages, and (3) addressed problems unrecognized by, or unresolved by, lower stages. A justice structure that organizes patterns of role taking in moral conflict situations is the common core at every stage, culminating in the Stage 6 capacity to consistently derive moral decisions from the generalized principle of justice; that is, to use it as a consistent guide to situational role taking independent of the arbitrary specifications of the particular cultural order of the moral judge. These ideas outline our psychological theory of moral judgment, a theory that assumes certain philosophical postulates for the sake of psychological explanation. Now, what philosophic support can we give to these postulates themselves?

Commenting on the built-in normative implications of my theory, Alston (1971, pp. 273–274) says,

What is crucial is the claim that the processes involved in stage transition involve the person's coming to realize that certain modes of thinking are more adequate ways of handling the subject matter, that they represent a more finely articulated grasp of the field in question. Thus, the kind of psychological explanation of stage sequence favored by Kohlberg has built into it claims about the relative worth of the stages as ways of moral thinking.... The crucial question, then, is as to just what claims of superiority Kohlberg makes, and whether he has adequately justified them.

I must now take up the "crucial question(s)" raised by Alston. I will first clarify the sense in which I claim that the higher moral stage is the philosophically better and then turn to the "is" to "ought" issue; that is, the sense in which it is permissible to use psychological findings and concepts to support philosophic claims.

First, note that my "claims of superiority" for higher stages are not claims for a system of grading the moral worth of individual people but are claims for the greater adequacy of one form of moral thinking over another. In my view, the basic referent of the term *moral* is a type of *judgment* or a type of *decision-making process*, not a type of behavior, emotion, or social institution. Second, note that Stage 6 is a *deontological* theory of morality. The three primary *modes* of moral judgement, and the corresponding types of ethical theory, deal with (1) duties and rights (deontological), (2) ultimate aims or ends (teleological), and (3) personal worth or virtue (theory of approbation). My claims of superiority, then, are claims for the superiority of Stage 6 judgments of duties and rights (or of justice) over other systems of judgments of duties and rights. I make no direct claims about the ultimate aims of people, about the good life, or about other problems that a teleological theory must handle. These are problems beyond the scope of the sphere of morality or moral principles, which I define as principles of choice for resolving conflicts of obligation.

The general criterion I use in saying that a higher stage's mode of judgment is more adequate than a lower stage is that of morality itself, not of conceptions of rationality or sophistication imported from other domains. Stage 6 is not necessarily more cognitively complex (by nonmoral criteria of complexity), nor need it be based on a philosophically more congenial metaethical position. Accordingly, a philosopher may not judge Stage 6 as more adequate than lower stages because it is not more scientifically true, is not more instrumentally efficient, does not reflect more metaethical or epistemological sophistication, or is not based on a more parsimonious set of normative ethical postulates. Only a philosophical formalist who views morality as an autonomous domain, with its own criteria of adequacy or rationality, is likely to evaluate moral arguments by moral criteria rather than by philosophical criteria of rationality imported from nonmoral domains. I assume a metaethic that says that moral judgments are not true or false in the cognitive-descriptivist sense, that higher moral conceptions cannot be judged more adequate by technical-economic criteria of efficiency; for example, as better means of maximizing the happiness of the self or of society.

I am arguing that a criterion of adequacy must take account of the fact that morality is a unique, *sui generis* realm. If it is unique, its uniqueness must be defined by general formal criteria, so my metaethical conception is *formalistic*. Like most deontological moral philosophers since Kant, I define morality in terms of the formal character of a moral judgment, method, or point of view, rather than in terms of its content. Impersonality, ideality, universalizability, preemptiveness, and so on are the formal characteristics of a moral judgment. These are best seen in the reasons given for a moral judgment, a moral reason being one that has these properties. But I claim that the formal definition of morality only works when we recognize that there are developmental levels of moral judgment that increasingly approximate the philosopher's moral form. This recognition shows (1) that there are formal criteria that make judgments moral, and (2) that these are only fully met by the most mature stage of moral judgment, so that (3) our mature stages of judgment are more moral (in the formalist sense, more morally adequate) than less mature stages.

Moral judgments, unlike judgments of prudence or esthetics, tend to be universal, inclusive, consistent, and grounded on objective, impersonal, or ideal grounds. Statements such as "Martinis should be made five-to-one, that's the right way" involve "good" and "right" but lack the characteristics of moral judgments. We are not prepared to say that we want everyone to make them that way, that they are good in terms of some impersonal ideal standard shared by others, or that we and others should make five-to-one Martinis whether we wish to or not. In similar fashion, when a ten-year-old at Stage 1 answers the moral question "Should Joe tell on his younger brother?" in terms of the probabilities of Joe getting beaten up by his father and by his brother, he does not answer with a moral judgment that is universal or that has any impersonal or ideal grounds. In contrast, Stage 6 statements not only use moral words but also use them in a specifically moral way: "regardless of who it was" implies universality; "Morally I would do it in spite of fear of punishment" implies impersonality and ideality of obligation; and so on. The individual whose judgments are at Stage 6 asks, "Is it morally right?" and means by "morally right" something different from punishment (Stage 1), prudence (Stage 2), conformity to authority (Stages 3 and 4), and so on. Thus, the responses of lower-stage subjects are not moral for the same reasons that responses of higher-stage subjects to esthetic or other morally neutral matters fail to be moral. In this sense, we can define a higher-stage judgment as "moral" independent of its content and of whether it agrees with our own judgments or standards.

This is what I had in mind earlier when I spoke of the stages as representing an increased differentiation of moral values and judgments from other types of values and judgments. For example, with respect to the moral value of the person, the Stage 6 argument has become progressively disentangled from status and property values (Stage 1), from the person's instrumental uses to others (Stage 2), from the actual affection of others for the person (Stage 3), and so on. With each stage, the obligation to preserve human life becomes more categorical, more independent of the aims of the actor, of the commands or opinions of others, and so forth. This is why I appealed to two of the formal criteria of moral judgment—prescriptivity and universality—and paralleled these to the criteria of differentiation and integration, which entail a better equilibrium according to developmental theory. I developed this in detail in the preceding section, where I showed that the Stage 6 response, being more prescriptive and more universal, generated a more stable and consistent response. In contrast, each Stage 5 philosopher (qualified attitude and rule utilitarian) generated a somewhat different solution to the dilemma, stopping at varying points in asserting the universal and prescriptive nature of obligation.

I am claiming that developmental theory assumes formalistic criteria of adequacy, the criteria of levels of *differentiation* and *integration*. In the moral domain, these criteria are parallel to formalistic moral philosophy's criteria of *prescriptivity* and *universality*. These two criteria combined represent a formalistic definition of the moral, with each stage representing a successive differentiation of the moral from the nonmoral and more full realization of the moral form.

My developmental definition of morality is not a system for directly generating judgments of moral worth, just as Piaget's developmental definition of stages of intellectual adequacy is not a system for grading single acts of people as better or worse along an IQ scale. A developmental definition seeks to isolate a function, such as moral judgment or intelligence, and to define it by a progressive developmental clarification of the function. Thus, intelligence, as defined by Piaget, is both something present from the start of life (in the infant's adaptive sensory motor behavior) and something whose ultimate structure or form is only given in the final stages (for example, the formal operational thought of the adolescent as experimenter and theorist). Similarly, in my view, there is a moral judgmental function present from age four to five onward in judgments of "good and bad" and "has to" (Stage 1), but this function is only fully defined by its final or principled stages.

I am stressing that my developmental *metaethical* conception of the higher or later as the more moral is not a *normative ethical* principle generating moral judgments. Some formalistic philosophers, notably Kant, have attempted to construct rules of punishment or blame and a theory of the good or of virtue from deontological principles. But I make no such claims and do not think a Stage 6 normative ethic can justifiably generate a theory of the good, a theory of virtue, or rules for praise, blame, and punishment. In order to engage in moral education and social control, society may need rules of punishment and reward and rules for labeling virtues and vices (Stage 5). But Stage 6 principles of justice do not *directly* obligate us to blame and punish, even though it is necessary or expedient in terms of social utility.

I have been arguing that, both by Stage 6 normative ethical standards and by formalist metaethical criteria, Stage 6 is a more moral mode of judgment than Stage 5 or 4. One may define an act as moral if it is in accord with Stage 6 principles in a particular situation, but this does not generate rules for grading the worth of individual people or of actions. Nor does my formalist metaethic answer such questions as "Why be moral?" or "What good is justice?" Such questions cannot be answered by a normative ethical theory or by using moral concepts. Just as a theory of formal logic is a theory of what logical inference is and ought to be, but does not answer the question "What good is logic?" or "Why be logical?" so answers to these metaethical questions are not given by a Stage 6 normative ethical theory. A formalistic normative theory says, "Stage 6 is what it means to judge morally. If you want to play the moral game, if you want to make decisions which anyone could agree upon in resolving social conflicts, Stage 6 is it." It cannot give a justification of Stage 6 morality in nonmoral terms.

In the present section, I have clarified my claim that Stage 6 is the most adequate exemplification of the moral, supporting it with a few of the many arguments advanced by formalist (deontological) theories. In this connection, Alston's comment that "it is notorious that moral philosophers agree no more about what is distinctive of the moral than about anything else" (1971, p. 276) is somewhat misleading. Although there are an infinite variety of definitions of the moral, there is a fairly high degree of agreement among formalists as to the formal properties of moral judgment (compare Frankena, 1963). Philosophers who offer alternative definitions of morality do so because they ignore formal features of morality and define it instead in terms of the particular content of the normative morality they advocate. To my knowledge, those who object to a formalist definition of morality have no positive alternative to offer except (1) morality is what is in accord with my own system, or (2) morality is relative. Regardless of psychology, then, our conception of morality has a strong philosophical base. Anyone who tries to criticize it must provide a stronger positive alternative.

The Claim for Principles of Justice

I now turn to the defense of my substantive definition of Stage 6 in terms of principles of justice. Although every domain of thought, from grammar to music, implies "principles" (that is, abstract rules), moral principles have unique features and functions. If a "bad" painting is made according to principle, so much the worse for the principle. But the whole notion that there is a distinctively moral form of judgment demands that moral judgment be principled; that is, that it rely on moral principle, on a mode of choosing that is universal, that we want all people to adopt in all situations.

By "principle," I mean something more abstract than ordinary moral rules of the Ten Commandment variety. Conventional college students say, in regard to the drug theft story, "The principle of loyalty to your family comes ahead of obeying the law here," and so on, but, on the face of it, they do not wish to universalize these rules. For one thing, not everyone has a family; for another, it is doubtful that if one's uncle were Hitler one could claim loyalty to be a relevant or *prima facie* principle. We know it is all right to be dishonest and to steal to save a life because one person's right to life comes before another person's right to property. There are always exception to such rules. By "moral principle," all thoughtful people have meant a general guide to choice rather than a rule of action. Even our college student who talks of "the principle of loyalty to your family" means something like "a consideration in choosing," rather than a definite rule prescribing a class of acts.

It has sometimes been thought that principles such as the utilitarian maximization of happiness or Kant's categorical imperative are not only universalizable to all people and all situations but are also absolutely definitive of right action in any situation. Thus far we have never encountered a live human being who made moral judgments in terms of principle in this sense. Yet we do find people judging in terms of principles in a weaker sense, illustrated in the writings of the principled intuitionists, such as Sidgwick and Ross. In this weaker sense, a person may consistently hold more than a single principle of moral judgment, and these principles may not be definitive of a choice in all situations (that is, alternative choices may be derived from them). In our empirical work, I and my colleagues considered the term *principles* to refer to considerations in moral choice, or to reasons justifying moral action. We found empirically that almost all these reasons easily fall into the categories outlined by principled intuitionist philosophers.

Accordingly, in our detailed coding of categories of moral judgment, we have the following categories of "principles," which correspond to those of Sidgwick (1887), except that we add the psychological category of "respect for authority": (1) prudence (and self-realization); (2) welfare of others; (3) respect for authority, society, or people; and (4) justice. As I suggested in preceding sections, all of these "principles" are present in one form or another from Stage 1 onward, except that prudence and authority have dropped out as reasons by Stage 6. From the start, these reasons have two characteristics: they refer to states of affairs that are involved in all moral situations and are potentially relevant to all people. Still, benevolence and justice do not become genuine moral principles until Stages 5 and 6. At the conventional stages, the reasons for choices include considerations of benevolence and justice, as well as of prudence and social authority. But not until Stages 5 and 6 is there an effort to systematically and consistently derive *prima facie* rules or obligations from these principles or to view obligation as fundamentally directed by them rather than by concrete rules.

In my view, mature principles are neither rules (means) nor values (ends) but are guides to perceiving and integrating all the morally relevant elements in concrete situations. They reduce all moral obligation to the interests and claims of concrete individuals in concrete situations; they tell us how to resolve claims that compete in a situation, when it is one person's life against another's. If my formal characterization of the functioning of mature principles is correct, it is clear that only principles of justice have an ultimate claim to being adequate universal, prescriptive principles. By definition, principles of justice are principles for deciding between competing claims of individuals, for "giving each person his due." When principles, including considerations of human welfare, are reduced to guides for considering such claims, they become expressions of the single principle of justice.

The only general principle of content seriously advanced by philosophers, other than justice, has been the principle variously termed *utility* or *benevolence*. Although benevolence can be universalized (that is, everyone should care for the welfare of all other humans), it cannot resolve a conflict of welfares, except by quantitative maximization. The content of moral concerns and claims is always welfare, but maximization is no true moral principle, as I attempted to show in the analysis of Stage 5 rule utilitarianism. Concern for the welfare of other beings, "empathy," or "role taking," is the precondition for experiencing a moral conflict rather than a mechanism for its resolution. The moral question is "Whose role do I take?" or "Whose claim do I favor?" The working core of the utilitarian principle is the maximization principle. As everyone knows, and our studies document, "Consider everyone's happiness equally" is not a working principle of justice. Stage 6 subjects will say, "Steal the drug for anyone; whether it's his wife or not, every person has a right to live," but they do not claim that a husband should treat the happiness of his wife and of a stranger equally. Neither do they rationalize the husband's preference for his wife's happiness on "rule utilitarian" grounds. Instead, they speak of a marriage tie, or "contract," or relationship of reciprocal trust and love; that is, a claim of commutative reciprocity or justice, not one of utility.

My argument for justice as the basic moral principle is, then, as follows:

1. Psychologically, both welfare concerns (role taking, empathy) and justice concerns, are present at the birth of morality and at every succeeding stage and take on more differentiated, integrated, and universalized forms at each step of development.

2. Of the two, however, only justice takes on the character of a principle at the highest stage of development—that is, as something that is obligatory, categorical—and takes precedence over law and other considerations, including welfare.

3. "Principles" other than justice may be tried out by those seeking to transcend either conventional or contractual-consensual (Stage 5) morality, but they do not work, either because they do not resolve moral conflicts or because they resolve them in ways that seem intuitively wrong.

4. The intuitive feeling of many philosophers that justice is the only satisfactory principle corresponds to the fact that it is the only one that "does justice to" the viable core of lower stages of morality.

5. This becomes most evident in situations of civil disobedience for which justice, but no other moral principle, provides a rationale that can cope with the Stage 5 contractual-legalistic argument that civil disobedience is always wrong.

6. The reason that philosophers have doubted the claims of justice as "the" moral principle is usually that they have looked for a principle broader in scope than the sphere of moral or principled individual choice in the formal sense.

Denial that justice is the central principle of morality thus tends to coincide with a refusal to accept a formal deontological concept of morality but is not backed by an alternative positive definition of morality.

In identifying the core of principled morality with justice, I follow a line of normative ethical argument advanced recently by Raphael (1955) and Rawls (1963, 1971). Formalists who disagree with the primacy of justice usually do so because they wish to keep morality completely content-free. In one sense, justice is itself content-free; that is, it merely prescribes that principles should be impartially applied to all. However, I have also argued that the Stage 6 form implies justice as equity; that is, as a treatment of people as morally equal (compare Frankena, 1963). Second, I have argued that it also implies commutative justice as reciprocity, contract, and trust. In this chapter, I cannot show that the moral form of universality, tied to the notion that obligations are to people, logically implies the principle of justice, a task that Raphael (1955) has attempted. I simply point to the fact that no principle other than justice has been shown to meet the formal conception of a universal prescriptive principle.

Let me briefly consider Alston's (1971, p. 277) criticism that

What Kohlberg really wants most to recommend to our acceptance is the principle of justice (in his interpretation) as a supreme moral principle. But stages of prescriptivity will not advance that cause. A judgment based on a principle of racial destiny, or on no principle at all, can be just as prescriptive as a judgment based on an application of Kohlberg's principle of justice.

For most of us, it is counterintuitive to believe that racial destiny could be held as a universal prescriptive principle. This is because no human being held it or similar beliefs as such a principle, at least none in research studies done by my colleagues and myself. Hitler himself explicitly said, "Might makes right"—that is, his judgments were nonprescriptive. And he explicitly held that Nazi morality was non-universal—that is, it was not designed to govern the decisions of Jews or others. The fact that psychological study shows that no one does use unjust "principles" in a formally principled way, is no proof that they cannot. However, it is of more moment that no philosopher ever has seriously attempted to demonstrate that an alternative substantive principle to justice could function in a universal prescriptive fashion in a satisfactory way. Alston is correct in saying that I have not proved that justice is the only possibility, but he neglects to point out that no one has successfully argued for an alternative.

In summary, if a formalistic definition of moral principle is unjustified, no one has proposed a better definition. And if an equation of moral principle with justice is injustified, no one has proposed a satisfactory alternative. In that sense, it is clear that my definition of Stage 6 as the way people ought to reason is more than what Alston suggests, namely "some arbitrarily selected criterion . . . [based on] congeniality to his predilections" (1971, p. 277).

From "Is" to "Ought"

Let us consider the sense in which our description of what morality is tells us what it ought to be. To begin with, there are two forms of the naturalistic fallacy I am not committing. The first is that of deriving moral judgments from psychological, cognitive-predictive judgments or pleasure-pain statements, as is done by naturalistic notions of moral judgment. My analysis of moral judgment does not assume that moral judgments are really something else, but insists that they are prescriptive and *sui generis*. The second naturalistic fallacy I am not committing is that of assuming that morality or moral maturity is part of biological human nature or that the biologically older is the better. The third form of the naturalistic fallacy, which I *am* committing, is that of asserting that any conception of what moral judgment ought to be must rest on an adequate conception of what it is. The fact that my conception of the moral "works" empirically is important for its philosophic adequacy. By this I mean first that any conception of what adequate or ideal moral judgment *should* be rests on an adequate definition of what moral judgment *is* in the minds of people. If all Ph.D. philosophers showed a Stage 6 concern for universal and autonomous moral principles, while all other people were Durkheimian asserters of the authority of the group or were Benthamite hedonists, it would be, I believe, impossible to construct a plausible account of why people should adopt a Stage 6 morality. Contrariwise, neither a Benthamite construction nor a Durkheimian construction of what morality ought to be, based as they are on the assumptions that morality really is Stage 2 (Bentham) or Stage 4 (Durkheim), is viable, because both ignore the reality of what morality is at Stages 5 and 6. Every constructive effort at rational morality, at saying what morality ought to be, must start with a characterization of what it is, and in that sense commits the naturalistic fallacy.

What I am claiming about the relation of "is" to "ought" in moral development comes to this:

1. The scientific facts are that there is a universal moral form successively emerging in development and centering on principles of justice.

2. This Kantian moral form is one that assumes the fact-value distinction; that is, moral people assume that their moral judgment is based on conformity to an ideal norm, not on conformity to fact.

3. Science, then, can test whether a philosopher's conception of morality phenomenologically fits the psychological facts. Science cannot go on to justify that conception of morality as what morality ought to be, as Durkheim attempted to do. Moral autonomy is king, and values are different from facts for moral discourse. Science cannot prove or justify a morality, because the rules of scientific discourse are not the rules of moral discourse.

4. Logic or normative ethical analysis can, however, point out that a certain type of moral philosophy—for example, Stage 4—does not

handle or resolve certain problems that it acknowledges to be problems that it ought to handle, whereas another type of morality (for example, Stage 5) can do so. Here, factual investigation of people's beliefs must support internal logical analysis of why the developmentally higher philosophy can handle problems not handled by the lower ones. Science, then, can contribute to a moral discourse as to why one moral theory is better than another.

5. The scientific theory as to why people factually *do* move upward from stage to stage, and why they factually *do* prefer a higher stage to a lower, is broadly the same as a moral theory as to why people *should* prefer a higher stage to a lower. In other words, a psychological theory of why people move upward in moral ideology is not like a psychological theory of why they move from the anal to the genital stage. It is the naturalistic fallacy to say that a Freudian theory of an instinctual progression is an ethical justification of why genitality is better than anality. But the theory of *interactional* hierarchical stages of cognition and morality and the theory of *maturational* embryological stages are critically different in their logic, as I have discussed in detail elsewhere (Kohlberg, 1969).

Claims 1–4 are simply claims that moral psychology and moral philosophy should work hand in hand. This unexciting conclusion is represented in this chapter where I have tried to give normative ethical answers to problems set by developmental findings. As Alston (1971) regards my claim that any constructive effort at rational morality must start from a characterization of what it is as "a very innocuous sense" (p. 273) of the "naturalistic fallacy," he probably does not object to them. Alston does object to claim 5 and thinks that I am trying to "pull a moral philosophy out of a hat" (p. 277). What is not completely clear to me is whether he means that it is logically impossible to derive anything for moral philosophy out of a hat of developmental facts, or whether he is arguing that I have not been completely successful in a logically possible enterprise, because it is a hard trick to pull off. (I agree with his latter conclusion; if my argument were completely successful, it would have solved the basic problems of moral philosophy.) The former notion—that is, that facts of development cannot be of any use in arguing for moral "oughts," because the distinction is absolute and "Thou shalt not use facts in the development of principles"—is an untenable position, as Scheffler (1953) seems to me to have demonstrated.

At any rate even the claim that normative theories need to be grounded on a firm view of the facts of moral judgment carries us quite far. First, our findings indicate that philosophical analysts are justified in asserting universal features, as against the arguments of ethical and cultural relativists. They also show that the philosopher's task cannot be merely to clarify moral language or moral common sense, since there are six such systems of moral language. Furthermore, because the highest stage includes the basic positive features of lower stages, only a normative ethical theory that includes all these features can tell us how we ought to make moral judgments.

However, I do hold a stronger position, claiming that, although psychological theory and normative ethical theory are not reducible to each other, the two enterprises are isomorphic or *parallel*. In other words, an adequate psychological analysis of the structure of a moral judgment and an adequate normative analysis of the judgment are made in similar terms. In the context of our work, psychological description of moral stages corresponds to the "deep structure" of systems of normative ethics. The logical relations between stages represent indifferently the structure of an adequate theory of moral judgment development, or the structure of an adequate theory as to why one system of moral judgment is better than another. Thus, I have argued for a parallelism between a theory of psychological development and a formalistic moral theory on the ground that the *formal psychological* developmental criteria of differentiation and integration, of structural equilibrium, map into the *formal moral* criteria of prescriptiveness and universality. If the parallelism were correct in detail, then formalist philosophers could incorporate an equilibration concept as part of their normative ethical theory, and vice versa. The ultimate result would be a theory of rational moral judgment like current economics theory, in which the theories of how people ought to make economic decisions and the way they do make decisions are very closely linked.

What can warrant such a "parallelist" claim is only the fruitfulness of its results. I have argued that the fruitfulness of the parallelist assumption is revealed in the clear success of the psychological work based on it. Its fruitfulness in solving philosophic problems will, I optimistically believe, be apparent when moral philosophers begin to use the new moral psychology to help pose and solve their problems.

Let me be concrete about the way in which our stage psychology provides guidance for the moral philosopher's task. Critical or analytic moral philosophy sees its task as the clarification of ordinary consciousness. But if there are six stages and each stage is a reconstruction of moral "principles" of lower stages, then moral principles are active constructions, and moral philosophy must construct, not merely analyze or clarify. Confronted by the task of constructing a rational morality, philosophers have usually taken one of two metaethical positions: (1) that a rational system for moral choice must consist of deductions from principles that are self-evident to an actor who accepts nothing but rational methods of inference and of optimizing choice (the classic Benthamite utilitarian stance, leading to a naturalistic form of descriptive metaethic) or (2) that moral principles are dimly intuited by the common human being (ordinary morality) and the philosopher's task is simply to codify and make consistent the morality derived from these principles (Kant or Sidgwick). How far off this was is documented by the Rest (1968) study, which shows the lack of comprehension of subjects at conventional stages for even the most concrete and palatable statements of Kant's categorical imperative. On the basis of our research, we reject both the Benthamite (naturalistic) position and the Kantian notion that principles are innate, universal, and *a priori*.

From my developmental perspective, moral principles are active reconstructions of experience; the recognition that moral judgment demands a universal form is neither a universal *a priori* intuiton of humanity nor a peculiar invention by a philosopher but, rather, a portion of the universal reconstruction of judgment in the process of development from Stage 5 to Stage 6. An analogy to grammar may clarify this point. Kantian moral intuitionists see their task as like that of Chomsky, who attempts to delimit the principles, the deep structure transformations, which define competent syntax in any language. In grammar, the codification of these principles does not, however, transform syntax itself. Chomsky speaks the same syntax he spoke at age five. It is for this reason that he is able to hold a Kantian epistemology of grammar. There is only one grammatical system of intuition, known to all children of five. In contrast, I am arguing that the codification of principles is an active reconstruction of morality, that Stage 6 principled morality is a radically different morality rather than a codification of conventional Stage 4 morality. The task of both the psychologist and the philosopher, then, is very different in the sphere of morality than in grammar. If my position is correct, the only "competent moral speakers" are the rare individuals at Stage 6 (or, more tolerantly, at Stages 6 and 5), and normative ethical codifications and metaethical explanations of conventional moral speech will miss their true task. Like neo-Kantian intuitionists, ordinary-language moral philosophers, particularly formalists such as Hare, think their task is to analytically define and clarify ordinary (Stage 4) moral language. If the form of ordinary moral language is, however, qualitatively different from that of the language of a normative ethical philosopher, the problem is different.

Another implication of our stage psychology for moral philosophy is that arguments for a normative ethic must be stepwise. Rawls (1971) has taken a formal set of assumptions that I term Stage 5—namely, that society is ordered by a constitution defined by a social contract—and he shows how such a society must be based on principles of justice or of equal rights, because these are the only principles to which rational individuals in the imaginary original state could consent. These principles are, in a sense, prior to law and social institutions, and in certain conditions justify civil disobedience. In other words, Rawls has used a formal argument to derive Stage 6 morality from Stage 5 and to systematize Stage 6 morality insofar as Stage 6 morality is defined by sociopolitical choices. In contrast, one of the classical arguments for Stage 5 morality has been that of deriving it from Stage 2 morality. Assuming instrumental egoistic people (Stage 2), earlier moral theories attempted to show that it is rational for such people to create a social contract with social welfare conditions. This argument fails to be fully convincing, because it ignores the Stage 4 to which it "ought" to be addressed. From this, one can conclude that there is no one line of argument for Stage 6 (or Stage 5) morality, but only a family of arguments that move from one stage position to the next.

In essence, there is a "deep logical structure" of movement from one stage to the next; a structure tapped by both a psychological theory of movement and by families of philosophical argument. If these contentions are correct, they provide a new definition of the moral philosopher's task, a definition more exciting than that implied by much recent philosophic work.

From Thought to Action

A moral decision, we usually think, involves a conscious conflict between two lines of action, and a strong emotional component. Psychology's notion of conscience comes from the prophets through Saint Paul to Freud's conception of the battle between the id and the superego. Saint Paul's "The flesh lusteth against the Spirit and the Spirit against the flesh so that ye cannot do the things ye would," and St. Augustine's "O Lord, give me strength to give up my concupiscence, but not just yet," have passed into the clichés of most psychology text books: moral behavior is construed as resistance to temptation, the algebraic outcome of two forces, the lusts of the flesh (needs), and the anticipation of the guilt (superego), mediated by a slightly overwhelmed ego, self, or will.

To get an indication of the battle of conscience, one of my students (Lehrer, 1967) built a ray gun test following Grinder's (1962) rationale. Grinder's gun was preprogrammed to yield a marksmanship score just a little below that needed to get a handsome prize, and the twelve-year-olds tested had the opportunity to fudge their scores. Grinder (1962) reports that 80 percent of the children end up cheating. Lehrer wanted to tempt the children even more, by improved gadgetry that leads them to the brink of success in a realistic but random fashion. To our surprise, when Lehrer ran the test on 100 children, only 15 percent cheated (Lehrer, 1967). This was hardly a decision of conscience; the machine obviously struck the children as being a computer that kept its own score, while the Grinder machine did not.

What I am trying to show is what Hartshorne and May (1928–1930) showed forty years ago, although it has been ignored ever since. As I noted in "Education for Justice" (Chapter 2),

1. *You cannot divide the world into honest and dishonest people. Almost everyone cheats some of the time.* Cheating is distributed in bell-curve fashion around a level of moderate cheating.

2. *If people cheat in one situation, that does not mean they will or will not in another. There is very little correlation between situational cheating tests.* It is not a character trait of dishonesty that makes a child cheat in a given situation; if it were, you could predict from one situation to another.

The emphasis on moral virtues that are acquired by habit derives from Aristotle, whose bag of virtues included temperance, liberality, pride, good temper, truthfulness, and justice. Hartshorne and May's bag included honesty, service, and self-control. The Boy Scout bag is well known—a Scout should be honest, loyal, reverent, clean, and brave. My quick tour through the ages indicates that the trouble with the bag of virtues approach is that everyone has his own bag. The problem is not only that a virtue like honesty may not be high in everyone's bag, but that my definition of honesty may not be yours. When I have given Hartshorne and May cheating tests to children, I have been lying and cheating them, saying I was testing their aptitude. I cheat and lie to them so that I can catch them cheating me. Nevertheless, I would argue that my cheating does not indicate a lack of consistency between my self-concept as honest and my behavior but reflects the consistency of this particular kind of cheating with my moral principles. Your moral principles might be inconsistent with giving these tests to children, but you will probably believe that I am generally moral even though I cheated in this situation.

The objection of the psychologist to the bag of virtues should be that virtues and vices are labels by which people award praise or blame to others, but the ways people use praise and blame toward others are not the ways in which they think when making moral decisions themselves. You may not find my cheating children "honest" or moral, but I find it in accordance with my moral principles and thinking. To illustrate the point another way, Edmund Wilson (and Thoreau) failed to pay income taxes as a "matter of conscience," while millions of their fellow citizens fail to do so for reasons of "expedience." The behaviors are the same, and no psychologist can tell them apart; it is only what the people involved think they are doing that sets their behavior apart. There simply is no valid psychological definition of moral behavior, in the sense that no observation and categorization of behavior "from the outside" or "behavioristically" can define its moral status in any psychologically valid sense. But, although there is no such thing as moral behavior as such, there is such a thing as behavior that is consistent with an individual's moral principles or that springs from a moral decision. Before we can know anything about such behavior, however, we must first know what a person's moral judgments or principles are.

I can now relate moral judgment to moral action in light of my earlier contention that the major general individual and group differences in moral judgment are developmental differences. What I am ready to predict is not that people in a moral situation will do what they said they should do outside that situation but that maturity of moral thought should predict to maturity of moral action. This means that specific forms of moral action require specific forms of moral thought as prerequisites, that the judgment-action relationship is best thought of as the correspondence between the general *maturity* of an individual's moral judgment and the maturity of his or her moral action. This implies the cognitive-developmental contention (Kohlberg, 1969) that maturity of moral judgment and action have heavy cognitive components and suggests a broader developmental notion of moral action than that represented by the "bag of virtues."

In our first study (Kohlberg, 1958), 72 Chicago boys aged ten to sixteen were rated by their teachers on a variety of character traits including conscience strength or internalized conformity. The product moment correlation between maturity of moral judgment scores and ratings of conscience was .46. Experimental studies by Krebs (1967) and by Schwartz, Feldman, Brown, and Heingartner (1969) bear out these correlational trends. In the latter study, a short form of my moral judgment instrument was administered to 35 undergraduates, who could then be divided into two moral judgment levels, the conventional and the principled. Principled subjects appear much less likely to cheat than conventional subjects. Only one of nine principled subjects cheated, while about one-half of the conventional subjects did so. The former study reports similar results with 120 sixth-grade children (20 percent of the principled subjects cheated, as compared to 67 percent of the subjects at lower stages).

On the usual attitude test measures of cheating, principled subjects were no more opposed to cheating than conventional subjects; those strongly opposed to cheating were just as likely to cheat as those who were indifferent. So the greater resistance to cheating of the principled subjects was not due to their greater endorsement of conventional rules about cheating. To understand why the principled subjects did not cheat while many of the conventionals did, one must remember that the experimental situation is Mickey Mouse (it does not matter much whether one cheats or not) and that it is fishy (the experimenter explicitly leaves the child unsupervised in a situation where one would expect supervision). Even if the conventional subject is taken in by the experimenter, there is the more basic ambiguity as to whether anyone cares or not. The experimenter indicates he does not care whether cheating goes on; he almost suggests its possibility and desirability. If an adult experimenter takes a casual attitude, not only is the possibility of punishment minimized but a far more important thing is also minimized: *the concept that the authority or the group is damaged or that it cares whether you conform or not.*

While conventional children care about maintaining social expectations and order regardless of punishment, their reasons for not cheating ("It is wrong," "You should do your own work," "The other fellow may not have the right answer," and so on) carry no force as soon as they are not supported by the expectations and sanctions of the authority or of the group. In contrast, a Stage 5 or 6 person defines the issue as one of maintaining an implicit social contract with the tester and the others taking the test. The more unsupervised, the more trusting the experimenter, the more contractually obligated this principled person is. Also, the principled person defines the issue of cheating as one of inequality, of taking advantage of others, of deceptively obtaining unequal opportunity; that is, in terms of justice.

This interpretation implies that *moral judgment determines action by way of concrete definitions of rights and duties in a situation.* Moral attitudes as measured by attitude tests do not indicate the way an individual defines moral conflict situations. Because "Cheating is always wrong" means "You always get caught" for Stage 1 but "It's good to be honest because nice people are honest" for Stage 3, a Stage 1 subject cheats when there is no punishment, a Stage 3 subject when other nice people are cheating. Implicit in Stage 3's definition of "good" is a stereotypical conception of "what most people do" and "expect," which is much more potent in defining the situational conditions of cheating or not cheating than are variations in the intensity of statements about the value of honesty.

Because moral stages are defined as *structure* of values, not as *content* of values, choice on our dilemmas is not always determined. Stage 4 law-and-order subjects may opt for not stealing the drug out of respect for law and property rights, just as they may opt for stealing out of respect for marital responsibility and for the value society puts on human life. We call the choice *content* and the stage characteristics *structure*. But many aspects of value hierarchy are determined by stage structure. Stage 2 subjects recognize nothing higher than individual needs, so say they will steal. Stage 4 places social order over individual needs, but it is uncertain whether law and property or an individual human life is more primary to the social order. Stage 6 again has a clear hierarchy in which moral principles demanding respect for life are higher than the social order. Prediction to action thus requires that the alternatives are ordered by a hierarchy related to the individual's basic structure. In the case of Stage 4, we could only predict how a subject would choose when social order stands clearly on one side and other values on the other, as in civil disobedience. Again, however, if authority is on the side of civil disobedience, as it is in Southern racist areas, the choice becomes ambiguous.

An even more basic way in which stage defines choice is by bringing sensitivity to new aspects of the moral situation, while ruling out other aspects of the situation. Principled subjects are sensitive to justice aspects of the cheating situation that are ignored by conventional subjects. In the case of cheating, there is no conflict between "law and order" and justice, so the principled subject is not required to choose justice over law and order. It is, however, the principled subjects' sensitivity to justice that gives them a reason to not cheat when law-and-order reasons have become ambiguous or lost their force because of the confusion and indifference involved in the experimental situation.

I am arguing that moral judgment dispositions influence action through being stable cognitive dispositions, not through the affective charges with which they are associated. Textbook psychology preaches the cliché that moral decisions are a product of the algebraic resolution of conflicting quantitative affective forces. Although efforts to predict moral decisions by this model have yielded slim results, the metaphor continues to have currency. I am claiming instead that the moral force in personality is cognitive. Affective forces are involved in moral decisions, but affect is neither moral nor immoral. When the affective arousal is channeled into moral directions, it is moral; when not so channeled, it is not moral. The moral channeling mechanisms themselves are cognitive. Effective moral channeling mechanisms are cognitive principles defining situations. It is no more inspiring to find that cognitive moral principles determine moral choice in a cheating situation than it is to find that cognitive physical principles determine choice in a situation dealing with physical objects. In playing pool, or billiards, one does not follow the principles of physics because of one's affective identification with them. Although more than truth value is involved in moral principles, the analogy is that one follows moral principles in a situation because one feels they correctly define that situation, not because of an abstract affective identification with these principles as verbal abstractions. The motivational power of principled morality does not come from rigid commitment to a concept or a phrase. Rather, it is motivated by awareness of the feelings and claims of the other people in the moral situation. What principles do is to sort out these claims, without distorting them or canceling them out, so as not to leave personal inclination as the arbiter of action.

This leads us to an even more basic point about moral action. The conception that difficult moral choices are difficult because of the conflict between the flesh and the spirit, the id and the superego, is misleading. If we attend to literature and history instead of textbook personality psychology, it appears that real moral crises arise when situations are socially ambiguous, when the usual moral expectations break down. The traditional social psychology example is the mob. The book *Lord of the Flies* gives a better example, a group of well-behaved young British boys who became moral savages when left on a desert island. It is apparent that maintenance of morality in such situations depends on principles that make sense in spite of the fact that external social definitions do not support them. We have interpreted our experimental cheating situation as simply the most trivial of such situations, claiming that conventional subjects cheat not because their restraint of impulse is less than that of principled subjects, but because their cognitive definition of right and wrong is less independent of what other people think.

Psychology has assumed that action is determined by emotional and social forces associated with belief, that the relation of belief to action is independent of the cognitive adequacy of the belief, that a rational or cognitively mature moral belief affects action in the same way as an irrational belief. If this is not the case, we must start theorizing about thought and action in a new way. Yet although the way is new, it seems clear. The study of the relation of social cognitive structures to social action seems in principle much like the study of the relation of physical cognitive structure to actions upon physical objects, including the fact that both take place in social fields. The issue of sacrifice, however, raises a fundamental difference in the moral area. Because much morality involves basic sacrifice, it has been consigned to the realm of the irrational by Nietzsche, Freud, Kierkegaard, and their followers. If, however, a mature belief in moral principles in itself engenders a sacrifice of the rational ego, apart from other personality and emotional considerations, we are faced with a conception of the rational and of cognitive structure that has no parallel in the realm of scientific and logical thought.

To summarize, I believe that our studies support what in Chapter 2 I called the Socratic view, including the following propositions:

- *First*, virtue is ultimately one, not many, and it is always the same ideal form regardless of climate or culture.
- *Second*, the name of this ideal form is justice.
- *Third*, not only is the good one, but virtue is knowledge of the good. He who knows the good chooses the good.
- *Fourth*, the kind of knowledge of the good which is virtue is philosophical knowledge or intuition of the ideal form of the good, not correct opinion or acceptance of conventional beliefs.

5. Justice as Reversibility: The Claim to Moral Adequacy of a Highest Stage of Moral Judgment

In CHAPTER 4, "From *Is* to *Ought*," I have outlined (1) the extensive research facts concerning culturally universal stages of moral judgment, (2) the psychological theory of development that I believe best fits those facts, and (3) a metaethical view that attempts to bridge the gap between naturalistic and non-naturalistic, moral philosophic theories. This chapter elaborates a claim made in the previous chapter, that a higher or later stage of moral judgment is "objectively" preferable to or more adequate than an earlier stage of judgment according to certain *moral* criteria.

In Chapter 4, I attempted to show that a higher stage (such as Stage 5) is an objectively better way of making moral judgments than a lower stage (such as Stage 4). I said that the betterness of Stage 5 is partly a *cognitive* betterness, that the judgments of Stage 5 are more cognitively complex (differentiated) and more cognitively inclusive than Stage 4 judgments (*inclusive* meaning that Stage 5 ideas include Stage 4 ideas as elements or parts). I cited, as an example, the cognitive perspective of Stage 5 as compared to Stage 4. I claimed that Stage 5 ideas arose from a social contract, utilitarian, "prior-to-society" *law-making perspective,* while Stage 4 judgments arose from a "member-of-society" *law-maintaining* perspective. As contrasted to Stage 5, at Stage 4 the authority of laws does not rest on free contract but rests directly on divine, natural, or societal authority. Laws are not judged functionally as revisable in the light of maximizing utility or public welfare, but maintaining laws is necessarily utilitarian in preventing disorder. In including Stage 4 considerations of authority and functions of law, the Stage 5 perspective is cognitively better.

I also claimed, however, that Stage 5 was better not only by cognitive criteria, but also by *moral* criteria. The two are not the same, I said, because a certain cognitive-logical stage (as defined by Piaget) and a certain stage of social cognition or role taking (as defined by Selman) are necessary but not sufficient for the parallel moral judgment stage. Presumably the Pentagon "best and the brightest" (and perhaps also less "well-intentioned" people such as Hitler and Stalin) were capable of the highest levels of logical thought and of social perspective taking. Their decisions and reasoning on Vietnam reflected an advanced cognitive perspective corresponding to Stage 5 morality but would not be called particularly moral if they did not reflect Stage 5 moral reasoning resting on a social contract to maintain human rights, which are "natural" or common to all humanity. Their reasoning, then, reflected a high level of cognitive but not of moral development.

Recognizing this distinction, in the previous chapter I argued Stage 5 is not only cognitively more sophisticated but that it is more moral than Stage 4. I said that it is more moral in the sense that its judgments come closer to the formal criteria distinguishing moral from nonmoral judgments. These criteria have been elaborated by a tradition of "formalist" moral philosophy running from Kant to contemporaries such as Hare, Frankena, Brandt, Rawls, and Raphael. These criteria of morality include prescriptivity (a distinct concept of an internal duty), universalizability (a sense that judgments should be those all people can act on), and primacy (of moral over nonmoral considerations). Such formal criteria define judgments and reasoning as involving "a moral point of view" or as being "principled" (where moral principles are distinguished from concrete moral rules and laws). From this formalist point of view, I said that Stage 6 moral judgments are more moral than Stage 5 in the same sense in which Stage 5 judgments are more moral than Stage 4.

I also reviewed my psychological theory and findings and then went on to make certain *metaethical* claims. As a piece of philosophy, Chapter 4 is a statement of metaethical theory (a theory as to the nature, function and grounds of validity of moral judgments). I argued, for instance, that moral judgments should not be viewed from a relativistic perspective or metaethic but from a perspective of methodological nonrelativism. Philosophers usually distinguish between a metaethical theory, which defines the nature and grounds of validity of moral judgments, and a *normative ethical* theory, which defines actual principles of moral judgments and attempts to justify the principles as valid or rational. In this sense, Chapter 4 was fundamentally an enterprise tying my psychological theory to a statement of contemporary formalist metaethical theories in philosophy in such a way as to justify the claim that a higher stage is a better stage.

In Chapter 4, I touched on, but did not develop, the relation of my psychological theory to contemporary normative ethical theory. To do so, in this Chapter I elaborate the parallels between our psychological theory and Rawls's (1971) normative ethical theory of justice.

Rawls's theory has two aims. The first is to construct a systematic structural model for explaining or generating "considered" moral judgments analogous to the models of structural linguists generating the rules of grammatical speech of competent speakers. Rawls's second aim is to use his model to *justify* and *prescribe* principles of justice that he claims should underlie competent or considered moral judgments. With regard to Rawls's first aim, this chapter claims that, as an explanatory structural model, Rawls's theory does successfully describe the method and the substantive principles used in the considered moral judgments of all human beings in any culture, with one major qualification. The qualification is that it successfully generates the judgments of only the human beings who have completed the sequence of moral development and are at the highest stage of moral judgment (Stage 6, attained by less than 5 percent of adult Americans). In this sense, Rawls's notion of "considered judgment" or "reflective equilibrium" corresponds to judgments at our highest moral stage. This capacity of Rawls's model to generate moral judgments at the highest stage springs from a correspondence between his explanatory theory and my explanatory or psychological theory presented in Chapter 4. This correspondence is hardly surprising, because my theory and Rawls's grew out of the same roots; Kant's formal theory in moral philosophy and Piaget's formal theory in psychology. As our theory is tied to empirical data on the moral judgments of hundreds of subjects, while Rawls's theory has no data except philosophic introspection, this correspondence strengthens Rawls's theory as an explanation of moral judgment.

With regard to Rawls's second aim, Rawls's theory does something I have not tried to do—to prescribe and justify to a rational person the principles of considered moral judgments. Insofar as Rawls has succeeded in doing this, he has, I claim, demonstrated why a higher stage is a better stage. A higher stage is a better stage because its judgments more closely approximate Stage 6 judgments generated from the principles or model that Rawls's theory undertakes to justify.

The present chapter, then, elaborates the way in which I believe the substance of Stage 6 principles of judgment to be better than the substantive principles of lower stages, not just the sense in which they are formally "more moral." It elaborates my claim that the Stage 6 structure or method of reasoning actually leads to more just or "morally right" conclusions about specific dilemmas than do lower-stage methods of reasoning. I argue that just or "morally right" principles or just decisions are those which all rationally moral people would or could agree on.

The Stage 6 method of reasoning can do this, I argue, if there is common agreement on the facts and probabilities. Not only are Stage 6 principles designed to be acceptable to all rational people, but all those who were using Stage 6 methods and principles will eventually agree on the "right" solution in concrete situations, our empirical data suggest. The people we have studied whose reasoning is at Stage 6 have agreed on the dilemmas we have presented them. In contrast, Stage 5 people all agree on certain dilemmas but not on others.* In this chapter, I take up some dilemmas on which Stage 5 subjects disagree but on which Stage 6 subjects agree. I then attempt to show why the Stage 6 reasons are "right," using some extrapolation from Rawls's normative theory.

Common Assumptions of Rawls's Theory and of that of Piaget— Reversibility and Equilibrium

Chapter 4, "From *Is* to *Ought*," presented our psychological theory of moral development. Here I briefly review the theory with attention to the similarities in assumption between Rawls's theory and my own.

Over a period of twenty years, my colleagues and I have rather firmly established a culturally invariant sequence of stages of moral judgment, summarized in the Appendix.

As described in the Appendix, the last stage, Stage 6, has a distinctively Kantian ring, centering moral judgment on concepts of obligation as these are defined by principles of respect for persons and of justice. In part, this corresponds to an initial "formalist" or "structur-

---

* The general claim that the higher the stage, the more the determination of content by structure, and the more the agreement among people, is elaborated empirically in Chapter 7, which reports an empirical study of moral judgments on capital punishment.

alist" bias of both our moral and our psychological theory. Our psychological theory of morality derives largely from Piaget (1948), who claims that both logic and morality develop through stages and that each stage is a structure that, formally considered, is in better equilibrium than its predecessor. It assumes that each new (logical or moral) stage is a new structure that includes elements of earlier structures but transforms them in such a way as to represent a more stable and extensive equilibrium. Our theory assumes that new moral structures presuppose new logical structures; that is, that a new logical stage (or substage) is a necessary but not sufficient condition for a new moral stage. It assumes, however, that moral judgments (or moral equilibrium) involves two related processes or conditions absent in the logical domain. First, moral judgments involve role taking, taking the viewpoints of others conceived as *subjects* and coordinating those viewpoints, whereas logic involves only coordinating viewpoints on objects. Second, equilibrated moral judgments involve principles of justice or fairness. A moral situation in disequilibrium is one in which there are unresolved conflicting claims. A resolution of the situation is one in which each is "given his due" according to some principle of justice that can be recognized as fair by all the conflicting parties involved. These "equilibration" assumptions of our psychological theory are naturally allied to the formalistic tradition in philosophic ethics from Kant to Rawls. This isomorphism of psychological and normative theory generates the claim that a psychologically more advanced stage of moral judgment is more morally adequate by moral-philosophic criteria. The isomorphism assumption is a two-way street. Moral philosophical criteria of adequacy of moral judgment help define a standard of psychological adequacy or advance, and the study of psychological advance feeds back and clarifies these criteria. My psychological theory as to why individuals move from one stage to the next is grounded on a moral-philosophical theory that specifies that the later stage is morally better or more adequate than the earlier stage. My psychological theory claims that individuals prefer the highest stage of reasoning they comprehend, a claim supported by research (Rest, 1973). This claim of my psychological theory derives from a philosophical claim that a later stage is "objectively" preferable or more adequate by certain *moral* critera. This philosophic claim, however, would for us be thrown into question if the facts of moral advance were inconsistent with its psychological implications.

My assumption of isomorphism implies first the assumption of continuity between the context of discovery of moral viewpoints (studied by the psychology of moral development) and the context of justification of moral viewpoints (studied by formal moral philosophy). This implies that the philosopher's *justification* of a higher stage of moral reasoning maps into the psychologist's *explanation* of movement to that stage, and vice versa. The isomorphism assumption is plausible if one believes that the developing human being and the moral philosopher are engaged in fundamentally the same moral task.

Let us approach Rawls's normative or justifying theory from this perspective. From Rawls's point of view, as from ours, the task is arriving at moral judgments in reflective equilibrium. For Rawls, the notion of "reflective equilibrium" has three meanings. The first is an equilibrium between espoused general moral principles and particular judgments about situations. The relation between the two is back and forth (always the meaning of something in equilibrium). We extract or induce principles that seem to lie behind our concrete judgments and try to make new judgments by them. This process continues to lead to revision, sometimes of our principles, sometimes of our intuition as to what is right in a concrete situation.*

For Piaget, science or cognition as well as morality develop through a reflective equilibrium between "principles" and concrete experience. Stages represent "theories" or principles within which facts or concrete experiences are interpreted or to which they are assimilated. Experience can only be stretched so far so that a theory may assimilate it; eventually an inadequate theory or stage will be caught in contradiction, and the individual will then generate a new principle or theory to accommodate the experience. Stages, then, represent equilibrium points in the successive revisions of principles and concrete experiences in relation to one another.

There are two additional meanings of the equilibrium idea elaborated by Rawls. The first is the idea of a social contract arrived at as

---

*This notion of reflective equilibrium implies a somewhat different relation between principles and the "facts" of concrete experience in morality than in cognition or science. We can attain consistency by revising the "facts" (our intuitions about what is right in a concrete moral case) where it conflicts with the principle of our moral theory in a way that we cannot revise the experiential facts when they conflict with the principles of our scientific theory. In the sense "moral law" or principles bend the facts of moral experience, although not in the absolutist sense implied by "moral law."

the equilibrium point among a group of rationally egoistic bargaining players. Here Rawls draws on the idea of equilibrium of mathematical and economic theories of competitive games, the idea of a *maximin*. He asks, "Is there a ground rule or principle for the distribution of income in a society that represents the equilibrium point of egoistic proposals?" This equilibrium point would give each individual the most he could get if he were at the top of the income distribution under a condition that minimizes the risk of loss if he ends at the bottom of the distribution. If individuals did not know in advance what place they would have in the income distribution, there is a rule that generates an equilibrium and is in this sense fair. The principle or rule rational egoists would choose is "the difference principle"; that is, "Inequalities are unacceptable or arbitrary unless it is reasonable to expect that they will work out for everyone's advantage." The reason that the difference principle represents the equilibrium or maximin point for people setting up an income distribution and not knowing the place they will hold in it may be verbalized as follows:

I want as much as I can get. Hence I will try for a set of principles tailored to advantage me, but the other participants will reject such slanted proposals or even bring in ones that slant in their favor. They will not give me more than them and I will not take less. So I must insist on, and settle for equality of income. But wait a moment. Suppose some unequal distribution can so increase the output that there is an "inequality surplus." Suppose someone suggests a distribution which by eliciting greater effort, increases the output so much that there is "an inequality surplus," so that after the lowest-paid roles are paid at the previous level of equal distribution, the newly raised roles are paid more, and there is still a surplus enough to raise at least marginally the payoff of the lowest-paid role. In that case I should insist not on equality but on a distribution of the surplus that benefits every man. In that case I will certainly be better off than under a pattern of absolute equality. I will allow such inequalities to work to everyone's benefit. But I will not accept any unequal distribution that pushes some roles beneath the equality baseline in order to raise others above it. Since I am not willing to take the chance, I will be stuck with that lower role. [Wolff, 1977, p. 33]

A second example of Rawls's equilibrium of maximin is a method of distribution that exemplifies "pure procedural justice." This is a practice in which one person cuts the cake and a second person distributes it. If the person cuts the cake to advantage himself, he must anticipate that he may receive the disadvantaged portion from the distribution. This practice would lead to equal shares except where there is an inequality surplus, where it would lead to the difference principle.

For Rawls, then, principles of justice thus represent an equilibrium among competing claims. Justice, however, represents equilibrium only under the assumption that each player is choosing in an "original position" prior to the establishment of a society or a practice and under a "veil of ignorance" so that no one knows his position in society, nor even his place in the distribution of natural talents or abilities. The "veil of ignorance" represents a statement of the fundamental formal condition(s) of the moral point of view, the conditions of impartiality or universalizability. Impartiality means a judgment made without any bias based on knowing that the judge or one of his or her friends is one of the players being judged. Universalizability is exemplified in Kant's maxim of the categorical imperative "So act that the outcome of your conduct could be the universal will" or "Act as you would want all human beings to act in a similar situation."

Kant wanted the form of universalizability to generate actual substantive principles of justice for a society or principles of moral decisions in concrete dilemmas. Rawls's effort to exemplify the form of universalizability in the idea of the original position works better. This is because the "original position" exemplifies an idea of equilibrium distinguishable from, although related to, Rawls's idea of a contract resulting from an equilibrium in a bargaining game. This is the idea of *reversibility*, as a property of a system in equilibrium. The veil of ignorance exemplifies not only the formalist idea of universalizability, but the formalist idea of Hare and others that a moral judgment must be reversible, that we must be willing to live with our judgment or decision when we trade places with others in the situation being judged. This, of course, is the formal criterion implied by the Golden Rule: "It's right if it's still right when you put yourself in the other's place." In Rawls's theory, a possible principle of justice is the *fair* principle of justice if it is the one that would be chosen under the original position, if one would choose it if one did not know who one would be in the society or situation after the principle was used. In this sense, the choice is reversible; we chose it in such a way that we can live with the choice afterward, whoever we are, as was the case for the procedure of cutting the cake.

We can clarify the idea of reversibility implied by Rawls's concep-

tion of the original position by citing the use of reversibility in defining choice in the Heinz dilemma. (See Table 4.2, Chapter 4.)

In Chapter 4, I cited a "Stage 6" response to the dilemma by Philosopher 3. He started by saying, "I believe that one has a moral duty
to save a life whenever possible and the legal duty not to steal is
outweighed by the moral duty to save a life. One can often "see" or
intuit that one "ought" to break a law in order to fulfill a moral
duty."

As stated, the intuition that one ought to break a law because of a
moral duty to save a life is one shared by "Stage 6" Philosopher 3
with the two other philosophers cited in Chapter 4 as thinking at
Stage 5. Philosopher 3, however, goes on to use "a moral theory of
Stage 6" to justify his intuition. He says, "If intuition is not clear or
convincing and if someone claims not to recognize a duty to save life
whenever possible, then one can only point out that he is failing to
make his decisions both reversible and universalizible; that is, he is not
seeing the situation from the role of the person whose life is being
saved as well as the person who can save the life (reversibility) or from
the point of view of the possibility of anyone filling these roles
(universalizability)."

The idea of reversibility in the Heinz dilemma invoked by Philosopher 3 may be clarified in this way. Philosopher 3 is saying, "Start
with the Golden Rule, change places with the wife in deciding. Is your
denying a duty to save the woman's life consistent with the Golden
Rule?" The wife, we may say, holds that her right to life is higher or
prior to the druggist's right to property. She claims that the husband
has a duty to steal to protect the right, because she cannot. The druggist denies that the husband has a duty to steal the drug and asserts he
has a right to property equal to or greater than the wife's right to life.
Is the druggist's denial of the husband's duty to steal reversible? No,
this denial could not stand if he exchanged places with the wife. In the
position of the druggist, he holds his right to property higher than the
wife's right to life. Presumably, however, if it were his life at stake,
not the wife's, the druggist would be rational enough to prefer his
right to life over his property and would sacrifice his property. If the
druggist tried to make his conception of rights and duties reversible by
imaginatively changing places with the wife, he would give up the
idea that the husband had a duty to respect his property rights and
would see that the husband had a duty toward his wife's life. In contrast, the wife's claim that her husband has a duty to preserve life and

that her right to life is prior to the druggist's right to property is reversible.*

Another word for reversibility is "ideal role taking" or "moral musical chairs." Moral musical chairs means going around the circle of perspectives involved in a moral dilemma to test one's claims of right or duty until only the equilibriated or reversible claims survive. In "nonmoral" or competitive musical chairs, there is only one "winning person." In moral musical chairs, there is only one "winning" chair, which all other players recognize if they play the game, the chair of the person with the prior claim to justice.

It is clear that Rawls has embodied the idea of reversibility as well as universalizability in the idea of "the original positon" or the "veil of ignorance," although he does not develop the idea of equilibrium implicit in the reversibility criterion, because he is bent on developing an equilibrium to be found in a bargaining game conception of the social contract.

An intuitively more appealing statement of reversibility as equilibrium comes from the conception of ideal role taking as "moral musical chairs" just elaborated. This first reversibility process of reaching fairness through ideal role taking is as follows:

1. The decider is to successively put himself imaginatively in the place of each other actor and consider the claims each would make from his point of view.
2. Where claims in one party's shoes conflict with those in another's, imagine each to trade places. If so, a party should drop his conflicting claim if it is based on nonrecognition of the other's point of view.

I claim that such a process of equilibrated and complete use of Golden Rule role taking is formally equivalent to Rawls's idea of decision in an original position or in a position of ignorance of one's own identity and the set to maximize the ego's interests.

This second reversibility process for reaching fairness as stated by Rawls is as follows:

---

* Suppose the husband, or the wife or the druggist were to try to choose a relevant principle of justice from the veil of ignorance, not knowing who they were to be. They would choose the principle that there is a natural duty to preserve life or that a human's right to life comes before another human's right to property. Rawls assumes such a natural duty to preserve life as implied by his original position, prior to any contracts about rights and duties in particular roles in any society.

The decider is to initially decide from a point of view that ignores his identity (veil or ignorance) under the assumption that decisions are governed by maximizing values from a viewpoint of rational egoism in considering each party's interest.

In the first procedure, the decider is assumed to start with an altruistic empathic or "loving" orientation; in the second case, the decider is assumed to start with an "egoistic" orientation to maximize his own values, canceled out by the veil of ignorance. To indicate that the two approaches to reversibility lead to the same solution, let us consider the Heinz dilemma from the original position, as we did from the process of ideal role taking.

In the Heinz dilemma, let us imagine someone making the decision under the veil of ignorance; that is, not knowing whether he or she is to be assigned the role of husband, wife, or druggist. Clearly, the rational solution is to steal the drug; that is, this leads to the least loss (or the most gain) to an individual who could be in any role. This corresponds to our intuition of the primacy of the woman's right to life over the druggist's right to property and makes it a duty to act in terms of those rights. If the situation is that the dying person is a friend or acquaintance, the same holds true. In the Heinz dilemma, a solution achieved under the veil of ignorance is equivalent to one obtained by ideal role taking, or "moral musical chairs," of an altruistic person in the husband's position asking the wife and druggist to trade places.

Having considered reversibility in Rawls's philosophic theory, we can now relate it to its central meaning in Piaget's theory. In Piaget's equilibrium theory, the fundamental formal condition of equilibrium in logic as well as morality is reversibility.

A logical train of thought is one in which one can move back and forth between premises and conclusions without distortion. Mathematical thinking is an example; $A+B$ is the same as $B+A$. Or again, the operation $A+B=C$ is reversible by the operation $C-B=A$.

Piaget defines a stage of logic as a group of logical operations; that is, as a group of reversible transformations of ideas, classes, or numbers that maintain certain relations invariant. Moral reasoning or justice in Piaget's theory represents decisions that are not "distorted" or changed as one shifts from one person's point of view or perspective to another's. As I said in Chapter 4 (see section on the cognitive-developmental theory of moralization), morality is the "logic" for coordinating the viewpoints of subjects with conflicting interests, as logic is the coordination of points of view on objects or symbols of objects. An example of a reversible moral operation is reciprocity. There is a parallel to morality in logic in the idea of a reciprocal relationship. If I have a brother, my brother has a brother—me. The relationship of brother to brother is reciprocal. As I noted, logical reciprocity is necessary but not sufficient for moral reciprocity. All children who have some moral idea of reciprocity, as given by the Stage 2 notion of the obligation to return a favor, have some idea of logical reciprocity; that is, they answer correctly the question "Does your brother have a brother?" The reverse is not the case, however. Children may pass the logical item but fail to show reciprocity in moral thought.

Piaget and I hold that the core structure of stages of moral reasoning consists of the set of operations or ideas that define justice or fairness. The two principal justice operations are the operation of equality and of reciprocity, both of which have logical parallels. Justice is a matter of distribution, involving the operations of equality and reciprocity. Distribution is by equality (equity, distributive equality proportionate to circumstance and need), or it is by reciprocity (merit or desert, reward in return for effort, virtue, or talent). Each stage defines and uses these operations differently, and each higher stage uses them in a more reversible or equilibrated way. Both Rawls's theory and theories of Piaget and myself, then, are theories of "reflective equilibrium." Both identify justice with equilibration in valuing. Piaget's theory is explanatory or psychological; it explains (1) why justice is a compelling, obligatory, "natural" norm and (2) why concepts of justice change, moving to greater equilibrium. Rawls's theory is justificatory; it undertakes to prove that certain principles of justice held at Stage 6 (and important at Stage 5) are the ones that would be chosen in a condition of complete reflective equilibrium; that is, the ones that would be chosen in the original position. In that case, Rawls claims, they are the right or true principles of justice. My psychological claim, parallel to Rawls's claim, is that something like his principles of justice are chosen by those at Stage 6, and they are chosen because they are reversible, or in better equilibrium than justice principles used at previous stages.

Reversibility as the Criterion of Stage Advance

In the Piagetian framework, the core of a social judgment is a structure of justice, a structure including operations of reciprocity and equality. Each higher stage redefines these operations in a more reversible way. The operation of reciprocity is closely related to reversibility, but reciprocity can be used or defined with varying degrees of reversibility. A low degree of reversibility characterizes early stages of reciprocity.

In Chapter 4, I noted the Stage 1 idea of reciprocity, justice as talion. My young son thought that if Eskimos killed and ate seals it was right to kill and eat Eskimos. Such an early notion of reciprocity is not reversible in the sense that it does not meet the criterion of the Golden Rule. Although Eskimos may not be doing to other (seals) as they would be done by, clearly killing Eskimos is not doing to others as one would wish to be done by. My son interpreted reciprocity not as reversibility (doing as you would wish to be done by) but as exchange (doing back what is done to you). This is generally the case for children at Stages 1 and 2. We have systematically asked children who "know" or can repeat the Golden Rule the question "If someone comes up on the street and hits you, what would the Golden Rule say to do?" Children at moral Stages 1 and 2 say, "Hit him back. Do unto others as they do unto you."

In contrast to Stage 1 and 2 concrete reciprocity, Stage 3 equates reciprocity with reversibility, with the Golden Rule. The Golden Rule implies (1) ideal role taking or reversing perspectives ("trading places," "putting yourself in his shoes"), not exchanging acts, and reversing perspectives in terms of the *ideal* ("What you would like in his place?"), not the real ("What you would do in his place?").

The meaning of Golden Rule reversibility is well expressed by a ten-year-old subject at our third moral stage, who replied, "Well, it's like your brain has to leave your head and go into the other guy's head and then come back into your head but you still see it like it was in the other guy's head and then you decide that way." This Golden Rule ideal role taking as reversibility entails differentiating the self's perspective from the other's and coordinating the two so that the perspective from the other's view influences one's own perspective in a reciprocal fashion. At Stage 3, then, reversibility is reciprocity of perspectives, not actions.

Let us now consider how the increased reversibility of moral stages from Stage 1 to Stage 3 leads to a more adequate valuing of human life in one moral dilemma. This increased reversibility of the valuing of life is illustrated by Tommy's response to life dilemmas, reported in Table 4.2 of Chapter 4.

At Stage 1, Tommy's thinking fails to pass the test of the Golden Rule reversibility even at the level of Stage 2 egoistic exchange. Whether to save the life of another person depends not only on rigid rules ("don't steal," "don't kill") but on the wealth of the person to be saved. This is a failure to take the viewpoint of the dying person even at the level of egoism, in which the dying person would egoistically value his or her life regardless of its relation to furniture.

At Stage 2, Tommy's "instrumental egoism and exchange view" of the value of a friend or a wife's life, ignoring rigid rules, does not pass the test of Golden Rule reversibility. On Dilemma 4, he has the doctor take the "selfish" viewpoint of the husband, who cannot replace his wife, rather than the "selfish" viewpoint of the wife, who would be better off out of her pain. He does not have either the doctor or the husband look at the situation from the wife's shoes.

At Stage 3, Tommy engages in ideal role taking but the role taking is not complete. There is a conflict between the wife's point of view and the husband's. According to Tommy, the husband does not want to allow mercy-killing because he loves his wife and will grieve for her. This lack of reversibility between the perspective of husband and wife leads us to feel Tommy's view of the husband's love is still "selfish" or "nonmoral"; the husband will let his wife suffer pain to avoid grief to himself. If the husband really loves his wife, we would say, he would put himself in her place and then would want her death if that were what was best for her. We sense that a "more loving" or "more moral" attitude would lead to a solution to this dilemma. But we can only define a more moral solution in terms of fairness or reversibility. Why is the implied perspective of the husband in Tommy's response selfish? If the husband should consider the wife's pain, the wife (if she loves her husband) must also consider the husband's grief at her death. If the wife puts herself in the husband's place, the grief she anticipates about her own death is more than matched by the grief a husband should feel at her pain.

I am here applying to the mercy-killing dilemma the idea of reversibility as "moral musical chairs," which, in the last section, I said Philosopher 3 used in the Heinz dilemma and which I said would require the druggist to trade places with the wife and the wife with the druggist before making claims on the husband. In the mercy-killing dilemma, we also imagine the husband and wife trading places before making claims on the doctor. This Stage 6 process of ideal role taking or "moral musical chairs" is a "second-order" use of the Golden Rule. Before the doctor (in Dilemma 4) or the husband (in Dilemma 3) are to base action on Golden Rule empathy with any one actor, they must imaginatively have that actor trade places with any other interested party in the situation. Intuitively, we feel that the "second-order" interpretation of the Golden Rule leads to a solution to the two dilemmas (if we allow the wife with cancer to be the best judge of her rights and interests).*

If we interpret reversibility as Rawls's original position, we get the same solution for the mercy-killing dilemma as we get using "moral musical chairs." The doctor, not knowing who he would be, would choose the solution he could live with in the position of the least advantaged, the dying woman in pain.

A more difficult case yields the same results. This is the case of an individual drowning in the river. A passerby can save him, but at a 25 percent risk of death (and a 75 percent chance that both will be saved). Should the passerby jump in with a 25 percent chance both would drown? From the viewpoint of simple Golden Rule empathy with the drowing person, the passerby should. But is such empathy fair or reasonable, or is it ultimate sacrifice? To see, we ask, "If the drowning person put himself in the bystander's shoes and returned to his own position, could he still make the claim?" Here moral musical chairs is augmented by a Rawls-type calculation. Stated in terms of the "veil of ignorance" (if an individual did not know whether he was the bystander or the drowning person), the right decision is that of jumping in as long as the risk of death for jumping was definitely less than 50 percent. Egoistic maximization (or maximin) leads to the choice of jumping in if the actor does not know the probabilities of which party he will end up being but does know the minimum probabilities of being alive is greater than 50 percent if the bystander jumps in, less than 50 percent if he does not.

I have enunciated a criterion of fairness as reversibility and have applied it to three dilemmas. In light of this criterion, the Stage 2, 3, and 4 solutions to the Heinz and mercy-killing dilemmas, reported in

---

*In other situations, like the Talmudic dilemma of two parties in the desert and only one having a water bottle with just enough water to save one, the "second-order" interpretation of the Golden Rule leaves one difficulty as the first-order one does. The first-order Golden Rule interpretation leaves each party passing the bottle back and forth to the other like Alphonse and Gaston. An equilibrium at the second-order level requires something, like a precedence or fairness principle under the veil of ignorance; for example, drawing shares or recognizing ownership rights even in a life or death situation.

Table 4.2 of Chapter 4, are judged to be unbalanced. What about Stage 5? Stage 5 solutions in terms of human rights usually generate reversible solutions to the dilemmas (steal the drug, permit mercy-killing, and save the drowning person). Stage 5 solutions in terms of rational act-utilitarianism (integrated with some concepts of rule-utilitarianism) also usually generate reversible solutions. For instance, the "fair" solution to the river dilemma under the veil of ignorance is also the fair solution as utility, maximizing numbers of lives, each to count as one. Because the utilitarian maximization principle has built into it the justice principle, each life or person to count as one, it usually leads to reversible solutions. Rawls, however, stresses that in issues of justice dealing with the distribution of goods or income "justice as aggregate utility" differs from justice as equality or the difference principle and that by the criterion of reversibility or of the original position, justice as the difference principle should be preferred.

In Table 5.1, I present a dilemma pitting aggregate utility against the difference principle not in regard to income, but in regard to life. Philosopher 2, cited in Chapter 4 as having a rule-utilitarian Stage 5 normative ethic, opts for aggregate utility. Considering justice in the eyes of the other person is not a direct basis of choice, it is one utilitarian consequence with others to be weighed by the captain. In contrast Philosopher 3 classified as Stage 6 feels a utilitarian solution by the captain is not reversible; that is, it doesn't consider the viewpoint of the expert, and opts for the lottery.

Table 5.1. Philosophers' Responses to Two Alternative Versions of a Life Dilemma

Variation 1—The Captain's Dilemma

A charter plane crashed in the South Pacific. Three people survived, the pilot and two passengers. One of the passengers was an old man who had a broken shoulder. The other was a young man, strong and healthy. There was some chance that the raft could make it to the safety of the nearest island if two men rowed continuously for three weeks. However, there was almost no chance if all three of the men stayed on the raft. First of all, the food supply was meager. There was barely enough to keep two men alive for the three-week period. Second, a storm was approaching, and the raft would almost certainly capsize unless one man went overboard. This man could not cling to the raft and in all likelihood would drown. A decision had to be made quickly.

The captain was strong and the only one who could navigate. If he went over, there was almost no chance the other two would make it to safety. If the old man with the broken shoulder went, there was a very good probability, about 80 percent, that the other two could make it. If the young man went overboard and the old man and the captain stayed, chances were a little less than 50:50. No one would volunteer to go overboard.

	Chance of Survival	
	Old Man Goes	Draw Straws
Outcome for old man	0%	50%
Outcome for young man	80%	50%

What should the captain do? Should he (1) order the old man overboard, (2) should they draw straws (*Note:* the captain has the option of including himself in the draw or not), or (3) let all three of them stay? Why?

Variation 2—Suicide Mission Dilemma

In Korea, a company of ten marines was outnumbered and was retreating before the enemy. The company had crossed a bridge over a river, but the enemy were still on the other side. If someone went back to the bridge and blew it up, the company could then escape. However, the man who stayed back to blow up the bridge would not be able to escape alive. The captain asked for a volunteer, but no one offered to go. If no one went back, it was virtually certain that all would die. The captain was the only person who could lead the retreat.

The captain finally decided that he had two alternatives. The first was to order the demolition man to stay behind. If this man were sent, the probability that the mission would be accomplished successfully was 80 percent. The second alternative was to select someone to go by drawing a name out of a hat with everyone's name in it. If anyone other than the demolition man were selected, the probability that the mission would be accomplished successfully was 70 percent.

Which of the two alternatives should the captain choose and why?

Two Responses to the Captain's Dilemma

Philosopher 2 (Stage 5):

He should order the expert, and himself do his own job of captain in the hope of preserving the company. He should not draw lots because this would not yield as skilled and reliable a man. The expert has no right to refuse, because he has undertaken to serve in the war and to be trained as a demolition man. The main consideration is who is most likely to perform the job and preserve the most lives. The captain might consider, in addition, the factor that the death of one man with a family might be a greater loss than the death of another. An important consideration would be the effect on the other men. Whatever the captain's own views about justice, he would have to regard his men's views because an act thought by them as unjust would be harmful to morale.

Philosopher 3 (Stage 6):

The lottery. If you choose the expert, you are denying him the same chance to pull through. I think that he would want to live as much as anyone else and would claim the same chance as everyone else. It would be nice to maximize the chances of saving lives but that should be secondary to the justice considerations at hand. Justice means treating the people in the situation as having the same intrinsic value or claim to life without distinctions that are utilitarian or are subjective on the part of the captain. The expert has an equal claim to life. He wants to preserve his life, he expects the others to have the same claim. He feels he ought to exert his own claim to the extent that it is no greater than anyone else's. He just doesn't want it subordinated to the others'. Sending the expert is using the demolition man for other people's welfare, to maximize the probability of saving all lives. I think that utilitarianism, trying to maximize life so the most people should survive, is a consideration that should be taken into account only after the justice one.

Let me clarify why I agree with Philosopher 3 that the lottery is better because it is the fair solution by the test of reversibility.

The dilemma (in either form) poses a choice by the captain between (1) ordering a man to his death by a utilitarian criterion that would maximize the probability of saving the remaining lives or (2) leaving the choice to a lottery. It presupposes a prior choice, that the captain should order someone to go, at gunpoint if necessary, rather than having everyone die. Such a choice assumes that the captain (or anyone else) has an obligation to preserve each person's life and that the obligation to the rights of each to life are not exhausted by respecting any particular individual's wish not to be ordered. Whether the utilitarian or "equal chance" version of justice is accepted, justice would be taken to involve respecting the lives of each, counting each person as one. Because a person refuses to risk his life so that all may be saved does not mean his life can be treated as of greater value than the others. Why do we say this? Why not argue that respect for persons implies allowing all to go down? The right to life is not so different from the druggist's property rights in the Heinz dilemma, if we interpret rights in terms of moral musical chairs. I said the druggist's claim to property rights could only be upheld if he could be imagined to maintain them after trading places with the wife or to maintain them choosing under a veil of ignorance as to his position, including ending in the least favored position, the wife's. In the captain's dilemma, does the

old man have a right to refuse to go, or at least to draw straws? He
could not maintain the right to refuse if he were to change places with
the others. If he did not know who he was in the situation, the old and
weak man or the strong man, a rational man would still want someone
to go.

Given that the captain should order someone to go, should he select
the person who would maximize the probability of survival, or should
he use a lottery? The lottery is not the best solution from a utilitarian
viewpoint. Is it the fair solution? We can get an answer by asking,
"Does the weak man (or the expert) have the right to insist on a
lottery? Could he insist on the claim if he were to consider the claim
in the strong man's (or the captain's) shoes?" In making the claim, he
is saying he has the right to an equal probability of living to the probability the other man has, even if this lowers the average probability
for all.

He claims that this is implied by the assumption that he has a right
to equal treatment of his life to that of others. This claim seems to
hold up even if he trades places imaginatively with the captain or the
strong man. In terms of the Rawls original position, we ask, "What
would be chosen by the captain (or the strong man or the weak man)
in an original position, with an equal probability of being the weak
man or the strong man (or the captain)? If a lottery is used, the old
man's probability of living is 50 percent; if he is ordered, the probability of living is 0 percent. From the standpoint of the least advantaged
position, the old man's, the lottery increases his life chances 50 percent. The choice of the lottery is not offset by a decline in life chances
in the other positions. The strong man's chances of life decrease only
30 percent by the use of the lottery, compared to the 50 percent decrease in life chances of the weak man if he is ordered to go, instead of
using a lottery. Both the strong man the weak man, then, would
choose the lottery in an original position. Alternatively stated, they
would choose to apply the difference principle, stating that no inequalities in life chances are justified unless they are of benefit from the
viewpoint of the least advantaged—here, the weak man.

In this dilemma, then, justice as reversible role taking agrees with
utility in denying an absolutist concept of the right to life, which
would allow all to die in order to avoid coercion. It disagrees with
utility in what it means to count each person's life as one. This cannot
be arrived at by aggregating lives to find a solution but requires taking

the viewpoint of each individual claiming his right to life as equal to that of others.

These considerations are more or less explicit in Philosopher 3's response to the dilemma, which we label "Stage 6" and which contrasts with Philosopher 2's rule-utilitarian solution to the dilemma.

So far the test of reversibility agrees with utilitarianism unless a dilemma raises an issue of the difference principle, in which case the difference principle is preferred, or fairness takes priority over utility. In such dilemmas, Stage 5 and Stage 6 lead to different solutions. I need now to indicate that "Stage 5" utilitarianism deviates from our intuitions as to how to approach moral dilemmas and the sense in which "Stage 6" tests of reversibility correspond to our natural intuitions of how to proceed in making moral decisions. To do so, I will use a dilemma that does not lead itself to rational calculation or counting, whether the counting be of utilitarianism or the counting of Rawls's maximin in the original position. The dilemma is one developed by Selman and myself for high school students, not for a moral discussion but for a discussion that would require and develop empathy or role taking. In reading it, one's first question is "Is the dilemma or choice a moral one, requiring a morally right answer?" Because the dilemma is trivial, and deals with minor consequences and minor rules, many adults we have presented it to are uncertain as to whether it is a "moral dilemma" or a dilemma of social etiquette and courtesy. We would hold it is a moral dilemma with a "morally right" answer.

The dilemma is as follows:

Joanne is trying out for the school play. After her audition, she rushes to her friend, Charlene, to thank her for her moral support and to ask for her opinion of her performance. Charlene assures Joanne that she was very good, but Joanne worries that a newcomer to the school, who is trying out for the same role, will get the part. The new girl, Tina, comes over to congratulate Joanne on her performance and asks if she can join the two girls. She says that she's trying hard to make friends. Charlene asks her to join them for a snack. Joanne is more reserved.

When Tina leaves, Joanne and Charlene arrange to get together on Saturday because Joanne has a problem she'd like Charlene to help her solve. However, later that day, Tina calls Charlene and asks her to go to Washington to see a play on Saturday. Charlene is faced with a dilemma: she would like to go with Tina but has already made plans to see Joanne. Joanne might understand and be happy that Charlene has the chance to go, or she might feel she's losing her best friend. What should Charlene do?

Usually discussion of the dilemma with adults eventually leads to the conclusion that (1) it is a moral dilemma and (2) the right action is for Charlene is keep her date with Joanne, the old friend.

The reasoning for such a conclusion comes from "Stage 5": (1) keeping contract and promises as the foundation of social obligations and relations (with a rule-utilitarian rationale for contract) and (2) act-utilitarian considerations that the old friend's need to see her friend Charlene is greater than the new friend's need.

Stated in these ways, fairness and altruistic utilitarianism coincide with the solution to the dilemma. Suppose, however, that it is the new friend (Tina) who has the clearly urgent need for counseling, but the promise had been made to the old friend. Act-utilitarianism would say, "Break the date or promise." Most would agree, but not for act-utilitarian reasons. Few will intuitively accept an act-utilitarian rationale for breaking promises. Few, however, would accept a rigid rule-utilitarianism about promises, either, which would hold Charlene to see Joanne "because a promise is a promise, and the practice of promise breaking generally has bad consequences." To see this, let us imagine the utilities as originally defined (the old friend with the greater need) but the prior date or commitment has been made to the new friend, to see the play. Few would hesitate to think the right thing is to help the old friend with the need even if it entails breaking an appointment.

The whole use of utilitarian thinking is far-fetched because intuitively we would decide through "moral musical chairs" and test our imaginative role taking with reality. If the prior date were made with the new friend Tina and the old friend Joanne had the urgent need, we would call up the new friend and explain. We would expect her to trade places with Joanne, the old friend, and, because her need was not as great, release her from the promise. Even if Charlene could not reach her until the last moment, we would expect Tina to understand.

If we reverse the situation and the new friend has the more urgent need and the date is made with the old friend, the situation is more difficult. This is because we don't know whether the old friend will understand and accept our reasons for breaking the date in order to counsel a new friend about college.

We expect, like Rawls, that envy should not be allowed to determine the fair solution. We also expect an old friend to role take the viewpoint of the new friend as well as vice versa. In the end, then, keeping the promise is not a matter of rule utility but of the personal meaning of friendship and trust in a world directed toward ideal role taking. Utilitarianism, we intuitively feel, is unempathic, it does not start with respect for people. It does lead to relatively clear and principled solutions. Starting moral decision making with an act of empathy, the criterion of moral musical chairs or the original position leads to a clear solution of justice and is more completely reversible.

An Experimental Test of the Reflective Equilibrium Hypothesis

In the two previous sections, I have made the following claims:

1. Moral judgments that are not reversible by the test of the original position or moral musical chairs are not in equilibrium.
2. Moral judgments that are not based on the principle of equality or equity (the difference principle) are not reversible and so are not in equilibrium.
3. When people become aware of the lack of reversibility of their judgments, they will change these judgments or principles to reach a more reversible solution.
4 This search for equilibrium is a basis for change to the next stage.
5. Our final stage, Stage 6, is in complete equilibrium; its judgments are fully reversible. This is not true of Stage 5 and even less of lower stages.
6. Because Stage 6 judgments are reversible, all Stage 6 subjects agree, given common understanding of the facts of the case.

Erdynast (1973) undertook to empirically examine these hypotheses. His research subjects were twenty adult business executives and ten graduate students in philosophy. Their stage of moral reasoning was established on three "standard" dilemmas, including the Heinz dilemma. They were then asked to deal with two dilemmas pitting aggregate utility against equality or the difference principle. One dilemma involved distribution of income in a new cooperative business. The second was the suicide mission dilemma presented in Table 5.1. After initially "pretesting" subjects on these two dilemmas, subjects were asked to test the reversibility of their solutions, by being asked (1) to ideal role take or take the viewpoint of each party in the situation in turn and (2) to choose from an original position of ignorance as to which party the chooser would end up being. They were then reinterviewed some days later to see if the test of reversibility would change their solution.

The first subjects of interest were the five Stage 6 subjects. These subjects were defined as Stage 6 from their responses to dilemmas that did not directly pit utility against equality. All five of these subjects agreed in choosing the equity solution on the two experimental dilemmas; for example, the lottery on the captain's dilemma. As we expected, on the dilemmas used all the Stage 6 subjects agreed in the content of the principle chosen, as well as in form of reasoning, and the content chosen was equity. Not only did our Stage 6 subjects agree, but all were in equilibrium by the reversibility criterion. None switched his choice or thinking when asked to ideal role take or choose from the original position. All gave signs of having considered reversibility in their original responses to the dilemma.

In contrast, subjects at Stage 4 and 5 responded differently. They did not start in agreement in the content of choices. A little more than half initially chose the utilitarian solution; the remainder chose the equity solution. Many of those who chose the utility solution felt disequilibrium when asked to test the reversibility of their choice through ideal role taking. Wherever a different solution was reached under the ideal role taking or original position set than was found on pretest, it was a shift to the equity principle. Often this shift was retained on the post-test interview after a delay.

Here is one example of a Stage 4 executive (with some Stage 5 thinking). His first response to the dilemma is:

If I was the captain I'd order the expert to maximize the probability of getting the job done and assure the survival of the company. The survival of the organization should be dominant.

Under the experimental instruction, he is first asked to consider his solution from the point of view of the expert. He then says,

I would think my going doesn't improve the chances of success of the group. I shouldn't be singled out to sacrifice for the organization, it should be done in a more equitable way. The lives of all are involved, they should all contribute equally and jeopardize themselves through the lottery.

He is then asked, "Imagine you didn't know which man in the company you were. If you could be anyone, which choice is best?" He replies,

If I didn't know who I were going to be, it would switch me over to the lottery, if I didn't already choose it. As soon as I thought I might have a chance of being the expert, it forces me to consider his claim if I were him. It forces me to see that if I advocated sending the expert it's not balanced. The lottery is best. It would diminish the chance that I would go as the expert without seriously diminishing the probability of survival if I were someone else.

Days later, asked how he would now resolve the dilemma, he replies,

My choice would depend on who I am. I would waiver. But the lottery would seem now to be best for all concerned, whereas my original choice was the expert. I can see where the lottery is better because everyone is jeopardized equally.

This subject, then, moved from a Stage 4 idea of right as survival of the organization to a more Stage 5 idea of right as equity to all through being stimulated to reversible role-taking.

A Stage 5 executive moved from preference for a Benthamite act-utility principle to a preference for a more Stage 6 Kantian respect for people principle after original position role-taking. On the posttest, he said,

Originally I chose sending the expert, thinking of the probability factor, the Bentham principle. But if you give equal weight to the principle regarding human beings as an end rather than as a means, the lottery is preferable. I don't think the probabilities justify sending one person who happens to be in the position he is in. The consideration of each human having an equal chance is most important here.

In summary, the study supported a claim derived from Rawls (1) that equality (or respect for persons) was indeed the principle chosen under an original position set as opposed to the utility principle and (2) the principle chosen in the original position set is in better equilibrium than a competing principle and tends to be preferred, once articulated. In the words of the first subject quoted, the original position "forced me to see that if I advocated sending the expert, it's not balanced." The study also supports the claim I made at the beginning of the chapter, that Rawls's theory is a theory justifying the "considered judgments" not of all people, but only those at our highest moral stage. Only the Stage 6 subjects consistently chose Rawls's equity principle, and only they spontaneously used a perspective close to that of the original position in articulating and justifying this principle. In this sense, we can say that only Stage 6 moral judgments are in reflective equilibrium and that, if we accept Rawls's theory, Stage 6 judgments are better than judgments at lower stages.

Differentiation and Integration of Moral Categories at the Highest Stage

So far I have given two formal reasons for saying that our highest stage is best or better than Stage 5. First, all Stage 6 thinkers agree; all Stage 5's do not. If the purpose of moral judgment structures is to yield choices on which all reasonable people could agree, then they should use Stage 6 rather than Stage 5 structures. Second, and related, all Stage 6's can agree because their judgments are fully reversible: they have taken everyone's viewpoint in choosing insofar as it is possible to take everyone's viewpoint, where viewpoints conflict. Again, if principles of moral judgment are to be chosen, they should be principles on which all rational people could agree.

Rawls's theory and our findings suggest that the principles on which all ideally rational people could agree are the principles of justice chosen by Stage 6. The formal criterion of reversibility, or ideal agreement that I have stressed also entails other formal criteria in terms of which Stage 6 is best. Two such criteria are differentiation and integration. In the previous chapter, "From *Is* to *Ought*," I elaborated the formal concepts of differentiation and integration that apply to both the psychological and the normative analysis of moral deliberation, and linked the concepts to formalistic concepts of moral judgments as prescriptive and universal. Increased differentiation and integration are anchored in the "is" side by their explanatory power in the study of the development of directed thinking, and on the "ought" side by their necessary inclusion in rational justification and choice. To illustrate how and why this might be the case, I will consider some usages of the categories of "rights" and "duties" at Stages 5 and 6, and the sense in which this suggests that moral theories derived from Stage 6 structures are more advanced than moral theories derived from Stage 5 structures. Table 5.2 shows usage or "rights" and "duties" at each stage.

Table 5.2 suggests that each higher stage's usage of the categories of rights and duties is *more differentiated and integrated* than the prior stage. I list, in the parentheses, the differentiation of the concept of

Table 5.2. Six Stages in the Usage of Categories of Rights and Obligations

STAGE 1. *Having a right* means having the power or authority to control something or someone or is confused with being right (in accordance with authority).

Obligation or "should" is what one "has to do" because of the demands of external authorities, rules, or the external situation.

STAGE 2. *Having a right* implies freedom of the self to choose and to control the self and its possessions. One has a right to ignore the positive claims or welfare of others as long as one does not directly violate their freedom or injure them. (Having a right is differentiated from being right, and from being given the power to, by a status one holds.)

Obligation or "should" is a hypothetical imperative contingent on choice in terms of an end. In this sense, obligations are limited to oneself and one's ends. ("Should" or obligation is differentiated from "has to" from external or authoritative compulsion.)

STAGE 3. *Having a Right* implies an expectation of control and freedom that a "good" or natural person would claim. A right is based either on a rule or on a legitimate expectation toward others; for example, you have a right to have your property respected, because you worked hard to acquire the property. Rights are earned. (Having a right is differentiated from the freedom to control and choose.)

Obligation ("should" or "duty") equals a role obligation, what it is incumbent on a member of a social position to do for his role partners as defined by rules, by the expectation of the role partner, or by what a good role occupant (a good husband, a good doctor) would do. (Obligation is differentiated from being a means to a desired end.)

STAGE 4. *Having Rights* means having (1) categorical general freedoms and expectations that all members of society have, and (2) rights awarded to particular roles by society. General rights usually take primacy over role rights. (Having a right is differentiated from a particular legitimate expectation.)

Obligations are responsibilities; that is, welfare states of others or of society for which one is accountable. These responsibilities arise through (1) being a member of society and (2) voluntarily entering into roles that entail these responsibilities. (Obligation or duty as commitment and responsibility is differentiated from what is typically expected of a role occupant.)

STAGE 5. *Having Rights* entails an awareness of human or natural rights or liberties that are prior to society and that society is to protect. It is usually thought by Stage 5 that freedoms should be limited by society and law only when they are incompatible with the like freedoms of others. (Natural rights are differentiated from societally awarded rights.)

Obligations are what one has contracted to fulfill in order to have one's own rights respected and protected. These obligations are defined in terms of a rational concern for the welfare of others. (Obligations are conceived of as required rational concern for welfare differentiated from fixed responsibilities.)

STAGE 6. *Having Rights* means there are universal rights of just treatment that go beyond liberties and that represent universalizable claims of one individual on another.

Obligations are correlative to any right or just claim by an individual that gives rise to a corresponding duty for another individual.

"right" and "obligation" made by each stage not made at the prior stages. At Stage 2, a right as a freedom is differentiated from a physical or social power; at Stage 3, it is differentiated as an expectation to be supported by others from an actual physical or psychological freedom; and so on. The sense in which each stage is *better integrated* is seen in the fact that only at Stage 6 are rights and duties completely correlative. The meaning of correlativity of rights and duties is suggested in the following passage by Raphael (1955, pp. 47–48):

We have accepted the deontological view that the moral use of "ought" is a basic concept that cannot be derived from the idea of goodness. We turn next to the notion of "rights." There are two senses of the word, the first meaning, "I have no duty to refrain from so acting," the second in which I describe the same fact as I describe by saying, "Someone else has a duty to me." The second kind of a right might be called "a right of recipience." Whenever I have a right of action, I also have a right of recipience. In virtue of the second definition of rights, the two forms of expression: "A has a duty to B" and "B has a right (or recipience) against A" are correlative in the sense of analytically implying each other. They may not be connotatively tautologous in ordinary speech, though they are in the more precise language we are recommending.

Let us accept, for the moment, Raphael's view that using rights and duties on correlative terms is either more "precise" or more "integrated." Such usage, consistently maintained, is found only at Stage 6. At Stage 5, "rights" categories are completely reciprocal; that is, the concept and limits of rights are completely reciprocal with the rights of others, but individual rights and individual duties are not completely correlative.

An example is Longitudinal Case 2, age twenty-four, who said, "Morality to me means recognizing the rights of others first to life and then to do as they please as long as it doesn't interfere with somebody else's rights."

Although Case 2 is able to define rights clearly, he is unable to specify clearly the conditions under which awareness of rights generates correlative duties. At Stage 5, for every right, society has some duty to protect that right. Duties to other individuals, however, are not clearly specified in the absence of either individual contract or social contract. At Stage 5, there are obligations to the law and to the welfare of others, of a rule- or act-utilitarian sort. But recognition of individual rights does not directly generate individual duties; that is, rights and duties are not directly correlative. Even moral philosophers, like our "natural" Stage 5 subjects, need not accept that rights directly imply duties. This is indicated in philosophers' responses to the Heinz dilemma.

In general, subjects whom we classify on other grounds as Stage 5 recognize the woman's right to live but do not believe that it directly generates an obligation to steal to save her. Or they may recognize a duty to steal for the wife, based on contract, but recognize no duty to steal for the friend or stranger who equally has a right to life. This, too, is the position taken by a number of moral philosophers, two of whom are quoted in Chapter 4.

Examples are as follows:

Philosopher 1: What Heinz did was not wrong. The distribution of scarce drugs should be regulated by principles of fairness. In the absence of such regulations, the druggist was within his legal rights, but in the circumstances he has no moral complaint. He still was within his moral rights, however, unless it was within his society a strongly disapproved thing to do. While what Heinz did was not wrong, it was not his duty to do it. In this case it is not wrong for Heinz to steal the drug, but it goes beyond the call of duty; it is a deed of supererogation.

Philosopher 2: It is a husband's duty to steal the drug. The principle that husbands should look after their wives to the best of their ability is one whose general observance does more good than harm. He should also steal it for a friend, if he were a very close friend (close enough for it to be understood that they would do this sort of thing for each other). The reasons are similar to those in the case of wives. If the person with cancer were a less close friend, or even a stranger, Heinz would be doing a good act if he stole the drug, but he has no duty to.

These philosophers agree that stealing to save a life in the situation is right, but disagree on when it is a duty. Using rule-utilitarian criteria of duty, it is difficult to make duties and rights correlative. In contrast, here is the response of Philosopher 3, who responds quite differently to duty questions about this dilemma:

Q.: If the husband does not feel very close or affectionate to his wife, should he steal the drug?

A.: Yes. The value of her life is independent of any personal ties. The value of human life is based on the fact that it offers the only possible source of a categorical moral "ought" to a rational being acting in the role of a moral agent.

Q.: Suppose it were a friend or an acquaintance?

A.: Yes, the value of a human life remains the same.

In general, Philosopher 3's conceptions of rights and duties were correlative. In this sense, his thinking appears more differentiated and integrated than that of the other two philosophers. However, the greater integration of a structure making rights and duties correlative is not a mere matter of increased logical or analytical tidiness, as Raphael suggests, but imposes a severe price. The price in question is, baldly, that Philosopher 3 must be prepared to go to jail to steal for a friend or acquaintance, and Philosophers 1 and 2 do not. According to Raphael (1955, p. 51):

From an objective point of view, the so-called duties of supererogation are not duties. For the agent, they are duties but from the objective standpoint; that is, from the standpoint of what we take to be the average moral agent, they are thought to go beyond duty. Correspondingly, in the eyes of the agent, the beneficiary has a right while from the objective standpoint (of the average impartial spectator) the person benefited does not have a right.

I would question whether duties and rights could be made correlative, as Raphael wishes, if the moral point of view adopted is that recommended by Raphael; that is, "the average moral agent" or "the average impartial spectator." To make duties and rights correlative, we must take, not the standpoint of the "average moral agent," but Philosopher 3's standpoint of the "rational moral agent." Rational moral agents are not self-sacrificial saints, because saints' duties do not imply that they have corresponding rights. Rational moral agents are fair, not saintly; they do as a duty only what they are rationally prepared to demand that others do as a duty, or that to which they have a right. The fact that a dying acquaintance in need of the medicine has the right to life does not define a duty for the average moral agent, but it may for the rational or just moral agent.

In summary, there are certain basic categories used by every moral stage structure or every moral theory, such as the categories of rights and duties. Development through the stages indicates a progressive differentiation of categories from one another—for example, of rights from duties—and a progressive integration of them, expressed in the correlativity of rights and duties. This correlativity is not merely a matter of the analytic tidiness of an abstract normative or metaethical theory but leads to very different judgments of obligation, judgments that are in better equilibrium with judgments of rights.

As a result, Stage 6 moral judgments are able to differentiate, among the amorphous wastebasket of "actions of supererogation," those actions which are duties prescribed by the rights of others from those which are not.

As stated, a problem remains for Stage 6 moral judgment. If the rights of every human define duties for an individual moral agent, this seems to open up the abyss of the existence of infinite and simultaneous duties to support the rights of every human being wherever he or she is. The problem here entailed is partially solvable, though complex. The individual moral agent has rights, and these rights are incompatible with having duties to every right of every other. Because a human being has a right to life, other humans have a duty to save that life. The conditions under which one human being has a duty to save the life of another human being require clarification of what it means for a "rational moral agent" to choose between conflicting duties, because the agent cannot be an omnipotent saint.

The Formal Concept of Principle at Stage 6

In the previous section, we saw two different orientations to the correlativity of rights and duties, one stemming from the viewpoint of expectations for the average moral agent or husband, the other from the viewpoint of what Philosopher 3 terms "a categorical moral 'ought' to a rational being acting in the role of moral agent." "This 'ought' viewpoint," Philosopher 3 goes on to say, "is that of someone making a 'principled decision; that is, one made from a viewpoint that is consistent with the decision of any rational agent in a similar situation.' " Philosopher 3 has a somewhat different conception of principle from Philosopher 2, who cites "the principle that husbands should look after their wives to the best of their ability."

Philosopher 2's conception of principle is closer to that of the notion of a moral rule than is that of Philosopher 3. A moral principle has some of the properties of a moral rule, but a principle is different from a rule. We need to clarify the distinction and indicate the necessity of principles for an equilibrated morality:

1. *A moral principle is a rule or method of choosing between legitimate alternatives.* A rule says, "Don't do that" or "Do that"—it prescribes an action. A principle is some rule that tells us how to make a choice between two more-or-less legitimate or ruleful alternatives. A rule tells us we must not steal and a rule tells us we must maintain the lives of others in our family, but there is no set rule that tells us which to prefer if we must choose one. A rule for such choice must prescribe a way of thinking or evaluating, not simply demand or prescribe a kind of action. A principle, then, must not only dictate a choice but must also be a reason for such a choice.

2. *Moral principles imply a universalistic and general basis for choice.* A principle implies the universality of such a reason or such a decision rule; the basis of choice is one that it would be desirable for all to use. Further, it must be general: it must order all the relevant decisions, or it will lead to inconsistency or conflict.

There are fundamentally two ways in which moral principles may be used in moral judgment. The first is as "second-order" principles; that is, as procedural principles or principles for generating rules. This is the usage of principles in the ordinary forms of appeal to rule-utilitarianism or to social contract. In this form, the individual actor is to abide by rules, but only such rules as are justified by, or consistent with, either rule-utilitarian calculation or a social contract. Principles here are legislative guides rather than guides to the individual decision-making actor. Second-order principles may also be thought of as "qualified attitude" criteria of moral judgment, criteria including various checks or tests in making moral rules or moral judgment as elaborated by Brandt (1968) and Baier (1965). Brandt, who combines a "qualified attitude" and a "rule-utilitarian" approach, says that rule-utilitarianism can be viewed either as a "true principle of normative ethics or as a rule for valid inferences in ethics." A "rule of valid inference" is a procedural or second-order principle of moral judgment much as procedural principles of the social contract are second-order principles limiting the formation of concrete moral rules.

Both Philosophers 1 and 2, quoted in the last section, used principles in this second-order way. Philosopher 2 defined duties in terms of what we would term *rules*—for example, "Husbands should look after their wives to the best of their ability"—and formulated this rule in terms of the general second-order principle of rule-utilitarianism—for example, that "its general observance would do more good than harm." Philosopher 1 says that "scarce goods should be distributed by principles of fairness," but this principle does not directly define the husband's duty for him. Philosophers 1 and 2 view a decision of duty as one that is legislated from a principled perspective, but the principles governing the legislator and the husband (the legislated) are not the same. For Philosopher 2, husbands are to follow the rule "Look after your wife to your best ability." This rule is legislated on the basis of the principle of utility; that is, the "rule's general observance does more good than harm." The individual in the husband's shoes is not, himself, to follow the utilitarian principle.

In summary, for the first two philosophers principles are second-order determinants of decision. In contrast, Philosopher 3 defines duty in terms of what an individual in the husband's shoes should decide from a principled, universalizable, or impartial basis. The application of principles to the husband's decision is direct, not second order. Insofar as, in fact, decisions can be made by substantive principles, the resulting decisions are more fully determined and in that sense more equilibrated.

It is this first-order conception of principles that Rawls's theory is essentially defining and justifying. Rawls's two principles of justice are substantive principles of justice agreed on through the social contract. Other versions of social contract theory use social contract as a second-order principle or procedure to justify laws, rather than using a second-order principle to arrive at first-order substantive moral principles of justice. Similarly, rule-utilitarianism is usually a second-order procedure or principle for arriving at rules, not for arriving at a limited and ordered set of principles. The same is to be said for Kant's use of the categorical imperative, which is used as a second-order principle for justifying and interpreting rules such as "Never lie," rather than itself leading to a substantive principle of decision.

Moral Theories and Moral Stages

I have so far argued that our highest stage is better by various formal criteria: it is more reversible, more integrated, more principled. Because it meets these criteria better, its principles are the principles that would lead all rational people to moral agreement. This is Rawls's fundamental claim, that the principles of liberty and equality (defined by the difference principle) are those on which all people could agree starting from an original position guaranteeing impartiality.

My argument, although resting on a theory, has not been about moral theories, but about moral stages, conceived as structures generating concrete normative moral judgments. It is important to distinguish claims about stages from claims about theories. My claim, for instance, that stages of moral judgment are culturally universal does not mean, for instance, that my theory or that of Rawls is culturally universal. It may be true that Rawls's theory, or my own, may spring from the Western liberal tradition, but this does not mean that Stage 5 or Stage 6 principles are Western rather than universal. Put differently, the validity of moral principles does not depend on the validity of any particular theory justifying these principles.

Scholarly critiques of Rawls or others hardly put into question the principles of liberty and equality. Rather than the adequacy of principles deriving from the elegance of theories supporting them, in my view the adequacy of moral theories derives from the adequacy of the principles they support. In this sense, the central achievement of Rawls's theory is that it represents the first clear systematic justification of the principles and methods of decision I call "Stage 6," principles and methods only partly articulated by Kant. In Chapter 6, "The Future of Liberalism as the Dominant Ideology of the Western World," I view Rawls's theory as an expression of a historical movement toward a more radically principled and egalitarian "Stage 6" political ideology than that represented by older versions of the liberal tradition. The great value of Rawls's theory lies not in its technical perfection in performing a task but in the fact that the task it tries to accomplish is new and important. This, I believe, is true of any moral theory, because the task set to a theory is given by the evolution of the moral structures it attempts to systematize.

Our major empirical studies define stages in terms of the structure of concrete normative judgments of moral situations by subjects rather than defining stages in the formulations of moral theories. In addition to concrete moral judgments, we also ask subjects questions to elicit their moral theories; that is, (1) their metaethical theories as to the nature of moral rules and judgment and as to the objectivity or universality of moral rules and the grounds of such objectivity and (2) their normative theories or their general definitions and justification of principles of justice, duty, and so on. I view an individual's moral theory as a conscious reflection on his or her actual normative judgments. In this sense, a certain type of moral theory presupposes a certain moral judgment stage structure.

Two examples may be given of the relation of an individual's moral theory to his or her concrete moral judgment stage. The first example is that of the types of moral category that are primary for a theory. It is customary to classify normative moral theories according to the categories they stress; for example, consequential, deontological, and perfectionistic. Hardly surprising, when an individual's moral theory is classified in this way it is found to reflect the stressed categories in his or her actual normative judgments. The exact categories used are listed in Table 4.1 in Chapter 4, "From *Is* to *Ought*."

The second example is that of the "level of reflectivity" or "level of social perspective" of a moral theory in relation to "the level of reflectivity" of a stage structure of moral judgment. A given level of social perspective in concrete judgment stage is necessary but not sufficient for the parallel level of moral theory: that is, a given type of moral theory requires a given level of reflectivity or level of social perspective underlying a given parallel stage structure. These levels of reflectivity or perspective are defined in the Appendix.

To illustrate our stages as levels of reflectivity, I will quote one of our fifty longitudinal subjects replying to the same question at various ages. A question asked at each age was "Why shouldn't someone steal from a store, anyhow?"

At age ten, Case 2 was Level I, primarily Stage 1. He answered, "It's not good because there might be someone who could see you and call the police."

The concern with punishment suggests Stage 1, but this concern is content. If we ask, "To *whom* is punishment of concern?" it is *you*, the concrete, self-interested actor. The perspective involved, then, is that of the atomistic individual. At age thirteen, Case 2 was Stage 3 and entering Level II, the member-of-society perspective. He answered, "Well, the man who owns the store probably has a nice business and earns the money."

The answer is in terms of an individual in a social role (storekeeper) with shared role norms, and expectations. At age sixteen, Case 2 firmly takes the Level II member-of-society perspective at Stage 4 and answers, "Because it opposes another individual's rights to property. If property isn't protected, our whole society would get out of kilter."

Here the ultimate reference point is that of a member of society concerned about the maintenance of the whole society.

As an example of the Level III (Stage 5) prior-to-society perspective, Case 2 at age twenty-four answers,

It's violating another person's rights, in this case to property.

Q.: *Does the law enter in?*
A.: Well, the law in most cases is based on what is morally right so it's not a separate consideration.
Q.: *What does morally right mean?*
A.: Recognizing the rights of other individuals; first to life, then to do as he pleases as long as it doesn't interfere with somebody else's rights.

Viewing our stages as levels of reflectivity makes it clear that the familiar concerns of moral philosophy correspond to the "natural" concerns or modes of reflection at our highest stages, the "prior to society" level of reflection. This is implied by writers such as Dewey and Tufts (1932) and others who see a post-conventional level of "reflective" moral discourse as the matrix from which moral philosophy or formal moral theory emerges. As an example, Case 2 had developed a rudimentary normative moral theory of the social contract at age twenty-four, to justify and systematize his "prior to society" perspective that individual rights were the grounds for law and social morality. At sixteen, in contrast, he had little moral theory because the implicit theory of a "member of society perspective" is that the right is what all moral members of society believe.

Case 2's moral theory is a "deontological" theory stressing the category of rights, as he does in his concrete moral judgments. At sixteen, he had no moral theory stressing one category of judgment. His judgments sometimes oriented to teleological consequences, sometimes to duties and rights, sometimes to approbation.

Our longitudinal study of development suggests that in ontogeny, as in the history of philosophy, the transition to the level of moral theory starts with the awareness of the inconsistencies among the rules of any given social system and between the rules of one's own system and those of others: the problem of the relativity of morals. It suggests that the answers provided at the level of natural moral theories in ontogeny

are much the same as those provided by the answers of formal philosophic theories of social contract, utility, and so on. In this light, we
have interviewed moral philosophers concerning our moral dilemmas
and tried to relate their published theory to their reasoning on the
dilemmas. We feel that our results justify the notion that a philosopher's formal moral theory is an elaboration of certain portions of his
or her "natural" moral stage structure. A given philosopher's theoretical writings are understandable as part of a more general moral structure, exhibited in responses to our moral dilemmas as well as in
responses to questions about moral theory. Furthermore, hardly to our
surprise, all philosophers interviewed reason at the two highest stages,
being Stage 5, Stage 6, or some mixture of the two. This would be
expected if concrete normative judgments at Stage 5 or 6 imply a level
of reflectivity necessary but not sufficient for formal moral theories.

We believe our data on philosophers are consistent with our assumptions that (1) stages are structure generating families of moral
theories and (2) the two major families of formal normative theory
tend to be generated by two natural structures that we term "Stage 5"
and "Stage 6."

Without formal moral theory, people naturally attain to a "Stage 5"
in which they judge laws by the light of a social contract, by rule-
utilitarianism, and by some notion of universal or natural rights.
Much moral philosophy may be understood as a systemization of this
mode of thought, and most moral philosophers have in some sense
assumed this to be their task. Other philosophers, however, have attempted to generalize or raise to a higher level of reflectivity these
"Stage 5" postulates to define a basis for individually principled moral
decision. As G. H. Mead (1936) put it,

Kant generalized the position involved in the theory of natural rights and
social contract, which was that one could claim for himself only that which he
recognized equally for others. He made a generalization of this the basis for
his moral doctrine, the categorical imperative that every act should be of such
a character that it could be made universal for everyone under the same
conditions.

As Rawls (1971, p. viii) states it, "My aim is to present a conception of justice which generalizes and carries to a higher level of abstraction the familiar theory of the social contract as found, say, in
Locke, Rousseau, and Kant." Rawls does so by suggesting a contract

to define principles rather than a contract to define authority and law.

In my view, the task of moral theory attempted by Rawls is not merely one of "generalization and abstraction" of a prior moral theory (a theory of Stage 5) but is the task of moving from a theory justifying Stage 5 to a theory justifying Stage 6 moral thought.

Rawls's motive, presumably, in moving to a higher level of abstraction was to make a better moral theory, one that would have less assumption or have a clearer deductive structure. In fact, however, the movement in level of theory corresponds to justifying new normative justice principles that define justified civil disobedience or radical income equalization in a way quite different from the normative principles of Rousseau or Kant. Thus, we believe that Rawls's leap in level is not a leap to a better theory for generating and justifying the considered moral judgments of a reflective people or philosophers at both Stage 5 and 6, but is only a better theory for generating and justifying judgments at Stage 6.

PART THREE

Moral Stages and
Legal and Political Issues

⊱⊰

In the introduction to Part Two of this book, I said that Stage 6 is less an empirical psychological finding than a theoretical direction of movement of ethical thought. The first chapter in Part Three, "The Future of Liberalism as the Dominant Ideology of the Western World," takes up this theme. Chapter 6 was originally written in 1977 for a conference on "The Future of the West" at the University of Southern California's Annenberg School of Communications. The conference brought together historians and statespeople as well as social scientists to speculate on a large question: "Is the economic, political, and cultural future of the Western world to be progress or decline?"

In Chapter 6, I note that one aspect of Western liberal ideology has been a faith in progress in societies governed by constitutional democracy. Another aspect of liberalism has been the moral principle of Stage 5—the principle of equal liberty and opportunity defined and justified by a social contract. These liberal ideas shaped the Declaration of Independence and the U.S. Constitution. The current mood in the United States is one of disillusionment with liberalism. Chapter 6 suggests, however, that the liberal faith in progress still has an empirical foundation, that there are long-range sociocultural trends of evolution toward Stage 5 and 6 principles.

More fundamental than a lack of faith in progressive movement is the widespread feeling that classical statements of Stage 5 liberal principles do not deal satisfactorily with the moral problems facing our times. The chapter suggests that the somewhat more radical Stage 6 vision of justice addresses the questioning of classical liberal doctrines that occurred in the 1960s and 1970s. It further suggests that Rawls's book is one example of a new structural development of liberal ideology, more radical than its predecessors but still operating as a new stage in the development of liberal thought. I conclude the chapter by briefly illustrating how this new stage or level in liberal thought might apply to the issue of capital punishment faced by the U.S. Supreme Court.

In Chapter 7, "Moral Judgments about Capital Punishment," I examine in detail the application of a liberal ideology to this issue. Capital punishment is a good issue for detailed analysis, because the liberal tendency to reject capital punishment is often largely argued on utilitarian grounds—on the grounds that capital punishment fails to deter murder. However, the facts about deterrence are ambiguous and do not clearly support the liberal view. For this reason, opponents of capital punishment must turn to a more principled or Stage 6 type of reasoning to make their case, rather than relying on utilitarian considerations of deterrence. In the chapter, I also present in detail the argument that there are evolving standards of justice in this area, continuing the line of thought initiated in Chapter 6, on the future of liberalism.

Since 1975, when the paper was written, the U.S. Supreme Court has recognized as legal new state laws that make capital punishment more uniform or "procedurally just" by mandating it for certain types of crime. As long as procedural justice is maintained, the Court majority holds, capital punishment is not "cruel and unusual punishment." In part, this may reflect the greater conservatism of the Burger Court majority; in part, it reflects the greater conservatism of public opinion as manifested through state legislatures.

This decision by the Burger Court highlights the fact that in the *Furman* decision only a minority based its decision on "evolving standards of justice," recognizing the continuing dignity of the human personality of the murderer; the majority rested its decision against capital punishment on the grounds of procedural injustice. It also highlights the fact that my claim that there is a slow evolution of liberal thought toward principles suggested by Stage 6 is far from being a claim that this is the dominant current trend in American society, which is presently in a conservative mood.

The last chapter in Part Three, "Moral and Religious Education in the Public School," offers a bridge to Part Four, which deals with religious issues. Fundamentally, however, Chapter 8 limits its focus to the implications of the Supreme Court *Schempp* decision for moral education in the public schools. The *Schempp* decision prohibits required prayers in the public schools as a violation of the rights of students and their families to freedom of religion. Some interpreters of the *Schempp* decision have argued that the decision prohibits moral education or teaching in the public schools, as well as religious teaching, on the grounds that moral education is a form of teaching the religion of secular humanism. Using both philosophic argument and empirical data, I argue that moral and religious education are separable. Furthermore, I argue for the importance and legitimacy of engaging in a *secular moral education* in the public school, in order to maintain the fundamental civil rights that the *Schempp* decision held were threatened by *religious ceremony or training* in the schools.

The chapter on capital punishment was an exercise in futility, as regards it's influence on the climate of legal opinion. In contrast, the chapter on moral and religious education was quite influential in establishing educational policy, not in the United States but in the province of Ontario, Canada. This influence is described in an unpublished paper, "Moral Values Development and Education, the Ten-Year Perspective in Ontario 1968–1978," written by V. J. Cunningham (1978) of the Ministry of Education, Research and Evaluation Branch. He says (pp. 5–6, 57, and 59),

The Mackay Committee was appointed in 1966, not only to study the question of religious education in the public schools, but also to "study means by which character building, ethics, social attitudes and moral values and principles may best be instilled in the young; [and] to consider the responsibility of the public schools in these matters." In its report *Religious Education and Moral Development* (1969), the committee noted that its findings

should take into account recent conclusions of educational research . . . [and] should be in harmony with the discoveries of developmental psychology.

The committee recommended that moral development become "an explicit objective throughout our public school system," and that

The primary concern of moral education should be to stimulate the development of the young person's powers to make value judgments and moral decisions, and that its least important purpose is to teach fixed virtues.

The committee particularly cited Lawrence Kohlberg:

The school is no more committed to value neutrality than is the government or the law. The school, like the government, is an institution with a basic function of maintaining and transmitting some, but not all, of the consensual values of the society. The most fundamental values of society are termed moral values, and the major moral values, at least in our society, are the values of justice.

The major statement of Kohlberg's occurs in his essay on "Moral and Religious Education and the Public School: A Developmental View," published in T. Sizer (ed.), *Religion and Public Education* (1967), a series of essays examining the implications of the U.S. Supreme Court decision against religious education in the public schools. . . . His differentiation—that religious education is primarily concerned with religious beliefs and sentiments, and moral education is primarily concerned with moral principles and concerns—was shared by the Mackay Committee in their *Report on Religious Education and Moral Development*, when they stated (p. 88),

> We have been at pains to present them (moral education, and religious education) separately, because they are separate programs. Moreover, neither of them will benefit if they are confused in any way. As an aspect of curriculum study, religious information should be interwoven with the general objectives of education (the child's understanding and developing respect for all men) and never distorted into a separate subject of instruction inviting specialization.

The committee concluded,

> Here, then, is the final rationale for a program whose purpose is to stimulate moral reasoning rather than to inculcate moral absolutes. The objective must always be to encourage the individual to weigh the justice of alternative courses of action of varying conclusions open to him. . . . If our willingness to look in the end for the benchmark of justice constitutes acceptance by us of an absolute, it is an absolute which we think enjoys the unique characteristic of being capable of being defended at every time in every situation. Henceforth in this report the concept of morality becomes synonymous with justice, and to reason morally means to reason justly. We believe that the high duty of public education to foster character building—and we hereby confirm that we consider this to be a duty of public education—should be discharged through a clearly understood, continuously pursued, universal program pervading every curricular and extracurricular activity in the public school system from the beginning of elementary to the close of secondary education.

I can only echo these conclusions and feel heartened by the ten-year effort to implant them in the Ontario schools. The fact that my expression of the liberal ideology underlying the American Declaration of Independence and Constitution could communicate across national boundaries helps support my own faith in "The Future of Liberalism as the Dominant Ideology of the Western World."

6. The Future of Liberalism as the Dominant Ideology of the Western World

IN THIS chapter I focus on the moral dimension of ideology. The term *ideology* refers to a very general pattern or structure of belief that defines evaluation and choice. One part of an ideology is its pattern of assumptions about factual matters, about the nature of human beings, society, and the cosmos. Of even more significance are the assumed moral principles, which, together with assumptions about facts, determine choice for that ideology.

My approach to ideology comes from a structural developmental perspective. Structuralism, as popularized for instance by Levi-Strauss, attempts to identify the invariants under transformation of a set of ideas or symbols. As structure, an ideology is a recurring system of logically interrelated general assumptions about facts and includes a set of general moral principles.

Let us take, as an example of a structure, liberalism, which I believe has been the dominant ideology of the past two centuries in the West. John Dewey's *Liberalism and Social Action* (1935) and Roberto Unger's recent critique of liberalism, *Knowledge and Politics* (1975) are particularly useful writings on the subject. Dewey traces liberalism from Locke's doctrine of the social contract and of natural rights to Bentham's and Mill's utilitarian philosophy of social reform and then to his own less individualistic and more organic philosophy of social reform.

Behind these historically varying doctrines is a structure. According to Unger (1975, pp. 8, 15),

"The Future of Liberalism As the Dominant Ideology of the Western World" first appeared in *Proceedings of the Annenberg Conference on the Future of the West,* Center for the Study of the American Experience, University of Southern California. Los Angeles, Calif.: Center for the Study of the American Experience, copyright © 1977, Center for the Study of the American Experience.

Liberalism is a way of thinking. To grasp a way of thinking, we have to understand the problems it is concerned with and the methods it uses to solve them in the context of an experience of the world. Problems, methods, and experience constitute the "deep structure" of the thought. This "deep structure" allows for a variety of philosophic positions, depending on which part of the underlying experience is illuminated.... It cannot be demonstrated that the different premises of the liberal doctrine follow from one another by a strict logical necessity. But one can analogize the relationships among the doctrines of liberal thought to logical entailments and the conflicts among them to logical contradictions.

From a structural point of view, liberalism is first of all a doctrine of social reform, of progressive or constitutional social change. Central to it are moral principles of justice, where justice is defined in terms of individual rights, all of which revolve around liberty. These principles of justice are usually defined and justified through a social contract theory. The theory of a social contract may be viewed as a set of premises about fact; notions that law and society did emerge from a contract of people living in a state of nature. But the theory of a social contract is actually neither history nor sociology; it is a way of specifying the moral principles adhered to by the liberal.

This view of the social contract has been elaborated best in one of the newest great books of the liberal tradition, John Rawls's *Theory of Justice* (1971). In Rawls's version, the state of nature—"the original position"—is arrived at by rational people contracting about the principles of justice or the moral principles that should govern a society. The original position imagined is that in which each person is under a "veil of ignorance" as to the position he or she will have in the society. Thus people must choose principles of justice that they are willing to live with, whether rich or poor, black or white, male or female, or whatever. Rawls contends that, under these conditions, the first principle chosen would be the right to maximum individual liberty compatible with the liberty of others; the second principle would be that there is no justification of inequalities unless they are to the benefit of the least advantaged. Rawls claims that his principles of liberty and equality are not just the principles of Western liberalism, but would be those chosen by rational people, acting under a veil of ignorance, as they worked toward development of a contract that would maximize their individual values in any society.

Rawls explicated the structure of liberalism in the direction in which liberalism is still evolving or developing as a dominant ideology of the West. The death of liberalism as an ideology and its replacement by a new ideology has been the theme of many books, the most popular of which has been Reich's *The Greening of America* (1970), and one of the most scholarly, Unger's book, previously discussed. I contend that Rawls's book is one example of a new structural development of liberal ideology, more radical than its predecessors but still operating as a new "stage" in the development of liberal thought. In that sense, I believe liberalism will not be replaced by a new ideology of the West but will continue to be its dominant ideology for the next century.

Application to the Special Problems of Our Times: The Direction of Moral Change in the 1970s

The "liberal" position holds that there is a tendency for both individuals and societies to move in a positive direction under normal conditions. A faith in progress is a core of the liberal tradition. The liberal faith is not a faith in the inevitability of progress by some iron law of social history or by some biological unfolding in the child. The liberal faith is, rather, that under conditions of open exposure to information and communication and of a degree of control by the individuals over their actions and the ensuing consequences, basic changes in both individuals and societies tend to be in a forward direction in a series of steps or stages moving toward greater justice in terms of equity or recognition of universal human rights. This seems a proper point at which to provide some documentation for the liberal faith in progress at a time in which such faith has come to seem naive or obsolete.

Historical and cross-cultural evidence supports the notion of a long-range moral evolutionary trend on the societal level. Do societies go through stages of moral evolution? Acceptance of the existence of these stages was popular in the nineteenth century and then supposedly disproved by early twentieth-century anthropology and sociology. The best early work on societal stages of moral evolution was done by L. T. Hobhouse in 1906 (1923). Hobhouse pooled cross-cultural ethnographic data with the limited data of written history to define cultural stages that roughly parallel our psychological stages. He found a strong correlation between these moral stages and the level of socio-technological complexity of a society. Elfenbein replicated Hobhouse's findings, using newer methods for scaling social complexity and using more precise definitions based on moral stages to classify ethnographic descriptions or institutions and beliefs.

This method of investigating cultural evolution is by a comparative study of a cross-sectional sample of societies at various levels of evolutionary development. In several cross-cultural studies, my colleagues and I have found that moral stage development tends to be arrested at lower stages in less developed, village cultures, whereas in highly developed, urban societies moral development proceeds to the highest stages, at least in some individuals. For example, in a study of moral reasoning among the black Caribs of British Honduras (Gorsuch and Barnes, 1973), all 84 subjects, who were town and village boys between the ages of ten and sixteen, were either Stage 1 or Stage 2 (one case was scored a mixture of Stages 2 and 3), and among the young male inhabitants (ages ten to twenty-five) of a primitive Turkish village we found no higher stage than Stage 4 (Turiel, Kohlberg and Edwards, 1978). These results may be contrasted with our finding that within the literate, urban sector of all societies complex enough to have one, including such less developed nations as Turkey (Turiel, Kohlberg, and Edwards, 1978), India (Parikh, 1975), and Zambia (Grimley, 1973), as well as highly developed countries such as the United States, Japan (Grimley, 1973), and Israel (Kohlberg, 1971c; Bar-Yam, Reimer, and Kohlberg, 1972), there are at least some individuals at every stage from Stage 1 to Stage 5. The most plausible explanation for these cross-cultural differences is that societies undergo moral stage evolution.

We obtained further support for the moral evolutionary hypothesis in a pilot study of ethnographic data collected for a small sample of fifteen primitive cultures (Elfenbein, 1973). The data for this study were taken primarily from published sources reproduced in the Yale University library's Human Relations Area Files. Our hypotheses were (1) that cultures have a specific moral stage orientation that cuts across the institutional systems of law, religion, and morality and (2) that the overall moral stage orientation of cultures is highly correlated with their degree of evolutionary advancement, as indicated by level of societal differentiation, political integration, and economic productivity. We collected all the data available on the moral reasoning, legal procedures, and religious practices of the societies in our sample. We found that the legal and religious modes of our societies did in fact have an underlying structure that could be analyzed in moral stage terms. The ideal stage typology we developed for scoring legal systems is presented in Table 6.1.

Table 6.1. Cultural Stages of Legal Systems

STAGE 1. Dispute settlement consists of physical retaliation by the victim or his representatives. Retaliation typically takes the form of talion—doing back to the offender what he did. Authority derives from physical strength in that the dispute remains unresolved unless the victim can muster sufficient strength to exact retribution. Sanctions are entirely physical and are intended to harm the offender, who deserves to be harmed, and to extirpate bad acts or bad people.

STAGE 2. Disputes are settled through negotiations in which the disputants press their respective claims and engage in bargaining and reciprocal exchange (for example, restitution for the offense), with each side trying to arrange a settlement that maximally accommodates its own interests. Authority is commensurate with the ability to drive a bargain. A settlement acceptable to both parties, typically a compromise, is eventually worked out, sometimes with the help of an intermediary. The outcome of the negotiations partly depends on strength, insofar as strength improves a disputant's bargaining position. The sanctions ultimately agreed on by the parties serve as appeasments of the victim and usually take the form of reciprocal quantitative compensation or damages.

STAGE 3. Disputes are settled in conformity with the expectations of an impartial mediator or with conventional social expectations or standards. In mediation, a third party who commands respect by virtue of personal qualities or impartiality intervenes in the dispute and persuades or compels the disputants to submit to a settlement that takes into account both of their viewpoints. The disputants abide by the mediator's decision in order to win his approval, to conform to conventional standards that he espouses, or because it is impartial. An alternative procedure by which the parties may be induced or compelled to abide by the shared expectations of society is dispute settlement by moots, informal tribunals comprised of members of the community. The moot typically conducts public deliberations and arrives at a consensus regarding the norms of conduct that should be upheld and the kind of settlement that is appropriate. The purpose of the sanctions imposed is to protect the interests of the group, to reconcile the disputants, and to reform the offender.

STAGE 4. Disputes are formally adjudicated in accordance with substantive and procedural rules uniformly enforced on a societywide basis by one or more individuals or agencies delegated by the state or by the society as a whole to fill the office of judicial authority (for example, judge or court). The office (usually that of judge) is typically one of several complementary legal roles that, together with the system of rules, comprise a legal order. The judge's duty, as defined by law, is to orient to representing the interests of the society as a whole and to maintaining the legal order as he applies legal rules to particular cases. The rules defining adjudicative procedures are fixed and general and are consistently followed. Such rules also delimit the scope of the judge's authority. There is typically a system of courts. The judges hear disputes and render impartial verdicts that are valid, and may be enforceable, throughout the society. Sanctions are specified by law and are intended to communicate society's outrage at the offense, to serve as a deterrent, and to force the offender to expiate his crime; that is, to "pay his debt to society." Punishment typically takes the form of a fine or imprisonment.

STAGE 5. Procedures for dispute settlement embody many of the structural features of Stage 4 procedures; cases are formally adjudicated in accordance with general rules impartially administered by a judicial authority. In contrast with Stage 4 modes, however, the function of the legal order is not primarily to maintain its own integrity and to advance the interests of the state or of the society as a whole. Rather, its prime function is to uphold universal individual rights and to promote collectively agreed-on values. Judicial authority is vested in the judges by the people; this authority is typically delimited by a constitution. The judicial system is institutionally differentiated from the authority of the state. Where the claims of individuals clash with the state's interests, the law provides for impartial adjudication by an independent judicial apparatus. Provision is also made (typically by the constitution) for procedural devices that ensure that individual rights are protected during the course of adjudication (for example, trial by jury or due process of law). The judge's duty is not merely to apply general rules to particular cases but to do so in such a way that fairness to individual disputants is achieved and the underlying purposes or policies of the law are served. In addition, the judge orients to the need for improvement of the law and of society. Only legal sanctions that fulfill a utilitarian purpose—such as deterrence and rehabilitation of offenders and restitution of victims—are imposed.

A similar typology was developed for scoring religious orientations. We scored the data on moral reasoning using standard scoring methods.

Both of our hypotheses in this study were supported by our results. In our sample, which was comprised of societies fairly selected to represent a cross-section of evolutionary levels, we found that cultures tended to be highly stage consistent across legal, religious, and ethical systems and that, the higher a society was on the evolutionary scale, the higher was its institutional moral stage.

The classic account of moral evolution given by Hobhouse (1923) also suggests very strongly that the overall progression has been toward higher moral stages.

Ideally, we would be able to study moral evolution historically or longitudinally, but such studies are immensely difficult to carry out. Generational studies may also afford us some opportunity to test the evolutionary hypothesis; fortunately, this type of research is much more feasible. If sociomoral evolution were taking place, we would expect that, in general, a larger proportion of the individuals in each succeeding generation would attain higher moral stages. The preliminary evidence suggests that there is in fact a tendency for more adults to reach Stage 5 in this generation than in the last one. The results of two studies (Haan, Langer, Kohlberg, and Kuhn, 1976), one of which is ongoing, show that about twice as many young male adults (ages twenty-six to thirty-four have reached Stage 5 as have their fathers. (The principles articulated in the Declaration of Independence and the Constitution are Stage 5 in that they rest on conceptions of universal human rights prior to law and on a social contract between the state and the individual the purpose of which is to protect those rights. Our finding that the modal stage of American adults is now Stage 4 means that the majority still do not embrace the moral principles that underlie their political system. If sociomoral evolution is taking place, however, then the number of Americans who do espouse these principles is steadily increasing. The fact that our government was founded on Stage 5 principles in the first place is remarkable, because people actually reasoning at Stage 5 were evidently in the minority at that time, as they are today.)

Thus, we have reason to believe that, beyond the cyclical variations of liberalism and conservatism, there is a social evolutionary trend toward a higher conceptualization of justice (the sense in which higher developmental stages represent higher conceptualizations of justice will be discussed later). The basic theoretical reason for such a trend is that lower stage structures are always imperfect resolutions of conflict; hence, the progression toward higher stages is a "natural" one.

Why should there be a cultural as well as an individual progression through stages of justice? Justice is both a sociological and a psycho-

logical concept. A just solution of a social conflict is a better equilibrated resolution of a conflict. By definition, justice is a resolution of
conflicting claims in light of principles and procedures that appear fair
to the parties involved in the conflict. When a society has arrived at a
relatively just solution to a conflict, that solution tends to be maintained, whereas a situation of injustice is always a situation in disequilibrium, particularly in a society whose sociopolitical institutions have
a constitutional democratic (Stage 5) or "open" basic structure so that
authority and force do not maintain arbitrary, unjust solutions. Quali-
fications regarding an evolutionary trend toward justice in an open
society, however, must be made first.

The concept of justice is relative; justice perceived as being at one
stage of development cannot be so perceived at another. The American
conventional majority perceived racial discrimination and prejudice as
compatible with justice. There was always a certain tension between
justice and discrimination for the Stage 4 individual, but not in the
sense that there was for the individual with a principled sense of justice. Second, the progress of a sociopolitical system formally at a certain stage or level is contingent on the moral level of the majority of
members of the system.

To classify an institution or a society at a certain moral stage does
not mean that all or even the majority of members of the society are at
that stage. The American constitutional system is a Stage 5 social system. It is founded on the premises of liberalism (whether of a Stage 5
or Stage 6 variety). Although the American social system is a Stage 5
system, the majority of Americans and sometimes their leaders are
conventional (Stage 4 law and order) in their moral reasoning. The
American constitutional system, of course, was never assumed to require that most members of society think and act in terms of liberal
moral principles. Rather, the system was designed to ensure that political and legal decisions compatible with liberal principles would
emerge from the constitutional democratic process itself. The Constitution was an integration of liberal moral principles with a carefully
suspicious sociology and psychology that attempted to consider all the
abuses of power to which Stage 2 instrumental egoistic human nature
was liable.

The agonizingly slow but relatively consistent trend toward greater
justice, civil rights, and racial equality is one of many historical indi-

cators of the directionality of a democratic system toward carrying its original premises of justice beyond the boundaries accepted by the founders of the system. Indeed, the major moral crises of the past twenty years have represented conflicts between universal justice and the boundary-maintaining demands of society-sustaining morality. From a liberal or morally principled view, the agony of Vietnam can be recognized as the first time a war engaged in for national security has been massively questioned in terms of universal human rights to life. On the whole, American history has supported not only the sheer viability of a Stage 5 sociopolitical system, but the fact that a sociopolitical system based on Stage 5 premises can move in a direction of moral progress even though the bulk of the members of the system and even sometimes its leaders may be Stage 4, or conventional. Such sociomoral progress, however, will always be accompanied by temporary waves of reaction as long as the majority of the society is conventional.

The notion that there is a trend toward moral advance in our society is supported by generational findings. Interviews conducted (keeping education controlled) with men in their twenties and with their parents found a higher proportion of the younger generation to be principled than of their mothers and fathers. these results can be explained largely in terms of increased awareness at an earlier age of value conflicts within conventional morality and of conflict between conventional morality and more universal value principles. Awareness of value conflict is not enough to stimulate movement toward principled morality. Even now, a relatively small percentage of people in their twenties reach principled thought.

Problems of Moral Change in the 1970s

The preceding exposition presents a liberal evolutional view of current moral change. From this perspective, the older generation's distress about the decline of the work ethic, the rise of the new sexual morality, the indifference to patriotism, and the decline of authority at first seems to be merely a reactionary or a conventional (Stage 4) law-and-order response to progress toward postconventional or principled morality. This is not, however, entirely true. The decline of conventional morality in the youth is more than the expression of movement toward a more principled stand. Although the movement toward principled morality starts with a questioning of conventional morality, such relativistic questioning can also occur without movement to principles. Here are two college student examples:

ELLIOT: I think one individual's set of moral values is as good as the next individual's. . . . I think you have a right to believe in what you believe in, but I don't think you have a right to enforce it on other people.

JOHN: I don't think anbody should be swayed by the dictates of society. It's probably very much up to the individual all the time, and there's no general principle except when the views of society seem to conflict with your views and your opportunities at the moment, and it seems that the views of society don't really have any basis as being right. In this case most people, I think, would tend to say, "Forget it and I'll do what I want."

The college students just quoted are, from the point of view of moral stage theory, in a transitional zone, "Stage 4½." They understand and can use conventional moral thinking, but they view it as arbitrary and relative. They do not yet have any clear understanding of, or commitment to, Stage 5 moral principles that are universal and have a claim to some nonrelative validity. Insofar as they see any "principle" as nonrelative or generally applicable, it is the principle of "Do your own thing and let others do theirs." This principle has a close resemblance to the principles characteristic of younger children's Stage 2 instrumental egoistic thinking.

In this decade, the extreme doubt and relativism that earlier characterized only a minority of college students has appeared both earlier in individuals' lives and much more pervasively. It is now often found toward the end of high school. A majority rather than a minority of adolescents now seem to be aware of relativism and of postconventional quesitioning, although it is still a minority who really attempt postconventional or principled solutions to these questions.

From the point of view of the contemporary middle-class adolescent, then, a questioning of conventional morality leads less to systematic rebellion or a search for ideal or universal values than it does to only partial acceptance of and commitment to the basic social institutions in which they participate. Adolescents, as well as adult liberals, currently question a faith in human institutions as agencies of human progress, human rationality, and human ethics. Part of this questioning is attributable to a basic distrust of technology (in which our institutions have invested so heavily) because of the potential technology offers for ecological and nuclear destruction. In addition, there is a postindustrial taking for granted of freedom from basic want, together with a questioning of whether technological progress will ever eliminate poverty, which today's youth views as an inherent aspect of injustice in society.

There is also in both adults and adolescents a widespread questioning of democracy, or of our fundamental political structure, as an agency of social progress. Our form of government, and the nation itself, is seen not only as the preserver of human rights but also as a system in conflict with the rights and needs of minorities within the country, of others abroad, and of the natural environment.

This is a questioning, I believe, of the inadequacies of the dominant Stage 5 liberal ideology of our constitutional democracy to resolve world moral problems, not a questioning of its inadequacies as an institutional system compared to some other possible system. To overcome these inadequacies requires reformulation of the liberal ideology in the more morally principled terms of our Stage 6, along the lines of Rawls's effort, as opposed to the more utilitarian or more laissez-faire individualistic views of social contract liberalism found at Stage 5.

Let me clarify with one specific example the need to find an ideological rationale for a constitutional guarantee of the right to human dignity. Compulsory desegregation and abolition of capital punishment are two issues that have faced the Supreme Court and been uncertainly decided on grounds of formal procedural justice and related notions of "equal opportunity." Both issues, however, represent a concern for a Stage 6 Kantian principle of equal respect for all humans as people, only tenuously supportable by a utilitarian or laissez-faire consideration of justice or equal opportunity.

The Supreme Court, in the *Furman* decision of 1972, rejected capital punishment as cruel and unusual punishment but did so primarily on Stage 5 grounds that as presently administered it violated procedural justice.

When legislation for fixed mandatory capital punishment was enacted in some states, the court then decided that capital punishment was constitutional because it did not violate procedural justice. The argument of some justices in *Furman* held that capital punishment was cruel and unusual by "evolving standards of justice." Against this argument was public poll data showing majority support for capital punishment. The notion of a sociomoral evolution supports Justice Brennan's and others' contention that capital punishment is cruel and unusual by evolving standards of justice. Although the majority of the adult research subjects (mainly conventional or "law and order") supported capital punishment, almost all at Stage 5 and all at Stage 6 rejected it.

At Stage 5 opposition to capital punishment, however, is contingent on the factual view that it fails to deter murder, that it is not utilitarian, or that it is procedurally unfair. At Stage 6 subjects reject capital punishment for the same reasons articulated by Justice Brennan, that capital punishment is cruel and unusual "because it treats members of the human race as nonhuman. It is inconsistent with the fundamental premise that even the vilest criminal remains a human being, possessed of 'common dignity.'"

Justice Brennan invokes what I earlier termed the fundamental universal principle of justice of Stage 6, formulated by Kant as the categorical imperative: to treat human beings always as ends, not as means. Kant himself believed in capital punishment as just retribution for murder. He believed that retribution is consistent with treating the criminal as an end not as a means. He believed that utilitarian views of punishment for deterrence do treat the criminal as a means, not as an end.

In contrast, Rawls's reworking of Kant's moral philosophy leads to a different solution. Would a rational person contract into capital punishment for his society if he didn't know who he was to be in the society, murderer or victim? Even by hard rational standards, no one does know whether he or his child might become a murderer. Given this ignorance, the additional protection of the deterrence of capital punishment over life imprisonment in the role of victim would hardly nullify the certain death through capital punishment in the role of the murderer. Neither Kant nor the constitutional Founding Fathers and early justices rejected capital punishment, just as the Founding Fathers failed to reject slavery. We see the movement from Kant to Rawls, or from Justice Marshall to Justice Brennan, as part of an ideological movement of the liberal social contract from Stage 5 to more consistently Stage 6 premises. Meanwhile, Watergate reminds us that the Stage 5 social contract still waits for the majority to evolve.

7. Capital Punishment, Moral Development, and the Constitution

with DONALD ELFENBEIN

WHAT CAN social science research contribute to the decisions that courts and legislatures make as to the constitutionality of capital punishment? Such decisions can usually be accounted for in terms of an interaction between two factors: the decision maker's beliefs about certain matters of fact and his or her moral standards or principles. Thus, for example, judicial decisions in this area may turn on whether the judge believes that the death penalty effectively deters murder and also on whether he thinks it is morally permissible for the state to take the lives of convicted murderers as a means of preventing future murders. Accordingly, social-scientific research on the facts of capital punishment and research on moral reasoning are both relevant to the legal decisions that must be made. Social scientists have been engaged for some time in research on the factual aspects of capital punishment but have paid little attention to the moral-psychological issues. In this chapter, we hope to fill a long-standing void by specifying the theoretical and empirical framework within which the psychology of moral judgments about the death penalty can most fruitfully be studied.

We report data from a twenty-year longitudinal study of the development of moral judgment in American men. This and related research has firmly established that moral reasoning develops through an invariant sequence of six universal stages. We show that the moral principles applied by individuals to the problem of capital punishment derive from their stage of moral development and discuss developmental trends in judgments about the death penalty in relation to general

This chapter is a revised version of Lawrence Kohlberg and Donald Elfenbein, "Moral Judgments about Capital Punishment: A Developmental-Psychological View," in Hugo Adam Bedau and Chester M. Pierce, eds., *Capital Punishment in the United States* (New York: AMS Press, 1976), pp. 247–296. Copyright © 1975, 1976, American Orthopsychiatric Association, Inc. Reprinted by permission.

stage development in moral reasoning. On the basis of our longitudinal data and our theory of moral development, we claim that the attainment of the most mature stages generates moral condemnation of the death penalty. We also rely on the evidence presented in Chapter 6 that societies evolve toward higher moral stages parallel to the stages of individual development.

These various findings lead us to make two fundamental claims—one empirical and one philosophical—that bear on the constitutionality of the death penalty. On the empirical side, we argue that taken together, the evidence of moral evolution and the finding that capital punishment is condemned at the highest moral stages suggest that American moral standards are gradually shifting toward the view that death is an unjust form of punishment. If such an objective, long-range evolution of moral standards is occurring, then under existing constitutional doctrine, we contend, capital punishment must be held to violate the Eighth Amendment's prohibition of "cruel and unusual punishments." On the philosophical side, we set forth in abbreviated form the argument, which has been elaborated in Chapter 4, that higher stage structures, in virtue of better satisfying the formal criteria of morality, are more adequate and more just modes of moral reasoning than lower stage structures and that the highest stage is the only one that defines a fully adequate principle of justice. We then outline a theory of punitive justice based on this principle and argue that under this theory capital punishment would be judged to be unjust and hence unconstitutional.

Research on Capital Punishment and the U.S. Supreme Court

The U.S. Supreme Court's most extensive discussion of the constitutionality of capital punishment occurs in a landmark 1972 case, *Furman* v. *Georgia* (408 U.S. 238, 1972). By a five-to-four vote, the Court held in *Furman* that the death penalty, as administered at that time, violated the cruel and unusual punishments clause. The grounds relied on by the five justices who comprised the majority were varied. Justices Douglas, Stewart, and White, concurring in separate opinions, objected to the manner in which capital punishment was being administered. Justice Douglas concluded that as of 1972 the imposition of the death penalty was highly discriminatory against minorities, Justice Stewart that it was capricious and freakish, and Justice White that it was so infrequent as to be of no substantial value to the state. Justices Brennan and Marshall, who also concurred separately, focused on the moral status of the death penalty itself. They took the position that the penalty does not comport with the moral values embodied in the Eighth Amendment. Justice Brennan reached the conclusion that capital punishment is cruel and unusual because it denies the executed person's humanity and dignity, violates contemporary moral standards, and serves no penal purpose more effectively than does imprisonment. Writing in much the same vein, Justice Marshall argued that the death penalty is unconstitutional because it is excessive, unnecessary, and morally unacceptable to the people of the United States. Justices Brennan and Marshall both rejected the argument that capital punishment is justifiable on grounds of retribution, stating that retribution is not a legitimate goal of criminal sanctions.

The justices who voted to sustain the death penalty in *Furman*, Chief Justice Burger and Justices Blackmun, Powell, and Rehnquist, argued in separate dissenting opinions for the legitimacy of retributive sanctions and for judicial deference to legislative judgments about capital punishment.

There was unanimous agreement among the justices in *Furman* that the constitutionality of capital punishment should be determined in light of relevant social science research. In justifying their decisions, the justices relied heavily on research concerning both the facts of and moral judgments about capital punishment. The factual research may be divided into two categories. The first has to do with the manner in which the death penalty is administered and the second with its effectiveness as a deterrent. In both areas, the justices agreed with each other as to which studies were relevant but disagreed sharply as to how to interpret the results.

The first of these lines of factual research showed to the satisfaction of several of the justices that as of 1972 the administration of capital punishment was formally unjust in that it was sporadic, arbitrary, and discriminatory. An example of this research, cited by Justice Douglas, is the study by Koeninger (1969) of capital cases in Texas. Koeninger concluded that "application of the death penalty is unequal: most of those executed were poor, young, and ignorant. . . . The Negro convicted of rape is far more likely to get the death penalty . . . whereas whites and Latins are far more likely to get a term sentence." Chief Justice Burger, dissenting, interpreted the available evidence differently; in his view, the contention that people were being sentenced to death "arbitrarily" was "unsupported by known facts."

The Court also divided in its interpretation of the second line of factual research, which dealt with the issue of deterrence. Some of the justices were persuaded by studies such as the one by Sellin (1959), who analyzed a large mass of homicide data and concluded, "Anyone who carefully examines the . . . data is bound to arrive at the conclusion that the death penalty, as we use it, exercises no influence on the extent of fluctuating rates of capital crimes. It has failed as a deterrent." Justice Powell, on the other hand, found himself in agreement with the British Royal Commission on Capital Punishment, which concluded that there was "some evidence" that the death penalty had "a stronger effect as a deterrent to normal human beings than any other form of punishment."

A third line of social-scientific research that the *Burger* Court found relevant to the constitutionality of capital punishment was that which has attempted, through public opinion polls, to measure the degree to which the death penalty is deemed morally acceptable by the American people. Most of the justices agreed that the constitutionality of the death penalty depends in part on whether this particular form of punishment "offends the conscience of society." On the assumption that public opinion polls might shed some light on this question, a majority of the Court took the position that this research was relevant to the issue presented in *Furman,* although once again the Court split on the question of how the research should be interpreted. This third line of research differs from the other two that have been mentioned in that it was relied on by the *Burger* Court, not as a source of *factual* information about capital punishment, but as a source of *moral* standards.

Why did the Supreme Court in *Furman* concern itself with popular ideas about the morality of capital punishment? The constitutional mandate that punishments may not be cruel and unusual rests on a moral judgment made in accordance with a principle of justice, a judgment that certain forms of punishment are inherently wrong or unfair. The language of the Eighth Amendment is so vague, however, that the Court cannot give it content except by some reference to society's moral standards. Now collective moral standards do not usually remain fixed; they evolve over time. Recognizing this, the Court has for some time interpreted the Eighth Amendment in accordance with the doctrine that the cruel and unusual punishments clause "must draw its meaning from the evolving standards of decency that mark the progress of a maturing society" (*Trop* v. *Dulles,* 356 U.S. 86, 1975). Under this doctrine, public opinion studies are relevant to the constitutionality of capital punishment insofar as they constitute evidence of "evolving standards of decency."

It should be noted that the Court did *not* say in *Furman* that the constitutionality of the death penalty depends on whether a majority of Americans approve of the penalty at any particular time. To determine the scope of a constitutional guarantee of individual rights merely by putting the question to a vote and abiding by the will of the majority would be altogether inconsistent with the political philosophy that underlies the Constitution, because the very purpose of the Bill of Rights, in the words of Justice Jackson, "was to withdraw certain subjects from the vicissitudes of political controversy, to place them beyond the reach of majorities . . . and to establish them as legal principles to be applied by the courts" (West Virginia, *Board of Education* v. *Barnette,* 319 U.S. 624, 1943). From a more practical standpoint, the consequences of construing the provisions of the Bill of Rights to mean whatever the majority thinks they should mean might prove to be disastrous indeed, because public opinion surveys have shown that under certain circumstances most Americans would be willing to dispense with many constitutional rights altogether (McClosky, 1964; Prothro and Grigg, 1960).

Nor did the *Burger* Court assert that the evolution of society's moral standards can be gauged solely on the basis of one or two public opinion polls. Moral evolution is a gradual process that can only be observed if a relatively long time frame is taken into account. Month-to-month or year-to-year fluctuations in public opinion do not necessarily reflect long-term evolutionary trends. What a majority of the Court did say in *Furman* is that public opinion polls might constitute *one* source of evidence of evolving standards.

Have moral standards in the United States evolved to, or are they evolving toward, the point where capital punishment is condemned? The *Burger* Court divided on this question. For example, Justice Brennan asserts that, to a large extent, "our society has in fact rejected this punishment," citing as evidence the increasing rarity with which capital punishment is imposed, whereas Chief Justice Burger argues that the death penalty comports with "current social values," citing public opinion polls showing a high degree of popular support for the penalty.

If we try to answer the question by consulting the public opinion research, we find that in a 1936 poll 62 percent of the participants said that they were in favor of capital punishment and that this percentage slowly decreased until 1966, at which time a poll showed that only 42 percent of Americans approved of the death penalty (Erskine, 1970). Considered by themselves, these findings might seem to support the hypothesis that standards have been evolving in the direction of greater opposition to capital punishment. But since 1966 public approval of the death penalty has sharply increased, possibly due to the "law-and-order" sweep of the Nixon era. A 1973 poll showed that the percentage of Americans supporting capital punishment had again risen to 59 percent (Vidmar and Ellsworth, 1974). At this point it becomes unclear whether the shifts in public opinion reflect the long-term evolution of "standards of decency" toward moral condemnation of capital punishment or merely short-term fluctuations in the political climate, which might occur for any number of reasons having nothing to do with moral standards.

Generally speaking, public opinion polls on the subject of capital punishment provide information about the moral *judgments* that are made in this area (for example, whether the death penalty is cruel or unjust) but not about the underlying moral *standards* that generate those judgments. Ordinarily it is extremely difficult to draw reliable inferences about moral standards from moral judgments. The judgment, for example, that capital punishment is cruel or unjust might derive from any of several standards of cruelty or principles of justice. Thus the question of whether society's moral standards are evolving can never be satisfactorily resolved solely on the basis of public opinion data; the question must be confronted directly. If the social sciences are to make any substantial contribution to Eighth Amendment jurisprudence, it can only be as the result of research that focuses not only on moral judgments about punishment but also on the modes of moral reasoning that underlie and generate those judgments. It is this kind of research that we report in this chapter.

It is sometimes thought that changes in the moral judgments that people make concerning capital punishment can occur as the result of the acquisition and dissemination of factual information. Justice Marshall, for example, argues in *Furman* that the constitutionality of the death penalty depends in part on "whether people who were fully informed as to the purposes of the [death] penalty and its liabilities would find the penalty shocking, unjust, and unacceptable." According to this view, if the majority of the population supports capital punishment, believing it to be an effective deterrent, and the facts are otherwise, the majority's opinion is not "informed" and hence need not be taken into account by the Court. Citing evidence that the death penalty is no more effective as a deterrent than life imprisonment, Justice Marshall argues that, if such evidence were widely publicized, most Americans would conclude that the penalty is "immoral and therefore unconstitutional." He further argues that the dissemination of information showing that capital punishment is imposed discriminatorily "would serve to convince even the most hesitant of citizens to condemn death as a sanction."

Justice Marshall thus takes it for granted that most Americans base their moral judgments about the death penalty at least in part on their factual assumptions as to whether or not it is effective as a deterrent and whether or not it is administered in a discriminatory manner. But this is true only if the moral standards that are employed recognize these factual matters as relevant to the morality of capital punishment. If most people evaluate the death penalty in accordance with the principle that anyone who intentionally takes a life simply deserves to die, then it would not be the case, as Justice Marshall supposes, that the dissemination of information showing that the penalty has failed as a deterrent would lead to its rejection by the majority. Most proponents of retribution would regard such information as irrelevant to the question of whether capital punishment is unjust. Research has shown that in fact, contrary to the assumption of Justice Marshall, a large segment of the American population does espouse retributive capital punishment and does regard the issues of deterrence and discrimination as beside the point. One survey found that about 55 percent of a sample of American and Canadian subjects who said they approved of capital punishment also said they would approve of it even if it had no greater deterrent effect than imprisonment. Most of these subjects expressed the opinion that capital punishment can be justified in terms of the idea of just deserts and biblical concepts of retribution (Vidmar and Ellsworth, 1974). In another study, it was learned that supporters of capital punishment tend not to value formal justice or nondiscrimination; this is evident for example, in the finding that such people tend to oppose open housing (Zeisel, 1968). In short, the growth of factual knowledge, in and of itself, will not necessarily bring about a change in public opinion. The impact that new facts will have on the evolution of attitudes toward capital punishment depends on the moral standards that prevail in society.

If society's attitudes toward capital punishment are evolving, it must be primarily as the result of the evolution of moral standards or principles. The Supreme Court has been aware of the possibility of moral evolution at least since 1910, when it stated that the meaning of cruel and unusual punishment may change as "public opinion becomes enlightened by a humane justice" *(Weems* v. *United States,* 217 U.S. 349, 1910). Justices Brennan and Marshall asserted in *Furman* v. *Georgia* that society's moral standards are in fact evolving toward a point where the death penalty would be viewed as immoral or unjust. In this chapter, we claim that this hypothesis has a sound basis in social-scientific research. It is our thesis that moral standards are slowly evolving toward principles of punitive justice that deny the value of retribution, uphold the importance of deterrence and formal justice, and condemn capital punishment on these and other grounds.

The Determinants of Attitudes Toward Capital Punishment

Our position is that the nonfactual cognitive components of attitudes toward capital punishment are determined by developing moral standards. An alternative view taken by many psychiatrists is that these attitudes are the product of irrational, purely emotional, factors. This is the conclusion reached by Gold (1961), who explains support for the death penalty in the following terms:

Murder is imagined as a horrible deed of such great and thunderous violence that man instinctively recoils from this concept because it is too painful to bear. His immediate reaction is obviously emotionally conditioned and it is this type of affective imprint which does not lend itself readily to rational and logical confrontation by words of wisdom or statements of fact.

Extending this interpretation, other researchers (Vidmar and Ellsworth, 1974) have marshaled evidence that many proponents of capital punishment exhibit features of the "authoritarian personality," a hypothetical clinical constellation of attitudes of prejudice, ethnocentrism, and conservatism organized around repression and displacement of impulses directed against authority (Adorno and others, 1950). Such interpretations must be regarded with extreme caution. Most liberal social scientists seem no more willing to accept evidence that capital punishment deters crime than are conservative or "authoritarian" people to consider evidence that it does not.

We hope to show that it is more fruitful to regard attitudes toward capital punishment as the product of an interaction between moral assumptions and assumptions of fact than to believe that support for the death penalty results from irrational, emotional complexes. We have already discussed the role that factual beliefs can play in the formation of attitudes toward capital punishment. In order to show more clearly how judgments about the death penalty derive from moral principles, let us consider two typical statements, one in favor of and one opposed to capital punishment.

As we have said, most proponents of the death penalty justify the penalty on the ground that retribution is a morally acceptable rationale for punishment. Throughout history, a belief in retribution has been a fundamental component of most people's conception of justice. An especially articulate statement defending the death penalty on the basis of retribution was made by Lord Denning, Master of the Rolls of the Court of Appeal in England, in testimony before the British Royal Commission on Capital Punishment:

Many are inclined to test the efficacy of punishment solely by its value as a deterrent: but this is too narrow a view. Punishment is the way in which society expresses its denunciation of wrongdoing: in order to maintain respect for law, it is essential that the punishment inflicted for grave crimes should adequately reflect the revulsion felt by the great majority of citizens for them. It is a mistake to consider the objects of punishment as being deterrent or reformative or preventive and nothing else. . . . The truth is that some crimes are so outrageous that society insists on adequate punishment, because the wrongdoer deserves it, irrespectieve of whether it is a deterrent or not.

This statement was cited with qualified approval by Justice Powell in his *Furman* dissent. Many people, however, do not subscribe to the view expressed by Lord Denning. Those opposed to capital punishment typically believe that retribution is not a legitimate goal of criminal sanctions. Justice Marshall took such a position in *Furman*:

Our jurisprudence has always accepted deterrence in general, deterrence of individual recidivism, isolation of dangerous persons, and rehabilitation as proper goals of punishment. . . . Retaliation, vengeance, and retribution have been roundly condemned as intolerable aspirations for a government in a free society. . . .

To preserve the integrity of the Eighth Amendment, the Court has consistently denigrated retribution as a permissible goal of punishment. It is undoubtedly correct that there is a demand for vengeance on the part of many persons in a community against one who is convicted of a particularly offensive act. At times a cry is heard that morality requires vengeance to evidence society's abhorrence of the act. But the Eighth Amendment is our insulation from our baser selves. The cruel and unusual language limits the avenues through which vengeance can be channeled. Were this not so, the language would be empty and a return to the rack and other tortures would be possible in a given case.

How can we best account for these two representative opposing views? Certainly not in psychiatric terms. The differences between Lord Denning's position and Justice Marshall's are moral and philosophical. The defense of the death penalty offered by Lord Denning rests on a distinct conception of punitive justice, according to which society has a right to administer retributive punishment as a means of maintaining respect for law and of expressing collective denunciation of crime, irrespective of deterrence. Justice Marshall's opposition to capital punishment is grounded in an altogether different principle of justice. In Justice Marshall's view, punishment that is imposed for the sake of retribution is immoral; punishment is justifiable, according to Justice Marshall, only if it serves a utilitarian purpose such as deterrence or rehabilitation.

As we explain in greater detail later, our research shows that moral reasoning of the sort found in the two passages just quoted develops ontogenetically through an invariant sequence of six and only six structurally distinct stages. (The stages are summarized in the Appendix.) Lord Denning's mode of reasoning exemplifies the fourth of these six stages (the modal stage of American adults), and Justice Marshall's way of thinking represents Stage 5 (a stage reached by approximately 15 percent of Americans). This means that the statements of these two jurists do not merely represent two competing principles of justice; they are hierarchically related, in two senses. First, the structure of Justice Marshall's position presupposes the structure of Lord Denning's position, although the converse is not true (see Chapter 4). Second, everyone who expresses a view that is structurally similar to Justice Marshall's view has already passed through a stage during which he or she took a position structurally similar to the one stated by Lord Denning; once again, the converse is not true (Kohlberg, 1969). These points, which have been made elsewhere, cannot be elaborated here. The three central claims we make in this chapter are (1) that society's conception of punitive justice is evolving away from Lord Denning's view and toward Justice Marshall's view; (2) that Justice Marshall's principle, which prescribes opposition to the death penalty (given that it is merely retributive and not deterrent), is a more adequate moral principle than Lord Denning's, which prescribes favoring the death penalty (given that it expresses society's abhorrence of the crime and does not deter); and (3) that there is another principle of justice, defined at Stage 6 of moral development, that is more adequate than either of these principles and prescribes opposition to capital punishment under all circumstances on the ground that it is unfair to the criminal.

Moral Evolution and the Eighth Amendment

There exists a considerable body of evidence that supports the hypothesis that the prevailing moral standards in the United States and in other societies are gradually evolving toward higher developmental stages and thus toward more adequate conceptions of justice. This evidence is presented in Chapter 6 and need not be rehearsed here. The basic theoretical reason for such an evolutionary trend is that lower stages provide inadequate modes of resolving moral conflict; hence the progression toward higher stages is a "natural" one, for societies as well as for individuals. The balance of our discussion is based on the idea that moral evolution is in fact taking place.

The relevance of a moral evolutionary trend to the constitutional test for cruel and unusual punishment should be evident. The Supreme Court's vague criterion—the compatibility of the punishment in question with the "evolving standards of decency that mark the progress of a maturing society"—acquires a very definite meaning when read in the light of our developmental theory and research on moral evolution. In our view, the most valid social-scientific construct in terms of which the moral progress of a maturing society may be measured is stage of moral development. If our society is in fact evolving toward higher moral stages, then we can assess the compatibility of any particular form of punishment with evolving standards simply by determining the attitude toward that punishment that is held by individuals who have attained those higher stages. Thus, in order to test the constitutionality of capital punishment, we need only ascertain its moral status among people who are in the vanguard, so to speak, of moral development in our society. We later present data indicating that, on the whole, the attainment of higher stages of moral reasoning leads to a rejection of capital punishment. This finding, together with the evidence for moral evolution, constitutes objective social-scientific support for the conclusion that the death penalty violates "evolving standards of decency." This is not to say that the moral standards of the majority of Americans *have evolved* to the point where capital punishment is condemned; the public opinion polls, as well as our own data, indicate otherwise. What we are claiming is that standards *are evolving* toward rejection of the death penalty, although only a minority of Americans have as yet attained a high enough developmental stage for this rejection to have taken place.

The Nature of Moral Stages

Before attempting to show how moral judgments about capital punishment develop through stages, we will attempt to define more precisely the general concept of moral stage development. A longitudinal study of fifty Chicago working-class and middle-class males has been central to the process of defining the moral stages. Aged ten to sixteen when first interviewed in 1955, the subjects have been reinterviewed every three years since. In the interviews, the subjects were asked to resolve nine hypothetical moral dilemmas. Two typical dilemmas, one about mercy-killing and one about stealing a drug in order to save a life have already been presented.

The data obtained from the longitudinal study and other research support the conclusion that moral reasoning—the modes of justifying moral judgments elicited by our interviews—develops through stages. The key elements of the concept of developmental stage may be summarized as follows (Piaget, 1960; Kohlberg, 1969):

1. Stages imply *qualitatively different modes of thinking* or of solving the same problem at different ages.
2. These different modes of thought form an *invariant sequence,* order, or succession in individual development; although cultural factors may speed up, slow down, or stop development, they do not change its sequence.

3. Each of these distinct, sequential modes of thought forms a *structured whole;* that is, each stage represents an underlying thought organization that determines responses to tasks that are not manifestly similar.

That moral stages are qualitatively distinct modes of reasoning is conveyed by the data presented in Table 7.1, as well as by the longitu-

Table 7.1. Relationship of Age, Moral Stage, and Stage of Reasoning about Capital Punishment: Thirty Longitudinal Subjects

Case	Age						
	10	13–14	16–17	19–20	22–23	25–26	28–29
1 Overall moral stage	2(1)	3	4(3)	4(3)	5	b	b
Capital punishment stage	a	2	4	4	a		
2 Overall moral stage	2(1)	2(3)	3	3(4)	4(3)	b	b
Capital punishment stage	a	a	3	3	3/4		
3 Overall moral stage	2(1)	2(3)	3(4)	3(4)	4(3)	b	b
Capital punishment stage	2	2	3	3/4	4		
4 Overall moral stage	1	2	3	2(3)	2(3)	b	b
Capital punishment stage	1/2	2	2	2/3	2/3		
5 Overall moral stage	1(2)	2	3(2)	3(2)	3(4)	b	b
Capital punishment stage	a	a	2/3	3	a		
6 Overall moral stage	1(2)	2	3	3(4)	b	b	b
Capital punishment stage	1	2	3	3			
7 Overall moral stage	2(1)	2	3	3	b	b	b
Capital punishment stage	a	2	3	3			
8 Overall moral stage	2(1)	3(2)	b	4	4	b	b
Capital punishment stage	2	3		4	4		
9 Overall moral stage	2(1)	3(2)	3(4)	4	b	b	b
Capital punishment stage	a	3	3/4	4			
10 Overall moral stage	2(1)	2(3)	3	4	4(5)	b	b
Capital punishment stage	a	2	3	3/4	4/5		
11 Overall moral stage	2	3	b	3	4	b	b
Capital punishment stage	a	3		3	4		
12 Overall moral stage	2	2(3)	b	2(3)	2(3)	b	b
Capital punishment stage	a	2		3	a		
13 Overall moral stage	2	2(3)	2(3)	3(2)	b	b	b
Capital punishment stage	a	2	2/3	2/3			
14 Overall moral stage	2	3	3	4	4	b	b
Capital punishment stage	2	2	3	3/4	4		
15 Overall moral stage	1(2)	b	4	b	4/5	b	b
Capital punishment stage	a		4		4/5		

Case		Age						
		10	13–14	16–17	19–20	22–23	25–26	28–29
16	Overall moral stage	2(1)	3(2)	3	4(3)	4(3)	b	b
	Capital punishment stage	a	2/3	3	3	3/4		
17	Overall moral stage	b	2(3)	3(2)	b	b	4/5	b
	Capital punishment stage		2	3			4/5	
18	Overall moral stage	b	2	3	b	3	3	b
	Capital punishment stage		a	3		3	3	
19	Overall moral stage	b	3	3	b	3	3	b
	Capital punishment stage		2	3		3	3	
20	Overall moral stage	b	3	4(3)	4(3)	4(3)	5	b
	Capital punishment stage		3	4(3)	3	3/4	5	
21	Overall moral stage	b	3(2)	3	4	4(5)	b	b
	Capital punishment stage		a	3	4	4		
22	Overall moral stage	b	2	3	4(3)	4(3)	4	b
	Capital punishment stage		2	a	3/4	3/4	4	
23	Overall moral stage	b	3(2)	4(3)	b	4/5	5(4)	b
	Capital punishment stage		2/3	3		4/5	5	
24	Overall moral stage	b	2(3)	3(2)	b	4	4(5)	b
	Capital punishment stage		a	2/3		4	4	
25	Overall moral stage	b	2(1)	2(3)	3(2)	3(2)	3(2)	b
	Capital punishment stage		1/2	3	3	3	a	
26	Overall moral stage	b	2(3)	3(2)	b	4(3)	4(3)	b
	Capital punishment stage		2/3	3		3/4	3/4	
27	Overall moral stage	b	b	3(2)	b	b	3(2)	3
	Capital punishment stage			a			3	3
28	Overall moral stage	b	b	1(2)	3(2)	b	3(2)	3(2)
	Capital punishment stage			1/2	2/3		2/3	2/3
29	Overall moral stage	b	b	2(1)	3	b	3	4
	Capital punishment stage			a	3		3	3/4
30	Overall moral stage	b	b	3(2)	3	b	3	3
	Capital punishment stage			2	3		3	3

NOTE: A stage score such as "3(2)" indicates that the subject's reasoning was primarily Stage 3 and partially Stage 2. A score such as "2/3" means that the subject's thinking was a mixture of Stage 2 and Stage 3. The scores in this table were obtained using the 1971 issue-rating scoring system (unpublished manual). These stage scores correlate highly with the scores obtained for these cases using standard form scoring (Colby and Kohlberg, 1982). See Volume 2, Chapter 5, "The History of Stage Scoring and the Results with Longitudinal Data."

[a] Data missing or unscorable.

[b] Subject not interviewed at this time.

dinal data on capital punishment that we shall discuss. The most important evidence of an invariant sequence of moral stage development is our longitudinal data, presented in Table 7.1 for the thirty subjects discussed in this chapter. Table 7.1 indicates that after every three-year interval subjects were either at the same stage or at the next higher stage. We have also found that the moral stages are structures in the sense that individuals reason at the same stage or, at most, one stage higher or lower, regardless of the verbal dilemma they confront.

Each moral dilemma involves two or more basic moral values or *issues* in conflict. For example, the mercy-killing dilemma presents a potential conflict among moral considerations having to do with the issues of law, punishment, family affectional relations, and the value of life. In every culture, we have found our dilemmas to be defined in terms of the following ten moral issues: (1) punishment and guilt, (2) property, (3) affectional relations, (4) authority and governance, (5) law, (6) life, (7) liberty, (8) distributive justice, (9) truth, and (10) sexual values. The elemental moral issues into which the problem of capital punishment may be analyzed are *life* and *punishment*.

The ten basic moral issues are conceived differently at different stages. The different conceptions of the value of life held at each stage are presented in Table 4.2 in Chapter 4 (p. 118), the different conceptions of punishment in Table 7.2.

Table 7.2. **Five Stages in Conceptions of the Morality of Punishment**

STAGE 1
Definition:
 Punishment is an automatic response to the commission of a bad act and is proportional to the badness of the act. The actor's reasons or intentions are not taken into account. The judge or punisher is seen as powerful in a physical or quasi-physical way. (He is big, important, can send you to jail forever, and so on). Punishment is not understood to have a positive function.
Example:
 Q.: Should Heinz be punished for stealing the drug that saved his wife's life?
 A.: He'd be a thief if they caught him and the police would put him in jail.
STAGE 2
Definition:
 Punishment is seen as inappropriate if the actor had a sensible reason for doing what he did. Where punishment is appropriate, its purpose is to

prevent the actor from repeating his act. The judge or punisher is seen either as an arbitrary authority figure whose legitimacy is rejected or as a person who can put himself in the actor's place and should not punish if he "would have done the same thing." Fair punishment is doing to the offender what he did to the victim. Restitution to the victim may be seen as important.

Example:

Q.: Should Heinz be punished?

A.: Let him go free if he needed the medicine. He didn't do anything wrong. I would have done the same thing.

STAGE 3

Definition:

The actor's motives are taken into account in imposing punishment. Punishment should be minimized if the actor's motives and character are socially acceptable. The purpose of punishment is rehabilitation, with the focus more on personality or attitude change than on prevention of future crime. The failure to punish may be seen as unfair to other offenders who are punished. The judge or punisher should be benevolent, sympathetic, and fair in the sense of trying to consider all points of view.

Example:

Q.: Should Heinz be punished?

A.: He had a good enough reason for stealing the drug, and he wasn't doing it just out of greed. He was doing it in order to help somebody, to save a life, and if the judge knew that he had already tried to talk to the druggist and buy the drug and he was trying to raise money, and he knows that he didn't just do it for doing it, he was really doing it for a real good cause.

STAGE 4

Definition:

The actor's good motives are seen as reasons for leniency in punishment, but these considerations are subordinated to societal considerations such as the maintenance of social order and legal consistency and the protection of property and other legal rights. The purpose of punishment is defined in terms of these societal objectives as well as in terms of the setting of legal precedent and the offender's paying his debt to society. The judge has a duty to maintain the law regardless of his own views because his social role as a judge does not permit him to base his decisions on personal opinion.

Example:

Q.: Should Heinz be punished?

A.: The judge should give Heinz a short sentence because, even though he was morally right, stealing is a criminal offense, and it is necessary to follow laws that are made for general cases to keep order in society. He has broken a law, and precedents must be set to give a basic structure to law enforcement.

STAGE 5

Definition:

The need to maintain legal consistency and to consider the effect of precedents is recognized, but these objectives are subordinated to considerations of fairness and utility. The role of the judge is to decide whether a particular application of the law is just in a particular case and whether it fulfills the purposes for which the law was conceived. Precedent is seen as a means of bringing about social change. Punishment is seen from a utilitarian or social contract perspective; reasons to punish and not to punish are evaluated according to their positive and negative consequences for society as a whole and their implications for the rights of individual citizens.

Example:

Q.: Should Heinz be punished?

A.: After announcing the appropriate sentence for the general case under the law, the judge describes the special circumstances surrounding the Heinz dilemma. He explains that Heinz fulfilled the requirements of justice, exhausting legal means, and of suitably limited consequences. Then he explains that principles supporting the general law also support exceptions to that law in appropriate circumstances. No group of individuals would agree to a general law and an administration of that general law that failed to allow for special circumstances.

Moral Judgments About Capital Punishment

To facilitate the scoring for moral stage of judgments about capital punishment, we constructed a detailed scoring manual. Because the capital punishment problem is a composite of the life and punishment issues, the scoring manual is based largely on the different stage conceptions of these two issues. The manual, containing examples of judgments about capital punishment scored at each moral stage, is reproduced in Table 7.3.

Table 7.3. Capital Punishment Scoring Manual

STAGE 1

Definition:

1. *Reasons for Capital Punishment:* Capital punishment is justified in terms of the idea that a murderer deserves to be given a punishment proportional in badness to his crime; that is, the death penalty is seen solely in

terms of its retributive function. The perspective is that of the punishing authorities or of the criminal who is concerned about physical consequences to himself.

Examples:[a]

(*Retribution*)

- When someone kills someone. He took someone's life, so you have to take his.
- If you go and kill a person, the police are going to catch up with you, and they're going to put you in the electric chair.

Definition:

2. *Concerns About the Value of Life:* The lives of the criminal and the victim are valued solely in physical or social status terms. Concerns about life are subordinated to considerations having to do with punishment.

Example:

- Yeah, if you kill somebody, he might be a very important person, and you will get the death penalty for sure.

STAGE 2

Definition:

1. *Reasons for Capital Punishment:* Capital punishment is seen in terms of reciprocity between the criminal and the victim; retribution is a matter of concrete physical exchange, a life for a life. Whether the death penalty is deserved depends on whether the killing was intentional or not. Deterrence and rehabilitation are conceived in terms of preventing repetition of the crime by the criminal or the commission of similar crimes by other individuals. The perspective is that of isolated, egoistic individuals—the criminal, the victim, and others.

Examples:

(*Responsibility and Motivation.*)

- Well, if he killed someone on purpose—say he just hated the person—well then, he should be given the death penalty. He knew exactly what he was doing, and he could have stopped himself but he didn't.

(*Retribution.*)

- Yes, one of these cases where somebody just shoots some people down and doesn't care at all, then the guy who does something like that should have his life taken away, just like he did to those people.
- Yes, like if somebody robbed a bank and shot the guy, then they should put him to death because he took another person's life when the person didn't want to die. He had a whole life ahead of him, things to do yet, and a person like that should be put to death.

(*Deterrence and Rehabilitation.*)

- Yeah, if there isn't a strict law, murderers could go around killing other people without even thinking about it.

Definition:

   2. *Concerns About the Value of Life:* The lives of the criminal and the victim are valued in terms of the instrumental satisfaction of their own needs and the needs of others.

Example:

- No, not the electric chair or the gas chamber. It is okay to give a life term, but no one should take a life away, because you might need them and they could always do something later on. Maybe they could help their country. They could get out of jail or something.

STAGE 3

Definition:

   1. *Reasons for Capital Punishment:* Capital punishment is evaluated in terms of a general prohibition against taking life and other norms shared by the group. Whether the death is deserved depends on the motives of the criminal—the extent to which he was acting out of kindness, malice, and so on. Retribution is appropriate when the killer's motives do not conform to group norms. The desirability of capital punishment depends partly on whether rehabilitation of the criminal is possible. Rehabilitation is defined in terms of reformation of the criminal's personality, not just in terms of recidivism. Deterrence is seen in terms of the prevention of social chaos. The perspective is that of the group or of the interpersonal relationship.

Examples:

   (Responsibility and Motivation.)

- No, never. A person who commits a murder isn't in his right state of mind to be put away, and just because one murder is committed is no excuse for taking some other life for another one. Killing in the first place is completely wrong. Just because one murder has been committed—it's just like committing another murder to get even.

   (Retribution.)

- I think so, for cold-blooded murder, where the person had no reason whatsoever to do it, just hatred. In murder, there is no sympathy, just hatred or disregard for the person. It's done in violence, if someone is leading a good life, and he just comes up and does away with him.
- Yes, I believe in it. Depending on the case, but if a person is just being cruel and takes a person's life, and doesn't have any feelings for the other person at all, he should give up his own life.

   (Deterrence and Rehabilitation.)

- Yes, otherwise other people will think they can get away with killing people, and then the whole society will break down. Nobody will be obeying any rules any more.
- Yes, for murderers who kill with malice. If a person can commit one

brutal murder, you have to figure he could do it again, and he'll always be this way.

- I think that if the murderer goes free, he actually hasn't seen any of his mistakes. With a life sentence, you have time to think over what you have done and what you could do to redeem yourself, but a man that goes to the chair can no longer redeem himself. I think everyone should have the chance to redeem himself.

Definition:

2. *Concerns About the Value of Life:* Capital punishment is seen in terms of a general prohibition against taking life. The value of the criminal's life and the victim's life is based on interpersonal affection and sympathy.

Examples:

- I feel in some cases it would be the best thing that could be done. "Death for he who takes another's precious life." One human being does not have the say of life or death over another human being.
- I cannot see how anyone, a judge or anyone, can have the power to say that you must die, so I'm against the death sentence.
- No, it isn't. If you were a criminal, you wouldn't want to go to the electric chair. Criminals have families and everything, and you have to consider them, too.

STAGE 4

Definition:

1. *Reasons for Capital Punishment:* Capital punishment is evaluated in terms of society's rights and responsibilities with respect to the taking of human life. Whether the death penalty is deserved is decided in light of the notion that citizens are responsible and culpable for knowingly violating duly established legal rules and harming others, regardless of their motives for doing so. Retribution is a matter of paying one's debt to society. Deterrence and rehabilitation are defined in terms of the need for society to maintain and protect itself by getting rid of murderers, enforcing a system of laws, etc. The perspective is that of society as a self-sustaining system or that of a general member of society whose rights and duties are defined by the society.

Examples:

(Responsibility and Motivation.)

- I think if you are convicted of murder, especially murder in the first degree, I think you should be given the death sentence. As I understand it, first-degree murders are those which you sit down and plan out, so that shows you have some reasoning and you have your rational faculties, and I think a person who does go to the trouble to plan out something like this should be executed.
- Yes, I think today's society has gotten into the habit of judging anyone

who commits an offense against society as being sick. Well, they may be sick and they have broken the rules of society, but that doesn't necessarily excuse them from a responsibility to society. There are, of course, the mentally ill, but that's a different story altogether. You don't go around and hang them, because they're completely incapable of carrying out a rational act. They're not responsible.

(Retribution.)

- Yes. I believe, offhand, there are certain instances where a man has been given more than one chance, and he has just proven himself not worthy of living in society, that he cannot live in society and at the same time go on with the laws and the customs of society as set up.
- Yes, for your multiple murders, your heinous crimes, whatever the hell they are. Now my reason for this is not necessarily keeping others from later committing the crimes. It's just simple revenge, I guess, or an eye for an eye—just obliterate this cancerous person. I think you're never going to change this thing in society, this thing that says obliterate him. The man on the street cannot cope with someone who can murder seven nurses walking around free. Maybe I can't cope with it, so I'm saying this man cannot live with me anymore. He must die. I think society has always felt this way.

(Deterrence and Rehabilitation.)

- Yes, for offenders against society: rapists, kidnappers, murderers—you know, premeditated murder, someone who sat around and thought it out for several days. If this is allowed to go unpunished, you know, it serves not as an encouragement exactly, but there's no restraint against this happening. And there are rapists who have been in jail and have gone and done it again. Society just cannot tolerate this kind of situation.
- I have never gone along with capital punishment. I feel that there is probably some degree of goodness in all of us, and I don't think we can completely lose it. Instead of killing criminals, we should rehabilitate them to the point where they can become useful members of society.

Definition:

2. *Concerns About the Value of Life:* Capital punishment is evaluated in terms of society's responsibility to recognize the absolute value or sacredness of human life.

Examples:

- I think capital punishment is necessary for first-degree murder. Otherwise, you are having a legal system placing a price on human life, if you only give a jail sentence of fifteen or twenty years. You are setting a term of human life, and I don't like setting any limits on human life.
- I just don't think that one human being has a right to sentence another

human being to his fate. We are going beyond our powers when we do that. We can't violate the sacredness of human life, even in a case of murder.

STAGE 5

Definition:

1. *Reasons for Capital Punishment:* Capital punishment is evaluated in terms of rational principles based on respect for individual rights and the promotion of human welfare. Retribution and the criminal's culpability are ruled out as justifications for the death penalty. Deterrence and rehabilitation are defined in utilitarian terms. Capital punishment is approved only insofar as it represents a positive contribution to the welfare of individual members of society. The perspective is that of a rational individual standing outside of society and entering into a social contract.

Examples:

(Responsibility and Motivation.)

- Well, when a person has knowingly violated the legal rights of someone else, the state has the responsibility of punishing him as a deterrent, but I don't think the state has the right to say to a person that what he has done is so morally reprehensible that they are going to kill him for it. Society doesn't have the right to judge a person morally and then take his life when there is nothing to be gained from it.

(Retribution.)

- No. Capital punishment is not that effective as a preventive thing. The only thing I can see that it has accomplished other than that is a retribution-type thing, revenge, an eye for an eye, which I don't think is too necessary. I don't think that is a civilized approach.

(Deterrence and Rehabilitation.)

- I don't think capital punishment is ever justified. How can you say, "Don't take a life," to a person, and then take his life? Society says if a guy kills someone, that threatens society, so society sets the consequences for doing that—saying we are going to protect ourselves from your doing that, we can't trust you not to do it. But I don't see that killing anybody does any real justice; it isn't necessary to protect society. Society can protect itself just by locking the guy up.

- No, I don't think so. Maybe if capital punishment worked as a deterrent to murder, if we could save a lot of innocent lives by executing murderers. But there are statistics that point out capital punishment is not that strong a deterrent.

- No, it's not right. Obviously, we can't let someone just go out and kill someone and then be turned loose. But there is a rehabilitation principle involved in a prison sentence. I guess I have a certain amount of the eternal optimist in me and like to think that as long as there is a finite chance that a person may be rehabilitated or has the opportunity to become a productive member of society again, we shouldn't deny him that. It is a difficult line because you can't get too lax, either, in the sense that the whole structure of the law and prison sentence serves the function of demonstrating to society that people cannot get away with killing other people.

Definition:

2. *Concerns About the Value of Life:* Capital punishment is evaluated in terms of the principle that the individual's right to life is prior to and to be protected by society.

Example:

- I would say it is never right. The purpose of the legal system—like the law against murder, for example—is to preserve life. Everybody has a fundamental right to life, including criminals, and the law is supposed to exist so that people can enjoy this right. The law should not be used to destroy the right to life.

---

[a] Examples are responses to the question "Is it ever right to give the death penalty?"

The responses of our longitudinal subjects on the capital punishment issue were scored separately from the rest of their moral judgment interviews. Our results, presented in Table 7.2, indicate an invariant longitudinal stage sequence of moral judgments about capital punishment similar in each case to that found for the case as a whole. In general, a subject's stage of reasoning about the death penalty at any particular time is highly correlated with his overall stage at that time. In fact, in only eleven cases out of 105 (10 percent) does the subject's major moral stage differ from his stage of reasoning about capital punishment; in these cases, the overall and capital punishment stages differ by one.

We now quote two cases at various points in their development to illustrate the sequence of stages through which individuals pass as their judgments about capital punishment become more mature. The first case, whom we call Tommy, is at Stage 1 at age ten. Tommy's orientation to capital punishment at that age is indicated by the following response to the Heinz dilemma.

Q.: Should the husband steal the drug to save his dying wife?

A.: Maybe his wife is an important person and runs a store, and the man buys stuff from her and can't get it any other place. The police would blame the owner that he didn't save the wife. He didn't save an important person, and

that's just like killing with a gun or a knife. You can get the electric chair
for that.

Q.: Would it be all right to put the druggist in the electric chair for murder?

A.: If she could be cured by the drug and they didn't give it to her, I think so,
because she could be an important lady like Betsy Ross—she made the flag.
And if it was President Eisenhower, he's important, and they'd probably
put the man in the electric chair because that isn't fair.

At Stage 1, Tommy looks at the capital punishment issue from a
single point of view, that of an egoistic individual concerned about
physical consequences to himself. His acceptance of the death penalty
is predicated on the idea that punishment should be or is (the distinction is not drawn at Stage 1) proportional to the "badness" of the
criminal act. Because the druggist caused the death of an important
person, he should be killed himself. As is evident from his remarks
about the importance of the dying wife, Tommy's conception of the
value of life is also Stage 1 at this age (see Table 4.2).

By age thirteen, Tommy has moved to Stage 2 in his thinking about
capital punishment. Now able to take the roles of the actors in the
dilemma, Tommy puts himself in the murderer's place and reasons
that he should not be executed unless the murder was intentional.
Asked, "Is it right or wrong to give the doctor the death sentence?" (in
the mercy-killing dilemma), he answers, "Well, I think it would be
wrong. It was really his fault for killing her, but they wanted her to be
killed, put to death and everything, so I don't think it would really be
right to kill him." When the killing is intentional, however, Tommy
takes the victim's point of view and argues that the murderer should
lose his life, just as the victim did:

Q.: Is it ever right to give the death sentence?

A.: If someone killed a couple of people and he was let off easy, the judge says,
"Oh, I'm just going to give you a light sentence in jail"—he's not really
punishing him right away like they did. They had their life taken away,
why don't they take his? They should do the same that he did to the other
person.

At thirteen, Tommy still accepts the principle of "an eye for an eye,"
but not because punishment should be proportional to the badness of
the crime as at Stage 1; he now advocates retribution as a means of
achieving reciprocity toward the victim. Tommy now has a Stage 2
instrumental conception of the value of life (see Table 4.2).

Tommy has moved to Stage 3 by age sixteen. The central advance in the movement from Stage 2 to Stage 3 is the adoption of a mutual or shared perspective, the perspective of the interpersonal relationship or the group. This perspective is evident in Tommy's reasoning about life's value, which he now conceives of in terms of familial empathy, love, and concern. The Stage 3 individual sees the law as something accepted and shared by members of society and sees those who violate the laws as "outside society." Society places certain limits on the behavior of all its members; if anyone is allowed to "get away with murder," society will break down, because others will think, "If he can kill, why can't I?" Tommy's Stage 3 response to the mercy-killing dilemma is as follows.

Q.: Well, would it be right to give the doctor the death sentence for mercy-killing the woman?

A.: The death sentence. I would have to say it would be right. No one consulted with anyone, and that's illegal, and I think if you are going to kill somebody with medicine, which is illegal, I think you should have the same punishment by death. I think that the same sentence should be applied to Ruby. What right has he got to kill Oswald, just because Oswald killed the President? He's no judge. If he has the right, everybody else has the right, then we wouldn't have any law.

At Stage 3, then, talion is still accepted but only if it is in accordance with law and is imposed by the judge, acting as a representative of society, punishment as simple revenge, a concept accepted at Stages 1 and 2, is no longer deemed moral. At the conventional level, the sin for which retribution must be exacted is breach of the social order, not concrete harm to others. Individual retribution is condemned because an ongoing vendetta is a threat to society. Sanctions that serve as collective retribution, however, are valued because they restore the social order and reassert the integrity of social rules, law, and morality. A well-known interpretation of this retributive tendency in conventional morality is that of Durkheim (1961).

We have said that central to the progression from Stage 2 to Stage 3 is the adoption of a group perspective. Although Stage 3 individuals do take such a perspective, they do not view the social order as a system distinct from particular norms. Not until Stage 4 do people orient to rules and institutions in terms of their function in the social system considered as a whole. Stage 4 individuals have a rudimentary sense of the social contract. Law-breakers are no longer considered to be outside society; rather, they are seen as having to pay the price of devi-

ation from rules because that is a requirement of social life that they
understand and accept as members of society. Tommy, who is at Stage
4 at age twenty, expresses it this way:

Q.: What punishment should the judge give the doctor for mercy-killing?
A.: I do think the doctor should get some sentence, because we are living in a
system of rules, and like I said before, I am willing to pay a penalty. I make
a move, like in chess—I make a move and you take my queen, that is my
penalty, and I am willing to pay a penalty for every move I make. And if I
was a doctor and I made the move to let the person die, I expect to take it. I
would hope, though, that the judge would not give me the stiffest sentence
possible. The death sentence would be too harsh.

Tommy's sense of the social contract at Stage 4 is rudimentary in
that he conceives of the contract as unilateral. The individual has chosen to be governed by rules and so has to be "willing to pay a penalty." But the contract contains no terms that bind society. Society has
no obligation, for example, to guarantee certain individual rights or to
uphold certain principles of justice as its part of the bargain. Taking
the role of the doctor, Tommy can only "hope" not to be given the
death penalty; he does not yet consider the possibility that the imposition of unduly severe punishment might be proscribed by the social
contract.

At Stage 4, Tommy still accepts the idea that society should have
capital punishment. But he thinks that the penalty of death should be
reserved for cases of murder involving the grossest disregard for the
value of human life. The Stage 4 individual thinks that the most des-
picable murderers must die in order to atone to society, which is out-
raged at their horrendous crimes. The rationale for capital
punishment at Stage 4 is differentiated from an eye-for-an-eye conception of retributive killing. Although the societal perspective is not
clearly articulated, elements of this conception can be detected in the
statements Tommy makes at Stage 4:

Q.: Do you think that the death sentence should be given in some cases?
A.: Yeah, I am in favor of capital punishment for blatant, out-and-out, cold-
blooded murders. I am.
Q.: Why?
A.: Well, here we have the life-for-a-life bit, but I would reserve that as a
special case for cold-blooded, premeditated murders. Something like the
deal where they killed two ambassadors. They were just held hostage and
murdered. Something like that I just cannot condone. I think years ago I

would have said an eye for an eye, a tooth for a tooth, whether it be a mercy killing or regular premeditated murder, but now I am willing to draw the line.

Q.: Why should they be given the death penalty?

A.: Fairness. It would be like the payment for the act.

To clarify the structure of Stage 4 reasoning about capital punishment and to illustrate the progression from Stage 4 to Stage 5, we consider another subject, whose reasoning about the value of life is also presented in Table 4.2. Richard, at age sixteen, has a Stage 4 conception of the sacredness of human life. He is against euthanasia because "God put life into everybody on earth, and you're taking away something from that person that came directly from God, and you're destroying something that is very sacred." Although Richard believes in the sacredness of life, his horror at its destruction also leads him to endorse capital punishment. At Stage 4, he is unable to resolve the contradiction:

Q.: Is it ever right to give the death sentence?

A.: Yeah. There are some people, and their minds are sort of twisted, and they go on these killing sprees. They're not really fit to live. They'll pay their punishment in some higher court, when whatever God thinks must be done. If he is killed by us, we're sort of passing over the decision to God.

Q.: Why should they be punished?

A.: For murder. Well, this is not a right or a privilege of man to decide who shall live and who shall die. He has gone against the will of God, or he has sinned against God. They say God is a forgiving God, but still, I don't really know what would happen.

By age twenty-five, Richard has moved to a Stage 5 view of capital punishment. The hallmark of the transition between Stage 4 and Stage 5 is a shift from the viewpoint of the social system to the perspective of a rational individual who exists prior to society and contracts into it. There exists at Stage 5 a framework of universal, second-order values or principles (such as, utilitarianism) that generate concrete rules and obligations. The Stage 5 individual sees a commitment to these values or principles as a prerequisite to defining and accepting the legitimacy of society's point of view and its rules. These principles define the basic terms of a bilateral contract between society and the individual; that is, they delimit societal as well as individual prerogatives. In this sense, society has lost the supraindividual authority it held at Stage 4. Stage 5 thinking generates opposition to capital punishment that is imposed for the sake of retribution or atonement. From a Stage 5 point of view, punishment rationalized in these terms is neither rational nor just because it does not serve to promote the rights and welfare of individuals. Retribution is seen, to borrow Justice Marshall's phrase, as "purposeless vengeance." Only punishment that upholds rights or makes a positive contribution to utility—punishment that prevents crime, deters crime, rehabilitates criminals, or restitutes victims—is justifiable at Stage 5. Another consideration that becomes salient at Stage 5 is formal justice; punishment must be administered in accordance with the principle that like cases are to be treated alike. We get a glimpse of this perspective in the statement Richard makes at Stage 5:

Q.: Is it ever right to have the death sentence?

A.: No, because it is too much of an eye-for-an-eye and a tooth-for-a-tooth kind of thing, and in a sense it is saying that it is all right for society to kill someone but it is not all right for you as an individual. I am more and more coming to feel that the death penalty is too harsh in any circumstance. In the sense that people's behavior is caused, it is a response to the environment, and in that sense society shares in the crime of anyone.

Q.: Is it the same thing for a state to demand a life as it is for an individual?

A.: I think it is very similar. I think I could see the existence of the death penalty if it would serve as a real deterrent to some type of crime that would involve life and death. But I don't think anyone has come up with anything that can really prove that it serves as a deterrent.

Beyond Stage 5 there is a higher stage of thinking, Stage 6, that orients to universal moral principles and respect for individuals. We postpone discussion of this stage, as it has not yet been attained by any of our thirty longitudinal subjects.

Content and Structure in Moral Reasoning

In our conceptualization of the stages, we distinguish between the *content* of a stage (the judgment formed) and its *structure* (the mode of reasoning employed). Whether or not a subject approves of capital punishment, for example, is a matter of content; the rationale he or she adopts is a matter of structure. Although structure is one thing and content another, there is a probabilistic tendency for certain stage structures to generate specific moral attitudes.

The relationship between content and structure in attitudes toward capital punishment is indicated in Table 7.4.

Table 7.4. **Relationship of Moral Stage to Judgment about Capital Punishment: Thirty Longitudinal Subjects**

Overall Moral Stage	N	Number Opposed to Capital Punishment [a]	Percent Opposed to Capital Punishment [a]
Stage 5	2	2	100%
Stage 4/5	6	6	100
Stage 4	11	4	36
Stage 3/4	17	7	41
Stage 3	25	5	20
Stage 2/3	31	0	00
Stage 2	9	1	11
Stage 1, 1/2	4	0	00

NOTE: Biserial correlation between moral stage and opposition to capital punishment is .76, $N = 105$. The moral stage scores are for thirty subjects tested between two and five times each, at three-year intervals (see Table 7.1).

[a] Subjects answering "No" to the question, "Is it ever right to give capital punishment?"

Table 7.4 shows the percentage of subjects at each stage (or mixed stage) who responded no to the question "Is it ever right to give capital punishment?" At Stage 3 and below, almost all subjects said that it was right to give the death penalty under certain circumstances, Stage 4 subjects were divided on the issue, and all subjects using Stage 5 reasoning rejected capital punishment. Our data thus supported the conclusion that, on the whole, the early stages of development are characterized by moral approval of the death penalty, but as individuals progress in their moral development their moral reservations about capital punishment multiply and they gradually come to condemn it as immoral (given certain factual assumptions discussed later).

To return to a point discussed earlier, one reason that the relationship between structure and content is only probabilistic is that the stand individuals take on the capital punishment issue depends on the factual assumptions they make as well as on their moral stage. For example, the pattern of unanimous opposition to the death penalty among the Stage 5 subjects in our sample reflects partly their moral principles (for example, rejection of retribution) and partly the assumption, which almost all of them explicitly made, that capital punishment had not been shown to be an effective deterrent to homicide. As we shall see, Stage 5 thinking does not necessarily lead one to oppose capital punishment when the assumption is made that it does deter potential murderers.

Another factor that accounts for the probabilistic relationship between structure and content is that the content of conventional (Stage 3 and Stage 4) attitudes is determined both by the structure of the individual's reasoning and by the values of his or her culture. (Jacquette and Carrick, 1971). We have found, for example, that the attitudes of conventional subjects toward capital punishment depend on the actual legal-moral status of the death penalty in their culture. As we can see from Table 7.4, only 30 percent of the conventional subjects in our longitudinal sample said that the death penalty was never justified; these data are from the United States, where capital punishment has been legal until recently. On the other hand, in Israel, where capital punishment is virtually nonexistent, most of the conventional subjects interviewed answered no to the question "Is it ever right to give the death penalty?" This rejection of capital punishment by conventional Israeli subjects was found to be derived from its legal status and not to be based on moral principles. A few executions have taken place in Israel—quasi-legal executions of fedayeen and the legal execution of Eichmann. Conventional Israeli subjects tended to accept these executions, regarding them as "special cases" in which retribution was justified. One of the implications of these findings is that if capital punishment were legally abolished in the United States, conventional opinion would eventually come around to supporting that position.

The Greater Adequacy of Higher Stages

The relationship that obtains between the content and the structure of attitudes toward capital punishment suggests one sense in which higher stages are more adequate modes of moral reasoning. In claiming higher stages to be more adequate, we are not referring to the age and stage progression toward rejection of capital punishment. We mean, rather, that the higher the stage, the greater the likelihood that individuals at that stage will agree not only in the structure of their reasoning but in the content of their judgments as well. All our Stage 5 and Stage 4/5 subjects agree that the death penalty is wrong; in contrast, the conventional (Stage 3 and Stage 4) subjects do not necessarily agree in their judgments on the subject. Whether they agree or not depends largely on the norms of their cultures and social roles. Where cultural values or values associated with social roles are inconsistent, the moral judgments of conventional individuals are likely to be inconsistent also. For example, a Stage 4 minister who orients to a religious ethic of mercy is likely to be against capital punishment, whereas a Stage 4 police chief who orients to the need for strict law enforcement is likely to be in favor of it.

In order to illustrate more vividly the capacity of conventional stages to generate judgments that are inconsistent in content, we now consider the statements of two Stage 4 individuals, one staunchly opposed to the death penalty and one vehement in his support of it. The statement opposing capital punishment is that of a dedicated and eloquent nineteenth-century abolitionist named Bovee (1878):

Human life should be invested with a reverence as sacred and as lasting as eternal truth. . . . The commandment, *"Thou shalt not kill,"* though delivered amid the thunders and lightnings of Sinai, thousands of years ago, is written freshly upon every heart, by the same Divine hand, and binds, with the same sacred power, both citizen and ruler. No system of reasoning, however specious or plausible, should ever induce men to depart from a broad principle, to stand upon a special instance. . . . [F]or all are the children of one common Father, and "God is no respecter of persons."

But how difficult to secure the universal observance of this grand principle, when government itself . . . will not practice the precept, "Thou shalt not kill," which it so solemnly enjoins upon others.

Compare this statement with F.B.I. director J. Edgar Hoover's enthusiastic defense of capital punishment (1967):

It is my opinion that when no shadow of a doubt remains relative to the guilt of a defendant, the public interest demands capital punishment be invoked where the law so provides. . . .

Where the death penalty is provided, a criminal's punishment may be meted out commensurate with his deeds. . . .

Maudlin viewers of the death penalty call the most wanton slayer a "child of God" who should not be executed regardless of how heinous his crime may be because "God created man in his own image, in the image of God created he him" (Genesis 1:27). . . .

In fact, in referring to man as the "image of God," the Old Testament, so freely quoted by opponents of the death penalty, also states, "Whoso sheddeth man's blood, by man shall his blood be shed" (Genesis 9:6). There are many passages in the Old Testament which refer to capital punishment being necessary to enforce the laws of society.

Bovee's reasoning and Hoover's are identical in structure; both statements are Stage 4. Yet with respect to the content of their judgments, the two could not disagree more completely.

This tendency for conventional stages of reasoning to yield conflicting judgments may be observed not only across individuals but within individuals as well. We have already seen an example of this in Richard's Stage 4 reasoning, which is characterized by an unresolved tension between the notion that taking life is categorically wrong and the idea that the state may legitimately execute murderers. Like Richard, most Stage 4 subjects vacillate uneasily between these two inconsistent ideas; they ordinarily resolve the inconsistency in accordance with the norms or values associated with their social roles. Bovee is atypical in that he takes a wholly consistent anti-capital punishment position. In Hoover's Stage 4 statement, however, we find the same tension that occurs in Richard's reasoning at age sixteen:

Certainly, penetrative and searching thought must be given before considering any blanket cessation of capital punishment in a time when unspeakable crimes are being committed. . . .

At the same time, nothing is so precious in our country as the life of a human being, whether he is a criminal or not.

Faced with a choice between these two opposed considerations, Hoover adopts the position that is consonant with the values that an F.B.I. director is expected to uphold, as we have seen.

The inadequacy of Stage 4 resides in the fact that at this stage a single mode of moral reasoning can generate contradictory conclusions about the morality of specific actions and institutions. This point may be restated in more formal terms. As we have argued in Chapters 4 and 5, one criterion of the adequacy of moral principles is *universalizability*. Morality represents a striving to decenter judgments of obligation, to make them from a "moral point of view" valid for all humanity. The principle we follow in a moral situation must be one we could want or expect all people to follow in that situation. This idea was expressed by Kant ([1785] 1959) in his first formulation of the categorical imperative: "Act only according to that maxim by which you can at the same time will that it should become a universal law." At heart, this concept of universalizability is a formalization of our intuitive sense that a moral principle cannot be adequate unless we would be willing for it to be applied across the board. Another criterion of moral adequacy, closely related to universalizability, is *consistency*. The goal of rational moral judgment is to arrive at moral decisions with which other rational moral agents could ideally agree. Insofar as a method of moral reasoning, or a set of moral principles, generates inconsistency or disagreement when applied to a concrete dilemma, it cannot be said to be adequate.

Applying these formal criteria, one can see that Stage 4 defines an inadequate moral principle. Faced with a moral dilemma, the Stage 4 individual says, "Act in accordance with society's norms and rules" or "Follow the Bible." But we would not want to universalize prescriptions such as these; if all people were to follow them, the result would be inconsistent judgments—moral disagreement—as in the examples just given.

Stage 5 reasoning better satisfies the criteria of universalizability and consistency than does Stage 4 reasoning. The Stage 5 individual makes an effort to take a point of view that transcends conventional social norms, to orient to values or principles that can and should be recognized by all societies and persons. This Stage 5 effort to embrace more universalizable principles can take two forms. One is the principle of utility or welfare maximization. The other is the idea of human rights and the social contract—the notion that individuals have rights that are prior to society and that the legitimate authority of the state must be limited in order that those rights may be protected. The greater universalizability and consistency of Stage 5 thinking is illustrated by the classic argument against the death penalty formulated by the eighteenth-century Italian philosopher Cesare Beccaria.

Writing in 1764, Beccaria (1963) argued that the parties to the social contract would never consent to a system of capital punishment:

What manner of right can men attribute to themselves to slaughter their fellow beings? Certainly not that from which sovereignty and the laws derive. These are nothing but the sum of the least portions of the private liberty of each person; they represent the general will, which is the aggregate of particular wills. Was there ever a man who can have wished to leave to other men the choice of killing him? Is it conceivable that the least sacrifice of each person's liberty should include sacrifice of the greatest of all goods, life?

Beccaria also orients to the principle of utility, which leads him to consider the facts of deterrence. His conclusion is that the death penalty serves no utilitarian purpose:

If we glance at the pages of history, we will find that laws ... never have ... been dictated by- a dispassionate student of human nature who might ... consider them from this single point of view: *the greatest happiness shared by the greatest number.*

The punishment of death, therefore, is not a right, for I have demonstrated that it cannot be such; but it is the war of a nation against a citizen whose destruction it judges to be necessary or useful. If, then, I can show that death is neither useful nor necessary I shall have gained the cause of humanity. ...

I see no necessity for destroying a citizen, except if his death were the only real way of restraining others from committing crimes. ...

[T]he experience of all the ages [shows that] the supreme penalty has never prevented determined men from injuring society. ...

Beccaria opposes retributive punishment and favors only those forms of punishment that can be justified in utilitarian terms:

[I]t is evident that the purpose of punishment is neither to torment and afflict a sensitive being, nor to undo a crime already committed. ... Can the shrieks of a wretch recall from time, which never reverses its course, deeds already accomplished? The purpose can only be to prevent the criminal from inflicting new injuries on ... citizens and to deter others from similar acts.

The principles invoked by Beccaria are clearly more universalizable than those relied on by the Stage 4 individuals quoted earlier. We would be much more willing for all people to resolve moral dilemmas in accordance with the principle of utility or the principle of the social contract than we would be for them consistently to obey Stage 4 rules. This is because Stage 5 principles are intrinsically appealing to any rational moral agent; their appeal, unlike that of Stage 4 modes of reasoning, is independent of extrinsic social norms. As we have already seen, Stage 5 utilitarian and contractarian principles are also more likely to generate moral agreement among people applying them to a particular dilemma than are Stage 4 principles. One manifestation of this is the greater internal consistency of the Stage 5 attitude toward retributive capital punishment. Beccaria's utilitarian opposition to retributive punishment is unequivocal. On the other hand, J. Edgar Hoover and Richard, our longitudinal subject, are ambivalent about the legitimacy of executing criminals retributively at Stage 4. When Richard reaches Stage 5, he eliminates from his earlier Stage 4 reasoning the contradiction between upholding the state's right to kill and simultaneously denying the individual's right to do so. In sum,

Stage 5 is a more adequate moral principle than Stage 4 and Stage 5 judgments about the death penalty, like those of Beccaria, are more adequate than Stage 4 judgments on the subject, such as those of Bovee and Hoover.

The Inadequacy of the Stage 5 Approach

Is Stage 5 a fully adequate mode of reasoning that can lead to universal agreement on whether capital punishment is just, given factual knowledge of its consequences? Unfortunately, it is not. We have seen that Beccaria's Stage 5 utilitarian condemnation of capital punishment was partly contingent on his belief that the death penalty was not an effective deterrent. But to this day the facts about deterrence, as we have noted, remain controversial. The potential inadequacy of Stage 5 reasoning becomes evident if we assume that capital punishment does deter murder. For the sake of argument, let us assume that the tentative findings reported by Tullock (1974) are correct:

Recently Ehrlich . . . by using a much more sophisticated method, has demonstrated a very sizable deterrence payoff to the death penalty for murder. His figures indicate that each execution prevents between eight and twenty murders. Unfortunately, the data available for this study were not what one would hope for, so not as much reliance can be put upon his results as one normally would give to work by such a sophisticated econometrician.

Now on these facts, the principle of utility prescribes acceptance of the death penalty, because a net saving of life would be achieved by executing murderers. In other words, although none of our subjects who are at Stage 5 support capital punishment (because they assume it serves no deterrent purpose), a convincing Stage 5 argument can be made for its retention if it does deter murders. Van den Haag (1969) has made such an argument:

Can any amount of deterrence justify the possibility of irrevocable injustice [resulting from the execution of innocent people]? . . . [H]owever one defines justice, to support it cannot mean less than to favor the least injustice. If the death of innocents because of judicial error is unjust, so is the death of innocents by murder. If some murders could be avoided by a penalty conceivably more deterrent than others—such as the death penalty—then the question becomes: which penalty will minimize the number of innocents killed (by crime and by punishment)? It follows that the irrevocable injustice, sometimes inflicted by the death penalty would not significantly militate against it, if capital punishment deters enough murders to reduce the total number of innocents killed so that fewer are lost than would be lost without it.

This Stage 5 utilitarian argument clashes directly with Beccaria's Stage 5 appeal to the social contract, to the notion that no one would consent to be governed by a regime that claims the right to take his or her life under certain circumstances. Once deterrence has been demonstrated, it is not clear which of these arguments is more convincing. The tension between them is evident in Beccaria's statement, quoted earlier. Beccaria seems unable to make up his mind about whether the death penalty can ever be morally justified. In the paragraph dealing with the social contract, he seems to argue that it cannot. But in another pasasage, he seems to admit that capital punishment might be justified if it were "the only real way of restraining others from committing crimes." Because his perception of the facts is that capital punishment does not deter, he is spared having to come to terms with the contradiction between his contractarian and utilitarian views. Stage 5 provides no principle according to which this contradiction may be resolved; hence, Stage 5 does not constitute a completely adequate basis for making moral judgments about capital punishment.

A further indication that Stage 5 conceptions such as Van den Haag's are not fully adequate is that they do not comport with the widely shared intuition that to execute a person for committing a crime, even if there are utilitarian grounds for doing so, is to violate his or her dignity as a human being. Justice Brennan articulated this view in the *Furman* case:

At bottom, then, the cruel and unusual punishments clause prohibits the infliction of uncivilized and inhuman punishments. The state, even as it punishes, must treat its members with respect for their intrinsic worth as human beings. . . .

The true significance of these [unconstitutional] punishments is that they treat members of the human race as nonhumans, as objects to be toyed with and discarded. They are thus inconsistent with the fundamental premise of the clause that even the vilest criminal remains a human being possessed of common human dignity. . . .

Death is truly an awesome punishment. The calculated killing of a human being by the state involves, by its very nature, a denial of the executed person's humanity. The contrast with the plight of a person punished by imprisonment is evident. An individual in prison does not lose "the right to have rights."

Kant ([1785] 1959) expressed the same moral idea in a slightly different way in one of his alternative formulations of the categorical imperative, the principle of respect for persons: "Act with reference to every rational being (whether yourself or another) so that it is an end in itself . . . and . . . never . . . a mere means." This attitude of respect for human dignity, for individual people as ends rather than means is missing at Stage 5. At the ultimate stage of moral development, Stage 6, however, the attitude is systematically elaborated into a general conception of justice. Central to Stage 6 reasoning is the idea of justice as equity or fairness to individuals. This idea integrates the two Kantian imperatives, universalizability and respect for people. If we say that all human beings should be treated as ends in themselves and insist on the universalization of this maxim, we arrive at a principle of justice that prescribes that in all moral dilemmas all individuals must always be accorded fundamentally equal consideration. Stage 6, we argue, is a method of moral reasoning that can resolve the contradictions between judgments about capital punishment still found at Stage 5.

Toward a Theory of Punitive Justice

Before we can elaborate the conception of justice as equity that we have just loosely formulated, we must state our basic assumptions about the nature of morality and the moral stages. Following Kant and other formalist moral philosophers (Baier, 1965; Hare, 1963; Rawls, 1971) we have argued in Chapters 4 and 5 that rational moral principles must satisfy certain formal criteria, including universalizability, consistency, and reversibility. The first two of these interrelated criteria have already been defined briefly. The criterion of *reversibility* refers to the capacity of moral principles to generate concrete judgments that do not vary across the perspectives of the actors in the dilemma; that is, do not depend on which role is taken by the person applying the principle. Our position is that each higher moral stage meets all of these formal conditions better than its predecessor and that only Stage 6 fully meets these conditions. In other words, only Stage 6 defines a fully adequate moral principle, given the quite reasonable formal constraints that we have placed on the concept of morality.

We now attempt to elucidate the claims we are making about Stage 6 by defining more precisely the Stage 6 mode of reasoning and illus-

trating how it best satisfies the formal criteria of rational moral judgment. We begin by tracing briefly the stage development of
progressively more reversible and consistent moral principles. For the
sake of clarity, we focus on the criterion of reversibility.

A moral dilemma may be defined as a state of social disequilibrium
characterized by the unresolved conflicting claims of individuals. A
nonreversible (unequilibrated) resolution of a moral dilemma is one
that is morally acceptable from the viewpoint of one or more of the
actors but not from that of all of them. In contrast, a reversible or fair
(equilibrated) resolution is one whereby everyone whose interests are
at stake is "given his due" according to some principle that everyone
judges to be morally valid, given that each person is not egoistic but is
willing to take a moral point of view; that is, to consider his own
claims impartially and to put himself in the shoes of the others. Such a
resolution is reversible in that one can move back and forth between
perspectives and still judge the resolution to be fair. This concept of
fairness as reversibility is the ultimate equilibration, at the highest
stage of moral development, of the idea of fairness as reciprocity, an
idea held in some form at every stage. At Stage 1, reciprocity is me-
chanical equivalence, an eye for an eye. At Stage 2, reciprocity means
positive (or negative) exchange of gratifications: "If you promote
(harm) my interests, it is fair for me to promote (harm) yours." Reciprocity becomes, at Stage 3, the Golden Rule—putting oneself in the
other person's shoes before making a moral judgment.

The trouble with these lower-stage modes of moral reasoning, as
was stated in Chapter 4, is that they are not fully reversible; as a
result, they generate resolutions of moral dilemmas that are neither
consistent nor fair. Consider, for example, the way in which Stage 3
handles the capital punishment problem: if we put ourselves in the
shoes of the murderer, we are opposed to the death penalty, but if we
put ourselves in the shoes of the victim whose murder would be deterred by the death penalty, we favor it.

At Stage 5, the concept of reciprocity of rights appears. In the Stage
5 subject's words, "Morality means recognizing the rights of other
individuals to do as they please as long as it doesn't interfere with
somebody else's rights." Like Stage 3 reciprocity, however, Stage 5
reciprocity can generate either of two conflicting attitudes toward capital punishment. On the one hand, a Stage 5 individual might argue
that the murderer has an equal right to life that takes precedence over

the claim that he should be executed for the sake of deterrence, as long as he does not kill anyone else. On the other hand, a Stage 5 person might claim that the murderer has forfeited his own right to life by violating the right to life of another person, given that executing him would result in a net saving of life.

Having noted that the criteria of reversibility and consistency are not satisfied at lower stages, we can now attempt to show that these criteria are fully met at Stage 6. In essence, Stage 6 is a second-order conception of Golden Rule role taking. Judgments are formed by role taking the claim of each actor under the assumption that all other actors' claims are also governed by the Golden Rule and accommodated accordingly. The steps involved in making a decision based on Stage 6 role taking are (1) to imagine oneself in the position of each person in the situation and to consider all the claims that a self-interested person could make in each position; (2) then to ask which claims one would uphold and which claims one would relinquish, imagining that one does not know which person in the situation one is to be; and (3) then to formulate a moral judgment in accordance with the fully reversible claims (those that one would uphold not knowing who one was to be).

If all the actors involved in a dilemma were to follow this hypothetical three-step procedure, they would necessarily give equal consideration to the claims of all before reaching a decision. Moreover, deliberating under these constraints, they would almost inevitably reach agreement with one another as to what the fair resolution of the situation would be. Thus, at Stage 6, the criteria of consistency and reversibility are fully met, because one and only one resolution would be agreed on and this resolution would be accepted as fair by all concerned. At the same time, the criterion of universalizability is fully satisfied, because a role-taking procedure based on the idea that equal consideration should be given to the claims of all whose interests are at stake commends itself as a principle we would want everyone to follow in resolving moral dilemmas. This is what it means to say that Stage 6 is a fully adequate moral principle.

A formal conception of justice as reversible role taking has been fully elaborated in Rawls's *A Theory of Justice* (1971). According to Rawls, valid principles of social justice are those that would be adopted by rational, self-interested people in an "original position," that is, behind a "veil of ignorance" as to who in society they are to be and having an equal (or unknown) chance of being anyone in particular, including the least advantaged member of society. "The idea of the original position," says Rawls, "is to set up a fair procedure so that any principles agreed to will be just."

[The veil of ignorance] ensures that no one is advantaged or disadvantaged in the choice of principles by the outcome of natural chance or the contingency of social circumstances. Since all are similarly situated and no one is able to design principles to favor his particular condition, the principles of justice are the result of a fair agreement or bargain.

Rawls's notion that principles of justice are to be drawn up in the original position coincides with Kant's alternative formulation of the categorical imperative, because, as Rawls puts it,

Treating men as ends in themselves implies at the very least treating them in accordance with the principles to which they would consent in an original position of equality. For in this situation men have equal representation as moral persons who regard themselves as ends and the principles they accept will be rationally designed to protect the claims of their person.

In Rawls's theory, the individual taking the original position must choose principles that "define the appropriate distribution of the benefits and burdens of social cooperation" without knowing "his class position or social status," "his fortune in the distribution of natural assets and abilities, his intelligence and strength, and the like." More specifically, Rawls proposes that the "justice of laws and policies is to be assessed . . . from the position of a representative legislator who . . . does not know the particulars about himself."

Rawls's theory of justice and Stage 6 are very similar in structure; the essence of both is the process of reversible role taking whereby a conflict of claims is resolved by deciding which claims would be regarded as most deserving of accommodation by an individual who is behind a veil of ignorance and must therefore give equal consideration to the points of view of all people whose interests are at stake. In order to determine how the death penalty would be evaluated at Stage 6, we must apply this role-taking procedure to the problem of capital punishment.

Before we can do this, we must decide whose claims are the relevant ones to consider. Borrowing and adapting for our own purposes a simplifying device employed by Rawls, we may assume that each legislative dilemma involves a conflict between the common interests of one class of people occupying a particular social position and the interests of one or more other such classes. In any dilemma, consideration must be given to all those conflicting claims that are advanced by representative people occupying the relevant positions. In the capital punishment dilemma, the potential conflict is between two social positions. One of these positions, that of capital offender, is occupied by all people who commit the crime that is to be punishable by death. The other position—which we shall call that of ordinary citizen—is the residual category, composed of all people in society other than capital offenders.

The Stage 6 principle of justice as fairness to individuals dictates that we evaluate capital punishment while imagining that we do not know which of these two positions in society we are to occupy and are just as likely to occupy one as the other. Only by doing this can we be assured of giving impartial and equal consideration to the conflicting interests of persons occupying both positions.

On the other hand, we would imagine that, once the veil was lifted, our circumstances might be such that we had no inclination whatsoever to commit a capital crime; that is, we might be an ordinary citizen. On the other hand, we would recognize that we might just as easily find ourselves in circumstances such that we were extremely likely to commit a murder or other crime punishable by death. This latter recognition would grow out of an awareness of several key facts about criminal behavior. Few people who commit capital crimes—murder, for example—decide to do so only after first weighing all the consequences that may befall them. Many social and psychological factors beside rational self-interest play a role in determining whether a person happens to commit such a crime. Most of these factors are not at all within a person's control. Indeed, criminality seems on the whole to be more a function of "natural chance" and "social circumstance" than of free will. Those who are less fortunate than others with respect to their natural endowment and socioeconomic status are much more prone to commit serious crimes. When we have taken all this into account, the rational thing for us to do behind the veil of ignorance is to protect ourselves against the worst consequences that might befall us if we turned out to be one of these less fortunate individuals. One way of doing this is to assess the death penalty from the point of view of someone who takes into account the possibility of being a capital offender himself.

It might be objected that if we take the view of law that Rawls takes—that law is a "coercive order of public rules addressed to rational persons" who know "what things it penalizes" and "can draw up their plans accordingly"—it becomes unnecessary for legislators deprived of knowledge of their own positions in society to take the capital offender's claims into account, because people behind the veil hypothetically know that they can avoid punishment altogether simply by conforming their conduct to law, no matter who in society they turn out to be. But this view of law and the psychology of criminal behavior is unrealistic, for the reasons just outlined.

Although Rawl's view of these matters appears to diverge from ours, his description of law as a system of rules addressed to rational people is qualified in a number of important respects, so that in the end the discrepancies are not very great. Rawls says,

> In the original position the parties assume that in society they are rational and able to manage their own affairs. . . . But once the ideal conception is chosen, they will want to insure themselves against the possibility that their powers are undeveloped and they cannot rationally advance their interests, as in the case of children; or that through some misfortune or accident they are unable to make decisions for their good, as in the case of those seriously injured or mentally disturbed. It is also rational for them to protect themselves against their own irrational inclinations by consenting to a scheme of penalties that may give them a sufficient motive to avoid foolish actions.

In arguing that the parties in the original position are to take into account the possibility that they might act irrationally once the veil is lifted, Rawls takes a position that is not very different from our contention that systems of punishment should be evaluated from the point of view of one who might turn out to be a criminal.

Now we must identify the major claims that would be asserted by the rational capital offender and the rational ordinary citizen. The rational capital offender, obviously, would claim that he should be allowed to remain alive; that is, would oppose capital punishment. On the other hand, the self-interest of the rational ordinary citizen, who knows that he is ineligible for the death penalty, would not dictate that he oppose it. On the contrary, the ordinary citizen may very well have reasons to support capital punishment. He might have a desire for retribution, for example. Or, if he knew that capital punishment served as an effective deterrent, the rational ordinary citizen would probably advocate it on the ground that his chances of becoming the victim of a capital crime would be lower with the death penalty in effect than it would be otherwise. The other claims that might be asserted by rational people in both positions would be relatively trivial and may be left aside.

In order to decide from a Stage 6 viewpoint which of these claims ought to prevail, we must keep in mind that the issue before us is whether the enactment of a system of capital punishment would yield a more just or less just state of affairs than that which would otherwise exist (the latter situation we shall refer to as the status quo), given the assumption that we are to live in an unjust society in which some crimes are committed. When we put ourselves behind the veil of ignorance, we must compare our prospects under a system of capital punishment with our prospects otherwise. Only if we would rather run whatever risks we would have to run under capital punishment than take our chances under the status quo, not knowing who in society we might turn out to be, is capital punishment a fair arrangement. The conflicting claims of the representative parties, just summarized, may be viewed as conflicting assessments of the relative attractiveness of a system of capital punishment and the status quo. In asserting a claim to life, the rational capital offender is expressing a preference for the status quo; in demanding that certain criminals be executed, the rational ordinary citizen is stating that he would prefer his prospects under capital punishment.

We can now attempt to determine which arrangement, capital punishment or the status quo, would seem more advantageous when one is behind the veil of ignorance. Let us first consider the rational ordinary citizen's proposal that capital punishment be enacted for the sake of retribution. The conflict of claims (life versus retribution) that arises in connection with this proposal is not difficult to resolve at Stage 6. If we put ourselves behind the veil, it appears that under a system of capital punishment we would run an extremely high risk indeed. To be sure, if we turned out to be ordinary citizens, we would have the opportunity to participate in collective retribution, for whatever that may be worth. But if we turned out to be a capital offender, we might be executed. On the other hand, under the status quo no such dire possibilities need be faced. If the death penalty were not instituted, then we would risk some punishment less severe than death if we turned out to be capital offenders and would forgo the satisfaction derivable from killing criminals retributively if we turned out to be

ordinary citizens. Facing these two alternatives would clearly be preferable to risking execution. Whatever appeal the idea of retributive
capital punishment may have in the abstract (as a means of revalidat-
ing the social order, and so forth) vanishes altogether once we take an
original position point of view. If we did not know which position,
that of capital offenders or that of ordinary citizens, we were to occupy, we would clearly relinquish the claim to retribution and uphold
the claim to life. The reversible solution to this aspect of the dilemma,
in other words, is to reject as unjust the proposal that certain criminals
be executed for the sake of retribution.

Assuming that capital punishment is an effective deterrent, how
does Stage 6 resolve the potential clash between the rational capital
offender's desire to remain alive and the rational ordinary citizen's
claim to maximal safety from capital crime? This problem is more
complex than that involving retribution, because deterrent sanctions
would be considerably more attractive to parties in an original position
than retributive punishments—attractive enough in some hypothetical
instances, perhaps, to warrant their adoption. The general conditions
under which a legislator behind the veil of ignorance would agree to a
particular deterrent sanction would be these: if the prospects of one
who did not know who in society he was to be were better under the
proposed system of punishment than under the status quo, then he
would rationally consent to such a system. This might conceivably be
the case if the risk of being victimized by crime under the status quo
were grave enough, the deterrent effect of the proposed penalty great
enough, and the penalty mild enough. Of course, in some cases it may
be difficult to determine the precise point at which the rational individual behind the veil would prefer prospects under the proposed system of punishment to prospects otherwise. But this problem does not
arise in the case of capital punishment. There are two considerations
that would lead a person in the original position to rule out the death
penalty as an acceptable criminal sanction.

The primary consideration that leads to rejection of the death penalty at Stage 6 is that, from an original position point of view, it would
never be rational to prefer one's prospects under capital punishment to
one's prospects under an alternative system, no matter how great a
deterrent effect the death penalty might have. Let us assume that capital punishment is as desirable as it could possibly be from the standpoint of the rational ordinary citizen; that is, it very effectively deters

the most heinous crime of all, murder, when made the mandatory penalty for that crime. Imagining ourselves behind the veil, we would see that, under capital punishment, our risk of being murdered if we turned out to be an ordinary citizen would be much lower. But we would also be aware that, if it so happened that we were destined to commit a murder, our chances of being killed by the state would be extremely high. These prospects are much grimmer than those we would face under the status quo. If capital punishment were not in effect, the possibilities would be (1) taking a higher risk of becoming a murder victim (if we turned out to be ordinary citizens) and (2) risking a penalty less harsh than death (if we turned out to be murderers). Any rational person would rather face the latter set of prospects than the former set. Because the prospect of being executed (the worst thing that could happen under capital punishment) would always be much less attractive than the prospect of being in greater danger of being murdered (the worst thing that could occur under the status quo), it would always be rational to forgo the additional protection against murder that we would enjoy as ordinary citizens in order to avoid taking the chance of being executed if we turned out to be murderers. If this reasoning is sound with respect to the crime of murder, it is correct *a fortiori* with respect to all lesser crimes. In short, at Stage 6 the rational capital offender's claim to life would be given priority over the claim to maximal protection from crime asserted by the representative ordinary citizen.

A secondary consideration that would preclude the adoption of capital punishment at Stage 6 is that from an original position point of view, the penalty of death would probably seem more severe than necessary to maximize deterrence. If we knew that we had the same chance of being the recipient of punishment as we did of being the beneficiary of deterrence, we would opt for the least severe punishment that would effectively deter the crime. It would be irrational to agree to sanctions more severe than this because they would carry no additional deterrence payoff and hence would provide no additional protection if we turned out to be an ordinary citizen but would pose an additional risk if we turned out to be a criminal. In order to find the approximate point at which further increases in the severity of a punishment cease to bring about additional deterrence, we must consider briefly the presuppositions about the motivation of prospective criminals that are implicit in the concept of deterrence itself.

When we speak of the deterrence of crime by punishment, we are assuming that at least some crimes are committed by people who take into account to some extent the consequences that may be in store for them before deciding whether to break the law. Furthermore, we are assuming that such people refrain from committing crimes whenever they perceive the risks as being too high. There is some evidence that some prospective criminals are rational in this sense and that deterrence does operate in this fashion (Tullock, 1974). Assuming that this is in fact the way deterrence works, the optimal punishment for a particular crime (the least severe penalty that would effectively deter rational criminals from committing that crime) from a Stage 6 point of view would be that which was just severe enough to offset the gains that might be realized from the commission of the crime in question, discounting for the probability of being arrested, convicted, and punished.

Keeping this upper bound on severity in mind when we put ourselves behind the veil of ignorance, we would probably conclude that the death penalty is excessively severe. At least in theory, a potential criminal acting rationally would be unlikely to decide that a particular crime was not worth risking his or her life to commit but was worth the risk of a lesser but extremely severe penalty such as mandatory life imprisonment without parole. Even if some people contemplating the commission of a crime would refrain from doing so only if they feared execution, the overwhelming majority of rational individuals would probably be deterred just as effectively by a punishment less harsh than death.

How should the case of irrational or impulsive criminals be handled? Because such criminals give less thought to consequences before committing a crime, they are less amenable to deterrent sanctions. Insofar as they are deterrable, however, less severe penalties than death should, on the whole, prove just as effective. Insofar as they are undeterrable, there would be no reason other than retribution for executing them.

For some prospective offenders, capital punishment probably would represent a more potent deterrent than any less severe punishment. To this extent, the enactment of capital punishment would carry an additional deterrence payoff. Even if the argument that the death penalty is excessively severe breaks down, however, the primary argument outlined previously (that it would never be rational to risk death for greater security) establishes conclusively that the death penalty would be ruled out at Stage 6.

Although here we can only sketch the reasoning that would occur at Stage 6, it should be clear that capital punishment is not an arrangement that we would feel we could live with no matter which members of society we turned out to be. For this reason, capital punishment is an unjust institution. This conclusion is not grounded in the language of the Eighth Amendment. Nor is it contingent on the uncertain facts of moral evolution or of deterrence. The judgment that capital punishment is unjust is unavoidable if we accept the Stage 6 proposition that murderers are to be treated as anyone in their position who also took the roles of others would wish to be treated (as an end rather than as a means). As we have stated, the Stage 6 principle is unique in that it yields a determinate and fully reversible solution to moral dilemmas and defines a mode of moral reasoning that we can justifiably urge all people to adopt. If all people were Stage 6, they would unanimously agree that the death penalty is morally wrong—on grounds that all who took a moral point of view could accept as fair.

The Eighth Amendment, Human Dignity, and Stage 6

Let us review the contentions we have made. The stance individuals adopt with respect to the morality of capital punishment is determined both by their stage of moral development and by their perception of the relevant facts. As moral development progresses, individuals acquire increasingly adequate moral principles, as well as new conceptions of which facts are relevant to a moral evaluation of the death penalty. On the whole, the progression through the universal, invariant sequence of moral stages is accompanied by a radical decline in support for capital punishment. This occurs largely because, as individuals develop more mature conceptions of justice, they systematically narrow the range of considerations that can justify taking the lives of criminals. When Stage 5 is reached, retribution and defense of the social order cease to be regarded as acceptable rationales for capital punishment; the death penalty, at this level, can only be justified in terms of utility or universal human rights. Even in the absence of clear evidence that capital punishment deters serious crimes such as murder, individuals at Stage 4 may nevertheless support it as a means of protecting society or of enforcing atonement for crimes, but on reaching

Stage 5 these proponents consistently change their minds and begin to oppose the death penalty on utilitarian or related grounds. This abandonment of support for capital punishment is the consequence of the factual assumption that the death penalty has not been shown to be an effective deterrent and of the acquisition of new moral principles—principles that are more reversible, more consistent, more universalizable, and more independent of cultural values than conventional modes of reasoning.

Moral evolution is evidently taking place in the United States. It can be described and theoretically explained as moral stage development across social institutions and individuals over time. In part, this evolution takes the form of a movement from Stage 4 to Stage 5. Evolution toward higher moral stages may be viewed as a scientifically precise referent for the Supreme Court's vague notion of "evolving standards of decency." If moral evolution is so viewed, our research points to the conclusion that, on the present state of the evidence for deterrence, the death penalty does not meet evolving (Stage 5) moral standards.

A very small but increasing percentage of individuals further elaborate the principles of Stage 5 and attain the ultimate moral stage, Stage 6, which defines wholly consistent and fully universalizable principles of justice as fairness. By applying Stage 6 principles to the problem of punishment, we can develop a theory of punitive justice based on reversible (original position) role taking. This theory, which provides, in essence, that the justice of penal systems is to be judged from a completely impartial point of view, prescribes the abolition of the death penalty on the ground that it is unjust.

Even if we can succeed in showing that Stage 6 is a fully adequate principle for defining just punishment and that this principle leads to the condemnation of capital punishment, it does not necessarily follow that death is a cruel and unusual punishment within the meaning of the Eighth Amendment. No matter how adequate Stage 6 may be, the Bill of Rights need not be interpreted in terms of this particular principle. We cannot fully explore this constitutional case here but can point out one highly relevant consideration.

Over the years, the Supreme Court has employed a variety of tests for deciding whether a particular punishment is cruel and unusual. When first called upon to construe the Eighth Amendment in 1878, the Court held the standard to be whether the punishment involved "unnecessary cruelty" (*Wilkerson* v. *Utah,* 99 U.S. 130, 1878). Shortly thereafter the Court announced that the test was whether the punishment was "inhuman and barbarous" (*In re Kemmler,* 136 U.S. 436, 1890). More recently, in *Trop* v. *Dulles* (356 U.S. 86, 1957)—the decision in which the "evolving standards of decency" criterion was announced—the Court said that a punishment was unconstitutional if it violated the "dignity of man." This standard was then taken up by Justice Brennan in *Furman* but, as we have seen, very little consensus was reached among the justices in that case as to what the test for cruel and unusual punishment ought to be. In *Furman,* Justice Brennan admitted that his "human dignity" test for cruel and unusual punishment "does not of itself yield principles for assessing the constitutional validity of particular punishments." This statement echoes the Court's long-standing recognition that "difficulty would attend the effort to define with exactness the extent of the constitutional provision which provides that cruel and unusual punishments shall not be inflicted" (*Wilkerson* v. *Utah*).

Wheeler (1972) has described the predicament in which the Court now finds itself:

[T]he tests for determining which punishments are constitutional are vague, apparently conflicting, and perhaps useless, since they do not clearly indicate how to determine whether a punishment is "unnecessarily painful," "inhuman and barbarous," or "contrary to human dignity." Each of these difficulties must therefore be resolved before the Eighth Amendment can be rationally applied to current "penological" problems.

Yet, despite these difficulties, the various standards promulgated by the Court seem to be based on a common theme. The cases suggest that the Court has long been groping for a way of articulating a single underlying moral principle, namely, that punishment incompatible with the criminal's human dignity ought not to be inflicted. One commentator ("Revival of the Eighth Amendment," 1964) has argued that the single "rational foundation for the notion of an inherently cruel punishment as it has developed in the cases" is the idea that

even the most loathsome criminal, justly convicted of a heinous offense by due process of law, has a moral claim upon the society which has condemned him: his humanity must be respected even while he is being punished. The state must not deny what is undeniable: that this man, though condemned, is still inalienably a man.

If, as Justice Brennan clearly believes, such an interpretation of the Eighth Amendment is called for, then a strong argument can be made that the Stage 6 conception of human dignity and fairness to individuals is the only available test for cruel and unusual punishment that is not only philosophically appropriate but also capable of generating agreement among the justices of the Supreme Court as to which forms of punishment are unconstitutional.

Postscript

Since *Furman* v. *Georgia* was decided, in 1972, the Supreme Court has decided several cases involving constitutional challenges to state capital punishment statutes enacted in the aftermath of *Furman*. A majority of the Court has now taken the position that some of these statutes are constitutional. It may be of interest to explain briefly how this new development has come about.

Recall that in *Furman* the reasoning relied on by the five-man majority in striking down the Georgia capital punishment law was varied. Justice Brennan reasoned in terms of what we have called Stage 6 principles, according to which even a convicted murderer has a right to human dignity. Justice Marshall adopted a Stage 5 utilitarian perspective, which favors punishment that is deterrent or rehabilitative but condemns punishment that is imposed for the sake of retribution. The other justices voting against capital punishment—Justices Douglas, Stewart, and White—did so on Stage 5 grounds of formal justice.

The four justices who voted to uphold the contitutionality of capital punishment in *Furman*—Chief Justice Burger and Justices Blackmun, Powell, and Rehnquist—based their decisions in part on their acceptance of the legitimacy of retributive punishment, quoting with approval Lord Denning's Stage 4 defense of the death penalty.

The decision of the *Furman* majority to declare capital punishment statutes unconstitutional was thus the result of an alliance between three justices who concluded that the administration of the punishment was formally unjust and two justices who objected to the death penalty *per se*, however administered, on substantive moral grounds. A number of state legislatures responded to the *Furman* decision by enacting new capital punishment legislation that was designed to render the administration of the death penalty less arbitrary, less capricious, and less discriminatory. Georgia, for example, passed a new law providing that juries could impose a death sentence in murder cases only if certain specified aggravating circumstances were found to exist and that death sentences were to be automatically reviewed by the state supreme court in order to safeguard against arbitrariness.

This statute was challenged in the Supreme Court in *Gregg* v. *Georgia* (428 U.S. 153, 1976). The Court voted seven to two that the law did not violate the Eighth Amendment. The majority in *Gregg* was comprised of the four justices who had dissented in *Furman*: Justices Stewart and White, who had voted with the majority in *Furman*, and Justice Stevens, who had joined the Court in 1975 following the resignation of Justice Douglas.

In *Gregg*, Justices Stewart and White concluded that the new Georgia statute was constitutional because the legislative guidelines to be followed by juries and the appellate review procedure provided adequate protection against the arbitrariness and capriciousness condemned by them and other members of the Court in *Furman*. This shift in position on the part of Justices Stewart and White can thus be attributed to factual differences between Georgia's pre-*Furman* and post-*Furman* capital punishment statutes. The shift illustrates the fact that judgments about capital punishment that are grounded in Stage 5 considerations are contingent on certain facts or factual assumptions.

Justice Marshall's opposition to capital punishment in *Furman*, which was also Stage 5, remained unchanged in *Gregg*, presumably because the factual assumptions on which that opposition was partly based had also remained unchanged. As of 1976, Justice Marshall continued to adhere to the view that there was no evidence to suggest that the death penalty is necessary as a deterrent to crime. Because the only other rationale for capital punishment is retribution—a rationale considered morally unacceptable at Stage 5—Justice Marshall voted in *Gregg* just as he had in *Furman*.

Like Justice Marshall, Justice Brennan was just as strongly opposed to capital punishment in *Gregg* as he had been in *Furman*. In his *Gregg* dissent, Justice Brennan reiterated the same Stage 6 arguments that he had put forward four years earlier. As we have seen, Justice Brennan's opposition to the death penalty rests on moral principles that are entirely independent of factual assumptions. It is therefore not surprising that his position on capital punishment has remained the same, despite efforts by state legislatures to reform the administration of the punishment.

8. Moral and Religious Education and the Public Schools: A Developmental View

THE MAJOR impetus for this chapter was the Supreme Court interpretation of the First Amendment. As an essay by William Ball (1967) indicates, it is possible to interpret the Court's Schempp decision as ruling out any form of moral or ethical, as well as religious, instruction in the school. He points out that the recent Court decisions define religion as embracing any articulated credos or value systems, including Ethical Culture or Secular Humanism, credos that essentially consist of the moral principles of Western culture. He concludes that the Court is in effect prohibiting the public school from engaging in moral education because such education is equivalent to the state propagation of the religions of Ethical Culture or Humanism.

My first reaction to the notion that moral education and religious education are identical in their implications for civil liberties was, like that of most laypeople, one of incredulity and shock. This reaction was especially intense because as a psychologist I have attempted to formulate a conception of moral education in the public schools based on research findings, a conception in which a complete separation of moral and religious education is implicit (Kohlberg, 1966). In this chapter, I focus explicitly on both the scientific findings and the philosophical reasoning that leads me to view moral education as completely separable from religion from the point of view of civil liberties.*

"Moral and Religious Education in the Public Schools: A Developmental View" first appeared in *Religion and Public Education*, edited by Theodore R. Sizer. Copyright © 1967 by Houghton Mifflin Company. Reprinted by permission of the publishers.

* My philosophical reasoning as to the relation of the schools to moral education is hardly original. It is largely a restatement of John Dewey (*Moral Principles in Education*, Houghton Mifflin, 1911) and "The Schools and Religion" in *Character and Events* (Holt, 1929). A recent statement by the philosopher Michael Scriven (*Primary Philosophy*, McGraw-Hill, 1966) forcefully develops a basically similar position, except that he advocates direct teaching of rational morality, whereas I advocate indirect stimulating of its development.

Justice as the Core of Morality

It appears to me that Ball's interpretation of the Supreme Court's ruling is possible only because of ambiguity and confusion in the Court's definition of ethical values as these relate to public institutions on the one hand and to religion on the other. It is clear that the Constitution and the law of the land compose or imply a "value system" or a body of norms, and it is equally clear that the government's maintenance of the Constitution and the laws does not mean the establishment of a religion. Accordingly, the public school's effort to communicate an understanding of, and intelligent respect for, the law of the land and the underlying conceptions of human rights on which it is based does not constitute the establishment of a religion. The school is no more committed to value neutrality than is the government or the law. The school, like the government, is an institution with a basic function of maintaining and transmitting some, but not all, of the consensual values of society. The most fundamental values of a society are termed *moral values*, and the major moral values, at least in our society, are the values of justice. According to any interpretation of the Constitution, the rationale for government is the preservation of the rights of individuals; that is, of justice. The public school is as much committed to the maintenance of justice as is the court. In my opinion, desegregation of the schools is not only a passive recognition of the equal rights of citizens to access to a public facility, such as a swimming pool, but an active recognition of the responsibility of the school for "moral education," that is, for transmission of the values of justice on which our society is founded.

In essence, then, I am arguing that Ball's interpretation of the Supreme Court ruling is possible only if morality or ethics is confused with "value systems" in general, and if it is not recognized that the core of morality is justice. Unless one recognizes the core status of justice, any conscious concern about the school's responsibility for developing the basic values of the society and making citizens as well as scholars will run into difficulties as soon as one tries to define the exact content of these basic values Obviously, the values transmitted by the school should not be the values of an organized minority. Once the school becomes engaged in teaching a particular moral doctrine belonging to a particular group of citizens organized as a religious, political, or ideological body, it may well be accused of establishing religion. The principle involved here would be unquestioned if the schools were to impose the moral beliefs of an organized minority on children; for example, the doctrine that it is wrong to receive a blood transfusion or that it is wrong to work on Saturday. It applies equally, however, if the moral belief happens to be that of an organized majority; for example, the belief of the majority in some Southern states that it is wrong for whites and blacks to mingle socially or to marry. Neither the government, the law, nor the schools represent a vehicle whereby the values of the majority may be imposed on the minority. Both prayer in school and segregated education were the will of the majority as determined by the Gallup Poll before the Supreme Court decision, yet the Court did not hesitate defending the rights of the minority. The basic values of our society are basic, not in the sense of representing majority or even unanimous consensus, but in the sense of representing universal values that either the majority or the minority must appeal to in support of their own beliefs.

The problems as to the legitimacy of moral education in the public schools disappear, then, if the proper content of moral education is recognized to be the values of justice, which themselves prohibit the imposition of beliefs of one group on another. The requirement implied by the Bill of Rights that the school recognize the equal rights of individuals in matters of belief or values does not mean that the schools are not to be "value oriented." Recognition of equal rights does not imply value neutrality; that is, the view that all value systems are equally sound. Because we respect the individual rights of members of foreign cultures or of members of particular groups in our society, it is sometimes believed that we must consider their values as valid as our own. Because we must respect the rights of an Eichmann, however, we need not treat his values as having cogency equal to that of the values of liberty and justice. Public instruction is committed to maintaining the rights of individuals and to transmitting the values of respect for individual rights. This respect should include respect for the right to hold moral beliefs differing from those of the majority. It need not include respect for "moral" beliefs predicated on the denial of the rights of others, whether of the majority or of a minority, such as the beliefs of the American Nazis or Ku Klux Klan.

Formulating Goals in Moral Education

So far, I have claimed that the schools cannot be "value neutral" but *must* be engaged in moral education. I have also claimed that the content of moral education must be defined in terms of justice rather than in terms of majority consensus, if the civil rights of parents and children are not to be infringed on by such education. These claims have been made in terms of the political philosophy underlying the school as a public institution.

When we consider the actual workings of the public school, the conclusions become more inescapable. All schools necessarily are involved in moral education. Teachers are constantly and unavoidably moralizing to children, about school rules and values and about students' behavior toward one another. Because moralizing is unavoidable, it seems logical that it be done in terms of consciously formulated goals of moral development. Liberal teachers do not want to indoctrinate children with their own private moral values. As the classroom social situation requires moralizing by the teachers, they ordinarily tend to limit moralizing to the necessities of classroom management; that is, the immediate and relatively trivial kinds of behavior that are disrupting to them or to the other children. Exposure to the diversity of moral views of teachers is undoubtedly one of the enlightening experiences of growing up, but the present thoughtlessness concerning which of the teachers' moral attitudes or views they communicate to children and which they do not leaves much to be desired.

Ambiguities in "Character Education"

The value problems of moral education, then, do not concern the necessity of engaging in moral education in the school, because this is already being done every day. Value problems arise from the formulation of the aims and content of such education. At an extreme, the formulation of aims suggests a conception of moral education as the imposition of a state-determined set of values, first by the bureaucrats on the teachers, and then by the teachers on the children. This is the "character education" employed in the Soviet Union, as described by Bronfenbrenner (1962). In the Soviet Union, the entire classroom process is explicitly defined as "character education"—that is, as making good socialist citizens—and the teacher appears to have a very strong influence on children's moral standards. This influence rests in part on the fact that the teacher is perceived as "the priest of society," as the agent of the all-powerful state and can readily enlist the parents as agents of discipline to enforce school values and demands. In part, however, it rests on the fact that the teacher systematically uses the peer group as an agent of moral indoctrination and moral sanctions.

The classroom is divided into cooperating groups in competition with one another. If a member of one of the groups is guilty of misconduct, the teacher downgrades or penalizes the whole group, and the group in turn punishes the individual miscreant. This is, of course, an extremely effective form of social control if not of moral development.

In contrast to the Soviet educators, American educators are not likely to take obedience to, and service to, the state as the ultimate content of moral education. Instead, when they have attempted to formulate some general notions of the content and aims of moral education, they have usually conceived of it as the inculcation of a set of virtues: honesty, responsibility, service, self-control, and so on. (Hartshorne & May, 1928–1930; Jones, 1936; and Havighurst & Taba, 1949). The implicit rationale for the definition of moral education in terms of virtues or character traits has been that it represents the core of moral agreement in the American community. In fact, however, community consensus on verbal labels such as "honesty" conceals a great deal of disagreement about what "honesty" is and when it should be compromised to serve another value or virtue. This is indicated by the results of a recent National Opinion Research Center survey of a representative sample of American adults concerning judgments of right or wrong in situations involving honesty.* While in general "dishonest" behavior was said to be wrong, lying, stealing, or cheating were said to be "all right" or not "dishonest" by very sizable proportions of the population in certain specific situations. A majority believe it is right to lie to spare another's feelings, a substantial minority believe it is right to steal to obtain expensive medical treatment for one's wife that is otherwise unobtainable, a considerable minority believe it is all rights to take hotel ashtrays and towels and so on. As soon as one leaves vague stereotypical terms such as "honesty" and attempts to specify concrete moral actions, it becomes very difficult to empirically establish consensus concerning moral values. Does 51 percent agreement represent moral consensus. Does 75 percent? Or does 100 percent? If the latter, our society has no moral consensus. The problem becomes worse if one considers virtues or character traits other than honesty. The lack of agreement about "moral character" appears when it is recognized that each educator draws up a different list of virtues. Havighurst and Taba (1949) include friendliness and moral

---

* Unpublished data, some reported on an NBC television special in January 1966.

courage in the list, while Hartshorne and May (1928–1930) leave these out and include self-control (persistence). "Religious" virtues (faith, hope, and charity) are hard to distinguish from "civil" virtues. What about "respect for authority"—is that a virtue or not? How about cleanliness—is it next to godliness?

Criticism of Present Content of Moral Education

My criticism of statements of moral education content in terms of moral character traits rests on three grounds. First, it is impossible to define the content of moral education in terms of factual majority consensus about good and bad behavior. Although the majority may agree on the value of cleanliness and proper dress, this does not answer the question of whether it is legitimate "moral education" for a school principal to expel boys whose families allow them to wear long hair. In the second place, even if one were willing to accept a majority opinion as defining moral education, vague character traits or labels do not represent majority consensus, because they conceal a great *lack* of consensus about specific actions and values. A parent will agree with a teacher that "cooperation" is a virtue but will not agree that a child's specific failure to obey an "unreasonable" request by the teacher was wrong, even if the teacher calls the act "uncooperative," as teachers are prone to do. In the third place, even if one were willing to ignore the lack of consensus concealed by moral character terms, these terms do not represent objective or observable behavioral outcomes of moral education. Psychologically, there are no such traits as honesty, service, responsibility, and so on. Research to date suggests that these words are only varying evaluative labels; they do not stand for separate consistent traits of personality. Insofar as consistencies of personality appear in the moral domain, they are quite different from labels of virtues and vices (Kohlberg, 1964).

The Development of Moral Judgment

I have so far objected to two conceptions of moral education. The first is the current thoughtless system of moralizing by individual teachers and principals when children deviate from minor administrative regulations or engage in behavior that is personally annoying to the teacher. The second is the effort to inculcate the majority values, particularly as reflected in vague stereotypes about moral character. I shall now present a third conception of moral education. In this conception, the goal of moral education is the stimulation of the "natural" development of the individual children's own moral judgment and of the capacities allowing them to use their own moral judgment to control their behavior. The attractiveness of defining the goal of moral education as the stimulation of development rather than as teaching fixed virtues is that it means aiding children to take the next step in a direction toward which they are already tending, rather than imposing an alien pattern on them. Furthermore, the stimulation of natural development as the basis of moral education coincides with my earlier statement that the legitimate moral values that the school may transmit are the values of justice.*

A Universal Definition of Morality

Moral development in terms of the stages is a progressive movement toward basing moral judgment on concepts of justice. To base a moral duty on a concept of justice is to base it on the right of an individual, and to judge an act wrong is to judge it as violating such a right. The concept of a right implies a legitimate expectancy, a claim that I may expect others to agree I have. Although rights may be grounded on sheer custom or law, there are two general grounds of a right: equality and reciprocity (including exchange, contract, and the reward of merit). At Stages 5 and 6, all the demands of statute or of moral (natural) law are grounded on concepts of justice; that is, on the agreement, contract, and impartiality of the law and its function in maintaining the rights of individuals. For reasons I have elaborated in Chapter 4, it is quite reasonable psychologically to expect similar conceptions of justice to develop in every society, whether or not they become the official basis of political morality as they have in the United States.

To a large extent, a conception of moral development in terms of justice coincides with a culturally universal definition of morality. In my view a culturally universal definition of morality can be arrived at if morality is thought of as the form of moral judgments instead of the content of specific moral beliefs. Although philosophers have been un-

---

* Justice (respect for the rights of others based on considerations of equality and reciprocity) includes the other cardinal American value of liberty. It also partially includes the second major moral value of benevolence (consideration of the welfare of all other individuals).

able to agree on any single ultimate principle that would define "correct" moral judgments, most philosophers concur on the characteristics that make a judgment a genuine moral judgment (Hare, 1952; Kant, 1949a).

Moral judgments are judgments about the right and the good of action. Not all judgments of "good" or "right" are moral judgments, however; many are judgments of esthetic, technological, or prudential goodness or rightness. Unlike judgments of prudence or esthetics, moral judgments tend to be universal, inclusive, and consistent and to be grounded on objective impersonal, or ideal grounds.

In similar fashion, when a ten-year-old answers the "moral should" question "Should Joe tell on his older brother?" in Stage 1 terms of the probabilities of getting beaten up by his father and by his brother, he does not answer with a moral judgment that is universal (applies to all about the situation) or that has any impersonal or ideal grounds. In contrast, Stage 6 statements not only specifically use moral words such as "morally right" and "duty" but use them in a moral way: "Regardless of who it was" or "By the law of nature or of God" imply universality, "Morally I would do it in spite of fear of punishment" implies impersonality and ideality of obligation, and so on. Thus the responses of lower-level subjects to moral judgment matters are not moral responses in somewhat the same sense that the value judgments of high-level subjects about esthetic or morally neutral matters are not moral. In this sense, we can define a moral judgment as "moral" without considering its content (the action judged) and without considering whether it agrees with our own judgments or standards. It is evident that our stages represent an increasing disentangling or differentiation of moral values and judgments from other types of values and judgments. With regard to a particular aspect—for example, the value of life—the moral value of the person at Stage 6 has become progressively disentangled from status and property values (Stage 1), from instrumental uses to others (Stage 2), from the actual affection of others for him or her (Stage 3), and so on.

A definition of the aim of moral education as the stimulation of natural development appears, then, to be clear-cut in the area of moral judgment, which has considerable regularity of sequence and direction in development in various cultures. Because of this regularity, it is possible to define the maturity of a child's moral judgment without considering its content (the particular action judged) and without considering whether or not it agrees with our own particular moral judgments or values or those of the American middle-class culture as a whole. In fact, the sign of children's moral maturity is the ability to make moral judgments and formulate moral principles of their own, rather than their ability to conform to moral judgments of the adults around them.

Moral Judgment and Moral Behavior

I have so far talked about the development of moral judgment as an aim of moral education. The sheer capacity to make genuinely moral judgments is only one portion of moral character, however. One must also apply this judgmental capacity to the actual guidance and criticism of action. Thus, in addition to stimulating the development of general moral judgment, a developmental moral education would stimulate children's application of their own moral judgment (not the teacher's) to their actions. The effort to force children to agree that an act of cheating is very bad when they do not really believe it will only encourage morally immature tendencies toward expedient outward compliance. In contrast a more difficult but more valid approach involves getting children to examine the pros and cons of their conduct in their own terms (as well as introducing more developmentally advanced considerations).

Although we cannot yet be sure that the stimulation of development of moral judgment will result in moral conduct, research indicating considerable correspondence between level of judgment and conduct in children provides some optimism on this score (Kohlberg, 1966).

Morality and Religion

It is clear that the conception of the words *moral* and *moral education* just advanced distinguishes moral judgment and development from other types of value judgment and development, including religious development. In fact, we find remarkably little use of religion in American children's responses to moral dilemmas, regardless of denomination. In less religiously pluralistic societies, such as Turkey, more religious concepts are introduced into moral responses, but mostly at lower levels of development (Stages 1 through 4). Preadolescent Turkish boys typically say that one should not steal because "Good

Moslems don't steal" and because "God would punish you." They also believe it is worse to steal from a fellow Moslem than from a Christian. As they develop further, they elaborate more intrinsically moral or justice-based reasons for not stealing and use less "religious" reasons. At higher levels, religion may be invoked as the ultimate support for universal human values, but moral action is not justified in terms of conformity to God or to the religious community. Because a morality of justice evolves in every society or religious group, then, a morality of justice cannot be said to represent the beliefs of religious sects such as Humanism or Ethical Culture or even to represent the "Judeo-Christian tradition."

Our evidence of culturally universal moral stages, then, is also direct evidence against the view that the development of moral ideologies depends on the teachings of particular religious belief systems. No differences in moral development due to religious belief have yet been found. Protestant, Catholic, Moslem, and Buddhist children go through the same stages at much the same rate when social class and village-urban differences are held constant. With regard to the content of moral beliefs, religious differences exist, such as differences in views of birth control, divorce, and eating pork. When members of given religious groups attempt to support these beliefs, however, they fall back on the general forms of moral judgment or moral principles described by the stages discussed earlier, forms that develop regardless of religious affiliation. The same distinctions between specific values and basic moral principles must be made in considering sociological studies of religious differences in values. For instance, values of educational and entrepreneurial achievement have been held to be favored by "the Protestant ethic" or the "Jewish ethic" as opposed to the "Catholic ethic." There is considerable evidence of such differential emphases in various religious traditions, but it should not obscure the common moral ideas and principles that seem to develop equally in all. All religious and nonreligious belief systems distinguish worldly achievement from conformity to moral principles and stress the latter regardless of different notions of the linkage between the two.

Religious people may readily accept the idea that moral principles develop regardless of religious belief. Since St. Thomas Aquinas, a great deal of theological doctrine has held that moral principles are grounded on natural reason rather than on revelation. It is more difficult, however, for most religious people to accept the thought that actual behavioral adherence to moral principles is independent of religious belief or commitment. They feel that their morality and their religion are closely bound together. In a recent nationwide National Opinion Research Center survey, a large majority of Americans stated that their morality was dependent on their religious beliefs. Subjectively, they may be correct. Objectively, however, empirical studies from Hartshorne and May (1928–1930) onward have found no relation between experimental measures of honesty and type or amount of religious participation or education. Cross-national comparisons suggest the same conclusions as the Hartshorne and May findings. Theft, deceit, and juvenile delinquency are low in some atheistic societies (Soviet Russia, Israeli atheistic kibbutzim) as well as in some Buddhist and Christian societies, while some strongly religious nations have high rates of dishonesty (Islamic Middle Eastern nations, Italy, Mexico, and so on). Although we should not conclude from these and other findings that there is no relation between religious experience and moral character, we can conclude that religion is not a necessary or highly important condition for the development of moral judgment and conduct.*

In summarizing findings suggesting the very limited influence of religious education on moral development, I am not attempting to argue that religious education may not be capable of playing a role in moral development. I am arguing that formal religious education has no specifically important or unique role to play in moral development, as opposed to the role of the public school and the family in this area. The primary purpose of religious education in our society is not to develop moral character but rather to develop religious beliefs and sentiments. The teaching of religious beliefs requires a teaching of their moral aspects as well as their theological aspects, because all

---

* Relations between conduct and religious experience may be more apparent where the given moral behavior depends largely on specific religious proscriptions than where it is based on general secular principles of justice. In contrast to findings on honesty, Kinsey (A. C. Kinsey and others, *Sexual Behavior in the Human Female,* Saunders, 1953) indicates that both premarital and extramarital sexual behavior is related to religious devoutness and, to a slighter extent, to religious denomination. The suggestion is also that subjective moral attitudes may be related to moral behavior even if the amount of institutional religious exposure is not. However, we cannot safely draw either of these conclusions because moral attitudes may determine religious ones rather than the reverse. For example, the Kinsey finding may be due to the tendency of young people who fear or condemn sexuality to become religiously devout, rather than vice versa.

religions stress an associated moral code. On the whole, however, the mark of success of such teaching is that it helps children to make religious and moral beliefs and sentiments an integrated whole, not that it leads to the formulation of basic moral values not formed elsewhere. Part-time religious education can hardly take as its goal fitting the child for moral citizenship and is fortunate if it can achieve its primary goal of creating religious meanings in the child's experience.

The Classroom Climate

In contrast to institutions of part-time religious education, the public school is the most important environment of the child outside the home. Although the Hartshorne and May findings did not show that specific religious or character education classes had a strong effect on moral conduct, they did demonstrate that the total school or classroom atmosphere had an extremely important influence on such conduct. By and large, basic morality develops "naturally" through a variety of intellectual and social stimulations in the home, the peer group, and the school; it does not require systematic programs of indoctrination. However, recent research suggests that the school may play a positive role in stimulating this development and suggests some lines along which this may be done (Kohlberg, 1966). Regardless of quantitative findings, the definition of the public school as fitting the child for citizenship and the pervasiveness of moral issues in classroom life and curriculum require explicit educational thought about the moral objectives of education. As an example, recent work by Blatt (Blatt and Kohlberg, 1975) suggests that discussion of moral dilemmas involving issues of law in the context of social studies curriculum for preadolescents entails just the sort of stimulation of upward movement of stages of moral thought one might elaborate if one were concerned with moral education as an explicit school function. It would be unfortunate, then, if the outcome of the recent Supreme Court decision were to inhibit our recognition that an ultimate statement of the social aims and processes of public education must be couched in moral terms.

PART FOUR

Moral Stages and
Problems Beyond Justice

॥

THIS BOOK thus far has dealt entirely with one set of problems, the problems of justice, and with stages of moral judgments of rights and duties as they help illuminate these problems. The field of ethics, as treated in such classics as Aristotle's and Spinoza's *Ethics,* deals with a much broader range of problems and ideas than is encompassed by the idea of justice. Ethics deals with statements about the nature of the good life and the good person resting on a general picture of human nature and the human condition, a picture that includes metaphysical or religious perspectives as well as the perspectives on which we have focused so far.

In a contemporary text called *Ethics,* Frankena (1963, p. 9) tells us that there are three kinds of normative or moral judgments studied by the field called *ethics:* "judgments of moral obligation or *deontic judgments,* which say a certain action is right or obligatory; judgments of morally good or *aretaic judgments,* which say that certain persons, motives, or traits of character are morally good, virtuous; and *judgments of nonmoral value* in which we evaluate not so much actions and persons but all sorts of other things, paintings, experiences, forms of government, and what not.

Our stages of moral development have been primarily stages of the development of deontic judgment, or judgments of obligation and of the right in action. At least at higher stages, the core of the structures of deontic judgments are justice structures or judgments of rights, such that the highest stage, Stage 6, achieves a correlation of duties and rights. The hypothetical (or real) dilemmas about which judgments are made by our subjects are justice dilemmas. They ask for judgments of right and of duty in situations involving conflicting claims of people.

It is quite possible that there may be something like stages in the development of ethical and religious thinking and attitudes. These stages may in some ways parallel our moral justice stages, but they may also differ from them, because they focus not only on justice or deontic judgment but also include thinking about the good life (judgment of nonmoral value) and the good person (aretaic judgments) as well. Furthermore, they may not only be stages of thinking about what ought to be or what is desirable but may also be stages in thinking about what human nature and the human condition is.

In Chapter 9, Clark Power and I outline an account of stages of ethical and religious thinking, drawing on the work of our friend and colleague, James Fowler. Fowler has been influenced by our account of moral stages in developing his stage conceptions. Because he is a Christian theologian as well as a developmental psychologist, he conceives of his six stages as stages of faith. In Chapter 9, we conceptualize aspects of Fowler's stages as stages of religious thinking paralleling the moral stages.

Our approach, like Fowler's assumes that there are universal religious issues or problems that all people attempt to answer with or without a belief in God and with or without religious affiliation or creed. These issues are limiting issues or issues that entail some reflection on life in relation to the infinite, unlimited, or eternal. With regard to morality, the fundamental issue that religious thinking may address is "Why be moral? Why be just in a universe that is not manifestly just?"

Essay 9 explores some answers to this question, including "Stage 7" (roughly equivalent to Fowler's sixth stage of faith), a metaphoric post-conventional stage of religious orientation attained after the achievement of principled morality. We report data and logical considerations suggesting that attainment of a given moral stage is necessary but not sufficient for attainment of the parallel stage of ethical and religious thinking.

From a philosophic point of view, the central issue raised by stages of ethical and religious thinking is how a highest or sixth stage of such thinking relates to our account of a highest moral stage focused on principles of justice. Many religious accounts suggest that a highest ethical and religious stage centers on *agape* or universal responsible love, forgiveness, and compassion "beyond justice" (or beyond our highest moral stage). From this point of view, agape may be viewed as a "competitor" for Stage 6, an alternative conception of a highest moral stage to the conception of Stage 6 justice. In Chapter 9, after presenting some examples of "Stage 7," of a highest stage of religious thinking with its own ethical implications, we try to show why it is not simply an alternative conception of a highest moral stage.

We argue that to view "Stage 7" as a competitive version of a sixth or highest stage of moral judgment leads to three problems. First, if a "Stage 7" agape is to be used to resolve moral conflicts, it cannot violate or ignore the basic principles of justice. Agape is, properly speaking, an orientation leading to acts of supererogation and not a substitute for principles of justice.

Second, if "Stage 7" were only an alternative form of morality, it could not take into account the religious problems that we think it must attempt to answer. Third, agape, unlike justice, arises out of a religious or metaphysical notion of the ideal unity of people with each other and with God or Nature. This religious perspective is then the basis for a mode of action in which the interests of the self and the other are no longer seen as antagonistic but as being in profound harmony.

In summary, issues left only partially answered by our account of moral development as the development of the idea of justice lead us to a more speculative treatment of religious development in a search for answers.

The tenth and final chapter is on tragedy. Why should a book on philosophy have a chapter on tragedy? As Walter Kaufman points out in *Tragedy and Philosophy* (1969), theories of tragedy have been shaped not by literary critics but by philosophers, by Plato, Aristotle, Hume, Hegel, Schopenhauer, and Nietzsche. This is because tragedy both calls into question the morality of its time and yet ultimately reaffirms morality. It is the task then, of a moral theory to deal with tragedy.

In Chapter 10, I stress that the tragic "wisdom learned through suffering" is the acceptance of injustice in a world in which justice still has meaning. It is in a sense religious, although not in any creedal sense. The tragic hero is one who attempts to take justice into his or her own hands. The tragic wisdom learned through suffering is that taking justice into one's own hands is not just and that it unleashes destruction on all whom the tragic hero most loves. This wisdom leads

the hero and the audience to a "Stage 7" orientation "beyond justice"—to an attitude of acceptance, humility, and forgiveness.

In conclusion, the treatment of some of the phenomena of both religion and literature helps clarify that our moral stages, culminating in
rational principles of justice, are not meant to be a complete or ultimate picture of the ethical life. It does suggest that any effort to present a more complete or ultimate picture, however, must find a place
within it for moral stages of justice.

9. Moral Development, Religious Thinking, and the Question of a Seventh Stage

with CLARK POWER

IN CHAPTER 8, I argued for the constitutional legitimacy of a moral education in the public schools that centered on principles of justice, independent of religion. In this chapter, we are not concerned primarily with the legal and constitutional issues involved in public moral or religious education. Instead, we focus on philosophic and psychological theories of the relation between moral judgment and religious thinking. In Chapter 4, I said that philosophic analysis and construction of the concept of moral development must precede empirical inquiry. The same is true for the study of religious development, so we start with a consideration of philosophic issues. I also said in Chapter 4 that the results of empirical inquiry could confirm, revise, or enrich its initial philosophic assumptions. In this chapter, after reporting some empirical findings, we again consider their implications for the philosophic issues raised.

In the introduction to this volume, I said that the best way to clarify philosophic issues and theories is to begin by considering their implications for education. In this chapter, we start by considering the educational implications of two extreme philosophic theories of the relation between morality and religion. The first theory is the fundamentalist theory that morality is ultimately defined by, or rests on, divine command as revealed by the Bible or other documents of revelation. The second theory is Freud's atheistic theory, stating that morality in part, and religion altogether, are "illusions," the product of irrational human fantasies and conflicts.

Divine Command Theory

Although moral development has a larger context that includes faith, it is possible to have a public moral education that has a foundation independent of religion. We believe that the public school should engage in moral education and that the basis of such education should be universal principles of justice, not particular religious and personal values. The American tradition of the separation of church and state is a doctrine of justice, or of the rights of all individuals to liberty of belief. Some have argued that children's rights prohibit any form of teaching moral values in the school. To say this is to forget that respect for children's rights is an expression of principles of justice to which our schools and government are committed. If the school is to have regard for the principles of justice, it must also take some responsibility for seeing that a sense of justice develops in children. To respect the rights of children is to be involved in developing their recognition of the rights of others. In summary, in Chapter 8, I argue for the independence of moral education from religion on legal and constitutional grounds, the principles of Stage 5, which underlie the U.S. democracy.

The constitutional argument for the independence of public moral education from religion made by myself and others is, as far as I know, uncontested by those familiar with the legal and philosophic issues involved. Although uncontested by scholarly argument, my assertion of the need for a secular Socratic and developmental approach to moral education in the public schools, has been intensely contested by a vocal minority among teachers, parents, and school board members. This has occurred in public school systems in which my colleagues and I have given consultation and teacher training toward establishing deliberate programs of moral education in the cities of Cambridge and Brookline in Massachusetts, Scarsdale, New York; Pittsburgh, Pennsylvania; and Tacoma, Washington.

The vocal minority who have opposed deliberate but nonindoctrinative public moral education have usually been literate, sane, and sincere morally concerned people. Their opposition has arisen because they strongly held a particular theory about the relation between morality and religion, the theory of divine command. As an example, at the end of a workshop I was holding for Cambridge teachers, one teacher said to me, "Professor Kohlberg, what you are purporting to do is very dangerous. You plan to engage in moral education. Before you engage in moral education, answer these questions: 'Is there a heaven? Is there a hell?' You should not dare to engage in moral education unless you are prepared to answer these questions." For this teacher, the very idea of separating morality and religion threatened to undermine the foundations of both. Accordingly, he went to the bishop of the city to engage the bishop's support in halting our effort at a secular program of moral education.

In a conversation I then had with the bishop, I found him rather uninterested in my summary of the legal and constitutional reasons for an autonomous moral education in the public schools. In contrast, he was very interested and supportive when I drew on a theory of moral theology other than the teacher's divine command theory. This theory was the natural law theory, which holds that there are universal or natural principles of justice that should guide all societies and that are known to us by reason independent of specific religious revelation or faith. It is such "natural law" morality, I said, that is the fit focus of moral education in the public schools. For the bishop and many other theologians, natural law morality is not the whole of morality. There are, in addition, moral attitudes and duties based on religious revelation, faith, or creed. From my point of view, I said, teaching this religious portion of morality may legitimately be undertaken by the family, the church, and by private parochial schools. It may not, on constitutional grounds, take place in the public schools.

Unlike the bishop, opponents of public moral education such as the concerned teacher often fail to distinguish the sector of morality called "natural law" from the sector based on religious creed or revelation. Failing to make the distinction, they feel that the teaching of "natural law" morality in the schools by rational inquiry will undermine the faith that they see as required for understanding and accepting the sector of morality based on religion. More correctly, they fail to distinguish different areas of morality, believing that all morality is based on divine command, and so will be undermined by Socratic teaching.

Divine command theorists are not opposed to public moral education as such. In Salt Lake City, Utah, where the majority of the population is Mormon, there is a public moral education closely linked to the tenets or creed of the Mormon Church and ultimately based on a form of divine command theory. In other cities and areas of the country, proponents of divine command theory are more likely to oppose any form of public moral education as a violation of the right to liberty of conscience of a given sect as a minority group. In discussions about public moral education, sophisticated divine command theorists often shift from moral-religious absolutism to moral-religious relativism with bewildering speed. Morality is in one context like the home, an absolute commanded by the God of their sect, and in another context like the public school, something totally relative to one's religious affiliation and hence an area without universals that might ground a public education. As one parent, a sophisticated, religiously orthodox, university professor, said to me after a school committee debate about moral education, "I have the right to indoctrinate my children until they are eighteen and the school should keep its cotton-picking hands off their values until that age."

This opposition of proponents of divine command theory to rational and Socratic moral education is as old as Socrates. The assembly of Athens voted to give Socrates the hemlock poison for corrupting the youth of Athens because the assembly was convinced to do so by proponents of divine command theory. Today, as in the days of Socrates, many proponents of divine command theory oppose the Socratic view that principles of justice must be forged in questioning and must be able to rationally withstand it, because they believe such questioning weakens a morality based on divine command and respect for divine authority.

In fact, divine command theorists are wrong in thinking that the Socratic approach weakens moral development. In Chapter 8, I briefly reviewed two bodies of research evidence. The first body of evidence showed that religious affiliation and religion-related indoctrinative "character education" failed to strengthen morality either in the area of moral conduct, as studied by Hartshorne and May (1928–1930), or in the area of development of moral judgment as studied by myself and my colleagues. The second body of evidence showed that a Socratic and developmental moral education did strengthen morality, clearly in the sense of development of moral judgment, less clearly in actual moral conduct (studies reported in Volume III).

In fact, divine command theorists are correct in viewing Socratic education as a danger, not to morality, but to their own views or theory—divine command theory is not a theory that can withstand Socratic questioning in a logical and consistent manner. In the *Euthyphro,* Plato records a dialogue between Socrates and Euthyphro, a believer in divine command theory. Euthyphro has denounced his father for what Euthyphro believes is an act of impiety. Euthyphro believes his own denunciation of his father is an act of piety. Socrates asks Euthyphro to define piety, and Euthyphro defines it as "acting in a way the gods approve (or that the gods command)." Socrates attempts to get Euthyphro to clarify whether an act is virtuous or pious because the gods command or approve the action or whether the gods approve the action because it is virtuous or pious in light of some standard or quality of the action independent of the gods' approval. Euthyphro is totally unable to address the question and gets lost in confusion as a result.

The logical confusion in Euthyphro's mind, as well as in the minds of modern proponents of divine command theory, is the confusion discussed at length in Chapter 4 as the "naturalistic fallacy." The naturalistic fallacy is the general fallacy that "ought" statements can be directly derived from, or reduced to, "is" statements. The particular form of the fallacy involved in divine command theory is the fallacy that "X ought to be done" or "X is just" can be derived from the statement "X is a command of God," "X is in the Bible," "X is one of the Ten Commandments," "X will be rewarded by God," and so on. Such statements are similar in form to statements that X is right because "X is approved by the majority on the Gallup Poll," critiqued in Chapter 4.

The starting point of rational discourse about the relation of morality and religion, then, is the recognition in some degree of the autonomy of morality and moral discourse from any other form of discourse, whether religious, scientific, or political.

In Chapter 4, I pointed out that our own approach to the study of morality started with the assumption of the autonomy of morality and moral principles rather than deriving moral development from, or reducing it to, something else, such as religious attitudes or principles.

Emotivistic Theories of Morality and Religion: The Freudian View

In Chapter 4, I also gave our reasons for philosophically rejecting emotivistic theories of moral judgment. Emotivism is an offshoot in ethics of the general philosophy called "positivism" or "logical positivism." Emotivists say that moral judgments have no meanings as statements of truth or falsity, in contrast to scientific judgments or statements that have meaning as predictors of sense data. Denying kinds of meaning and validity other than scientific truth meaning, emotivists say that the only meaning of moral judgments is as expressions of emotional states of approval and disapproval. In the religious domain, emotivists deny that "God-talk" has meaning other than as expressions of emotions such as adoration, penitence, and the need for security. Emotivists may think of themselves as either agnostics or atheists, because they deny that religion has any cognitive content.

Probably the most important and knowledge-producing emotivist theory of morality and religion is that of Freud. According to Freud, moral judgments are primarily expressions of the constellation of emotional structures termed the *superego*. The superego is conceived of partly as culturally universal in its direction against incest and aggression in the family, partly as arbitrary and relative in incorporating the arbitrary norms of the culture and the parents. In any case, the foundations of moral judgment are irrational and relative (Gilligan, 1976). Although the superego and the moral judgments and sense of guilt that arise from it, have no direct rational basis, the superego serves a necessary function, the control of antisocial impulses and desires. The superego and its guilt are according to Freud (1930) the origin of both *Civilization and Its Discontents.*

An even stronger emotivism is at the center of the Freudian account of religious judgment. Although morality has a necessary function of maintaining social order and survival, religion is an illusion analogous to a collective neurosis, according to Freud. One side of religion is mystical emotion, the "oceanic feeling" that derives from the primal sense of the union of infant and mother. A more important side is a mixed fear of, and love for, the father, which is the source of reverence for God, the heavenly father, and of religious rituals of appeasement.

A generation of neo-Freudian development has softened the impact of Freud's own courageous and harsh atheistic view of religion and morality. In the hands of Erikson, neo-Freudian interpretation gives rise to a sensitive psychology of the adult moral and religious development and attitudes of Luther and Gandhi. (Later in this chapter, we draw on Erikson's concepts of adult stages of generativity and integrity in relation to adult ethical and religious development.) Philosophically, however, Erikson does not really provide a way out from Freud's reduction of religious judgments and meanings to emotive states rooted in childhood illusions and conflicts.

From an educational point of view, the implications of a Freudian theory of morality and religion become rather similar to those of divine command theory. Both agree that psychologically morality is the product of, and rests upon, "divine command"; that is, morality consists of a set of arbitrary rules grounded in attitudes of respect for an ultimate authority figure. Both agree that rational inquiry weakens, rather than strengthens, a religiously colored morality. For Freud, the ideal is "Where id and superego were, there shall ego be." If the Freudian program were successfully carried out, the results would be a person who shares Freud's philosophy. The person would have an ego morality, an honest and consistent morality recognized as the necessary price of social order, and a view of religion as a set of universal myths perhaps necessary to support the morality of the unenlightened but not those able to think rationally and scientifically.

In summary, the Freudian theory and divine command theory agree in the view that religious thinking and scientific thinking are opposed to one another and that a rational and Socratic approach to moral and religious education is not viable. Dewey (Ratner, 1939, p. 1003) brings out the similarity of viewpoint between fundamentalism and militant atheism as follows:

Religions have traditionally been allied with ideas of the supernatural. There are many who hold that nothing worthy of being called religious is possible apart from the supernatural. The opposed group think that the advance of culture and science has completely discredited the supernatural and with it all religions that were allied with belief in it. But they go beyond this point. The extremists in the group believe that, with elimination of the supernatural, not only must historic religions be dismissed but with them everything of a religious nature. When anthropological and psychological knowledge has developed the all-too-human source from which religious beliefs and practices have sprung, everything religious must, they say, also go. There is one idea held in common by these two opposed groups: identification of religion with the supernatural.

Natural Law Theories of Morality and Religion

We have rejected two theories of the relation between morality and religion: divine command theory and atheistic emotive theory (in its Freudian form). We have suggested that there is a class of theories about the relations between morality and religion that we do accept: theories of natural law. We will try to be more exact about the meaning of natural law theory and the reasons we support it after we discuss the relation of religious thinking to the broader area of ethical reasoning and report some empirical data on the development of religious thinking. In a sense, however, an empirical investigation of the relations between moral and religious development might not even be undertaken without some prior commitment to natural law theory.

Investigation in this area was not initiated by ourselves but by James Fowler (1976, 1978), a Protestant theologian as well as a developmental psychologist. Although Fowler himself does not explicitly link his investigations to a prior natural law framework, the greatest understanding and acceptance of his work has come from Catholic theologians familiar with a natural law framework, from Protestant theologians familiar with Tillich's (1952) version of natural law theory, and from Jewish theologians familiar with a natural law framework that goes back to Maimonides.

We introduce our idea of natural law theory by noting that it has been the theory held by our exemplars of education for justice. In Chapter 2 of this volume, I cited two great moral educators who willingly sacrificed their lives to their mission as educators for justice—Socrates and Martin Luther King. Socrates, like Martin Luther King, was a profoundly religious man who held a natural law theory of the relations between morality and religion. Indeed, it is doubtful that either King or Socrates would have calmly faced his own death, or sacrificed his life for, principles of justice if his principles did not have some religious support. Their willingness to die for moral principles was partly based on their faith in moral principles as an expression of human reason and partly on their faith in justice, which had religious support. This support was not the support offered by divine command theory, which equates "higher law" with God's commandments. Rather, the support comes from seeing principles of justice as not only a social contract to resolve conflicts in a civil society but as the reflection of an order inherent in both human nature and in the natural or cosmic order.

Socrates and Martin Luther King recognized that their own questioning of society's laws must occur in a context in which civil disobedience was civil, public, and informed by respect for law. Both recognized, however, a natural "higher law" grounded in human reason and prescribing respect for human personality. In his "Letter from a Birmingham Jail" (1965), King explained his conception of the relation of civil law to natural law principles of justice.

One may well ask, "How can you advocate breaking some laws and obeying others?" The answer lies in the fact that one has not only a legal but a moral responsibility to obey just laws. One has a moral responsibility to disobey unjust laws, though one must do so openly, lovingly and with a willingness to accept the penalty. An individual who breaks a law that conscience tells him is unjust, and accepts the penalty to arouse the conscience of the community, is expressing in reality the highest respect for law. An unjust law is a human law not rooted in eternal law and natural law. A law that uplifts human personality is just; one which degrades human personality is unjust.

It should be noted that King had been a student of the "natural law" moral theology of Tillich. A first translation of King's natural law assumption into the theory developed in this volume would state that Stage 6 moral principles enjoining the uplifting of human personality are "eternal and natural law" in the sense that they are the universal outgrowth of the development of human nature. On the side of a psychology of human nature, my theory says that human conceptions of moral law are not the product of internalizing arbitrary and culturally relative societal norms. They are, rather, outcomes of universal human nature developing under universal aspects of the human condition, and in that sense they are "natural." King is assuming more than a psychology, however. He is also making an ontological or metaphysical assumption. He is assuming that our consciousness of justice or moral law is parallel to, or in harmony with, our consciousness of the ultimate power or laws governing the larger extrahuman or cosmic order.

King's natural law assumption is not specific to a particular theology or creed. We cite examples of natural law theory made by pantheists such as the Stoics and Spinoza. The pantheistic view equates ultimate power, being, or reality with the whole of nature or natural law as known by rational science. From the pantheist's perspective, human moral law is a part of the larger natural order or law embodied in the cosmos. We cite other examples of natural law theory made by more theistic thinkers, such as Teilhard de Chardin (1968). Finally, we cite agnostics with a religious attitude, such as Kant, who in a broad sense hold a natural law theory. Kant found the only *knowable* objects of reverence to be the "starry sky above and the moral law within" but felt that the consciousness of moral law required a faith in a parallelism between our consciousness of moral law and the nature of ultimate reality.

Our natural law assumption is perhaps best expressed as the assumption behind a journal for which I (Kohlberg) am an editorial

advisor. According to *Zygon's* statement of perspective, contained in
the front of each issue,

The word *Zygon* means the yoking of two entities or processes that must work
together. The journal provides a forum for exploring ways to unite what in
modern times have become disconnected—values from knowledge, goodness
from truth, religion from science.

Recent scientific studies of human evolution and development have indicated how long-standing religions have evolved well-winnowed wisdom, still essential for the best life. Zygon's hypothesis is that, when long-evolved religious
wisdom is yoked with significant recent scientific discoveries about the world
and human nature, there result credible expressions of basic meaning, values
and moral convictions that provide valid and effective guidance for enhancing
life.

At first sight, one might think that the natural law perspective of
Zygon represents another form of the naturalistic fallacy, like the divine command theory we have critiqued. One may argue that natural
law theories commit the "naturalistic fallacy" insofar as they deduce
moral prescriptions from "facts" about the natural order. The natural
law assumption that we endorse, however, is not the derivation of
moral principles from factual generalizations but is, rather, the assumption that there are certain shared features of the natural order as
known by science or metaphysics and of the moral order as known by
moral philosophy.

Morality as an autonomous domain of practical reason is distinct
from science as a domain of theoretic reason, but there are parallel
structures in the two. There are two levels on which our assertion of
parallelism between the structure of justice as known by moral philosophy and the structure of nature as given by science may be taken.
The first and most straightforward level was already implied by the
discussion of justice as equilibrium in Chapters 4 and 5. There I argued that the natural science study of human moral development is a
form of scientific knowing about morality that parallels the moral
philosophic form of knowing about morality. The argument did not
commit the naturalistic fallacy; it did not derive moral judgments
from, or reduce them to, the judgments of psychology as a natural
science. Instead, it assumed a structural parallelism between philosophic analysis and justification of moral judgment and (natural science) psychological analysis and explanation of moral judgment.

At a second, more epistemological level, the natural law assumption of parallelism suggests that our moral intuitions, or sense of moral order, have parallels in our metaphysical or religious intuitions of a natural order.

From this point of view, moral principles are autonomous; they cannot be derived from or reduced to scientific laws or metaphysical statements. Moral principles, however, are structures that have features that parallel ontological and scientific structures.

In summary, we argue that a structural-developmental account of moral principles and their development suggests some parallelism between well-developed moral intuitions and religious intuitions about nature or ultimate reality. These religious intuitions inform a general "natural law" ontological orientation and support principles of justice.

The Relationship of Religious Thinking to Stages of Moral Judgment

We have argued philosophically that in order to avoid falling into the "naturalistic fallacy" morality must be defined as an autonomous realm of discourse. We now wish to take up the psychological question of the relationship of religious thinking to stages of moral judgment. In order to do this, we must clarify the functions of moral thinking and of religious thinking. The function of moral thinking is to resolve competing claims among individuals on the basis of a norm or principle. The primary function of religious reasoning is to affirm life and morality as related to a transcendent or infinite ground or sense of the whole. Although the functions of morality and religion may be differentiated, they have been seen in the world religions of Christianity and Judaism as intimately related. These religions view God's principal concern as being not for cultic worship but for love and justice. They emphasize that to be in harmony with God people must act morally, but they also stress that people must rely on God in order to live a moral life.

In seeking to understand this reciprocal relationship of religion to morality, Toulmin (1950) points out that the domain of moral reasoning is not fully self-enclosed but that moral questions can point beyond themselves to the religious domain. He argues that if we continually ask for the reasons why a particular norm should be upheld (such as keeping promises), we will, after a time, exhaust the possible moral reasons supporting the norm. We will find ourselves asking "Why be moral at all?"—a question that can no longer be answered strictly on moral grounds. The "Why be moral?" question appears at the limit of moral inquiry and raises a new problem for consideration—the fundamental meaningfulness of human activity. Toulmin states that the religious problem is one in which the individual, finite and uncertain, seeks for assurance in the future. Religion helps us to accept our duty to be moral even in the face of evidence that acting morally will not lead to any tangible nonmoral rewards, such as pleasure.

It is important to note that the religious response to the limit question of morality respects the integrity of the moral domain in a way in which other nonmoral responses do not. The philosopher Bradley (1962) discusses the nature of the question "Why be moral?" in a way that is helpful to our presentation. He states that the question is reasonable but "strange" because "We feel when we ask it, that we are wholly removed from the moral point of view" (p. 60). Bradley refutes the answer of ethical egoism by showing that attempts to base morality on nonmoral ends, such as pleasure, contradict the very meaning of morality. "To do good for its own sake is virtue, to do it for some ulterior end or object not itself good, is never virtue; and never to act but for the sake of an end, other than doing well and right, is the mark of vice" (p. 62). Thus the question makes no sense if we take it to mean "What is the payoff for being moral?" The question "Why be moral?" is a question about the meaningfulness of one's existence as a rational being—a question at the heart of religion—and in some sense requires a religious answer.

Although the "Why be moral?" question may be raised philosophically, as we have demonstrated by referring to Toulmin and Bradley, it is more commonly raised existentially when one is confronted with the tension between one's duty and one's desire for happiness or between one's ethical ideals and the reality of injustice. Not only can we not justify being moral on the basis of a nonmoral end such as pleasure or divine reward, but human experience, as epitomized in the figure of the suffering, upright Job, also reveals that virtue does, in fact, go unrewarded and the just do suffer.

Religion in its theistic and pantheistic manifestations is a response to our uncertainty when faced with moral evil, suffering, and death. Religion offers a way of accepting reality as ultimately trustworthy in spite of the ambiguity occasioned by the gap between the moral ideal and the real, by the existence of suffering, injustice, and death. Religion then addresses questions that arise at the boundary of moral reasoning. These questions are peculiar, because they pertain to the moral domain and yet are not answerable in terms of moral discourse. These questions, as we have discussed them, ask in one form or another "Why be moral?" Thus religious structures presuppose moral structures but go beyond them in the search for answers.

Empirical Investigations of the Relationship of Moral Development to the Development of Faith and Religion

Now we will consider empirical efforts to study religion and its relationship to morality from a structural-developmental perspective. Over a number of years, Fowler (1976, 1978; Fowler and Vergote, 1980) has been engaged in interviewing about 400 people aged four to eighty with the expectation of defining stages of faith that would broadly parallel the moral stages. Fowler defines faith as people's orientation to the ultimate environment in terms of what they value as being most relevant and important to their entire lives. In Judeo-Christian thought, the ultimate environment is defined as a personal God and his kingdom, which is the end point of human history. However, the ultimate environment need not be linked to a personal deity—it is also reflected on in pantheistic and atheistic thought. Fowler distinguishes faith from religion. Faith is largely tacit, a universal quality of knowing and relating. Religion, however, is a particular expression of faith in which concerns about the ultimate environment are made explicit.

Fowler's stages are summarized in Table 9.1.

Table 9.1. Fowler's Stages of Faith Development

STAGE ONE: INTUITIVE-PROJECTIVE FAITH
(average ages: 4–7)

A. Locus of Authority

Fundamental dispositions and their expression depend principally on relations to "primal" other (parents, family, or surrogates). These persons represent power, nurturance, and security. The child's dependence on and affectional ties with them makes them prime authorities or references in his or her construction of a meaningful world. They convey both consciously and subliminally their own basic outlooks and commitment toward the ultimate conditions of life.

Where the faith of primal others is expressed congruently in the language, symbol, and ritual of a religious tradition, those media may take on a character of authority for the child, though the child's reliance on them is derivative and secondhand.

B. Criteria and Modes of Appropriation

Manifest interest in a child and the possession of visible (surface) qualities that attract the child's imagination and interest are required to qualify adults as faith models at this stage. Children attend to and imitate the moods, gestures, and visible practices of such primal persons. The "forms" so observed stimulate and give channels for the children's own projections of numinous intuitions and fantasies with which they try to come to terms with a world as yet unlawful, magical, and unpredictable. Cognitive understanding of the language and actions of commitment of significant others is limited, but affective investment in such often give them formative power in the child's normative awareness of ideal responsibility or adulthood.

C. Symbolic and Conceptual Functioning

Thinking is *preoperational* (Piaget), marked by egocentrism and by the use of symbols and concepts (or preconcepts—Vygotsky) in labile and fluid fashion. Typically there is little concern to separate fantasy from fact. Narrative ability is limited. Causal relations are vague to the child and notions of effectance in the world tend toward magical explanations.

Symbols of deity, where used, are frequently preanthropomorphic with an effort to use such ideas as invisibleness, soul, and air to depict a God who nonetheless acts physically and substantially on the world.

D. Role Taking and Extensiveness of Identification

There is little ability as yet to take the role of others. The child is not yet able to construct and interpret the inner feelings, intentions or reasoning of other persons. Interaction with others therefore is largely a matter of moment-to-moment parallel behavior, as in playing.

Prime identity and attachment are to family or caring group. While there is little consistent awareness of one's differences from other persons or groups, a sense of sexual, racial, and perhaps ethnic identity *is* already forming.

E. Prototypical Challenges with Which Faith Must Deal

A self-system is forming that begins to have both a conscious present and a vague futurity. With growing clarity about the self as separate from others comes a new kind of anxiety rooted in the awareness of death. Now the child knows that death threatens. Those on whom one is so vulnerably dependent can be removed by death. Faith, largely a matter of reliance on these others, needs to find a ground of hope and sustenance beyond them in order to "contain" the anxiety of possible abandonment through their death.

This is not to claim that the child is obsessed with these concerns. There are moments, of course, when they are obsessive and, for some children, actual. But they constitute an unavoidable shadow, an underside of life, which has to be dealt with in some fashion.

There must be some dim but potent locus for authority and forces beyond the immediate, tangible presence of parents or other significant adults. Death, sickness, bad luck as well as their opposites are not totally under control of those who "control" the child. Parents or their substitutes often give evidence of acknowledging power(s) and authority(s) beyond themselves. Some sort of deference must be paid to these powers that transcend and hold even parents in their grip and sway.

STAGE TWO: MYTHIC-LITERAL FAITH
(average ages: 6½–11)

A. Locus of Authority

The realm of worthy authority now extends beyond primal and others to include teachers, religious leaders, customs, traditions, the media, books, and the ideas of peers. The mythic lore, the ritual, the music and symbolism of a religious tradition can make powerful impressions on persons at this stage. As regards matters of perceptual experience the child's own logic and judgment are coming to be relied upon in a kind of empiricism.

Unless they have disqualified themselves, the primal familial group, now extended to take in others "like us" (in religious, ethnic, social class, and/or racial terms), typically still provide the most important models and validating sanctions for the form and content of faith.

B. Criteria and Modes of Appropriation

New role-taking ability enables one now to evaluate and respond to qualities in authorities that are no longer merely surface (as in Stage One). Potentially authoritative persons or sources for faith insights tend to be weighed by criteria like the following: (1) "fit" with the values, style, tastes, and commitments of those with whom one feels greatest emotional affinity and identification, (2) consistency in expressing real regard for the person, (3) appearance of competence and/or interesting qualities that promise access to a vaguely aspired to futurity, and (4) "orthodoxy" (the way "we" do it) as regards the style of religious action. The operation of such criteria is not self-conscious or self-aware at Stage Two, but is an implicit function of the person's belonging to a familial or extended familial group.

C. Symbolic and Conceptual Functioning

Concrete operational thinking has developed. Fluidity of concepts and symbolism has diminished. The child is concerned to understand lawfulness and predictability in relations between persons and in conditions affecting one's life. There is strong empirical bent fostering an experimental approach as regards the tangible world.

Symbols for deity, where used, are typically anthropomorphic. They have power to cause and make; but they also have feelings and will and are attentive to the intentions of humans.

Narrative ability is now well developed. There is interest in myths and heroic images. One-dimensionality and literalism mark efforts to "explain" that which myth and symbols try to convey.

D. Role Taking and Extensiveness of Identification

The ability to take the perspective of the other has developed, though mutual role taking (that is, "seeing myself as others are seeing me as we interact") is not yet possible. The person can take the role of the group, but does not see self through the eyes of the group. Interaction with others is now *cooperative* (H. S. Sullivan) in contrast to Stage One's parallelism.

The person's identity and faith still derive their parameters largely from ascriptive membership in the primal group and its ethnic, racial, social class, and religious extensions, which now have considerable clarity for the person. Those who are "different" are characterized in Stage Two thinking by fairly undifferentiated stereotypical images.

E. Prototypical Challenges with Which Faith Must Deal

The person's world now has a kind of order and dependability about it which results from the experience of continuities and from new cognitive abilities (inductive and deductive logic, capacities for classifying and seriating, understanding of causal relations, and a sense of time as linear). No longer does the person experience the world as potentially so capricious, arbitrary, or mysterious as before. The person operates with a more dependable understanding of the dispositions, intentions, motives and expectations of others— and of oneself. The orderliness or dependability of the (cognitively available) world makes possible a projection of order and intentionality onto a more cosmic theater. Reciprocity and fairness, lawfulness, and respect for intentions characterize ideas of God at this stage.

There are still, however, arbitrary elements and forces impinging on life beyond the ordering capacities of the child. Death, illness, accidents, and the unfolding of the person's own physical characteristics and capacities come as contingent elements of experience.

Faith helps sustain a sense of worth and competence by investing in ideal self-images which, though largely private, do include identification and affiliation with ideal persons and groups. Religious symbols, myths, ritual, music, and heroic figures can provide (where accessible) important vehicles of identification and affiliation. Where effectively offered, they can become means of evoking and expressing the child's or person's faith in a transmundane order or meaning, as well as being guarantors of present and future promise.

STAGE THREE: SYNTHETIC-CONVENTIONAL FAITH
(average ages: 12–adulthood)

A. Locus of Authority

Conventionally or consensually sanctioned authorities are relied upon in the various different spheres of one's life. Criteria for valid authority continue to be a blend of requirements of interpersonal virtues and competence, but now add credentialing by institutions, by custom, or through the ascription of authority by consensus. Authority tends to be external to self, though personal responsibility is accepted for determining the choice and weighing available sources of guidance or insight. Dissonances between valued authorities are solved either by compartmentaliztion or hierarchical subordination. Feeling tends to dominate conceptual reasoning.

B. Criteria and Modes of Appropriation

Criteria for truth are generated from what one feels or thinks on the basis of conventionally validated values, beliefs, and norms. The examples and expectations of "collective others" constitute important sources of criteria. Stage Three differs from Stage Two in that there is now a "collective other" which includes institutional and civil doctrines and law (as well as significant persons) which constitute an implicit value system against which authorities and insights can be evaluated. But there is no ground for other criteria by which one's own most deeply felt and held commitments can be critically evaluated. There is implicitly a continuing reliance on a community (or communities) which sponsor or nurture one's beliefs, attitudes, and values.

C. Symbolic and Conceptual Functioning

Early formal operational thinking is characteristic. Symbols are employed as having multiple levels of meaning, though there is little self-consciousness about this. There is a limited use of abstractions.

There is a tacit system to one's world view, but this system is legitimated by external authorities and inner feelings and is not a matter of critical reflection *qua* system. The person's beliefs and concepts that are expressive of faith function not as theoretical ideas but as existentially valued orientations.

The person is prepared to make do with rather global and undifferentiated ideas and symbols. A penumbra of mystery and deference to qualified authority compensate for the lack of conscious internal linkages and integration.

D. Role Taking and Extensiveness of Identification

Mutual role taking has developed in interpersonal relations. One can now see him- or herself through the eyes of a group or groups. Interaction with others now can be collaborative (H. S. Sullivan), involving full mutuality of role taking with each other and with groups to which there are common loyalties (though such loyalties as yet are not matters of critically self-conscious choice).

Role taking or identification with individuals beyond one's group(s) shows a limited development, but the inability to take the role of *groups* different than one's own is marked. Their world views are likely to be assimilated to one's own. Identity derives from *belonging* (family, ethnic groups, sex role, work unit) and/or *possessing* (respectability, competence, children, and so on).

E. Prototypical Challenges with Which Faith Must Deal

The existential challenges dominating Stage Three derive primarily from new cognitive capacities underlying mutual interpersonal role taking. The person, now able to see him- or herself *as being seen by a variety of significant others* who occupy a variety of disparate standpoints in his or her world, has the problem of synthesizing those mirror images. Moreover, congruence must be found between his or her own feelings and images of self and the world and those held by others.

An amalgam of conventional images, values, beliefs, and attitudes is fashioned to orient and provide boundaries for an as yet incompletely differentiated faith. In theistic expressions of faith at this stage, God is often the bearer of the role of the "collective other" who sums up the legitimate expectations and the individual loyalties of the significant others and groups in one's life. Faith is *derivative* at this stage, as is identity—a more or less promising variant of a larger group style. (*Group* may here be defined by any or all of the following: ethnic-familial ties, social class norms, regional perspectives and loyalties, a religious system, a technoscientific ethos, peer values and pressures, and sex role stereotypes.)

Faith, so expressed and buttressed, serves to provide a kind of coherence and comprehensive unity to one's experience of a now much more complex and ambiguous world. It also functions to sustain ideal self-images and bonds of affiliation with those significant others or sources of values and insights whose expectations, examples, and teachings provide orientation in a potentially overwhelming and chaotic world. By appropriating mainly *vicarious* solutions to life's besetting tensions and by screening out a fair amount of dissonant data, this stage of faith can provide powerful sustenance and a basis for decisive initiatives and action in life. But it has little way, other than denial or oversimplifying assimilation, to meet and take account of world views and lifestyles different than its own.

STAGE FOUR: INDIVIDUATIVE-REFLECTIVE FAITH
(average ages: 18–adulthood)

A. Locus of Authority

Charismatic representatives of ideological options, intensive (if selective) attention to the personal experience of oneself and peers, and/or the ideological consensus of intentional (as opposed to ascriptive) groups, are typical loci of authority for this stage. Authority has begun to be internalized, and criteria for its acceptance are no longer matters of convention. Loyalties are committed on the basis of the self's felt and ratified affinities of valuing, beliefs, style, and need fulfillment.

B. Criteria and Modes of Appropriation

Appropriation of truth or insight is guided by criteria of existential resonance and congruity with what one is becoming or has become. While previously one's world view was part of a matrix of experiencing, authority and an implicit and assumed coherence, now there is awareness that one holds (as do others) a point of view. The reference point for validating explanations has shifted from assimilating them to a nurturing ethos (Stage Three) to measuring them and that ethos against one's own experience, values, and critical judgments.

C. Symbolic and Conceptual Functioning

Full formal operations are employed. The ability to reflect critically on one's faith has appeared. There is awareness that one's outlook is vulnerable and can shift, and also of the relativity of one's way of experiencing to that of others whose outlook and loyalties are different.

There is an awareness of one's world view as an explicit system. There is a concern for inner consistency, integration, and comprehensiveness. Stage Four typically has an ideological quality. There is an excess of assimilation over accommodation, of subjective over objective content. Differences with other world views are sharply recognized and often dichotomized.

D. Role Taking and Extensiveness of Identification

Subject has the ability to treat other groups or classes as objects of mutual role taking. The continued existence and integrity of one's own group becomes an issue of concern, and conscious commitment is possible not only to other individuals (as in Stage Three) but also to norms, rules, and ideological perspectives that underlie groups or institutions.

Concern with group boundaries, exclusion, and inclusion is typical. Purity and consistency are matters of both personal and group concern. Ideal patterns of relation, interpersonal and social institutional, frequently are used to criticize existing patterns, with contrasts being sharply drawn. Derivative identity (Stage Three) has been supplanted by *awareness* identity.

E. Prototypical Challenges with Which Faith Must Deal

The existential challenges or crises activating Stage Four faith center around the issue of individuation. Telegraphically put, Stage Four develops in the effort to find or create identifications and affiliations with ideologically defined groups whose outlook is expressive of the self one is becoming and has become, and of the truth or truths which have come to provide one's fundamental orientation.

The transition to Stage Four involves becoming self-consciously aware of the boundaries of one's conventionally held outlook. This may arise either from confrontation with persons or groups who hold different coherent systems of belief and action, or it may come from experiencing the threatening of one's conventional synthesis under the impact of prolonged experiences of crises that expose its limits. Or it may come from a combination of both these.

The hope and need is for affiliation with a group and its ideology that provides a style of living and seeing which both express and hold up models for further development of one's own individuating faith. Where this cannot be found or where a dominant ethos negates recognition of the need, many persons move into a potentially long-lasting transitional posture, dissatisfied with former Stage Three conventionalities but without materials or models for construction of a Stage Four faith.

Stage Four faith provides channels and guidelines for religious or ideological orientation and for ethical and political responsibility in a world where the reality of relativism is threateningly real.

STAGE FIVE: PARADOXICAL-CONSOLIDATIVE FAITH
(average ages: minimum about 30)

A. Locus of Authority

Authority has now been fully internalized. Insights are derived through a dialectical process of evaluation and criticism between one's most profound experiences and intuitions and such mature formulations of the human-ultimate relationship as are available. Multiple communities and points of view contribute to one's complex world view, which is itself not reducible to any of these. While the normativity of tradition, scriptures, customs, ideologies, and the like is taken seriously, these no longer are solely determinative for the person. Personal methods and discipline have developed for maintaining a living relationship with, participation in, or deference to the transcendent of the ultimate conditions of life.

B. Criteria and Modes of Appropriation

Criteria for truth and adequacy of faith claims or insights now derive from a holding together of intentions for oneself and one's community (as in Stage Four) with intentions and hopes for a more inclusive community or humanity. There is tension between the claims of egocentric or "group-centric" loyalties and loyalties to a more comprehensive community; similarly between "objectivity" and "subjectivity" in the use of concepts and symbols. Stage Five embraces these tensions, accepting paradox when necessary, as essential characteristics of truth.

C. Symbolic and Conceptual Functioning

Stage Five affirms and incorporates existential or logical polarities, acting on a felt need to hold them in tension in the interest of truth. It maintains its vision of meaning, coherence, and value while being conscious of the fact that it is partial, limited and contradicted by the visions and claims of others. It is not simply relativist, affirming that one person's faith is as good as another's if equally strongly held. It holds its vision with a kind of provisional ultimacy: remembering its inadequacy and open to new truth, but also committed to the absoluteness of the truth which it inadequately comprehends and expresses.

Symbols are understood as symbols. They are seen through in a double sense: (1) their time-place relativity is acknowledged, and (2) their character as relative representations of something more nearly absolute is affirmed.

D. Role Taking and Extensiveness of Identification

The person has the ability not only to take the role of another person or group but also to take the role of another person's or group's world view in its full complexity.

Stage Five must sustain political-ethical activity that has a more complex character than at Stage Four. It has a double consciousness not required of Stage Four. With opposing groups, it must acknowledge a significant measure of identification—both in rights and wrongs—strengths and weaknesses. It has the burden of awareness of the degree to which "free will" or choice is always limited in fateful ways by a person's or group's history and situation. It must decide and act, but bears inevitable anguish due to a role taking that transcends its own group's limits. Its imperatives of love and justice must be extended to *all* persons or groups.

E. Prototypical Challenges with Which Faith Must Deal

If Stage Four had to deal with the issues arising out of the individuation process, Stage Five's characteristic existential challenges grow out of the experiences of finding the limits of one's Stage Four ideological and communal identifications.

First there is the issue of a loneliness now experienced as cosmic. One may have relationships with other persons or groups of great intimacy, yet there comes the recognition that one is never fully known nor capable of fully knowing others. Though one may work out patterns of loyalty and commitment with other person or persons, such loyalty is always limited either by will, capacity, or death. Great similarities and commonalities may be found or created with others, justifying celebrations; but even with those who are closest there may be deep-going differences which underscore the final aloneness and uniqueness of the person. One becomes aware of, and faith must deal with, the loneliness arising from the recognition of uncloseable gaps of experience, perspective, and emotional structure between the self and even those who are closest.

Faith must come to grips with the tensions of being ethically responsible but finite. Whereas Stage Four faith generally offers solutions that promise to solve the polar tensions between self-fulfillment and commitment to the welfare of others, Stage Five faith has to come to terms with the tragic character of that polar pull. Stage Five faith must sustain commitment to the worth of ethical action and its costliness even while accepting the realities of intractable ignorance, egocentricity, and limited abilities and interests—in oneself and in human beings generally.

Stage Five maintains its faith vision without the props of authority or ideological certainty that provide guarantees for Stages Three and Four respectively. Faith is a volitional act of paradoxical commitment at Stage Five. Stage Five is faith that has taken its own doubt and despair seriously.

Stage Six: Universalizing Faith
(average age: minimum about 40)

A. Locus of Authority

The matter of authority is now contained within a relationship of unmediated participation in and complementarity with the ultimate conditions of existence. There is a post critical at-one-ness with the ultimate conditions of one's life and of being generally. The paradoxical quality of this in Five is overcome.

The ultimate conditions are differentiated from the mundane; they are kept in creative tension and interpenetration.

Usually some disciplined means is employed to restore a sense of participation in or permeation by the transcendent.

B. Criteria and Modes of Appropriation

Criteria for truth now require incorporating the "truths" of many different standpoints into a synthesis that reconciles without negating their particular or unique contributions. In contrast to Stage Five, this reconciliation of the one and the many is no longer paradoxical, but has a quality of simplicity. For these criteria to be fulfilled the person must have an identification with being in which love of self is genuinely incorporated and fulfilled in love of being.

C. Symbolic and Conceptual Functioning

One is directly and immediately aware of the ultimate context of life. Symbols and concepts play a secondary function, making communication possible, though inevitably distorting. Stage Six draws on insights and vision from many sources, valuing them as helpful, if partial, apprehensions of truth.

Conflicts and paradox are embraced as essential to the integrity of being (similarly to Stage Five) but are unified in a no-longer-paradoxical grasp of the oneness of being.

D. Role Taking and Extensiveness of Identification

Stage Six has the ability to respond to and feel commonality with the concreteness and individuality of persons while also relating to and evoking their potential.

There is the capacity for a meaningful (that is, tested and hard-won) taking the role of a universal community. Active compassion for a commonwealth of being is expressed, including but transcending group differences and conflicts.

E. Prototypical Challenges with Which Faith Must Deal

Faith at Stage Six must meet the temptation to transcend and give way to complete absorption in the *all*. Ethical and historical irresponsibility can result from a genuinely universalizing perspective. Too complete a merging with the eternal now can result in the abdication from time and concrete responsibility.

Stage Six bears the burden and challenge of relating to persons and issues concerned at quite other stages and levels of development. It must do so with patience, compassion, and helpfulness. Faith at this stage must bear the pain and potential despair of seeing ethical causes and movements of compassion exploded or subverted by less universalizing interests.

There is a crucifixion involved in seeing and having to accept the inevitability of certain tragic denouements in history. Stage Six faith must cope with seeing and understanding more than others, and with the challenge and responsibilities of universal identifications.

Faith at [Stage] Six must resist the subtle temptations to pride and self-deception and the danger of corruption by adulation.

Faith must overcome the danger of ethical and political paralysis while at the same time being a source of solutional approaches that introduce genuine novelty and transcendent possibilities into situations of conflict and bitterness and deeply contested interests.

Faith must endure the misunderstandings and slanders and violent potentials (and actualities) of those who cannot comprehend, or of those who do comprehend and are threatened to the core by the person's vision and way of being.

There is the burden of being a mediator, teacher, or semidivine model for others. Faith must maintain, generate, and renew the vision of a cosmic meaning that will help sustain others. This is the frightful burden of being a "Savior of God" (Kazantzakis).

SOURCE: This table was reprinted from J. W. Fowler, "Stages in Faith: The Structural-Developmental Approach," in T. C. Hennessy, ed., *Values and Moral Development*. New York: Paulist Press, 1976, pp. 191–203.

The parallelism Fowler expects between his faith stages and the stages of moral judgment is given in Table 9.2.

In fact, work by Shulik (1979) and by ourselves (Power and Kohlberg, 1980) shows high empirical correlation between the two sets of stages. Shulik reports a correlation of .75 between independently made ratings of moral stage and of faith stage, a correlation almost as high as one would find between two alternative forms of the moral dilemma instrument.

Although there are both theoretical and empirical correlations between our moral stages and Fowler's faith stages, it is uncertain what this means. Fowler's conception of faith stages is holistic and includes, as components of their definitions, Piagetian logical levels and the

Table 9.2. Faith Stages By Aspects

ASPECT:	Form of Logic (Piaget)	Role Taking (Selman)	Form of Moral Judgment (Kohlberg)	Bounds of Social Awareness	Locus of Authority	Form of World Coherence	Role of Symbols
STAGE: One	Undifferentiated combination of basic trust, organismic courage, premonitory hope with admixtures of their opposites—preconceptual, prelinguistic mutuality						
	Preoperational	Rudimentary empathy (egocentric)	Punishment, reward	Family, primal others	Attachment-dependence relationships; size, power, visible symbols of authority	Episodic	Magical-numinous
Two	Concrete operations	Simple perspective taking	Instrumental hedonism (reciprocal fairness)	"Those like us" (in familial, ethnic, racial, class, and religious terms)	Incumbents of authority roles, salience increased by personal relatedness	Narrative-dramatic	One-dimensional; literal
Three	Early formal operations	Mutual interpersonal	Interpersonal expectations and concordance	Composite of groups in which one has interpersonal relationships	Consensus of valued groups and in personally worthy representatives of belief-value traditions	Tacit system, felt meanings symbolically mediated, globally held	Symbols multidimensional; evocative power inherent in symbol
Four	Formal operations (dichotomizing)	Mutual with self-selected group or class (societal)	Societal perspective; reflective relativism or class-biased universalism	Ideologically compatible communities with congruence to self-chosen norms and insights	One's own judgment as informed by a self-ratified ideological perspective; authorities and norms must be congruent with this	Explicit system, conceptually mediated, clarity about boundaries and inner connections of system	Symbols separated from symbolized, translated (reduced) to ideations. Evocative power inherent in meaning conveyed by symbols
Five	Formal operations (dialectical)	Mutual with groups, classes, and traditions "other" than one's own	Prior to society, principled higher law (universal and critical)	Extends beyond class norms and interests; disciplined ideological vulnerability to "truths" and "claims" of outgroups and other traditions	Dialectical joining of judgment-experience processes with reflective claims of others and of various expressions of cumulative human wisdom	Multisystemic symbolic and conceptual mediation	Postcritical rejoining of irreducible symbolic power and ideational meaning; evocative power inherent in and beyond symbol and in the power of unconscious processes in the self
Six	Formal operations (synthetic)	Mutual with the commonwealth of being	Loyalty to being	Identification with the species; transnarcissistic love of being	Personal judgment, informed by the experiences and truths of previous stages, purified of egoistic striving, and linked by disciplined intuition to the principle of being	Unitive actuality felt and participated unity of "one beyond the many"	Evocative power of symbols actualized through unification of reality mediated by symbols and the self

SOURCE: Fowler (1976), p. 205, in T. Hennessey, ed.

moral stages. At the same time that Fowler's stage definitions include the moral stages, Fowler (1976) conceives of his faith stages as being necessary for the grounding of a particular pattern of moral reasoning. In order to engage in making moral judgments, he claims a person must hold a broader system of beliefs and loyalties.

Every moral perspective, at whatever level of development is anchored in a broader system of belief and loyalties. Every principle of moral action serves some center of value. Even the appeal to autonomy, rationality, and universality as justifications for Stage 6 morality are not made *prior* to faith. Rather they are expressions of faith—expressions of trust in, and loyalty to, the valued attributes of autonomy and rationality and the valued ideal of a universal commonwealth of being. There is, I believe, always a faith framework encompassing and supporting the motive to be moral and the exericise of moral logic. [Fowler, 1976, p. 209]

Fowler then argues that his stages of faith or stages of a person's "center of value" provide a more extensive framework for understanding moral motivation and accountability than the stages of moral judgment alone. He points out that one's commitments, loyalties, and sense of meaning in life inform the way in which one acts as a moral agent. In Fowler's approach to faith, no clear distinction may be drawn between one's stage of faith and one's stage of morality, because each moral stage presupposes faith even if such faith is tacit. Fowler is correct in objecting that moral stages alone cannot provide a sufficient answer to the question "Why be moral?" He is also correct in pointing to stages of faith as adding to our understanding of the person's actual moral decisions and actions. We believe, however, that Fowler's broad definition of faith, which does not distinguish it from moral judgment, leads to confusions—confusions that make the empiricial study of the relationship of religion to morality difficult.

Within the broad matrix that Fowler calls *faith* or *center of value* (and Loevinger, 1976, and Erikson, 1950 call *ego development*), we would point to two separable spheres, moral judgment and reasoning and religious judgment and reasoning. In separating these spheres, we do not deny a certain unity to the development of the valuing activity of the human personality. This unity might be best termed *ethical development* rather than either *moral* or *religious development*. Such an ethical unity is reflected in such classical writings as the *Ethics* of Aristotle or Spinoza, which present general pictures of the good life based in part on moral principles, in part on a psychology of human nature and in part on a religious or metaphysical perspective on the human condition. Accordingly, the unity of development that Fowler calls *faith development* we call *ethical development,* within which we shall distinguish partially separable domains of moral and of religious thinking.

In our view, then, moral judgment is a distinguishable area within what psychologists, following Loevinger (1976), tend to call *ego development* and we have just called *ethical development,* a distinction elaborated and examined in Volume II, Chapter 3. Just as moral judgment is a distinguishable area in the overall development of the person, so too is religious judgment or thinking. Although moral and religious thinking are distinguishable from one another, there are parallel stages in the two domains. Furthermore, there are important relationships between moral and religious thinking. Even as we logically differentiate morality from religion, we are also concerned with understanding how the two are related. This chapter's central claim is that religion is a conscious response to, and an expression of, the quest for an ultimate meaning for moral judging and acting. As such, the main function of religion is not to supply moral prescriptions but to support moral judgment and action as purposeful human activities. If this is true, it implies that a given stage of solutions to moral problems is necessary, but not sufficient, for a parallel stage of solutions of religious problems.

Moral Development Is Necessary but Not Sufficient for Religious Development

The notion that moral stage development is necessary but not sufficient for development of a parallel stage of religious judgment is a psychological hypothesis that can be empirically tested. The hypothesis, however, derives from two philosophic assumptions we make. The first assumption is the autonomy of the moral.

The "necessary but not sufficient" hypothesis is consistent with our view that morality should be a logically independent realm rather than the application of religious thinking to moral issues. A small percentage of individuals explicitly appeal to religious concerns in order to justify their moral judgments, but the vast majority do not. It is also apparent that moral development occurs whether individuals have particular religious beliefs or not and that individuals at the highest moral stages differ widely in their religious views. Our hypothesis, then, is almost the direct opposite of divine command theory, which derives moral judgment or consciousness from religious judgment and consciousness.

Our second philosophic assumption is that the development of metaphysical reasoning presupposes the development of more certain moral or practical reasoning. In our view, religious structures are in large part metaethical or metaphysical structures that presuppose the normative or moral structures that they interpret and justify. In Chapters 4 and 5, I tried to clarify the distinction made by modern moral philosophers between normative moral judgments, principles or theories, and metaethical theories. The question "Why be moral?" is metaethical. It presupposes the existence of a normative structure (or stage) of morality that is being called into question. The existence or development of moral judgment, then, is presupposed by, or is necessary for, the development of metaethical judgment and theories. It is not sufficient, however, because metaethical theories or answers to the questions "What is morality?" and "Why be moral?" do not follow from moral principles themselves—they require additional social-scientific, metaphysical, or religious assumptions.

Put in slightly different terms, the idea that the development of moral principles is necessary but not sufficient for a metaphysics of morals (to use Kant's terminology) represents the idea that one moves from the better known or more certain to the more unknown and speculative. Kant held that what was well known or clearly grounded in reason was the (Stage 6) principle of the categorical imperative: "Treat each person as an end, not as a means." Analysis of, and speculation about, the grounding of this principle led him to develop *The Metaphysical Foundations of Morals* (1959) and *Religion Within the Limits of Reason Alone* (1949b).

A similar position is developed in a more psychologically profound manner by the major cognitive-developmental theories of religious development of J. M. Baldwin (1906), John Dewey (Ratner, ed., 1939), and G. H. Mead (1934). These theories hold that the ultimate object of religious faith is an ideal, unified self; an ideal, harmonious, or unified society (or kingdom of heaven); or an ideal, harmonious cosmos. These ideals of harmony are primarily expressions of moral structures or principles: an ideal self is a moral self, and an ideal deity or society is just. As moral structures or principles change and develop, so do the images of the ideal self, society, and deity. These ideal images are speculative and imaginative; they go beyond the certainties of our moral structures themselves. As stated by Dewey (Ratner, ed., 1939, p. 1016),

The connection between imagination and the harmonizing of the self is closer than is usually thought. The idea of a whole, whether of the whole personal being or of the world is an imaginative, not a literal, idea. The limited world of our observation and reflection becomes the universe only through imaginative extension. The whole self is an ideal, an imaginative projection. Hence the ideal of a thoroughgoing and deep-seated harmonizing of the self with the universe operates only through imagination. The intimate connection of imagination with ideal elements in experience is generally recognized. Such is not the case with respect to its connection with faith. The latter has been conceived as a substitute for knowledge. But the authority of an ideal over conduct is the authority of an ideal, not of a fact, of a truth guaranteed to intellect. Such moral faith is not easy. Moral faith has been bolstered by all sorts of arguments intended to prove that its object is not ideal and that its claim upon us is not primarily moral and practical, since the ideal in question is already embedded in the existent frame of things. Starting from such an idea as that justice is more than a moral ideal because it is embedded in the very makeup of the actually existent world, men have gone on to build up vast philosophies and psychologies to prove that ideals are real not as ideals but as antecedently existing actualities. They have failed to see that in converting moral realities into matters of intellectual assent they have evinced lack of *moral* faith. Faith that something should be in existence as far as it lies in our power is changed into the intellectual belief that it is already in existence. When physical existence does not bear out the assertion, the physical is changed into the metaphysical. In this way, moral faith has been inextricably tied up with intellectual beliefs about the supernatural.

Dewey's position on the relation of morality to religion is close to Kant's. Morality is a normative rational structure, but its "grounding" in speculative metaphysics or religion is uncertain and imaginative. Dewey's conception of *A Common Faith,* consistent with agnosticism, is that of the sharing of moral ideals about the truths of speculative metaphysics and religion. After exploring religious development and its relation to a necessary but not sufficient development of moral stages, we take up the extent to which it is possible to go beyond the agnosticism of Dewey and Kant to the natural law perspective.

Empirical Findings on Moral Stage as Necessary but Not Sufficient for Religious Stage

Having explored some of the theoretical issues concerning the relationship of religion to morality, we now turn to an empirical investigation of the hypothesis that a stage of moral judgment is a necessary but not sufficient condition for a given stage of religious reasoning.

In order to compare moral with religious stages, we (Power and Kohlberg, 1980) adapted Fowler's scoring scheme to focus more exclusively on "religious reasoning." The stages of religious thinking were constructed to parallel, as closely as possible, the moral stages, so that they would reflect the logic of the moral stages but represent something more. This is similar to the approach taken toward the relation between logical and moral stages in Chapter 4, "From *Is* to *Ought*."

In Chapter 4, I said that logical and moral stages have parallel structural features and that the moral structure presupposes the logical structure, although the logical structure does not presuppose the moral structure. I based this assertion on an empirical trend we found for a given logical stage to be necessary but not sufficient for the parallel moral stage. Individuals can be at a higher logical stage than the parallel moral stage but the reverse cannot be true. Although this relationship was partly an empirical finding, it eventually became a matter of the prior definition of the moral stage itself. As an example, individuals at the fourth, society-maintaining stage generally showed Piagetian formal operational or "systems" reasoning. Finding this trend, we sharpened the definition of Stage 4 reasoning to include more explicitly this form of thinking as necessary for assignment to Stage 4.

In considering the relation of moral to religious judgment, we followed a similar course. We developed a definition of religious stages that is independent in content of moral judgment but includes structural features of the moral stages. In the Judeo-Christian tradition, in which religious thinking centers on a personal God, it is easy to see how the religious relationship between God and people could be based on the same structure as the moral relationship of people to each other. Beginning with a definition of religious stages as paralleling but going beyond moral stages, we compared the scores of twenty-one individuals who had been interviewed on morality and faith. We found an 81 percent overall agreement. The only cases in which there were differences were in the higher stages (Stages 4 and 5). In all these cases, the moral stage was higher.

Now let us turn to a summary description, based on an analysis of the data, of the parallel structures of religious and moral conceptions at each stage. Our description of the parallel relationship of religious and moral conceptions stresses theistic versions of each stage of religious thinking. This is because it is easiest to draw these parallels of moral relationships between people and of relationships between a person and a personal God. We also sketch pantheistic versions of religious stages from Stage 4 onward. In the case of pantheism, there is a parallel between conceptions of (1) the moral order in human relationships and (2) a cosmic order. We do not yet have data that can deal with thinking about religious issues by atheistic subjects, so we cannot yet trace such thought through stages of reasoning about religious issues. In discussing the stages of religious reasoning, we refer to the work of Oser (1980), who has formulated stages of religious judgment based on administering religious dilemmas to a cross-sectional sample of children, adolescents, and adults in Switzerland.

Stage Descriptions

Stage 1

At this stage of moral judgment, children's thinking is rooted in a sense of obedience to adults, whose authority is based in their superior physical characteristics. God is depicted at the parallel religious stage as also having superior physical characteristics, greatly exaggerated. Thus God is pictured as larger in size, older, and more powerful than the adult figures in the child's experience. For example, one child described God as having the unique ability to "spread himself out" or "split himself up." Oser and his colleagues (1980) note that children think that God caused everything to happen, without ascribing purposes to God's actions. Children are more interested in *how* God creates than in *why*. For instance, one child explained that God created objects by magically saying their names or putting his thumb on them. This failure to ascribe intentionality to the actions of another is a characteristic of both moral and religious thinking at this stage.

Stage 2

At Stage 2, children base their moral reasoning on a sense of fairness in concrete exchanges. At the corresponding religious stage, they appreciate that the relationship with God also involves an exchange. If God is to act in ways that benefit an individual, then that individual must do what God wants. One child put it this way: "You be good to God, and he'll be good to you." Oser and his colleagues (1980) term this a *Do ut des* ("Give so that you receive") orientation. God is depicted as acting purposefully for his own good and the good of individuals. Individuals can influence God to act on their behalf through personal prayer and religious practice. We found that religious crises frequently occur at this stage when an individual perceives his or her prayers to be inconsistently answered. God is seen in such cases as being arbitrary and unfair. This moral judgment of God is an illustration of how moral reasoning can shape a religious expectation.

Stage 3

At this stage, one's moral judgments are based on a desire to meet the expectations of one's community and to do what is necessary to maintain relationships of affection and trust. At this stage of religious reasoning, God is conceived as, in Fowler's (1976) words, "a personal deity"; for example as a "friend" or a "caring shepherd." In relationships with humans, God's love surpasses the love of any human being. God is infinitely loyal, kind, and trusting. God's authority is supreme but tempered by understanding and mercy and guided by a concern for what is truly best for individual people. For individuals at this stage, God is interested not only in making people happy but also in helping them to become virtuous. Breaking moral norms hurts God and brings about shame in God's eyes: "He sees everything. If you don't do what he wants, you are offending him."

Stage 4

At the fourth stage of moral judgment, there is a concern for maintaining the social system. At the parallel religious stage, God is viewed as a lawgiver not only for the social order but also for the natural order. Thus God is conceptualized in abstract philosophical terms such as a "supreme being" or "a cosmic force," which refine the personalistic notions of Stage 3. For example, one young man said, "I don't have an understanding of God in the sense that God intervenes personally in my life. I think the metaphor that I like best is (that my life is like) a compass that is sensitive to the lines of force (God)." In moral reasoning at this stage, subjects conceive of the self as orienting toward internalized moral rules—a conscience. They see the practice of religion as an expression of reverence for both God's order and moral law. There is some sense of what Kant described as a "reverence for the starry skies above and the moral law within." God is viewed as an inner source of order, not solely as a partner in dialogue, as at Stage 3.

Stage 5

This stage of moral judgment is based on a concern for resolving moral conflicts through an appeal to the social contract recognizing universal human rights. What is crucial at this stage is the recognition that a "just" society must respect the rights of individuals. At this stage of religious reasoning, God is seen as an "energizer," supporting and encouraging autonomous moral action. In contrast to what we found at Stage 4, in which human activity was directed toward the fulfillment of a preordained plan, Stage 5 presents God and human beings as mutually involved in a "creative" activity that consists of establishing a community in which the dignity and freedom of each person may flourish.

An interesting religious metaphysic was used by one subject to ground the value of personhood as the basis of ethics. He argued that God, understood as the Trinity, is an "interpersonal being in relationship." If God is the source of values, then it follows that all ethical judgments must be based on this value. He advanced similar arguments in support of human autonomy ("Man is made in the image of God") and human dignity ("Man is becoming God"). The impact of these religious concepts is that they enhance the meaning of moral principles by providing them with ultimacy.

Stage 6

As Table 9.1 indicates, Fowler defines a sixth stage of faith partially designed to parallel a sixth moral stage of judgments of justice and love. His definition of this sixth stage is largely made in terms of charismatic examplars, including Martin Luther King, Mahatma Gandhi, Mother Teresa of Calcutta, Abraham Lincoln, and Dag Hammarskjöld. Before Fowler had started his research on faith stages, I had speculated about a "Stage 7" that would "answer" the unsolved questions left unanswered by Stage 6 moral principles (Kohlberg 1973a, 1973b). Its essence involved, I speculated, the adoption of a cosmic as distinct from (a moral Stage 6) universal human perspective. Exemplars held a "natural law" view of the relation between moral principles of justice and the ultimate. This could be either a theistic or a pantheistic orientation. Spinoza was a pantheistic exemplar.

Spinoza held a Stage 5 or Stage 6 social contract, human rights conception of a social order but articulated a pantheistic conception of the ultimate order. In Spinoza's vision, ultimate happiness or self-realization depended not only on accepting one's place in nature but also on "the active union of the mind with the whole of nature." Experiences of union are cultivated through moral and scientific as well as metaphysical reasoning about the natural order. Spinoza had a Stage 5 or Stage 6 sense of justice and law as being a purely human, rational construction, rather than being created through divine lawgiving. In spite of his notion of morality as a human construction, he still is what we consider a believer in a natural law view as the ultimate support for morality. Thus both pantheistic and theistic reasoning reflect the parallelism between moral and religious reasoning.

These stage descriptions of conceptions of God and the God-humankind relationship illustrate how elements of moral reasoning are taken up in religious considerations. Our data support the hypothesis that it takes additional time after the attainment of a moral stage to construct an organized pattern of religious belief and feeling at a parallel religious stage. Religious thinking involves a reflection on moral reasoning such that one's moral understanding is given religious significance. In this process, ordinary moral language is qualified and transformed to refer to the extraordinary. For example, at Stage 3 the ordinary moral langugage of interpersonal caring is transformed to indicate the unrestricted nature of God's love. In order for these extraordinary, religious conceptions to develop, it appears necessary that first the ordinary moral conception must develop. Furthermore, given the "limit" nature of religious reasoning and its function as providing a transcendent or infinite ground for rational human activity, religious reasoning must comprehend moral conceptions and go beyond them.

In summary, moral and religious reasoning may be investigated as separable domains. However, we believe that there is a parallel development of structures of moral and religious reasoning. Reaching a given structure of moral reasoning is "necessary but not sufficient" for reaching a parallel religious structure. The ethical function of religious thinking is to support the structures of moral reasoning that develop in some autonomy from religious structures. The parallelism between moral structures and metaphysical or religious structures is so pervasive as to give rise to various expressions of natural law thinking. The acknowledgment of this relationship between morality and the nature of ultimate reality does not depend on specific "natural law" theological traditions in either theistic or pantheistic ways of thinking.

The Question of a "Stage 7," a Sixth Religious Stage Going Beyond Justice Principles

We have argued that religious reasoning answers the "Why be moral?" question as it is raised at each stage. Nevertheless, there is a sense in which at the lower stages this question could also be answered with nonreligious reasoning. For example, at Stage 1 an appeal can be made to human as opposed to divine authority and punishment, at Stage 2 to one's self-interested needs, at Stage 3 to the approval of others, at Stage 4 to one's self-respect or to one's role within society, and at Stage 5 to the protection of one's right to pursue one's own happiness socially or individually with due regard for the rights and welfare of others. At Stage 6, however, universal ethical principles cannot be as immediately justified by the realities of the human social order. Such a morality uniquely "requires" an ultimate stage of religious orientation and moves people toward it. As we noted, the religious orientation required by universal moral principles I have in the past called "Stage 7" (Kohlberg, 1973a, 1973b), although the term is only a metaphor—used because it presupposes the conflicts and questions that arise at moral Stage 6. It is roughly equivalent to what Fowler calls a sixth stage of faith and what we call a sixth stage of religious reasoning. This religious orientation does not basically change the definition of universal principles of human justice found at moral Stage 6, but it integrates these principles with a perspective on life's ultimate meaning. One part of the notion of a "Stage 7" comes from Erikson's discussion of an ultimate stage in the life cycle in which integrity is found and despair ultimately confronted. Even awareness of universal principles of justice, typically attained in young adulthood, does not remove the possibility of despair; indeed, it may enhance the sense of the difficulty of finding justice in the world. As we would phrase the problem, after attaining a clear awareness of universal ethical principles valid against the usual skeptical doubts there still remains the loudest skeptical doubt of all: "Why be moral? Why be just, in a universe that is largely unjust?" At this level, the answer to the question "Why be moral?" entails the question "Why live?" and the parallel question, "How face death?" Thus, ultimate moral maturity requires a mature solution to the question of the meaning of life. This, in turn, we argue, is hardly a moral question *per se;* it is an ontological or a religious one. Not only is the question not a moral one, but it is also not a question resolvable on purely logical or rational grounds. Nevertheless, we use a metaphorical notion of a "Stage 7" to suggest some meaningful solutions to this question that are compatible with rational universal ethics. The characteristics of all these solutions is that they involve contemplative experience of a nondualistic variety. The logic of such experience is sometimes expressed in theistic terms of union with God, but it need not be. Its essence is the sense of being a part of the whole of life and the adoption of a cosmic, as opposed to a universal, humanistic Stage 6 perspective.

In religious writing, the movement to "Stage 7" starts with despair. Such despair involves the beginning of a cosmic perspective. It is when we begin to see our lives as finite from some more infinite perspective that we feel despair. The meaninglessness of our lives in the face of death is the meaninglessness of the finite from the perspective of the infinite. The resolution of the despair which we have called Stage 7 represents a continuation of the process of taking a cosmic perspective whose first phase is despair. It represents, in a sense, a shift from figure to ground. In despair we are the self seen from the distance of the cosmic or infinite. In the state of mind we have metaphorically termed Stage 7 we identify ourselves with the cosmic or infinite perspective itself; we value life from its standpoint. At such a time, what is ordinarily background becomes foreground and the self is no longer figure to the ground. We sense the unity of the whole and ourselves as part of that unity. This experience of unity, often mistakenly treated as a mere rush of mystic feelings, is at "Stage 7" associated with a structure of ontological and moral conviction.

"Stage 7" and Natural Law Justice—Marcus Aurelius

Our first example of our metaphoric "Stage 7" or of a sixth religious stage is the Roman emperor Marcus Aurelius. We choose him partly because he is outside the Judeo-Christian tradition, which helps

define universals in religous thinking. And we choose him partly because in the world of the Roman empire, in which absolute power
corrupted absolutely, this man with absolute power was the only man
who was absolutely incorruptible, absolutely principled. In days that
at times seem like the decline of the American empire, in which there
are so many examples of power corrupting, we need to look at universal foundations of integrity.

Marcus Aurelius, by nature a philosopher who hated war and killing, felt compelled by his sense of principle to exile himself from
Rome to lead the army in order to preserve what he saw as human
civilization and rights against barbarian attack. He found himself surrounded by men and women who had no understanding of his principles. Those closest to him betrayed him. Nevertheless, he found his
way not only to forgive but also to love his betrayers. His statement of
faith is given in his personal journal, usually called the *Meditations*.

The content of the faith of Marcus Aurelius, like that of all Stoics,
is simple and almost stark. It starts with the belief that the universe is
lawful, knowable, and evolving. In referring to the ultimate, lawful,
rational, and evolving principle of the universe, Marcus Aurelius does
not attempt to separate God from nature. Sometimes he calls the principle *God,* sometimes *nature.* From this belief, he derives a natural
law view of morality that gives him the strength to act in terms of
universal principles of justice in an unjust world. It also gives him the
peace that comes from sensing oneself as a finite part of an infinite
whole.

With regard to principles of morality, he says,

The power of thought, the potential of reason, is universal among mankind. It
follows that this reason speaks no less universally to us all with its "Thou
shalts." There is then world law, we are all fellow citizens and the world is a
single city. Is there any other citizenship than can be claimed by all
humanity?

With regard to the place of the individual person in the cosmos, he has
this to say:

Mortal life cannot offer you anything better than justice and truth; that is,
peace of mind in the conformity of your actions to the laws of reason. Your
destiny you cannot control. Even the vagaries of chance have their place in
nature's scheme. You yourself are part of that universe. Remember always
what the world-nature is and what your own nature is and that your nature is
such a small fraction of so vast a whole. Then you will recognize that no man

can hinder you from conforming each word and deed to that nature of which you are a part.

We present a different version of "Stage 7" in which the cosmic vision has a larger influx of union, love, joy, and grace as well as moral force. Marcus Aurelius, however, in stating the cosmic perspective in its starkest, simplest form, we think succeeds in illuminating how, in any culture, a person without special gifts or inner light, but with the courage and thoughtfulness to think through the human condition, can achieve moral and spiritual maturity.

Stage 7 and Agape—Andrea Simpson

Marcus Aurelius represents a version of natural law thinking in which principles of justice are in harmony with or parallel to the larger cosmic order. Another version of the striving for a cosmic perspective on morality is closer to the Christian perspective in which agape is the moral attitude that parallels the ultimate environment or order.

The Greek word *agape* means "love" or "charity" and is used frequently throughout the New Testament. *Agape* has two essential characteristics: first, it is nonexclusive and can be extended to all, including one's enemies; second, it is gracious and is extended without regard for merit.

In Chapter 12 of Volume II, "The Aging Person as Philosopher," Kohlberg and Shulik present in detail the life and thought of Andrea Simpson, a woman of seventy-eight, as an example of "Stage 7" movement out of despair to a cosmic perspective. For Andrea Simpson, this movement starts from mid-life despair, moves to contemplative experiences of identification with a cosmic perspective, and generates a viewpoint that both supports ethical action and allows a sense of peace or integrity about personal disease and death associated with aging.

Brought up as a Unitarian, Andrea Simpson became associated with the Quakers in her college years because she was a pacifist in World War I and found fellow feeling about the moral issue only among Quakers. Her account of this period in her life leads us to two interpretations. First, her pacifism and activism in its behalf indicated that in early adulthood she had attained a postconventional principled (Stage 5 or possibly Stage 6) stage of moral judgment. Second, her change of religious affiliation from the Unitarians to the Quakers rep-

resented the relation of moral orientation to religious orientation that
we have hyphothesized. Her religous activity and development presupposed a moral or ethical orientation for which she sought religious
support.

After college, her life centered directly neither on ethical concerns
nor on their religious support or elaboration. She drifted away from
religious affiliations and concerns, centering her life on art "and my
religion became a search for beauty," partly represented by her studies
and work as an art teacher.

The continuation of her religious concerns and searching came
about not so much from new moral awareness or problems arising
from the question "Why be moral?" as it did from her more general
existential despair about the meaning of her life that arose in her early
forties. The considerations and events precipitating the period of despair and "nervous breakdown" were her mother's death, her brother's psychosis, and her own failure to form a stable, intimate
relationship with a man. In this period of despair, she turned to an
Indian Vedanta teacher from whom she "learned the Oriental view
that it doesn't matter what you call it—'God' or 'Jesus' or 'cosmic
flow' or 'reality' or 'love'—and what you learn from that source will
not tie your life in creeds that separate you from your fellow man."

During this time, she came to have experiences of contemplation or
meditation centered on the sense of oneness with "God, cosmic flow,
or reality." In meditation, her experience was that "you stop using
your mind, deliberately, like a flower that opens itself to the sun, and
let this dimension in. Whatever dimension you call it, that is not just
overhead in the sky but in the heart and the whole surrounding world,
it's in everyone. You open yourself to that which surrounds totally and
is totally within."

She elaborated this experience in terms of a metaphysic, as follows:

We start by seeking a power that is greater than ourselves. I don't think
anyone can fail to recognize that there is a power beyond themselves when
they look out at the scene of their own neighborhood, to say nothing of the
cosmos. I don't think it matters a bit what you call this power, but it is within
every mind, and experience and makes one aware of this oneness, not only of
all people but all of life.

Moving from this conception and experience of oneness, Andrea
Simpson endeavored to perceive the existence of death, suffering, and
injustice from a cosmic or infinite perspective by combining the East-

ern metaphor of Karma and reincarnation with the scientific metaphor of evolution.

If there ever was a pure, sinless soul, it was my brother. Why he had to have a life like this, I don't know. I said to myself, "I've got to solve this if I'm going to believe in a good God." And I came out of it this way: human life is but a brief moment in eternity. I studied astronomy, and you get a broadened vista if you study astronomy, it opens out to incredible degrees. I've also studied anthropology, and you get some idea of the development of the human being on the planet Earth. If a human being's life is his moment in eternity, William's life may be the cocoon stage, to use a figure of speech, in his evolving into a spiritual butterfly. We think of life and death as a pair of opposites—you make your entrance and you make your exit from this material place—and that's death. But life is something contained in the hand of life.

Although she attributed the resolution of her existential crisis of despair to her experience related to the Oriental philosophy, she found the Oriental philosophy only a limited support for her moral or ethical concerns. Preeminent in this ethical concern was the need to do something to help her psychotic brother. "That was one of the things that brought me back to Quaker Christianity; the Hindu way of religion wasn't enough to actively help sick people." The religious orientation she evolved helped her to devote herself not only to her brother but also to other patients in the mental hospital where her brother was, for whom she developed programs, and to long-term efforts to improve race relations between blacks and whites. Her religious orientation, then, was an effort to integrate two forms of mysticism, the Eastern contemplative form and the Western form, which identifies inward spiritual union with God with active love for, and service to, fellow human beings.

She called her mystical meditative experiences "openings." She said, "William James clarifies that people have religious experiences that are openings, that do something to their personal lives. It makes them more understanding of people, more aware of their oneness, not only with people but with all of life."

The shape that her ethical orientation took as a result of her religious experience and thinking was the orientation called *agape* in Christian theological ethics, an ethic of responsible universal love, service, or sacrifice—an ethic of supererogation. For Andrea Simpson, the ethic of agape represented an interpenetration between religion and ethical action.

Her actual actions she describes as follows:

The undercurrent of my whole life in California was to get back to William as soon as I was well enough to tackle work in a mental hospital. I
decided the thing for me to do was to take up residence in the town and work
hard with William and see if I could get him out of there. That experience
was very trying for a raw recruit, when I wasn't too far from a nervous
smash-up myself. The ward was shocking to see, and they said "There's your
brother." And here was a little old man all bent over sitting there, and I got
down on my knees in front of him so I could look into hs face, and he saw
who it was, and I saw a smile right out of heaven, a smile of an angel. He'd
found his old sister.

She went on to describe how her concern for her brother led to a
new career in the mental health field.

This is one reason I say the path chose me. I never would have gone near a
mental hospital if I hadn't had somebody I loved who got stuck in it. I worked
with the patients with no background in mental health training at all; I was
scared to death that somebody was going to come along and say "What do you
think you're doing with these people?"

She recalled how she felt when she was first observed by the director of the facility:

I was really in a cold sweat, I didn't know if it was going to be approved or
disapproved. Dr. R. it was, had brought a head nurse with him. They were
both behind me, and when the thing was over he shook my hand and said,
"Miss Simpson, you have done a most remarkable thing with these women."
Well, it took an awful long time for me to know that the people who came to
watch my group came to watch because they thought it was remarkable, not
because they were going to throw me out.

She reflected on the religious significance of her acts as follows:

I think it's terribly important not only to give what help we can but not to feel
we are doing it. If you give love and sustain a joyous attitude, you have probably helped a lot more than if you've preached. They will be helped because
in a sense love is God, and if you give love you give something much more
than yourself.

The case of Andrea Simpson illustrates "mystical" experience of
identification with the eternal, or with the whole of what she says can
be called *God* or *reality*. She exemplifies the striving for a cosmic or
infinite perspective to answer the problems and questions raised but

left unsolved by principled (Stage 5 or 6) morality itself, the problem of undeserved injustice and suffering.

In these ways, Andrea Simpson is an example of "Stage 7" or of a sixth stage of religious thinking, as is Marcus Aurelius. However, differences between the two examples raise a number of theoretical issues not yet addressed. First, for Andrea Simpson religious thinking and experience not only support a moral orientation but inform it, unite with it, or give it new direction. Second, the moral principle to which this thinking and experience leads is agape, something different from, or more than, our Stage 6 principles of justice.

Agape: Not an Alternative Stage 6 Morality

The questions raised by Andrea Simpson may be phrased in two ways. First, the case suggests that there is an alternative conception of a sixth and highest moral stage other than principles of justice as reversibility, a conception of a sixth stage as an attitude or principle of agape or responsible love. Second, the case raises the possibility that there is a seventh moral stage, based on an ethic that goes beyond, and is higher than, an ethic of justice.

Let us consider the first phrasing, that agape is an alternative or competitive moral principle to that of justice, another and previously unacknowledged version of a sixth moral stage. We argue that this is not correct, because agape is an ethic that presupposes justice principles and maintains their integrity. Rather than replacing principles of justice, agape goes beyond them in the sense of defining or informing acts of supererogation (acts beyond duty or beyond justice), acts that cannot be generally demanded or required of all people, acts that freely give up claims the actor may in justice demand. The attitude of agape presupposes an understanding and acceptance of the logic of duty and justice for its own definition. As Outka (1972) and Frankena (1963) point out, the attitude of agape shares equal respect for human personality and dignity with the attitude of justice. If agape minimizes the differential merit, deserts, or social utility of people, so does justice as reversibility that centers on equality and consideration of the perspective of the least advantaged.

In the second place, agape is not a principle of justice competing with the principle of fairness as reversibility. An attitude of responsible love still requires our sixth-stage principle of fairness as reversibility to resolve justice dilemmas. In Chapter 5 ("Justice as Reversibility"), I argued that in most dilemmas of justice (the distribution of scarce resources) the principle of fairness as reversibility (moral musical chairs or the original position) is both required by, and yielded, the same dilemma solution, whether one coming to the dilemma started with a fundamental ethical attitude of rational egoism, an attitude of love and sacrifice, or an attitude of fairness. An example used was the captain's dilemma, where I claimed the fair solution was drawing lots. One might think that the attitude of agape might solve the dilemma in a different way, by the loving person volunteering to sacrifice himself for the others. This might be a solution, if everyone else on the boat was completely selfish. If others on the boat were oriented either to agape or to fairness, simply volunteering would not solve the justice problem of who should go. In a company of saints, all would volunteer. In a company of people with an attitude of fairness, all would insist on taking a chance. In such a situation, a justice procedure such as drawing lots, which recognizes the equal value of each human life, would be not only the fair solution, but the one consistent with the attitude of agape.

In summary, although an ethic of agape goes beyond justice to supererogation, it still requires principles of fairness to resolve justice dilemmas. Furthermore, our Stage 6 principles of reversible fairness are the only principles on which the ethic of agape could rest, in contrast to utilitarianism or desert principles of justice. Agape, then, is not a principle competing with the principle of fairness in the sense in which I defined the idea of principles in Chapter 5. It is an attitude inspiring acts of supererogation, rather than a principle on which there could be exact agreement or which could lead to just expectations. Acts of agape cannot be demanded or expected by their recipients but are, rather, acts of grace from the standpoint of the recipient.

We have stressed the consistencies between principles of fairness and the ethic of agape in response to problems of justice. In this way, our view is somewhat different than that of Rawls. Rawls's account starts from the premise that justice principles arise out of a social contract among rational egoists, or rational people with conflicting views of the good.

Amongst an association of saints, if such a community could really exist, the disputes about justice could hardly occur; for they would all work selflessly together for one end, the glory of God as defined by their common religion, and reference to this end would settle every question of right. The justice of practice does not come up until there are several different parties who press their claims on one another and who do regard themselves as representatives of interests which deserve to be considered. [In Outka, 1972, p. 75]

Our discussion of the captain's dilemma suggests that even an association of saints would require some principles of justice. This becomes more apparent if we accept that an association of saints might all share the attitude of love or agape but might disagree in their conceptions of the good life or "in their conceptions of God or the end of the greater glory of God." Our highest moral stage and its justice principle does not directly answer questions about the nature of the good person or the good life and does not assume that such questions have, or require, universalizable answers that they must provide. Following Rawls, we define principles of duty and justice that could be agreed on by rational agents while still holding differing conceptions of the good life (and of the good person). Social life at least ideally, requires universal agreement about judgments of justice (or about the domain of conflict between the claims of people) that we claim our sixth stage would generate. However, our sixth stage need not, and should not, suppose universal agreement on conceptions of the good life or the good person or of "God and the greater glory of God."

An association of saints in the sense of people imbued with agape need not agree in detail in their religious views or in their views of the good life. Accordingly, they too, require, and could agree on, universalizable principles of justice in addition to sharing an attitude of agape.

We have pointed to areas of agreement about principles of fairness used to resolve justice dilemmas that are common to rational people with an ethic of agape and to those with an ethic of fairness (or even of rational egoism). From a research point of view, there may be ethical dilemmas that elicit differing solutions for those with an ethic of agape, of fairness, and of rational egoism, those dilemmas unlike our standard hypothetical dilemmas, would not focus on issues of justice. Shawver (1979) constructed some dilemmas of this sort, although he did not actually research responses to them. His purpose was to show that agape, fairness, and rational egoism each have differing but equal claims to defining a sixth stage of moral judgment. Gilligan (1977) also argues that an ethic of responsible love represents a different version of a sixth and highest moral stage from that defined by principles of justice. We do not deny the possibility that research on the resolution of dilemmas differing from our own might validly lead to different stage definitions from those suggested by our research on justice dilemmas. Such stages, however, we would construe as stages in the development of a broader ethic or valuing process such as Fowler has attempted to describe. Such an ethic or valuing process would include religious thinking about human nature and the human condition as well as moral judgment and reasoning. As our discussion of an ethic of agape as at least a part of a highest stage of religious thinking argued, such an ethic still must rely on Stage 6 fairness principles to resolve justice problems. In our view, then, Shawver and Gilligan have not worked out an alternative account of a highest moral stage but have, rather, pointed to alternative attitudes in the development of higher stages of ethical orientation. Thus there may be alternative ethics of justice and of agape, either of which might be stressed at a higher ethical and religious stage.

Agape and Natural Law Justice as Alternative Forms of a Highest Stage of Ethical and Religious Thinking

From our point of view, the case of Andrea Simpson suggests that there may be a somewhat different end point of ethical development from that described in our successive stages of justice. This end point or "Stage 7" is not a reconstruction of a Stage 6 justice structure that better resolves the problems also faced by Stage 6, as Stage 6 is a more adequate reconstruction of Stage 5. Our metaphoric Stage 7 is a religious or ontological stage, not a purely moral one. It elaborates an ethic of supererogation, leaving justice problems to be resolved by Stage 6 principles. Although it does not reconstruct Stage 6, its center lies elsewhere than in justice. Stage 7 may be content to "render unto Caesar that which is Caesar's," namely societal justice, and center rather on the ethical problems of "rendering unto God that which is God's," namely acts of sacrificial love and human brotherhood. Such a Stage 7 would be an ethical orientation arising from development in existential or religious experience and thinking rather than from moral experience alone. In this way, "Stage 7" agape would differ from our example of Marcus Aurelius, for whom the development of a "Stage 7" contemplation of natural law paralleled and supported rational moral principles of justice, rather than providing a new ethical focus.

In partial contrast to Marcus Aurelius, Andrea Simpson showed a development of religious insight and experience resolving her mid-life existential despair, insights that changed as well as supported her previous moral orientation. We suggested earlier that the development of religious thinking helps resolve the gap between "is" and "ought," the gap between a person's construction of moral principles or ideals and the person's construction of social and cosmic reality, in ways that must consider the existence of suffering, injustice, and death. This gap is faced anew with each new stage of moral ideals or principles, new stages arising primarily through the effort to resolve moral conflicts of duty and justice. This interpretation is consistent with the example of Marcus Aurelius. In the example of Andrea Simpson, her religious development resolved her existential despair through a sense of union with God or the whole of life, promoting a sense of union with all other human beings. This sense of ideal union promoted the development of an ethical orientation of agape to resolve the gap between is and ought in addition to supporting her sense of moral principles of justice.

From the standpoint of psychology, it may be that our hypothetical Stage 7 or a sixth and highest stage of religious thinking does not fit our psychological claim that moral and religious stages are parallel in structure and that attainment of a moral stage is necessary but not sufficent for attainment of the parallel religious stage. This relationship seems to fit easily the example of Marcus Aurelius as a hypothetical Stage 7 but does not as easily fit the example of Andrea Simpson.

From the viewpoint of philosophy, the two cases present two pictures of "ultimate religion," alike and different in equally important ways. The religion and ethic of agape held by Andrea Simpson is often portrayed as resting on, or arising from, a faith in the God of revelation as expressed in the Judeo-Christian tradition. Andrea Simpson's religion, however, is as universalistic as is that of Marcus Aurelius. Neither has a religion directly dependent on revelation or an ethic resting directly on divine command. Instead, the religious orientation of each rests on a sense of connectedness between the individual human mind and heart and the larger cosmic whole or order, which they call almost equally readily *God, Nature, Life,* or *ultimate Reality.* This sense of connectedness supports and inspires in both ethical action toward other human beings.

Equally evident are the differences between the two cases. The religion and ethic of Marcus Aurelius is a natural law perspective of the kind we argued for earlier. The God or Nature of Marcus Aurelius is the pantheistic God "known" or intuited by rational science finding law in natural events. The ethical laws or principles of Marcus Aurelius are the principles of justice "known" or intuited by rational moral philosophy.

The religion and ethics of Andrea Simpson does not rest as directly on rational science and rational moral philosophy as does that of Marcus Aurelius. It is inspired much more by the Judeo-Christian assumption that God or Ultimate Reality is a loving God than by the assumption that God is an impersonal order of natural law. It assumes that the attitude of love is the source of intuition both about ultimate ethical principles and about the nature of the cosmos.

"Stage 7" and Philosophic Theory

The religious experience at the heart of our highest stage of ethical and religious philosophy are the experiences called "openings" by Andrea Simpson and "the union of the mind with all of nature" by Spinoza. Both ethical and metaphysical intellectual convictions seem to spring from these experiences. To attempt to intellectually justify these convictions is to move into a region that agnostics with a religious attitude, such as Kant and Dewey, claim is beyond the limits of rational thought.

Dewey (in Ratner, ed., 1939) himself seems not to have had, nor to have cultivated, mystical attitudes or experiences. Dewey defines religious experience as anything that introduces perspective: "All religions have dwelt upon the power of religion to introduce perspective into the piecemeal and shifting episodes of experience. We need to reverse the ordinary statement and say that whatever introduces genuine perspective is religious, not that religion is something that introduces it."

He goes on to say,

Those who hold that there is a definite kind of experience which is itself religious mark it off from experience as esthetics, scientific, moral, political, from experience as companionship and friendship. But "religious" as a quality of experience signifies something that may belong to all these experiences. Religious experience takes place in different persons in a multitide of ways. It is sometimes brought about by devotion to a cause; sometimes by a passage of poetry that opens a new perspective; sometimes, as was the case with Spinoza, through philosophic reflection. [pp. 1012-1013]

With regard to mystical experience, Dewey says,

A clear and intense conception of a union of ideal ends with actual conditions is capable of arousing steady emotion. The functions of a working union of the ideal and the real seems to me identical with the force that has in fact been attached to the conception of God in all the religions that have a spiritual content. The sense of this union may, with some persons, be furthered by mystical experiences using the term *mystical* in its broadest sense. That result depends upon temperament. But there is a marked difference between the union associated with mysticism and the union which I have in mind. There is nothing mystical about the latter, it is natural and moral. Nor is there anything mystical about the perception or consciousness of such union. There is, indeed, even danger that resort to mystical experience will be an escape, and its result will be the passive feeling that the union of actual and ideal is already accomplished. But in fact this union is active and practical; it is a *uniting*, not something given. [pp. 1025-1026]

Dewey's position differs in two ways from our conceptualization or hypothesis of a "Stage 7," of a highest stage of ethical and religious thought and experience. First, Dewey denies any special or unique religious characteristics to mystical experience as distinct from other positive and perspective-giving experiences, all of which may be "religious" in Dewey's view. Second, he denies that there is any form of philosophic reflection that is either necessary for religious experience or is the result of such experiences. According to Dewey, for Spinoza religious experience comes from philosophic reflection; for someone else, it may come from a passage of poetry or a devotion to a cause.

In contrast to Dewey, our hypothesis of a "Stage 7" is that mystical experience does have a unique religious meaning and that it both depends on, and leads to, philosophic reflections or theories that agree in several fundamental ways. Our position also differs from that of Kant (1949b), whose viewpoint in many ways is similar to Dewey's. The major distinction between Dewey and Kant is that Dewey views moral structures as natural, whereas Kant views morality as resulting from a free or nonnatural principle of practical moral reason. Kant views religion "within the limits of reason alone" as (1) the imaginative construction of an ideal of a morally perfect person, embodied in the image of Christ, and (2) the idea of an ethical commonwealth or of a people of God under ethical laws. With regard to the first, Kant says (1949b, pp. 396–398),

Mankind or rational earthly existence in its complete moral perfection is that which alone can render the world the object of a divine decree and the end of creation. It is our common duty as men to elevate ourselves to the ideal of moral perfection; that is, to the archetype of the moral disposition in all its purity. The ideal of a humanity pleasing to God and hence of such moral perfection as is possible to an earthly being we can imagine only as the idea of a person willing not merely to discharge all human duties himself and to spread about his goodness as widely as possible by precept and example but to take upon himself every affliction for the good of the world and even for his enemies. We need no empirical example to make the idea of a person well pleasing to God our pattern; this idea as a pattern is already present in our moral reason. Moreover, if anyone, in order to acknowledge, for his imitation, a particular individual as such an example which conforms to that idea, and therefore demands more than what he sees, more, that is, than a course of life entirely blameless and as meritorious as one could wish; and if he goes on to require, as credentials requisite to belief, that this individual should have performed miracles or had them performed for him—he who demands this thereby confesses to his own moral unbelief, that is, to his lack of faith in virtue.

With regard to the second point, Kant says (1949b, pp. 405–409),

A *juridico-civil* (political) state is the relation of men to each other in which they stand alike under public laws (which are laws of coercion). An *ethico-civil* state is that in which they are united under noncoercive laws; that is, *laws of virtue* alone. Because the duties of virtue apply to the entire human race, the concept of an ethical commonwealth is extended ideally to whole of mankind and thereby distinguishes itself from the concept of a political community. It involves working toward a union of which we do not know whether, as such, it lies in our power. We can foresee that this duty will presuppose another idea, that of a higher moral Being through whose universal dispositions, the forces of separate individuals are united for a common end. This idea of a people of God can be realized through human organization only in the form of a church.

Kant, then, like Dewey, holds that religious ideas are the extension of moral structures to the idea of a perfect person and a perfect community or ethical commonwealth. Such an extension requires neither revelation and miracles nor mystical experiences of union but only requires faith in morality and moral reason. Kant gives us a version of "Stage 7" based on a metaphysics of morality and without further metaphysical or mystical insight. He starts with Stage 6 principles of moral reason, of the principle of treating each person as an end, not as a means. The imaginative extension of this idea, he claims, leads to the idea of a perfectly loving and virtuous person (imagined as the Son of God) and of an ideal community of virtuous people (imagined as the Kingdom of God). Thus Kant moves from a moral Stage 6 conception of justice to a religious imaginative ideal or "Stage 7" of a perfect person with an attitude of agape and a religious community based on this idea.

Both Dewey and Kant's metaphysically agnostic views are compatible with our hypothesis of moral structures as necessary but not sufficient for stages of religious judgment. Their "Stage 7," however, is independent of mystical experiences and of speculative metaphysics, grounded rather on faith in moral reason and ideals. Our examples of Stage 7 lead us rather in a "natural law" direction. We shall present two types of philosophic theory, more metaphysical than the theories of Kant and Dewey, which seem to us more faithful to the experience of our examples of development to a Stage 7.

The first philosophy is the natural law pantheism of Spinoza, the most complete statement of the ethical and religious philosophy of which Marcus Aurelius was an example. The second speculative philosophy is the evolutionary process philosophy expressed in different ways by Whitehead (1938), by Bergson (1958), and by Teilhard de Chardin (1968). These are comprehensive statements of the ethical and religious philosophy exemplified by Andrea Simpson.

Our brief review is not directed to any intellectual "proof" of any of these theories as metaphysical or theological systems. Rather, it suggests some notion of their adequacy to address the questions or tasks faced by speculative philosophies. As stated by Whitehead (1938, p. 4),

Philosophy attains its chief importance by fusing religion and science into one rational scheme of thought. Religion is the translation of general ideas into particular thoughts, particular emotions, and particular purposes; it is directed to the end of stretching individual interest beyond its self-defeating particularity. Religion is an ultimate craving to infuse into the insistent particularity of emotions that nontemporal generality which primarily belongs to conceptual thought alone.

Spinoza's Theory

We discuss Spinoza's theory both as an ethical system and as a metaphysic. Spinoza's *Ethics* (1930) was firmly grounded on a natural science psychology that was the great ancestor of Freud's rigorously deterministic theory. It was also grounded on a rational moral and political philosophy of a "natural rights" social contract variety. Spinoza's system logically combined these elements of an ethic with a metaphysical or religious view of rational mysticism. His ethical system had no less a purpose than salvation; that is, the development of a coherent scheme that if followed would make people free or happy.

Spinoza's voyage into salvation starts with the familiar despair, a despair based on the relativity of values and on the unavoidable truth of death and separation. Spinoza tells us that experience has convinced him that none of the objects that people usually set before themselves can yield complete satisfaction of desire. Pleasure, power, and wealth—all fail to serve as a source of permanent, unbroken enjoyment. And they fail because of their nature. It is their nature to be perishable and finite. Hedonism is no solution for Spinoza because we need not only a life of pleasure but also a real life. This is what the vague word *self-realization* ultimately means. According to Spinoza, self-realization is the fundamental striving of our nature, and to achieve self-realization is to *become real*. Pleasures in activities sensed as unreal are not abiding. If hedonism (taking our own pleasures as a central object of concern) does not solve the central problems of life and its meaning, neither does morality or altruism (taking the pleasures and pains of others as central concerns) fully solve these problems. Put differently, if we are to love others in a way satisfactory to themselves and others, it must be without possessiveness, domination, jealousy, or fear of loss. And how are we to do that? Says Spinoza,

When I became convinced that things are good and evil, not in themselves, but only as our affections are aroused by them, I finally decided to ask whether there is a true good, one that gives its goodness of itself and by which alone our affections might be aroused; nay, rather, whether there were something which when found and possessed, could be kept forever with perfect and unbroken joy.

Spinoza is convinced that we cannot escape the dominion of our affections. We are the slaves of the love of something. The loves that enslave can be overcome only if there is and can be found an object that inspires a love that frees. If pleasure and power are not intrinsic ends, only some sort of love can be an intrinsic end. We only attain a stronger and more stable state of the self if we attain a stronger and more stable love of something. This love, Spinoza says, involves the love of something eternal and infinite. Can such an object be found? Spinoza thinks that we ought rather to ask, "What is the way to find it? What does trying to find it involve?" His answer is "It involves the discovery of the union of the mind with the whole of nature." In other words, the ideal state of human nature is "that in which we know the union of man's mind with the whole of nature." What does Spinoza mean by "the union of the mind with Nature?" It is self-evident that our bodies are a part of nature. It is not so clear to us that our minds are also a part of nature. But, Spinoza says,

> Our mind is also a part of Nature; that is, Nature has an infinite power of thinking which contains subjectively the whole of Nature. The human mind is this power, not as infinite and perceiving the whole of nature, but as finite and perceiving only the human body.

Spinoza believed that the mind's capacity for true ideas implies an innate fit between the mind and nature. In contrast, the modern positivistic tradition equates the mind with error and nonrealilty. The positivist invokes mentality to account for distortion and error in the perception of truth, just as children develop their concept of mind to account for dream or illusion experiences, which are not considered real. This error concept of the mind leads to the notion that only matter is real and leaves unexplained the reality of the order of events, an order that is neither material nor mental.

The reality of order or structure as prior to either mind or matter is held by many philosophers, scientists, and poets who are to some extent Platonists by nature. They are Platonists in recognizing that the *a priori* mathematical ideas of the scientist are not simply inventions which fit nature because the ideas that did not fit nature were weeded out. They recognize also that the mathematicians' ideas did not fit nature because nature was fitted to them as a set of arbitrary *a priori* schemata. The geometry of Riemann and Lobachevski seemed inconceivable to the apriorist Kantians, and should not have worked for the positivist, because they were developed antecedent to any empirical problem. But every mathematical construction that makes mathematical sense seems to have some correspondence to the structure of empirical reality. Furthermore, every mathematical or scientific theory that is useful is also beautiful. The fact that true ideas are beautiful attests to the fact that structures originate and are experienced in a way different from that suggested by the usual theories of scientific idea construction. If the beautiful is a preliminary intuition of the true, then there is some fit between the mind and nature that is *given,* rather than wrested from nature by the experiment. More controversially, Spinoza claims that the order of the universe is known to humans because the human mind is part of the universe and partly shares universal mental properties.

The union of the mind with nature, then, is fundamentally only a fuller knowledge of mind and nature plus a self-awareness about the meaning of those states where we are in physical or mental harmony with nature. The mystical rapture and acceptance of life, which is sometimes seen as involving the postulation of a supernatural, can be had only if we see this life whole. To see life whole is to love and accept life because it is to see ourselves as necessarily part of life. Thus Spinoza's attitude toward nature as a whole is like that of a mystic toward a supernatural God. In Spinoza's metaphysics, the word *Nature* is taken to be the same as two other words: *God* and *substance.*

Spinoza is willing to admit that there is something over and above and beyond the aggregate of things that constitutes our physical universe. He is even willing to call that something by the name of *God.* But—and here his first "but" comes in—he is unwilling to admit that the something, unlike the constituent parts of the universe, is separate from the universe. Within the universe itself and inseparable from it, he maintains there is something unlike its parts. He proceeds to explain that by that something he means the wholeness of the universe, which, he contends, is not the mere aggregate of its parts. To support this contention, he uses two propositions. First, the universe is a system or organism. Second, in a system the whole is something different from the mere sum of its parts.

Spinoza draws some distinction between God and all the phenomena involved. God is substance, while phenomena are mere modes. By *substance,* he means the order of the universe, considered as an eternal system of natural laws that have a mental side (because laws entail knowability), as Curley (1969) points out, as well as a side of physical regularity or fact. Spinoza's concept of God as substance is the sort of concept that a modern scientist could still propose if he or she moved from using natural laws to explain events to asking, "What kind of ultimate reality is implied by the existence of scientific laws?" (Curley, 1969).

How can this metaphysic or vision of reality be used to save us from despair? Our normal joys are the results of our self-actualization, of activities in which our competence, power, and knowledge are enhanced, especially when our self-actualization is linked to the self-actualization of others. But ultimately our joy in self-actualization is crushed by our awareness that ourselves and the selves of others are only limited, dying parts of a larger reality. As we first become aware of the larger reality that is the background of our activities, we are likely to be oppressed by a sense of the futility of all that we do and have and are. The "once-born" reaction to this sense of futility is to refocus on our own activities and the present in which they exist. Spinoza recommends, rather, that we stop acting and that we shift figure and ground, that we focus our experience on the larger reality that is usually the background of our activities.

The most concrete example is physical nature, which we are usually more aware of as a background to our activities than as an experience of reality. The experience of nature's beauty is the experience of the beauty of something that is permanent in spite of our transience. The beauty of nature is the beauty of one eternal system, not of this or that specific view. The experience of beauty is the experience of perceived eternal objects, which in turn are to be responded to in terms of the unity they manifest and in which we are included. This beauty is represented from the mountaintop, in which we have that sense of distance where we seem to share Nature's eternal and inclusive perspective. Now, if we use this experience at the mountaintop as a visual analogy to focusing on the reality which is the background to our everyday life, we reach the essence of Spinoza's religious attitude. We are bound to be miserable and unhappy, Spinoza thinks, as long as we are ignorant of what our place in nature is.

The understanding of our place in nature is the way to the active acceptance and love of life. In part, Spinoza says, this acceptance depends on our own acceptance of events and our own actions as causally determined, of the limits of our power in the face of Nature or God. In part, he says, it depends on the more active love of God or Nature and sense of union with it which comes with awareness of ourselves as part of nature.

Spinoza, then, has applied to his own God the common utterances of theology about the God of tradition. He is arguing, in effect, that his own God has as much personality as the God of tradition, if by personality is meant a personal relation on the part of human beings toward God as it expresses itself in the attitude of love. Spinoza is saying that if we understand Life or Nature we cannot help but love it and all things in it. And if we love Life or Nature or God, we become capable of overcoming all the pains of life. The pains of life are caused by the disappointments or losses in our loves of particular people or aims. But if we are aware of the relationship of all people and things to the whole of Nature or to God, then we continue to love the whole in spite of the disappointments or losses. And if we love life or nature, we are even able to face our own death with equanimity, because we love life more than our own particular and finite life. The demand for our survival can be met only by identification or union with something more eternal. The knowledge of, and love of, Nature or God are a form of union. In a sense, half-poetic, half-logical, but never supernatural, our mind is part of a whole, Spinoza claims, and if we know and love the eternal we ourselves are in some sense eternal.

Teilhard de Chardin's Theory

An alternative position to Spinoza's that also seeks to develop a religion of natural law with the aid of science is that of Teilhard de Chardin, a paleontologist and Catholic priest. Like the philosopher Bergson (1958), whose work made a profound and lasting impression on his own, Teilhard emphasizes the creative process of evolution as the "key" to understanding the universe and the presence of God.

He constructed a metaphysics of evolution, or a "hyperphysics," as he calls it, that viewed the world not as developing by chance but as guided by a personal center. Teilhard thinks of the *telos* of evolution as universal convergence into God, whom he called the Omega Point of evolution. He argues that evolution had two facets to it that cannot be separated—a psychic "within" aspect and a physical "without." He proposes a central law of evolution linking the within and without of things—the law of complexity-consciousness. This law stipulates that every better organized structure will correspond to a more developed consciousness. Thus Teilhard's metaphysics addresses the dualism of mind and matter and offered a unitary understanding of both.

Teilhard describes the tendency of the evolutionary process when taken as a whole as directed toward the human person with the capability of reflective thought. The achievement of evolution is *Homo Sapiens*—and, retrospectively, the "aim" of evolution from its beginnings. Teilhard stresses that his main purpose in presenting his evolutionary metaphysics was that others might see the cosmic dimensions of this development and accept their responsibility for its continuation. In the preface to his most systematic presentation of his theory, *The Phenomenon of Man,* he writes (1965, p. 31),

Seeing—we might say the whole of life lies in that verb—if not ultimately, at least essentially. Fuller being in closer union: such is the kernel and conclusion of this book. But let us emphasize the point: union increases only through an increase in consciousness; that is to say, in vision. And that, doubtless, is why the history of the living world can be summarized as the elaboration of ever more perfect eyes within a cosmos in which there is always something more to be seen. To try to see more and better is not a whim or curiosity or self-indulgence. To see or to perish is the very condition laid upon everything that makes up the universe, by reason of the mysterious gift of existence. And this in superior measure is man's condition.

Teilhard's urgency that we try to "see more and better" or "perish" is rooted in his own struggle with the problem of death. A commentator, DeLubac (1968, p. 56), says, "There would be no exaggeration in presenting the whole body of his work as one long meditation on death." Teilhard's personal reactions to death are perhaps most poignantly expressed after his loss of a close friend and colleague, Davidson Black:

But what an absurd thing life is, looked at superficially: so absurd that you feel yourself forced back on a stubborn, desperate faith in the reality and survival of the spirit. Otherwise—were there no such thing as the spirit, I mean—we should have to be idiots not to call off the whole human effort. . . .

In my distress following Black's death, and in the stifling atmosphere of "agnostic" condolences that surrounded it, I swore to myself on the body of my dead friend to fight more vigorously than ever to give hope to man's work and inquiry. [1962, pp. 155–156].

This anguish over the prospect of a cosmic dead-end is a constant theme throughout his life. In response to it, he searches for an *issue,* an opening, or a "way out" that could promote the élan of humanity. For Teilhard, the only belief capable of promoting this élan and sustaining the tide of human evolution is a belief in a personal Omega, a center capable of bringing human beings into unity without destroying their centered selves. Belief in the Omega is not an assent to the presence of a being removed from the self or the world. Rather, that belief is the recognition of the attractive presence of the Omega in the evolutionary process drawing evolution to greater complexity and consciousness and finally to mystical union. Teilhard conceived of the active force or energy exerted by the Omega as love. Love is a general principle of unity; it is "the affinity of being in the being." At its most rudimentary level love is present in the unity of people with each other and Omega or God.

Teilhard's vision of the relationship of the person to nature and God is, in his own words, a form of mysticism. He often states that his life work is an attempt to bring about "the conjunction of reason and mysticism" or the simultaneous attainment of the universal and the spiritual. Teilhard elaborates his mysticism in his major treatise on religion, *The Divine Milieu* (1968). He noted that the perception of the divine in the world is a "seeing" or "taste," an intuition that goes beyond reasoning itself. He describes the mystical apprehension of the divine milieu as a conscious state affecting all dimensions of the psyche. In this state, there grows a sense of the unity common to all things and an awareness of a new dimension of reality. He describes this state in terms of a transformation in the way one relates to the world: "deeper still: a transformation had taken place for me *in the very perception of being*. Thenceforward being had become, in some way, tangible and savorous to me; and as it came to dominate all the forms which it assumed, being itself began to draw me and intoxicate me" (1968, p. 129). Teilhard grants that such an experience is accessible to the "pagan and Christian alike" and that even the Christian must "admit that this inward reversal seems to him to have occurred within the profane and 'natural parts of his soul' " (p. 129).

For Teilhard, Christian mysticism demands both a love of the earth and a surrender to God. Teilhard (1968, p. 120) writes that to reach the upper layers of the divine milieu

is to experience with equal truth that one has need of everything, and that one has need of nothing. Everything is needed because the world will never be large enough to provide our taste for action with the means of grasping God, or our thirst for undergoing the possibility of being invaded by him. And yet nothing is needed; for as the only reality which can satisfy us lies beyond the transparencies in which it is mirrored, everything that fades away and dies between us will only seem to give reality back to us with greater purity, everything means both everything and nothing to me; everything is God to me and everything is dust to me.

As we have seen, Teilhard's approach to religion as expressed in his mysticism draws on two sources: a scientific theory of evolution and Christian theology. Rather than perceiving these sources to be in opposition, as has often been the case in theological circles, Teilhard perceives them as different expressions of the same truth. Teilhard argues that his scientific theory of evolution leads to the hypothesis of a God, conceived as the Omega. This hypothesis does not require "supernatural knowledge" or "revelation," but only requires a natural or "psychological faith." The decision to accept or reject the hypothesis is rationally based on a determination of how well it accounts for the totality of experience. For Teilhard, rejection of the hypothesis of God is incompatible with the phenomenon of human reflectivity:

Hence this remarkable situation—that our mind, by the very fact of being able to discern infinite horizons ahead, is only able to move by the hope of achieving through something of itself, a supreme consummation—without which it could rightly feel itself to be stunted, frustrated, and cheated. By the nature of the work, and correlatively by the requirement (experience) of the worker, a total death, an unscalable wall, on which consciousness would crash and then forever disappear, are thus incompossible with the mechanism of conscious activity (since it would immediately break its mainspring). [1968, p. 231]

Thus Teilhard concludes that the affirmation of Omega is the only choice that satisfies the demands of intelligence for meaning.

Although Teilhard develops a "natural theology" and a mysticism without relying on revelation, he sees the revelation of Christ as central to his theology. For Teilhard, as for contemporary theologians and philosophers working within an evolutionary metaphysical framework, revelation presupposes theology of nature or creation.

Teilhard's evolutionary metaphysics provides the necessary framework for interpreting the Christian revelation. In addition, he finds that Christianity is the best historical expression of the mystery present within and at the culmination of the evolving cosmos. Teilhard's natural theology brings him to the notion of an Omega that must be both immanent and transcendent—the focus of evolutionary convergence and yet outside of evolution as a center of personal attraction.

However, once he establishes the personality of God, he has found revelation not only possible but "in conformity with things." Although Teilhard does not believe he could deduce Christian faith from his evolutionary scheme, he finds them in profound harmony. Christian faith serves to complete his system and to make explicit and clear what has been suggested but vague. The Christian revelation confirms his psychological faith and provides it with new depth and inspiration.

Commonalities in the Theories of Spinoza and Teilhard

In our description of Spinoza and Teilhard's theories, the following common characteristics emerge as features that we describe as Stage 7. First, Stage 7 presupposes Stage 5 or 6 principled morality. Spinoza articulated morality in terms of justice, social contract, and natural rights, while Teilhard developed a morality of agape that presupposes a basic concern for personality. These moral positions are rationally constructed and do not depend on revelation or divine command. Although they represent ideals of the moral order, they also represent structures of reality or nature as well. In this sense, reality or nature is interpreted in terms of what we have called *natural law*. The claim that reality is lawful and in some harmony with humanity's most highly developed notions of love and justice rests on a set of further assumptions that we have described as metaphysical, ontological, or religious. These assumptions are made most explicit when questions such as "Why be moral?" and "Why live?" arise. Properly understood, these questions are not moral but religious. They ask whether there is any support in reality, in nature taken as a whole or in the ground of Nature, for acting according to universal moral principles. The personal history and thought of our examples suggests that the transition to Stage 7 begins with despair; that is, with the consideration that human life and action is in the final analysis meaningless and doomed to extinction. The experience of despair calls into question the fundamental worth of human activity. The only response to the radical questioning inherent in despair is the construction of a metaphysics capable of reaffirming what has been denied.

Religious assertions imply a metaphysics because they refer to the common structure of all reality. This position, as we stated, leads us to disagree with advocates of emotive theories of religion and with fundamentalists who discount any natural knowledge of God. As opposed to emotivists, we share with Teilhard and Spinoza the assumption that religious views have a cognitive basis concerning a basic structure of being. As opposed to fundamentalists, we assume with Spinoza and Teilhard the view that revelation can only be accepted and judged as "true" on the basis of some prior understanding of the meaning of God or some prior metaphysics.

Such a metaphysics starts with experiences of the world as exhibiting a rational order, as we have seen in Spinoza and Teilhard's appeals to science as the beginning of metaphysical reflection. Although Spinoza and Teilhard develop a metaphysics that is in harmony with rational scientific knowledge about the world, their metaphysics is not based on a simple extrapolation from the knowledge. Rather, it assumes an underlying "substance" or ground of being and of nature. Intuition of this ground of being transcends the duality of subject and object; it involves a sense of union between the knower and the known.

At Stage 7, then, individuals construct a "natural theology" that is based on reason. Although rationally derived, one's metaphysical system at Stage 7 is also supported by mystical experiences of union with the whole of reality. This mystical component is present in the theories and examples we have cited. Mystical experience is present as an element of Stage 7 spirituality, but it is necessary to see this experience in the context of the other features of this stage. Mystical experiences may perhaps be induced in a variety of ways, such as through drugs or disciplined meditation. Mystical experiences that are religiously significant are those in which the oneness of being is disclosed and the subject-object duality is overcome. These experiences then represent an emotionally powerful intuitive grasp of a reality that a metaphysics can only in a limited way express conceptually.

Summary and Conclusions

At this stage of inquiry, we can only draw tentative conclusions. Psychologically, there are clear parallels between our moral stages and a stagelike development of religious thinking. We have interpreted these parallels as consistent with the hypothesis that structures of religious thinking depend on moral structures for their formation; that is, moral judgment development is necessary but not sufficient for development of religious thinking. This relationship is consistent with the postulation of the autonomy of morality or moral judgment, of the

nonreducibility of moral "ought" judgments to descriptive "is" judgments of natural or supernatural facts. It is also consistent with the
notion that religious judgments and orientations function to support
moral judgment in the face of such questions as "Why be moral?" as
well as of problems arising from the gap between moral structures and
judgments of the world as it is and from the gap between just conduct
and the existence of injustice, suffering, and death in the world.

The necessary but not sufficient relationship is readily derivable
from the cognitive-developmental theories of Dewey (in Ratner, ed.,
1939), Mead (1934), and J. M. Baldwin (1906). These theories, although broadly compatible with our "natural law" view, differ in
their seeing religious judgment as essentially imaginative constructions
of the ideal moral self and the ideal society. In a certain sense, their
theories are agnostic in that they imply that there is no source of
religious "knowledge" and experience independent of moral "knowledge" and experience. These theories, of course, take into account the
bodies of religious belief and creed to which children are exposed, but
assume that children will assimilate this body of knowledge and values
to their own developing moral structures. Religious experience leads to
new moral and religious structures only insofar as such religious experience is translatable into moral experience with other people in a
religious community.

The observed relationships between moral and religious development are consistent with the philosophies and psychologies of Dewey,
Mead, and Baldwin, which assume that religious reasoning ultimately
derives either from moral reason or from reasoning about the world of
society and nature. These relationships also fit our own "natural law"
approach, which diverges from these theories in attributing more
autonomy to religious experience and reasoning. In our view, there are
problems, experiences, and thinking that are centrally religious and
metaphysical, although the problems depend in part on moral structures for their formulation.

This view we are able to most clearly elaborate in terms of the
experience and judgments of people at what we think to be "Stage 7,"
a sixth or highest stage of religious judgment. The center of the highest stage is experiences that are most distinctively religious experiences
of union with deity, whether pantheistic or theistic. These experiences
we do not interpret in a reductionistic psychological manner, as does

the Freudian theory, of mystic experience as a survival of an early feeling of union with the mother. We treat it instead as both arising from, and contributing to, a new perspective. We term this new perspective "cosmic" and "infinite," although of course the attainment of such a perspective is only an aspiration rather than a complete possibility. The attainment of this perspective results from a new insight. Using Gestalt psychology language for describing insight, we term it a shift from figure to ground, from a centering on the self's activity and that of others to a centering on the wholeness or unity of nature or the cosmos. In Spinoza's view, the experience of "the union of the mind with the whole of nature" results from the cognitive ability to see nature as an organized system of natural laws and to see every part of nature, including oneself, as parts of that whole.

This act of insight is, however, not purely cognitive. One cannot see the whole or the infinite ground of being unless one loves it and aspires to love it. Such love, Spinoza tells us, arises first out of despair about more limited, finite, and perishable loves. Knowing and loving God or Nature as the ground of a system of laws knowable by reason is a support to our acceptance of human rational moral laws of justice, which are part of the whole. Furthermore, our love of the whole or the ultimate supports us through experiences of suffering, injustice, and death.

Spinoza centers on the love of God or nature; Teilhard, however, sees God not only as the ultimate object of love but also as ultimately loving. Central to his view is the idea of the cosmos as evolving to higher levels of consciousness and organization. The principle or end of this evolution is love.

In our view, then, a psychological theory of religious stages, particularly a highest stage, rests on a philosophic theory, a set of metaphysical and religious assumptions consistent with, but not reducible to, rational science and morality. This view parallels the claims we make about moral reasoning, which requires an autonomous moral philosophy for its definition. In the case of morality, we claim that there is a single definable structure defining a sixth or highest stage and that this structure can be interpreted and justified by various rigorous theories, of which Rawls's theory is the best example.

In the case of "Stage 7," a highest level of ethical and religious thinking, the structure is much less unitary and definable. Correspondingly, speculative theories such as those of Spinoza and Teilhard de Chardin arising from and justifying this structure are more diverse and less rigorous than moral theories.

These theories, however, derive from a qualitatively new insight and perspective we call "Stage 7." The speculative philosophies that formulate this insight are not meaningless metaphysics, then, as positivism holds, but constructions essential for understanding human development.

10. Moral Development and the Theory of Tragedy

CENTRAL TO tragedy is the idea of justice. As stated by Aeschylus, the first great tragedian, "Zeus, who guided men to think, has laid it down that wisdom comes along through suffering. . . . *Justice so moves that those only learn who suffer*" *(Agamemnon)*.

Aristotle on the Moral Nature of Tragedy

The first philosopher of tragedy, Aristotle, tells us that tragedy was a moral action to arouse moral emotions. Our definition of tragedy, he says, must start (1) with the *moral character* of the people in the plot. Types of drama, he tells us, are defined by the types of moral character of the people represented. The objects the dramatist represents are actions with agents who are necessarily either good or bad. The difference that distinguishes tragedy and comedy is "that the one makes its personage worse, and the other better than the men of the present day" (Aristotle, *Poetics*, 1448). Second, morality is central not only to the definition of the characters in tragedy, but also (2) to the definition of the plot or action, which is a *moral* action. The soul of tragedy is not in its character but in its plot, the "change in the hero's fortunes from happiness to misery, not because of depravity but because of a great error on his part." The elements of the tragic plot, then, are peripety, discovery, and suffering. The plot of a tragedy is a moral action, not only in that it is action springing from moral character but also in that the action of the play starts with a moral decision by the hero in which he makes a great moral error, and this error leads to suffering through discoveries revealing this error and its meaning. Finally, (3) the aim of the tragedy, emotional catharsis in the spectator, is the arousal and release of specifically *moral emotion* (as opposed to

This chapter was first published in S. Weintraub and P. Young (eds.), *Directions in Literary Criticism: Contemporary Approaches to Literature* (University Park: Pennsylvania State University Press, 1973). Reprinted by permission.

other emotions aroused by drama). The aim of the plot, "the tragic effect," is a moral emotion, "the tragic pleasure of pity and fear."

Olson (1966) a contemporary exponent of the Aristotelian view of tragedy clarifies the sense in which the "tragic effect" of catharsis is distinctively moral. To do so, he claims the tragic effect cannot be defined purely in terms of a type of emotion, where the emotion is defined without attention to the cognitive structure of moral judgment that is part of the tragic effect. The quality of an emotion aroused by a drama depends on the quality of the structure of moral judgment implicit in the play. Tragedy, as a genre, and the achieving of a dramatic effect, are defined by the type or quality of the structure of moral judgment or cognition (moral or practical wisdom) implicit in the play and aroused in the spectator.

Olson (1966) says,

Emotions are also not peculiar to any given form, although we usually speak as if they were. Aristotle himself seems to have given some support to this notion by his remark that pity and fear are peculiar to tragedy. I do not think he means what he appears to mean; however, Aristotle or no Aristotle, the facts say otherwise. Any dramatic form can and does arouse almost every sort of emotion. Pity and fear, for instance, are aroused not merely by tragedy, but by melodrama and certain sentimental forms as well. Indeed, they can be aroused even by comedy. Thus the effect of drama must involve something more than emotion. What is that "something more"? . . .

Every emotional experience must either confirm or alter in some way our system of values; and, in altering it, make it better or worse whenever it affects a moral value. This must hold true, also, of drama and the other arts, so that the effect of drama is its effect upon moral values. . . .

One kind of drama assumes the system of values of the person of ordinary morality. It proposes simply the arousing of emotions to the ultimate effect of giving pleasure, its aim is entertainment. Its effect is transitory, and its excellence consists simply in the intensity of the pleasure which it gives. That intensity is naturally dependent upon the intensity of the emotions produced; thus the serious forms of this kind tend to play upon extreme fear and other painful emotion, while the comic forms play upon the more extreme reactions of the ridiculous.

The second kind of drama goes beyond entertainment, and permits us perceptions which we should not otherwise have had; it goes beyond ordinary morality and offers us other and better systems of values; it, in some degree, alters us as human beings. To put this in a nutshell, there is a difference between works which give us an intense experience and works which give us a significant experience.

What is this meaning, this significance? Certainly not the verbal meaning of sentences in the work. And certainly not some *moral* to be derived from the work, in the style of old-fashioned schoolteachers. The moral of *Othello* is that women should be careful how they bestow their linen, said Thomas Rymer, thinking of Desdemona's troubles with a certain handkerchief; we laugh at this, precisely because this moral—or any other—is so far removed from the significance of the play. It is not the discovery of the moral principle or precept involved, after the fashion of the moral-hunting pedagog, but the recognition that such and such a specific action *has* a certain moral quality.

I shall say, therefore, that a work possesses significance or meaning as it promotes perceptions—perceptions based on feelings—which are conducive to practical wisdom; which would, if acted upon, eventuate in such wisdom. The condition of mind which it immediately promotes is a temporary alignment of passion, emotion, and desire with right principle.

I agree with Olson that a significant tragedy (although not all significant drama, as he claims) must "go beyond ordinary morality and offer us other and better systems of values," that it involves the "discovery of moral principle," not "after the fashion of the moral-hunting pedagog" but in the "recognition that such and such a specific action has a certain moral quality" and that a tragic work possesses significance as it promotes perceptions based on feelings conducive to practical wisdom, and as it immediately promotes a condition of mind in which passion is aligned with right principle.

The Freudian View of Tragedy

The psychological problem of the emotion aroused by tragedy is expressed by Hume (1757) as the problem as to why "there should be an unaccountable pleasure which the spectators of a well-written tragedy receive from sorrow, terror, anxiety, and other passions that are in themselves disagreeable and uneasy."

The doctrine of catharsis, of course, explains this paradox on the grounds that tragic catharsis is pleasurable because it is a release or purgation of unpleasant emotions. The doctrine of catharsis is essentially an "irrational" doctrine, release from unpleasant emotions is not a movement toward moral enlightenment or rational moral vision. The doctrine of catharsis is the doctrine that we have irrational moral emotions of pity and dread and that the tragedy purges us of these irrational moral emotions. It is not surprising, then, that the chief contribution of modern psychology to the understanding of catharsis

has come from moral psychologists of the irrational, in particular
Nietzsche and Freud. Freud and Nietzsche agree fundamentally that
morality is a matter of guilt and that guilt is irrational because it
arises from irrational instincts turned inward (for Freud, aggression;
for Nietzsche (1971), the will to power). Both Freud and Nietzsche
place the origin of morality in a mythical past in which man turns his
instinct of aggression (or will to power) inward instead of directing it
against his oppressors or authorities, and with this inward-turning
instinct was born the sense of guilt. Nietzsche sees the full birth of
morality as conscience occurring in the figure of Socrates and sees the
full development of such morality as ending Greek tragedy, which was
itself a transition to the morality of conscience. Freud sees morality as
born in that primal act in which the first men slew their father and
paid the price of guilt as the result. In its starkest form, the Freudian
analysis of tragedy is the story of Oedipus. The tragedy in drama is
the formation of conscience through parricidal rebellion and subsequent guilt. In this Freudian formula, the drama starts with the spec-
tatorself divided into the impulsive hero and the authority figure he
slays. The end of the play is a reunification of the divided self, of the
id, and the superego. The id, the impulsive portion of self, recognizes
that it is inextricably a part of the self that also includes a moral force,
the superego, a force of guilt that controls it. In submitting to this
force, the force of punishment and fate, this impulsive self becomes at
one with the moral self, and catharsis is achieved.

Whatever our final view of the Freudian psychology of tragedy, its
contributions are clear-cut. It provides, first, a partial explanation for
why certain plots are recurrent in tragedy. Those who completely
doubt the Freudian interpretation need only be asked why it is that all
great tragedies—Greek, Shakespearean and modern—involve the
murder of another member of the family. Of all the aspects of tragic
plot we could never guess from the Aristotelian analysis, this is the
most astounding. We need not accept the whole Freudian doctrine to
understand why our ultimate pity and terror are felt toward those who
murder a member of their family, but the fact needs to be noted and
dealt with. Second, the Freudian doctrine helps to explain why the
primitive views of sin and punishment by fate embodied in Greek
tragedy still move us today. It tells us that even O'Neill's audience,
"an intelligent audience of today, possessed of no belief in gods or
supernatural retribution" had surviving in it from childhood some

such beliefs or the emotions that corresponded to them. It tells us that not only do we harbor, at some level, the potentiality for the family-murdering acts of tragic heroes but that we also harbor conscience feelings that would punish or destroy us for those acts regardless of whether such acts were a free-will choice of evil or whether they were determined so that we were not morally responsible for them.

Third, and most important, Freudianism not only helps explain but also helps create tragedies. Among the best of modern tragedies have been those written self-consciously by Freudians intending to revivify the Greek formulas by psychoanalytic means, men such as Eugene O'Neill and William Faulkner. Freudianism has served its literary purpose not merely by calling attention to recurrent universal themes of content in tragedy, but by creating a world view in which tragedy is meaningful within a scientifically oriented and morally relativistic culture. Faithful to necessities apparent in its early Athenian form, tragedy requires a crime to be committed that is both willed and unwilled; both free and foreordained, a fated act for which the actor is yet responsible. As tragic crime is foreordained but willed, so tragic punishment is both doom and self-discovery. In Athenian tragedy, the fated aspects of crime and punishment were the result of cruel but moral external forces. In the modern "psychoanalytic" form of tragedy, the fated aspects of crime and punishment are the products of uncontrolled and unconscious internal forces. The crime is the fated result of immutable instinctual impulses; the inevitable doom that follows the crime is the result of unconscious and inescapable needs for punishment. Other "scientific" world views, such as the sociological determinism embodied in Dreiser's *An American Tragedy,* provide a sense of the inevitability of crime and punishment. This inevitability, however, is the product of purely external and amoral forces and cannot be combined with the willed self-discovery and repentance characteristic of classic tragedy.

Thus the Freudian psychology is part of a Freudian world view that is itself largely tragic. It provides a context for tragedy in a scientific, rationalistic, and morally relative world. Nevertheless, modern tragedy based on the Freudian view, such as O'Neill's tragedies, are not ultimate tragedies in the sense in which Greek, Shakespearean, or Russian tragedy is ultimate tragedy, and it fails to be such because it fails to grapple with moral meaning and simply accepts, ultimately, an amoral cosmos in which human morality is merely the neurotic fate of a social animal. Only a philosophy and psychology that invests human morality with rationality and meaning, and then pits morality against a human fate of death and injustice, is one that can create an ultimate tragedy.

The Developmental Theory of Tragedy

Such a philosophy and psychology I call "cognitive-developmental" (Kohlberg, 1969). It was born in Hegelian German idealism but became naturalistic and scientific in America with John Dewey, William James, and James Mark Baldwin, in Russia with Vygotsky, and in Switzerland with Piaget. Its best statement as a general philosophy and psychology of art comes in Dewey's *Art as Experience* (1937). Unlike Freudianism, developmental psychology stresses universal mental structures or forms that develop through invariant stages. These structures come into positions of conflict or contradiction with one another, and the conflict of these forms and their integration (rather than conflicts between hydraulic emotional forces) is the soul of art and of tragedy.

In the case of tragedy, the critical structures in conflict are *forms of moral thought or judgment*. In the Freudian view, the characters in drama represent the warring forces in the personality, the forces of impulse (id), conscience (superego), and of cognition or reason (ego). These forces have a certain developmental order, the id being most primitive, the superego next, and the ego most mature. In contrast, the cognitive developmental theory of personality sees all developmental stages of personality as having a moral component. There is an impulsive morality, but it is still a morality, not an "id"; there is a rational cognitive morality, but it is still a morality, not an ego. The personality is unitary; cognition and affect join in single structures rather than being divided into separate organs of impulse (id) and cognition (ego). Although the personality is unitary, it progresses through stages in a sequential order. Here I draw on my theory and findings concerning stages of moral development (Kohlberg, 1968, 1969, 1970). These stages are redefined in Table 10.1, together with quotations from dramatic characters to represent them. The stages are culturally universal.

Not only are the moral stages culturally universal, but they also correspond to a progression in cultural history. Principled moral thinking appeared first in human history in the period 600-400 B.C.,

Table 10.1 Definition of Moral Stages with Examples from Literature

A. PRECONVENTIONAL LEVEL

At this level the child is responsive to cultural rules and labels of good and bad, right or wrong but interprets these labels in terms of either the physical or the hedonistic consequences of action (punishment, reward, exchange of favors) or in terms of the physical power of those who enunciate the rules and labels. The level is divided into the following two stages:

Stage 1: The punishment and obedience orientation

The physical consequences of action determine its goodness or badness regardless of the human meaning or value of these consequences. Avoidance of punishment and unquestioning deference to power are valued in their own right, not in terms of respect for an underlying moral order supported by punishment and authority (the latter being Stage 4).

Guard (in *Antigone*):

I want to tell you first about myself.
I didn't do it, didn't see who did it.
It isn't right for me to get in trouble.

We couldn't see a chance of getting off.
He said we had to tell you all about it.
We couldn't hide the fact.

Stage 2: The instrumental relativist orientation

Right action consists of that which instrumentally satisfies one's own needs and occasionally the needs of others. Human relations are viewed in terms like those of the marketplace. Elements of fairness or reciprocity and equal sharing are present, but they are always interpreted in a physical, pragmatic way. Reciprocity is a matter of "You scratch my back and I'll scratch yours," not of loyalty, gratitude, or justice.

Iago (in *Othello*):

I follow him to serve my term upon him;
You shall mark many a duteous and knee-crooking knave,
that doting on his own obsequious bondage
Wears out his time, much like his master's ass,
for naught but provender and when he's old cashiered.
Whip me such honest knaves. Others there are
Who, trimmed in forms and visages of duty
Keep yet their hearts attending on themselves,
And throwing but shows of service on their lords
Do well thrive by them and when they have lined their coats
Do themselves homage; these fellows have some soul,
And such a one do I profess myself.

• • •

Since I could distinguish betwixt a benefit and an injury I never found man that knew how to love himself. Ere I would say, I would drown myself for the love of a

guinea-hen, I would change my humanity with a baboon. . . . We have reason to cool
our raging motions, our carnal stings, our unbitted lusts; whereof I take this, that you
call love, to be a sect or scion. . . . It is merely a lust of the blood and a permission of
the will— . . . Put money in thy purse.

B. CONVENTIONAL LEVEL

At this level, maintaining the expectations of the individual's family, group,
or nation is perceived as valuable in its own right, regardless of immediate
and obvious consequences. The attitude is not only one of *conformity* to
personal expectations and social order but also of loyalty to them, of actively
maintaining, supporting, and justifying the order and of identifying with
the people or group involved in it. At this level, there are the following two
stages:

Stage 3: The interpersonal concordance or "good boy–nice girl" orientation

Good behavior is that which pleases or helps others and is approved by
them. There is much conformity to stereotypical images of the majority of
"natural" behavior. Behavior is frequently judged by intention. Being good
or moral and being loving are equated.

Ismene (in *Antigone*):

If things have reached this stage, what can I do,
poor sister, that will help to make or mend?
We must remember that we two are women
so not to fight with men.
And that since we are subject to strong power
we must hear these orders, or any that may be worse.
So I shall ask of them beneath the earth
forgiveness, for in these things I am forced,
and shall obey the men in power. I know
that wild and futile action makes no sense.

Go, since you want to. But know this: you go
senseless indeed, but loved by those who love you.

Desdemona (in *Othello*):

Do not doubt, Cassio
But I will have my lord and you again
As friendly as you were.

You do love my lord,
You have known him long; and be you well assured
He shall in strangeness stand no further off.
If I do vow a friendship, I'll perform it to the
last article; my lord shall never rest
For thy solicitor shall rather die
Than give thy cause away.

Tell me, Emilia, Dost thou in conscience think that
there be women do abuse their husbands
In such gross kind?

Wouldst thou do such a deed for all the world?
In troth I think thou wouldst not
I do not think there is any such woman
Beshrew me if I would do such a wrong for the whole world.

Stage 4: The "law and order" orientation

There is an orientation toward authority, fixed rules, and the maintenance of the social order. Right behavior consists of doing one's duty, showing respect for authority, and maintaining the given social order for its own sake.

Creon (in *Antigone*):

You cannot learn of any man the soul,
the mind, and the intent until he shows
his practice of the government and law.
For I believe that who controls the state
and does not hold to the best plans of all,
but locks his tongue up through some kind of fear,
that he is worst of all who are or were.
And he who counts another greater friend
than his own fatherland, I put him nowhere.

Nor could I count the enemy of the land
friend to myself, not I who know so well
that she it is who saves us, sailing straight,
and only so can we have friends at all.

Such is my mind. Never shall I, myself,
honor the wicked and reject the just.

C. POSTCONVENTIONAL AUTONOMOUS, OR PRINCIPLED LEVEL

At this level, there is a clear effort to define moral values and principles that have validity and application apart from the authority of the groups or people holding these principles and apart from the individual's own identification with these groups. This level again has two stages:

Stage 5A: The social contract legalistic orientation

This stage generally has utilitarian overtones. Right action tends to be defined in terms of general individual rights and in terms of standards that have been critically examined and agreed on by the whole society. There is a clear awareness of the relativism of personal values and opinions and a corresponding emphasis on procedural rules for reaching consensus. Aside from what is constitutionally and democratically agreed on, the right is a matter of personal "values" and "opinion." The result is an emphasis on the "legal point of view" but with an emphasis on the possibility of changing law in terms of rational considerations of social utility (rather than freezing it in terms of Stage 4 "law and order"). Outside the legal realm, free agreement, and contract are the binding elements of obligation. This is the "official" morality of the U.S. government and Constitution.

Socrates (in the *Crito*):

Ought one to fulfill all one's agreements? Socrates asks. Then consider the consequences. Suppose the laws and constitution of Athens were to confront us and ask. Socrates, can you deny that by this act you intend so far as you have power, to destroy us. Do you imagine that a city can continue to exist if the legal judgments which are pronounced by it are nullified and destroyed by private persons? At an earlier time, you made a noble show of indifference if you had to die. Now you show no respect for your earlier professions and no regard for us the laws, trying to run away in spite of the contracts by which you agreed to live as a member of our state. Are we not speaking the truth when we say that you have undertaken in deed, if not in word to live your life as a citizen in obedience to us? It is a fact then that you are breaking covenants made with us under no compulsion or misunderstanding. You had seventy years in which you could have left the country if you were not satisfied with us or felt that the agreements were unfair.

Stage 5B: The human justice conscience orientation

Stage 5A is the "objective" form of Stage 5 thought; it starts with the rational social perspective, the perspective of a rational member of society. Stage 5B is the "subjective" perspective; it starts with the perspective of the individual moral self. Stage 5A stresses society, its laws and its welfare as what is real, as what exists, and what is and can be agreed on. Stage 5B tends to stress the ideal, the self as oriented to the "higher," to the "ideal self," to the "ideal moral law" or to "higher values." Stage 5B orients to the "authority" of an "ideal society," to utopia, not to society as it is. Within Stage 5B, there are the 5B "rules and conscience intuitionist" and the 5B "human realization existentialist."

Socrates (in the *Crito*):

But perhaps someone will say "Do you feel no compunction, Socrates, at having followed a line of action which puts you in danger of the death penalty?" I might fairly reply to him "You are mistaken, my friend, if you think that a man who is worth anything ought to spend his time weighing up the prospects of life and death. He has only one thing to consider in performing any action; that is, whether he is acting rightly or wrongly, like a good man or a bad one."

Thomas More (in *A Man for All Seasons*) (illustrating Stage 5B or Stage 6):

The law is not a light for you or any man to see by; the law is not an instrument of any kind. The law is a causeway upon which, so long as he keeps to it, a citizen may walk safely.

I am used to hear bad men misuse the name of God, yet God exists. In matters of conscience, the loyal subject is more bounden to be loyal to his conscience than to any other thing.

Stage 6: The universal ethical principle orientation

Right is defined by the decision of conscience in accord with self-chosen *ethical principles* appealing to logical comprehensiveness, universality, and consistency. These principles are abstract and ethical (the Golden Rule, the categorical imperative); they are not concrete moral rules like the Ten Commandments. At heart, these are universal principles of *justice,* of the *reciprocity* and *equality* of the human *rights,* and of respect for the dignity of human beings as *individual people.*

Martin Luther King ("Letter from a Birmingham Jail")

One may well ask, "How can you advocate breaking some laws and obeying others?" The answer lies in the fact that there are two types of laws, just and unjust. One has not only a legal but a moral responsibility to obey just laws. One has a moral responsibility to disobey unjust laws. An unjust law is a human law that is not rooted in eternal law and natural law. Any law that uplifts human personality is just, any law that degrades human personality is unjust. An unjust law is a code that a numerical or power majority group compels a minority group to obey but does not make binding on itself. This is difference made legal. I do not advocate evading or defying the law as would the rabid segregationist. That would lead to anarchy. One who breaks an unjust law must do so openly, lovingly, and with a willingness to accept the penalty. An individual who breaks a law that conscience tells him is unjust, and willingly accepts the penalty of imprisonment in order to arouse the conscience of the community over its injustice, is in reality expressing the highest respect for law.

---

when universal human ideals and rational criticism of customary morality developed in Greece, Palestine, India, and China. A sequence in historical and cultural evolution generally consistent with the stages of individual development was traced by Hobhouse (1906) using ethnographic material.

The development of morality generates moral structures that are conscious and cognitive, although they also have an emotional component. These structures are filters determining the writer's and the audience's perception of the characters and action of a drama. We retain all lower moral structures, but subordinate them to higher structures. Complex literature embodies these types of moral thought in characters but lets no type of moral thought triumph in a simple way. Ketto (1961) says,

While tragedy does not represent the triumph of a single higher moral point of view, there is an element of moral development, or movement to a higher stage of moral judgment, in the tragic process in which "wisdom comes alone through suffering." This is perhaps most apparent in the classic Greek tragedies. In these tragedies, there is a development or "education" of the chorus itself. This is especially evident in Aeschylus' *Oresteia* trilogy, which represents a movement from the endless cycle of blood retaliation to a morality of civic union and order. The progression represents the movement from the stage of morality of arbitrary taboo based on kinship, supported by tradition and by blood atonement [corresponding sometimes to Stage 1, sometimes to Stage 3] to more universal norms of a civic order [corresponding to Stage 4] supported by loyalty to the state and by impartial punishment in rational support of this order.

The modes of thought represented correspond rather exactly to Hobhouse's stages of moral evolution of cultures, less exactly to our parallel stages of individual development. (A comparison of the guard in *Antigone,* a "childish" Stage 1, as quoted in Table 10.1, with the Oresteian chorus suggests the difference between a cultural and an individual Stage 1.) The morality of each of the choruses in the trilogy is a morality of Stage 1 orientation to blood atonement. The chorus of the *Agamemnon* says, "The truth stands ever beside God's throne eternal, he who has wrought shall pay; that is law."

The chorus in the second play of the trilogy, the *Libation Bearers,* says, "For the word of hatred spoken, let hate be a word fulfilled. The spirit of right cries out aloud and extracts atonement due blood stroke for the stroke of blood shall be paid." The ultimate embodiment of blood atonement is the chorus of the Eumenides, who say, "You must give back for blood from the living man red blood of your body."

Associated with the morality orientation of blood atonement is a Stage 1 conception of moral rules as particular taboos linked to blood kindship. The Furies explain that Clytemnestra's murder of Agamemnon was not as evil as Orestes' murder of his mother because "the man she killed was not of blood congenital."

A third characteristic of the Stage 1 morality of the Oresteian chorus is the belief in a morality based on fear. The Eumenides (*Agamemnon*) say,

Here is overthrow of all the young laws, if the claim of this
matricide shall stand good, his crime be sustained.
  Should this be, every man will find a way to act at his own
caprice: There are times when fear is good.
  Should the city, should the man rear a heart that nowhere
goes in fear, how shall such a one anymore respect the right?

The conclusion of the trilogy, of course, is acceptance of a "new morality" of civic order by the chorus of the Eumenides:

Let not the dry dust that drinks the black blood of citizens through passion for revenge and for bloodshed be given our state to prey upon. Let them render grace for grace. Let love be their common will; let them hate with single heart. Much wrong in the world thereby is healed.

This new morality is, of course, the Stage 4 civic morality, which decries blood atonement for the sake of the state and for civic unity. It is the morality represented in the thought of Athena, as opposed to the Furies. My research-defined moral stages, then, allow me to rather exactly specify Ketto's statement that there "is an element of moral development, of movement to a higher stage of moral judgment in the tragic process in which wisdom comes alone through suffering."

Development and Justice in Tragedy—Tragedy as Beyond Justice

It is important to recognize, that the core moral concern in Aeschylean tragedy—and, indeed, in all tragedy—is justice.

As Nietzsche tells us, "The most wonderful thing is the Aeschylean yearning for *justice*. The double personality of the Aeschylean Prometheus might be expressed in the abstract formula: 'Whatever exists is alike just and unjust, and in both cases equally justified.' " (1971, p. 22).

It is important to note the centrality of justice because "the wisdom learned through suffering" in tragedy is not the wisdom of a generally higher stage of morality but a new attitude toward justice.

But even if the *Oresteia* does, in a sense, represent a movement to, or a triumph of, a higher morality over a lower morality, this is not generally the case of Greek tragedy. The tragedies of Aeschylus' successor Sophocles represent a tragic hero whose moral error is still an expression of, or connected with, the hero's Stage 4 conventional civic morality. The Stage 4 civic morality that terminates the *Oresteia* is the source of strain and tragedy in Sophocles. The Oedipus cycle commences with Oedipus endeavoring to search out, curse, and punish the murderer of Laius, in the name of his responsibilities for civic order.

The termination of *Oedipus the King* comes with his fulfillment of that punishment against himself. Starting in *Oedipus at Colonus* and moving through *Antigone* is the story of the destruction of Creon because of Creon's prideful civic morality and his use of it to justify punitiveness. In Table 10.1, I quoted Creon's speech as an embodiment of Stage 4 civic morality. In the passage, Creon (1) asserts loyalty to the state as the highest value, (2) asserts the need to punish and discipline all who do not hold this loyalty, and (3) equates civic loyalty with discipline and obedience in the family as well as the state and justifies such discipline as necessary to avoid civic disorder.

Creon uses this civic order morality to justify his own punitiveness. His niece Antigone's morality, which he denies, is a morality of loyalty to kinship and to the gods who support the norms of kinship. Her morality, although it questions Creon's man-made law, is not a morality of conscience or principle. She says, "Nor did I think your orders were so strong that you, a mortal man, could overrun the gods' unwritten and unfailing laws. So not through fear of any man's proud request would I be likely to neglect these laws and draw on myself the gods' sure punishment."

Her morality is essentially like that of the Jehovah's Witness who refuses to be drafted, or pledge the flag, or have a blood transfusion, because of God's word and God's authority. The nature of this morality is not conscience but respect for authority and divine sanction. The norms of the morality are not universal principles of human justice and welfare but respect for the dead, expressed in maintaining concrete and arbitrary rules. It is essentially a Stage 4 morality of divine order rather than of civic order.

Creon's blindness, then, was not a blindness to a higher justice, it was the blindness of taking justice into his own hands in the name of civic morality. In *Antigone,* as in every tragedy, the hero acts out of a misplaced sense of justice. The "lesson" the hero learns through suffering is that he has no right to demand justice or enforce it on others. If he enforces punitive justice on others, he punishes those he loves most and so, eventually, himself. In *Antigone,* Creon finds that his "justice" leads to the suicide of his wife and son and only then learns true justice. *Antigone* ends thus:

CREON: O crimes of my wicked heart, harshness bringing death.
You see the killer, you see the son he killed.
For you have died too soon.
Oh, you have gone away
through my fault, not your own.
CHORUS: You have learned justice, though it comes too late.

I have considered Greek tragedy as embodied in the Orestes and the Oedipus cycles. They start with a world in disorder and tragic heroes who will bring order into the world by a passionate act of "justice," where justice is a punitive reaction at one or another moral stage. This act of justice ends by destroying either someone the heroes love or themselves, or both. The "wisdom" the hero learns is "Judge not, lest you be judged." This wisdom does not bring the heroes to the principled moral stage, but only leads them to recognize the error of their misplaced demand for justice.

It is characteristic of almost all tragedies that their heroes are people of conventional morality. An example of a drama with a hero above conventional morality, a principled hero, is Bolt's *A Man for All Seasons* (1960). As quoted in Table 10.1 the hero, Thomas More, illustrates Stage 6 (or 5B). The drama appeals to our Stage 6 sense of principles of conscience and reaffirms them. Stage 6 people go to their deaths willingly in the service of their principles. The drama is not a tragedy, it is a reaffirmation of Stage 6. It tells us that people of principle will die for their beliefs and die in calmness. In so doing, it reaffirms our faith in moral principles and in the potential nobility of human beings. It is not a tragedy, because principled or Stage 6 heroes are able to live with the consequences of their actions, there is no wisdom they can attain through suffering; their suffering may redeem others, but they need no redemption themselves. The emotion aroused by *A Man for All Seasons* is similar to that aroused in the *Crito* by Socrates' calm acceptance of death on behalf of principle (as cited in Table 10.1). Of this death, Phaedo tells us,

I could hardly believe that I was present at the death of a friend, and therefore I did not pity him; his mien and language were so noble and fearless in the hour of death that to me he appeared blessed. I was pleased and I was also pained because I knew that he was soon to die and this strange mixture of feelings was shared by us all.

Phaedo's emotion is one response to the death of a principled man; blind shock, as at the death of Martin Luther King, is another. In the first case the emphasis is on the principled person's acceptance of fate, in the second case on its wanton undeservedness. In neither case is the reaction that of classical tragedy. Not only are the heroes of a tragedy not initially principled, but the wisdom they learn through suffering is not the wisdom of a higher or principled morality.

The problem tragedy faces is the problem of justice, but the tragic wisdom is not a higher principle of justice, a "right principle," or a better "system of moral values" in Olson's (1966) terms. The tragic wisdom is, rather, religious; it is the resignation of the demand for justice in order to accept life in a cosmos that is just in no humanly understandable sense.

The Ontological Meaning of Tragedy and "Natural Law"

To clarify that the tragic wisdom is the resignation of the demand for personal justice and the acceptance of a cosmos that is both just and unjust, let us turn to Shakespearean tragedy. Shakespearean characters are more concerned with personal justice and less concerned with civic morality justice than are the characters of Greek tragedy. As in Greek tragedy, Shakespearean tragic heroes are people of pride and strength as well as passion, and the tragic action is a result of moral error rather than loss of self-control. It is an act they believe is morally right when they commit it, and only later do they come to see it as morally wrong. The act in each case is a vengeful act to the person the hero most loves. In *King Lear,* the act is cutting Cordelia out of her estate and his life; in *Othello,* murder. In both cases, these acts are performed not out of sheer passion, but in the illusion of acting morally in the name of justice to correct the loved one's ingratitude or unfaithfulness. The tragedy terminates with the death of both the loved ones and oneself. This termination, however, involves a mutual forgiveness and a recognition of the supremacy of love over justice. It is in this context that forgiveness, the "Judge not, lest ye be judged," is presented.

CORDELIA: We are not the first
Who, with best meaning, have incurred the worst.

LEAR: No, no, no, no! Come, let's away to prison:
We two alone will sing like birds i' the cage.
When thou dost ask me blessing I'll kneel down,
And ask of thee forgiveness; so we'll live,
and pray, and sing, and tell old tales, and laugh
At gilded butterflies, and hear poor rogues
Talk of court news; and we'll talk with them too,
Who loses and who wins; who's in, who's out;
And take upon's the mystery of things,
As if we were God's spies, and we'll wear out,

> In a wall'd prison, packs and sects of great ones
> That ebb and flow by the moon.

EDMOND: Take them away.

LEAR: Upon such sacrifices, my Cordelia,
The gods themselves throw incense.

Lear tells us not only that he willingly renounces all desire for an influence in state affairs to "ask and give forgivness," but also suggests that he and Cordelia "talk of court news...as if we were God's spies." He does not believe in divine justice, he is not one of God's spies, but he renounces his demand for justice, for understanding the mystery of things that dictates who loses, who wins.

I have so far stressed the morality of the protagonists in tragedy and have only indirectly stressed the morality of the fate that befalls them. On this, it is useful to summarize A. C. Bradley's (1904, pp. 24–36) comments on the Shakespearean view of fate or justice as "alike just and unjust":

In this tragic world, then, where individuals, however great they may be and however decisive their actions may appear, are so evidently not the ultimate power, *what is this power?* It will be agreed that this question must not be answered in "religious" language. Two statements, next, may at once be made regarding the tragic fact as he represents it: one that it is and remains to us something piteous, fearful, and mysterious; the other, that the representation of it does not leave us crushed, rebellious, or desperate. The ultimate power in the tragic world is not adequately described as a law or order which we can see to be just and benevolent—as, in that sense, a "moral order," for in that case the spectacle of suffering and waste could not seem to us so fearful and mysterious as it does. Neither is the ultimate power adequately described as a fate, whether malicious and cruel, or blind and indifferent to human happiness and goodness, for in that case the spectacle would leave us desperate or rebellious. Yet one or other of these two ideas will be found to govern most accounts of Shakespeare's tragic view or world. These accounts isolate and exaggerate single aspects, either the aspect of action or that of suffering; either the close and unbroken connection of character, will, deed and catastrophe, which, taken alone, shows the individual simply as sinning against, or failing to conform to, the moral order and drawing his just doom on his own head; or else that pressure of outward forces, that sway of accident, and those blind and agonized struggles, which, taken alone, show him as the mere victim of some power which cares neither for his sins nor for his pain.

The sense in which the ultimate powers in the tragic world is moral may be argued as follows:

Whatever may be said of accidents, circumstances and the like, human action is, after all, presented to us as the central fact in tragedy, and also as the main cause of the catastrophe. That necessity which so much impresses us is, after all, chiefly the necessary connection of actions and consequences. For these actions we, without even raising a question on the subject, hold the agents responsible; and the tragedy would disappear for us if we did not. The critical action is, in greater or less degree, wrong or bad. The catastrophe is, in the main, the return of this action on the head of the agent. It is an example of justice; and that order which, present alike within the agents and outside them, infallibly brings it about, is therefore just. The rigor of its justice is terrible, no doubt, for a tragedy is a terrible story; but, in spite of fear and pity, we acquiesce, because our sense of justice is satisfied.

Now, if this view is to hold good, the "justice" of which it speaks must be at once distinguished from what is called "poetic justice." We might not object to the statement that Lear deserved to suffer for his folly, selfishness, and tyranny; but to assert that he deserved to suffer what he did suffer is to do violence not merely to language but to any healthy moral sense. It is, moreover, to obscure the tragic fact that the consequences of action cannot be limited to that which would appear to us to follow "justly" from them. The idea which this suggests, is that of an order which does not, indeed, award "poetic justice" but which reacts through the necessity of its own "moral" nature both against attacks made upon it and against failure to conform to it. Tragedy, on this view, is the exhibition of that convulsive reaction, and the fact that the spectacle does not leave us rebellious or desperate is due to a more or less distinct perception that the tragic suffering and death arise from collision, not with a fate or blank power, but with a moral power, a power akin to all that we admire and revere in the characters themselves. This perception produces something like a feeling of acquiescence in the catastrophe, though it neither leads us to pass judgment on the characters nor diminishes the pity, the fear, and the sense of waste, which their struggle, suffering and fall evoke. And, finally, this view seems quite able to do justice to those aspects of the tragic fact which give rise to the idea of fate. They would appear as various expressions of the fact that the moral order acts not capriciously or like a human being, but from the necessity of its nature, or, if we prefer the phrase, by general laws—a necessity or law which, of course, knows no exception and is as "ruthless" as fate.

Bradley here attempts to present the Shakespearean cosmos as a representation of the Hegelian world order. But the essential statement is accurate, the statement that the tragic world is neither just and moral nor is it morally neutral. In my own view, this view of the cosmos as both just and unjust is an expression of the fact that the human sense of justice is a universal natural emergent in life; it rests on "natural law" in the sense that is is not the arbitrary creation of culture and training. Just because it is "natural," human morality comes into painful and sharp contrast with society's law or society's justice. Just that contrast proves that it has its source in a larger cosmic "law."

Although the sense of justice is natural, nature or fate are not bent on reward for justice or morality. The world order, then, is one that has established humanity's sense of justice and then left it in conflict with the forces of nature and society. In that sense, my view is much closer to Bradley's Hegelian view than to psychoanalytic views of conscience as a cultural creation to restrain amoral impulses, and, in that sense, my view of morality supports a larger vision of the "tragic fact" that is still compatible with science.

The Moral Nature of Tragedy in a Postconventional World

If what I have said is correct, modern tragedy should present a new vision of the "tragic fact." In Greek and Shakespearean tragedy, the tragic heroes' misguided struggles for justice are generated from a conventional morality. The fate that strikes them down, like the heroes' own demand for justice, is both just and unjust and, like the heroes', is expressive of the framework of a conventional morality of civic and cosmic order. The modern literary consciousness is one increasingly aware of principled morality, but as we have noted, principled heroes do not make a tragedy. Modern tragic heroes, then, will express the demand for a justice at a level intermediate between conventional and principled morality, at the level where they can make a principled demand for justice but do not really accept or live by principles. The writer who has most clearly expressed this conception of the tragic hero is Dostoevsky.

The problem of tragedy is the problem of justice, it reaches its ultimate ideological statement for modern man in Dostoevsky. Dostoevsky's parricidal tragic hero, Ivan Karamazov, says,

With my pitiful, earthly, Euclidian understanding, all I know is that there is suffering and that there are none guilty; that cause follows effect, simply and directly; that everything flows and finds its level—but that's only Euclidian nonsense, I know that, and I can't consent to live by it! What comfort is it to me that there are none guilty and that cause follows effect simply and directly, and that I know it—I must have justice, or I will destroy myself. And not justice in some remote infinite time and space, but here on earth, and that I could see myself.

I understand, of course, that an upheaval of the universe it will be, when everything in heaven and earth blends in one hymn of praise and everything that lives and has lived cries aloud, "Thou art just, O Lord, for Thy ways are revealed." But it's not worth the tears of one tortured child who beat itself on the breast with its little fist and prayed in its stinking outhouse, with its unexpiated tears, to "Dear, kind God"! It's not worth it, because those tears are unatoned for. They must be atoned for, or there can be no harmony. But how? The sufferings of her tortured child the mother has no right to forgive; she dare not forgive the torturer, even if the child were to forgive him! And if that is so, if they dare not forgive, what becomes of harmony? Is there in the whole world a being who would have the right to forgive and could forgive? I don't want harmony. From love for humanity, I don't want it. I would rather remain with my unavenged suffering and unsatisfied indignation, *even if I were wrong*. Besides, too high a price is asked for harmony; it's beyond our means to pay so much to enter on it. And so I hasten to give back my entrance ticket, and if I am an honest man I am bound to give it back as soon as possible. And that I am doing. It's not God that I don't accept, Alyosha, only I most respectfully return Him the ticket.

In one way, Ivan Karamazov has stated the problem of justice in a way that is insoluble. The culmination of moral development is the formation of universal principles of justice before which the law of society is brought to the bar, as in Martin Luther King's statement in Table 10.1. The construction of moral principles is the construction of ideals that are independent of social and cosmic reality and by which reality is itself judged. Awareness of moral principle implies an ultimate division or gap between the *is* and the *ought*, the real and the ideal. Ivan Karamazov tells us that "God's law" heals this gap no more than "society's law." Even if there is a God, a moral power in the universe, his morality is not our morality because he has made an unjust world. No kingdom of heaven can atone for the injustice of this world.

The problem of the world's justice as it is raised in the name of autonomous moral principle can be compared with the problem as it is raised in the name of conventional (Stage 4) morality in the Book of

Job. Job asked Ivan Karamazov's question of justice, but he asked it egocentrically. Job asked the justice question: "Why me? Why should an upright man like me suffer?" Job's morality was a law-maintaining morality premised on divine reward and punishment, or eventually on respect for divine authority. Ultimately, then, Job can be satisfied with God's answer, a reassertion of his authority:

Where wast thou when I laid the foundations of the earth
Declare if thou hast understanding,
wilt thou disavow my judgment?
Wilt thou condemn me, that thou mayest be justified?

The Book of Job, then, is in a sense an assertion of the "higher" elements in Stage 4 law—maintaining morality. Satan induces Jehovah to test whether Job's uprightness is based on divine reward or whether it will be maintained in the face of disaster. Although Job's morality is not based simply on divine reward and punishment (Stage 1, in my terms), his morality is partly contingent on divine justice, on some equation between uprightness and the events of fate. This contingency is stripped away, leaving a morality of respect for divine authority that no longer demands "justice" because justice is limited, egocentric, human desire for rewards according to one's own scales.

For moderns such as Dostoevsky, the question of justice asked at the principled level cannot be answered by the revelation of a divine authority in the cosmos. Dostoevsky, of course, attempts to provide a number of answers to the question. One is Christian, that "there is a being who would have the right to forgive and could forgive." But he attempts to answer the question also along the lines of classical tragedy. He claims, that is, that when the sense of justice of the tragic hero dares to go beyond or to violate civil law and religious faith, it leads the hero to murder and self-destruction—in Ivan's case, to the classic crime of parricide. The tragic hero's principled sense of justice in Dostoevsky is fused with the notion that morality is relative and arbitrary, with a consequent sense of being beyond good and evil.

In understanding Dostoevsky's tragic heroes, it is helpful to understand that they have real-life counterparts understandable in terms of moral stages. Our longitudinal work has demonstrated that there is a twilight zone in the movement from conventional to principled moral thought. A prerequisite to moving from conventional to principled morality is awareness of the relativity of conventional morality. In the ordinary course of development, dissatisfaction with the arbitrariness of conventional morality leads the individual to search for, or construct, more universal and autonomous ethical principles. A number of the youths we have studied, however, do not move directly from conventional to principled thought. Instead, becoming aware of the relativity of conventional morality, they assume that all possible moralities are relative and arbitrary, that there is no validity to judgments of right and good. These subjects generally oscillate, like Dostoevsky's heroes, between railing at society's injustice and the assertion that all concepts of morality and justice are relative. Sometimes, like Dostoevsky's heroes, they not only question, but they also commit crimes to prove they are beyond morality (Kohlberg and Kramer, 1969). Longitudinal study indicates that most of the students eventually progress to principled morality and that their moral questioning and "crimes" are only transitional to a higher morality.

In Dostoevsky's works, the moral ambivalence and ambiguity of the hero requires that he have a double who collaborates in his crime and who is truly amoral (Kohlberg, 1963c). Parallel to Ivan is Smerdyakov, to Raskolnikov, Svidrigailov, to Shatov, Stavrogin. These figures both tempt or lead the tragic hero into crime and reveal that behind their sense of justice, which justifies crime, is not justice but amoralism. The doubles themselves are uninterested in justice and are completely amoral. These figures, too, have their real-life counterparts. In addition to adolescents in ambivalent passage to moral principle, there is another group of individuals in the twilight zone. These individuals, all extremely bright, never fully comprehend or believe in conventional morality and are primarily Stage 2 instrumental egoists throughout early adolescence. In late adolescence, they, too, philosophically discover the relativity of conventional morality. Rather than being torn between demands for justice and amoralism, they use relativity to freeze and harden their basic posture.

Because Dostoevsky's heroes are post conventional although not principled, and because of their relations to their doubles, Dostoevsky's novels do not fit the formula of tragedy applicable to Greek or Shakespearean drama. But it should be recognized that ultimately Dostoevsky presents, like all, tragedians, tragic heroes who violate law in a passionate demand for justice. This demand leads them to kill those they love, to recognize that themselves they were not free or informed, and to recognize that one cannot judge, lest one be judged.

In spite of the complexity of ideology in Dostoevsky's novels, then, his most essential tragic effects, like Shakespeare's, depend on the emotions aroused by the tragic heroes' murder, directly or indirectly, of someone they love. The demand for justice, the questioning of good and evil, can lead only to a murder, which in the end reasserts the supremacy of love over justice. Tragic heroes overvalue justice and their own honor connected with it, and this leads them to destroy those they love. In the termination, the heroes and the audience recognize the primacy of love over justice, and the heroes are willing, too late, to accept life under terms they originally rejected.

Catharsis in the Developmental View

In contradiction to the psychoanalytic view, I have presented a view of tragedy as an enactment in moral character, action, and fate of a dialectic (a sort of ballet) of Hegelian ideas centering around the problem of justice, and have used my moral stages and types to translate moral ideas into characters and action. I have also recognized, however that the central action of tragedy involves the murder of someone loved and suggested the relevance of Freudian ideas to this fact. The fact suggests that the tragic action involves the ultimate primary emotional conflict, the conflict between emotions of love and hate, and their resolution.

As Raphael (1960, p. 15) has pointed out,

Aristotle's doctrine is an answer to Plato's criticism of tragedy in the *Republic*. Tragic drama calls forth pity for the distress of its heroes, and this, Plato thinks, will render us liable to self-pity, instead of endurance, when we meet misfortune ourselves. Pity is therefore antagonistic to virtue and the attempt to control pity requires the banishment of the art that fosters it.

Accordingly, Raphael notes (p. 82), Plato replaces tragedy with a philosophic tragedy best represented by the trilogy of the death of Socrates *(Apology, Crito, Phaedo)*. It has the theme of tragedy, the death of a hero: it has the form of tragic drama, prologue, episodes, and chorus. But its effect is intended to be different. Phaedo says, *"I did not pity him . . . he appeared blessed."* In contrast (p. 15),

Aristotle seeks to defend tragedy while retaining Plato's criterion of justification. Harmful emotions must have some outlet; better to let them boil up at mere representation, and then the soul will be less troubled by them on real occasions of misfortune. Aristotle disagrees with Plato about the psychological effect of exciting emotion. In opposition to Plato's view that the capacity for emotion grows with exercise, Aristotle puts forth the doctrine that when our feelings are stirred we blow off steam and so are "purged."

As I have noted, Aristotle's doctrine of catharsis received a powerful new interpretation through Freudian psychology, in which tragedy was seen as the discharge of the negative emotions of antisocial lust and anger and primitive guilt. The debate between Plato and Aristotle as to whether artistic portrayal of negative emotions strengthens them by exercise or weakens them through catharsis has recently been a debate between behaviorists, supporting the Platonic notion, and the Freudians, supporting the Aristotelian notion, and has led to intense experimental inquiry by psychologists studying aggression, effects of the mass media, and so forth (Bandura, 1973). The results on the whole support the behaviorists and Platonists and give little comfort to the doctrine of catharsis.

Neither the Platonic-behavioristic or the Aristotelian-Freudian doctrines, then, adequately explain the positive emotional effects of tragedy. As Vygotsky (1971) stresses, catharsis is not the purgation of negative feeling, it is "the creative overcoming of the feeling, resolving it, conquering it, the transformation of the feeling into its opposite." This transformation depends on a conflict "between the violation of absolute law by absolute strength of heroic struggle." This notion is clarified by Raphael (1960, p. 25), who says,

Tragedy always represents a conflict between inevitable power or necessity and the reaction to necessity of self-conscious effort. In the case of tragedy victory always goes to necessity. The tragic hero, however, attracts our admiration because of some grandeur of spirit, a greatness in his effort to resist and our pity for his defeat. The inner conflict of tragedy is between the two forms of the sublime, the awe-inspiring strength of necessity and the grandeur of spirit which inspires admiration. Each triumphs on its own plane.

In my terms, both fate and the hero are both just and unjust. Both are in unresolvable conflict, both are (or achieve) a sublimity above justice.

More specifically, beneath the demand for justice of the hero is hatred and the desire for *death* of another and ultimately the self. Beneath the working of fate is another "justice" that equally represents the force of death. The force of death in the hero leads him in seeking vengeance or "justice" to hurt or kill these he loves. Once he has killed those he loves, he is ready to die himself. Equally, the force of death or fate kills not only the evil "villain," but also the innocent and lovable. In the end, then, the "catharsis" of tragedy is the transformation of emotions of hatred (demand for death of others) and of grief or fear of death into their opposite, love of life. The ultimate emotional source of tragedy is the fact of death, of the unfulfilled desire for immortality (Unamuno, 1954). The ultimate demand of justice is the demand that the just shall be immortal. The ultimate tragic fact is that death comes alike to the just and the unjust. Most religious ideologies of divine justice and of immortality deny this tragic fact and so are inconsistent with tragedy. I have pointed to the fact that the modern consciousness, resting on autonomous human principles of justice and a scientific view of human mortality, implies a tragic view of life. The effect of tragedy is to abandon our demand for justice, but it is also to abandon our demand for immortality and to love life as it is while accepting death. Tragedy achieves this emotional effect without religious ideology. It presents an insoluble conflict without an intellectual solution. The fact that an emotional solution is reached without an intellectual solution is what is meant by the mystery of "catharsis." It is what is meant in recognizing that tragedy and its characters are more than our Hegelian ballet of moral ideas around the theme of justice. Tragedy involves emotional conflict as well as intellectual conflict between ideas. In the psychology of Vygotsky and Dewey, however, emotional conflict (1) has a cognitive component and (2) leads to transformation and development of emotion, not mere purgation.

Let me, then, summarize the argument. Agreeing with Aristotle and his modern interpreter, Olson, I find tragedy to be a representation of moral action by a hero with a determinate moral character leading to a moral emotion of catharsis. This catharsis is not a mere purging of pity and fear but is a new and in some sense higher attitude to the moral qualities of life; it is a moral insight. I find myself however, unable to explain the moral insight on the basis of the Aristotelian moral psychology and moral philosophy, which identifies morality with habits of virtue and vice and with prudential, practical wisdom.

I turn then to the Freudian moral psychology of unconscious loves and hates in the family as these generate a conflict between impulse and conscience guilt. In this psychology, the tragic crime, usually a murder of someone in the family, is one that arouses pity (or identification) and fear because it is one that the spectator has unconsciously fantasized. The tragic crime leads to extreme punishment by fate that is both just and unjust because it is a crime that arouses the spectator's own superego, his or her primitive sense of guilt. The tragedy ends with a reconciliation or integration of impulse and conscience in the spectator on this basis.

I find the Freudian psychology illuminating but unable to cope with the conscious cognitive component of the moral insight involved in the tragic effect. I find it unsatisfactory also in its description of characters as stock representations of ego, superego and id. These defects become apparent when Freudian psychology is used, as by O'Neill, to write tragedy as well as to psychologize about it. There is a weakness in the moral insight of modern Freudian tragedy because its fundamental view is that there is no moral wisdom except the wisdom that morality is the fate of social animals bound by the arbitrary, relative standards of their culture.

Accordingly, I turn to the cognitive-developmental moral psychology, which defines universal stages of moral ideology. This psychology gives a better description or typology of dramatic characters than do the Aristotelian psychology of habit or the Freudian psychology of drives. Of more importance, it helps clarify the moral insight involved in the tragic effect. It explains why the problem of tragedy is the problem of justice. It explains why the hero, operating from a basis of conventional morality, demands a justice that violates conventional morality but is not truly a principled or higher justice. It explains why, then, the tragic insight is the insight into the limits of conventional conceptions of justice, a realization of the meaning of "Judge not, lest ye be judged," which is a moral, rather than a relativistic, or amoral, meaning of "judge not." It suggests that the problem of modern tragedy, best handled by Dostoevsky, is the problem of the post conventional tragic hero who demands justice but who cannot live by principles of justice. It suggests that this problem is one that parallels the state of many modern adolescents.

My own interest in tragedy is part of my interest in literature's role in education, in literature as stimulating human development. For education, the ultimate literature is tragedy because it, alone, can help individuals with life's central problems—not merely help them to cope with suffering but also to develop through suffering. In that sense, the tragic vision is one that every human being needs to feel and understand.

Even more than for the critical understanding of literature, the teaching of literature depends on a moral psychology that goes beyond Aristotle and Freud.

There are three theories of the moral educational effects of literature. The first is that literature is valuable because it has a "moral" in the conventional sense, that it conveys true moral and political doctrines and stimulates virtuous habits and emotions—the doctrine of Plato, of Tolstoy, and of the Marxists. The second doctrine, that of Aristotle, retains part of this notion but stresses "practical wisdom" as opposed to moral ideology and "catharsis" as opposed to stimulation of virtuous emotions. As stated by Olson, "Tragedy promotes perceptions conducive to practical wisdom and a temporary alignment of passion, emotion, and desire with right principle." The third doctrine, the cognitive-developmental, stresses that literature stimulates new stages, qualitatively new forms, of moral and esthetic thought and feeling. The value of tragic literature is that it invests life with a meaning beyond conventional morality and conventional emotion, that it gives a new meaning to morality rather than supporting the old meanings of conventional moral or religious ideologies.

EPILOGUE

Education for Justice:
The Vocation of Janusz Korczak

⚛⚛

In Chapter 2, called "Education for Justice: A Modern Statement of the Socratic View," I cited two Stage 6 moral educators, Socrates and Martin Luther King. Although King was a religious man, he taught and lived justice and died for it. The same was true of Socrates. Their religious willingness to face death inspired their vocation as moral educators and was a source of their inspiration for others.

The first chapter in the last part of this book, "Moral Development, Religious Thinking, and the Question of a Seventh Stage," suggested that what empowers a person to live a life of justice, and to face death for it, is itself something "beyond justice," something I metaphorically call a "Stage 7." People at this "stage" affirm life from a "cosmic perspective"; feel some mystic union with God, Life, or Nature; and accept the finitude of the self's own life, while finding its meaning in a moral life, a life in which a sense of love for, and union with, Life or God is expressed in a love for fellow human beings. The ethical and religious philosophies suggested by the metaphor of a seventh stage were illustrated with both the pantheistic natural law and justice philosophies of Marcus Aurelius, and of Spinoza (to which I could add the philosophy of Socrates or Plato) and the more theistic and love or

Ann Higgins and Clark Power contributed vitally to the writing of this epilogue. I also want to acknowledge with gratitude Betty Jean Lifton's discussions of Korczak with me. It was she who called to my attention the significance of Korczak as a moral educator. This epilogue relies heavily on her article in *The New York Times Magazine*, April 20, 1980.

agape-centered philosophy of Teilhard de Chardin and others in the Christian theological tradition.

In this epilogue, I discuss a man whose vocation was education for justice but whose energy and devotion to this vocation was based on development to the metaphoric seventh stage. His life illustrates the fact that the truest and most inspired moral educators possess something more than a philosophy of justice—they possess a "Stage 7" ethical and religious perspective of agape. His life also illustrates, however, that a "Stage 7" vocation as a moral educator still leads to a focus on education for justice. This "Stage 7" moral educator wisely did not attempt to explicitly preach or morally educate for "Stage 7," for a religious vision of universal love. This vision is communicated by example, not by systematic education. He understood that what he could expect or demand of children was less than what he was ready to give them himself. Rather, he educated for justice, something that could be expected of others and that could be educated for.

Like the death of Socrates and the death of Martin Luther King, the death of Janusz Korczak expresses both his vocation as a moral educator and his progress in a spiritual journey that few undertake and fewer succeed in making. He died during the Warsaw Ghetto uprising of World War II. For many years Korczak, trained as a pediatrician, had directed two orphanage schools in Warsaw, one for Christian children and one for Jewish children, expressing a universal concern that went beyond his Jewish heritage. With the coming of the Nazis, Korczak and his Jewish orphans were herded into the ghetto along with the rest of Warsaw's half-million Jews. His daily life became a round of seeking food and medicine for his charges. Although in ill health and starving himself, in his last year Korczak volunteered to take responsibility for the 1,000 children in the ghetto's public orphanage. He and his devoted colleague, Stepha Wilczynska, invited actors and musicians to perform as a way of raising funds. They organized a school in which caring and justice guided the daily lives and experiences of the children, a place in which the children could still study and learn despite the war.

On the morning of August 6, 1942, German and Ukrainian guards surrounded the orphanage as part of the plan for elimination of "nonproductive elements" to the Treblenka death camp. Prepared for death, Korczak led the 200 children from his own orphanage to the train station where the freight cars waited. Each child, neatly dressed and carrying a favorite doll or book, marched the two miles in a parade of quiet dignity. Korczak led the column, holding the two youngest by the hand. Stepha and the other teachers walked not far behind. His attitude toward his own impending death is expressed in two statements: "You do not leave a sick child in the night, and you do not leave children at a time like this." In a diary entry August 4, while watching a guard outside his window, he said, "What would he do if I nodded to him? Waved my hand in a friendly gesture. Perhaps he doesn't know that things are as they are. He may have arrived only yesterday, from far away."

Korczak's acceptance of death put him beyond fear or hatred. His acceptance of death was not an acceptance of indignity for himself or his charges. From his first days in the ghetto he was a resister, refusing to wear the Star of David and protesting the lack of food and medicine. However, the day Korczak and his children marched to the trains, they carried proudly a banner with the blue Star of David.

Korczak's journey with the children began with his career as a medical student concerned about the conditions under which poor children lived. This concern is documented in a semiautobiographical novel, *Child of the Salon*, written in 1906. Between 1906 and 1911, he established a successful medical practice, and although his services were in demand by wealthy clients, he cultivated a practice with the poor and charged them only token fees.

Korczak became increasingly concerned about working with areas of children's lives that medicine did not touch. At thirty-three, a literary and medical success, Korczak accepted the directorship of a Jewish orphanage. Some of the thinking that led him to take this position is indicated by a book he wrote three years later as a Russian medical officer during World War I, *How to Love a Child*. One theme of this book is that love for children means a concern for their psychological development—"becoming a sculptor of the child's soul." A second theme is that genuine love for the child implies a concern for justice, for treating the child with equal respect.

The orphanages that Korczak ran were prototypes of what in America in recent years we have called the "just community school." Korczak called his experiment a *Children's Republic*. It had its own parliament, court, newspaper, and work schedules. He saw these not only as embodying respect for the child but as the vehicles of moral education or education for justice. According to Lifton, "he was concerned not with teaching the children their *ABC*'s but with the grammar of ethics. He organized his *Children's Republic* as a just society governed by the young citizens themselves. In the course [of governing themselves], they would learn that it was possible to live in harmony with others." Of particular interest was the children's court, in which the rules made by the parliament were applied to individual cases. All children took their turn in serving as members of this court. Korczak hoped that children would learn through it to judge fairly. In devising disciplines, the emphasis was not on retribution but on understanding and on communicating the spirit of the rules and the community. The court also functioned as a collective review of the individual's progress in the school, guided by a notion of ethical levels of contribution to the community. The children's court reviewed the progress not only of the children but also of Korczak and the other members of the staff in terms of these levels. Although familiar with the psychological theories of his day, Korczak relied on his practical intuitions about justice and the child's sensitivity to justice for developing his educational practice.

Korczak's dedication to justice was part of his family background. His father, a lawyer, wrote on Talmudic and ethical interpretations of the law in Polish. In his *Ghetto Diary,* Korczak recalled that as a young child he had a dream or plan of life that included "to throw away all money so that there will be no more dirty, ragged, or hungry children with whom one is not allowed to play in the courtyard." Korczak's sensitivity to justice became part of a life commitment of service to children resulting from an anguished spiritual journey through despair reminiscent of Andrea Simpson's life course, discussed in the last chapter.

As an adolescent, Korczak first experienced despair in relation to his father's insanity and subsequent death in a mental hospital. Several years later during World War I, while working as an officer in a hospital, he contracted typhus. His mother came to nurse him and caught the disease and died. Being driven even further into despair, he came close to suicide at that time. We saw in the case of Andrea Simpson that a cosmic despair after her mother's death was conjoined with the conviction that she could never have a family. For Korczak also, these two sources of despair became combined. Because he defined himself as "the son of a madman," he had decided he should never marry or have children. In addition to his despair about personal loss, Korczak felt a moral and metaphorical despair about recurrent war, suffering, and injustice. Andrea Simpson resolved her despair by committing her life to her mentally ill brother and his fellow sufferers. Similarly feeling (as he wrote) "disordered, lonely, and cold," Korczak recommitted himself to "the abandoned child of Warsaw," taking him "as his son."

Although Korczak's development was in some sense religious, as was that of Andrea Simpson, it was not grounded in identification with his traditional faith. Korczak's acceptance of his Jewish identity was associated with an assimilationist acceptance of Polish culture and Western culture in general. His simultaneous directorships of both Christian and Jewish orphanages indicates this dual allegiance.

His adult religious orientation was not specifically Jewish nor even specifically theistic. It was expressed in terms of a somewhat mystic pantheism that celebrated nature and the manifestations of what Bergson calls the "life force." His searching for religious meaning after his mother's death gave rise to a book *Tête-à-Tête with God: Prayers for the Unbelieving,* dedicated to his mother and father. He thought of leaving Poland in 1938 to settle in Israel to study the Bible and meditate. He felt the tension between social and moral responsibility and the desire for inward spiritual experience. He wrote, "A man is responsible to his own spirit, to his own mode of thought—that is his workshop. I ask myself, Is it too late? No. Had I gone earlier, I would have felt like a deserter. One has to remain at one's post till the very last moment." Although feeling this tension, like Andrea Simpson, he also achieved some integration between his spiritual love of life or the life force with an ethical love for other human beings, expressed in his life's service to children.

My presentation of the life of Janusz Korczak stresses the similarities between his educational philosophy and the philosophy of justice that has guided other great moral educators from Socrates to Martin Luther King. This philosophy is, on the surface, secular and rationalistic and does not rely on authority or revelation. As Korczak's life illustrates, however, this educational philosophy of justice is supported and inspired by an ethical and religious attitude and world view. This ethical and religious orientation governed Korczak's commitment to the vocation of a moral educator and allowed him to die for it with equanimity. As in the case of Andrea Simpson, Korczak's ethical and religious development proceeded through a crisis of despair and was resolved through adoption of a "Stage 7" orientation that united an attitude of agape with the embracement of a cosmic perspective on life's meaning.

The life of Janusz Korczak illustrates the way in which Stage 6 principles of justice give shape and content to moral education but do not give an answer to the question "Why make a commitment to being a moral educator?" Such a commitment does not occur through simple acceptance of a social contract and principles of justice. Just as Stage 6 cannot answer the question "Why be moral?" it also cannot answer the question of commitment to moral education. To engage such questions is to enter the domain of ethical and religious philosophies, the domain of "Stage 7."

I have made a distinction between the rational principles of justice, which should guide the practice of moral education, and the "Stage 7" ethical and religious philosophy, which optimally underlies the teacher's commitment to the practice of moral education. This distinction is important for the moral educator, because it protects moral education from three false expectations. The first false expectation is that the child develops an ethical and religious philosophy in the same sense one would expect the child to develop a moral viewpoint or a sense of justice. Even though Janusz Korczak's vocation as a moral educator was rooted in a deeply religious attitude and commitment, his practice of moral education was based on democracy and respect for the equal rights and rationality of the child. Undoubtedly Korczak taught his underlying religious and ethical philosophy as well as teaching principles of justice. But he did not expect his students to develop or adopt a particular ethical and religious philosophy in the same sense he expected them to develop or adopt principles of justice. He taught his philosophy implicitly by his example—by living it. In a pluralistic society, we cannot expect a particular ethical and religious philosophy—to do so would be sectarian. In contrast, we *can* expect development of principles of justice that are or should be common for all members of the society. An ethical and religious philosophy represents the development of a set of personal meanings and values, and in that sense cannot be expected by teachers or schools.

The second false expectation is that of inculcating students with the attitude that underlies Korczak's ethical and religious philosophy, the attitude of agape. Educators cannot expect of students the attitude of agape because it is supererogatory and because it is by definition beyond the claims of duty of what can be demanded. Self-sacrificial devotion enacted by a Korczak represents an act of freely chosen "grace."

The third false expectation, unlike the first two, is primarily a burden on the educator rather than on the child. This is the burden of having to live up to the demand that the teacher be an ethical exemplar. Janusz Korczak truly was an exemplary moral educator. But he did not define his role in those terms. He did not define himself as a role model, to use the current jargon. To think of one's role as exemplary is to risk hypocrisy by inconsistent displays of virtue; it is to risk arrogance and an attitude of superiority to the students; and it is to risk a recurring sense of failure for those who are not saints. If an educator like Korczak, capable of saintliness, did not premise his approach to education on it, how much more should nonsaintly mortals like the majority of us avoid this expectation! It is a great deal to ask of teachers to put aside their own needs, including their need to be in a position of unquestioned authority, in order to meet the questions and demands of justice in the school. We can hope that an educator's commitment to teaching is supported by an attitude of agape toward the child and by a personal ethical and religious philosophy, without expecting teachers to be moral exemplars or saints. We as educators had best teach that which we can at least partly live—the demands of justice—without pretending to be able to teach more.

In the last few years and in the UNESCO Year of the Child, Janusz Korczak's memory has been honored in a number of ways. In part, this recent recognition of Korczak as a moral educator reflects the slow but continuing effort of world society to make some moral response to the Holocaust, in which he perished. The Holocaust is the event in human history that most bespeaks the need for moral education and for a philosophy that can guide it. My own interest in morality and moral education arose in part as a response to the Holocaust, an event so enormous that it often fails to provoke a sense of injustice in many individuals and societies. Janusz Korczak, in the midst of the Holocaust, reacted with both a normal sense of injustice and a perspective beyond justice that allowed him to live as a moral educator and to die with equanimity.

This last part of Volume I has tried to make clear both some of the limits of our theory and the limits of the sense of justice itself. The example of Janusz Korczak illuminates the limits of justice in a world of tragedy and the strength of a sense of justice for living in such a world. Korczak, then, helps to exemplify the ideal of moral development that this volume has struggled to clarify. His life does not help to answer many of the questions that theory must eventually address. The theory has, I hope, framed the problems of moral philosophy in terms that the study of lives can help answer. I hope that this volume may have helped the reader to do just that—begin to bring together the problems of philosophy with the study of human lives.

Appendix. The Six Stages of Moral Judgment

Level A. Preconventional Level

Stage 1. The Stage of Punishment and Obedience

Content

Right is literal obedience to rules and authority, avoiding punishment, and not doing physical harm.

1. What is right is to avoid breaking rules, to obey for obedience' sake, and to avoid doing physical damage to people and property.
2. The reasons for doing right are avoidance of punishment and the superior power of authorities.

Social Perspective

This stage takes an egocentric point of view. A person at this stage doesn't consider the interests of others or recognize they differ from actor's, and doesn't relate two points of view. Actions are judged in terms of physical consequences rather than in terms of psychological interests of others. Authority's perspective is confused with one's own.

Stage 2. The Stage of Individual Instrumental Purpose and Exchange

Content

Right is serving one's own or other's needs and making fair deals in terms of concrete exchange.

1. What is right is following rules when it is to someone's immediate interest. Right is acting to meet one's own interests and needs and letting others do the same. Right is also what is fair; that is, what is an equal exchange, a deal, an agreement.
2. The reason for doing right is to serve one's own needs or interests in a world where one must recognize that other people have their interests, too.

Social Perspective

This stage takes a concrete individualistic perspective. A person at this stage separates own interests and points of view from those of authorities and others. He or she is aware everybody has individual interests to pursue and these conflict, so that right is relative (in the concrete individualistic sense). The person integrates or relates conflicting individual interests to one another through instrumental exchange of services, through instrumental need for the other and the other's goodwill, or through fairness giving each person the same amount.

Level B. Conventional Level

Stage 3. The Stage of Mutual Interpersonal Expectations, Relationships, and Conformity

Content

The right is playing a good (nice) role, being concerned about the other people and their feelings, keeping loyalty and trust with partners, and being motivated to follow rules and expectations.

1. What is right is living up to what is expected by people close to one or what people generally expect of people in one's role as son, sister, friend, and so on. "Being good" is important and means having good motives, showing concern about others. It also means keeping mutual relationships, maintaining trust, loyalty, respect, and gratitude.
2. Reasons for doing right are needing to be good in one's own eyes and those of others, caring for others, and because if one puts oneself in the other person's place one would want good behavior from the self (Golden Rule).

Social Perspective

This stage takes the perspective of the individual in relationship to other individuals. A person at this stage is aware of shared feelings, agreements, and expectations, which take primacy over individual interests. The person relates points of view through the "concrete Golden Rule," putting oneself in the other person's shoes. He or she does not consider generalized "system" perspective.

Stage 4. The Stage of Social System and Conscience Maintenance

Content

The right is doing one's duty in society, upholding the social order, and maintaining the welfare of society or the group.

1. What is right is fulfilling the actual duties to which one has agreed. Laws are to be upheld except in extreme cases where they conflict with other fixed social duties and rights. Right is also contributing to society, the group, or institution.

2. The reasons for doing right are to keep the institution going as a whole, self-respect or conscience as meeting one's defined obligations, or the consequences: "What if everyone did it?"

Social Perspective

This stage differentiates societal point of view from interpersonal agreement or motives. A person at this stage takes the viewpoint of the system, which defines roles and rules. He or she considers individual relations in terms of place in the system.

Level B/C. Transitional Level

This level is postconventional but not yet principled.

Content of Transition

At Stage 4½, choice is personal and subjective. It is based on emotions, conscience is seen as arbitrary and relative, as are ideas such as "duty" and "morally right."

Transitional Social Perspective

At this stage, the perspective is that of an individual standing outside of his own society and considering himself as an individual making decisions without a generalized commitment or contract with society. One can pick and choose obligations, which are defined by particular societies, but one has no principles for such choice.

Level C. Postconventional and Principled Level

Moral decisions are generated from rights, values, or principles that are (or could be) agreeable to all individuals composing or creating a society designed to have fair and beneficial practices.

Stage 5. The Stage of Prior Rights and Social Contract or Utility

Content

The right is upholding the basic rights, values, and legal contracts of a society, even when they conflict with the concrete rules and laws of the group.

1. What is right is being aware of the fact that people hold a variety of values and opinions, that most values and rules are relative to one's group. These "relative" rules should usually be upheld, however, in the interest of impartiality and because they are the social contract. Some nonrelative values and rights such as

life, and liberty, however, must be upheld in any society and regardless of majority opinion.

2. Reasons for doing right are, in general, feeling obligated to obey the law because one has made a social contract to make and abide by laws for the good of all and to protect their own rights and the rights of others. Family, friendship, trust, and work obligations are also commitments or contracts freely entered into and entail respect for the rights of others. One is concerned that laws and duties be based on rational calculation of overall utility: "the greatest good for the greatest number."

Social Perspective

This stage takes a prior-to-society perspective—that of a rational individual aware of values and rights prior to social attachments and contracts. The person integrates perspectives by formal mechanisms of agreement, contract, objective impartiality, and due process. He or she considers the moral point of view and the legal point of view, recognizes they conflict, and finds it difficult to integrate them.

Stage 6. The Stage of Universal Ethical Principles

Content

This stage assumes guidance by universal ethical principles that all humanity should follow.

1. Regarding what is right, Stage 6 is guided by universal ethical principles. Particular laws or social agreements are usually valid because they rest on such principles. When laws violate these principles, one acts in accordance with the principle. Principles are universal principles of justice: the equality of human rights and respect for the dignity of human beings as individuals. These are not merely values that are recognized, but are also principles used to generate particular decisions.

2. The reason for doing right is that, as a rational person, one has seen the validity of principles and has become committed to them.

Social Perspective

This stage takes the perspective of a moral point of view from which social arrangements derive or on which they are grounded. The perspective is that of any rational individual recognizing the nature of morality or the basic moral premise of respect for other persons as ends, not means.

References

Adorno, R., Frenkel-Brunswik, E., Levinson, D., and Sanford, R. *The Authoritarian Personality.* New York: Harper, 1950.

Alston, W. P. "Moral Attitudes and Moral Judgments." *Nous 2* (1968): 1–23.

Alston, W. P. "Comments on Kohlberg's 'From Is to Ought.'" In T. Mischel, ed., *Cognitive Development and Epistemology.* New York: Academic Press, 1971.

Asch, S. E. *Social Psychology.* Englewood Cliffs, N.J.: Prentice-Hall, 1952.

Ausubel, D., and Sullivan, E. *Theory and Problems of Child Development.* New York: Grune & Stratton, 1970.

Baier, K. *The Moral Point of View: A Rational Basis of Ethics.* Rev. ed. New York: Random House, 1965.

Baldwin, J. M. *Social and Ethical Interpretations in Mental Development.* New York: Macmillan, 1897.

Baldwin, J. M. *Thoughts and Things.* 3 vols. New York: Macmillan, 1906.

Ball, W. "Religion and Public Education: The Post-Schempp Years." In T. Sizer, ed., *Religion and the Public Schools.* Boston: Houghton Mifflin, 1967.

Bandura, A. *Aggression: A Social Learning Analysis.* Englewood Cliffs, N.J.: Prentice-Hall, 1973.

Bar-Yam, M., Reimer, J., and Kohlberg, L. "The Development of Moral Reasoning in the Kibbutz." Unpublished manuscript, 1972.

Beccaria, C. *On Crimes and Punishments.* Trans. H. Paolucci. Indianapolis: Bobbs-Merrill, 1963. (Originally published 1764.)

Bereiter, C. "Educational Implications of Kohlberg's Cognitive-Developmental View." *Interchange 1* (1970): 25–32.

Bereiter, C. "Moral Alternatives to Education." *Interchange 3* [1972]: 25–41.

Bereiter, C., and Engelmann, S. *Teaching Disadvantaged Children in the Preschool.* Englewood Cliffs, N.J.: Prentice-Hall, 1966.

Bergson, H. *The Two Sources of Morality and Religion.* Garden City, N.Y.: Doubleday, Anchor, 1958.

Berkowitz, L. *Development of Motives and Values in a Child.* New York: Basic Books, 1964.

Bettelheim, B. "A Psychoanalytic View of Moral Education." In T. Sizer, ed., *Moral Education: Five Lectures.* Cambridge, Mass.: Harvard University Press, 1970.

Blatt, M. "The Effects of Classroom Discussion on the Development of Moral Judgment." Ph.D. dissertation, University of Chicago, 1969.

Blatt, M., and Kohlberg, L. "The Effects of Classroom Moral Discussion upon Children's Level of Moral Judgment." *Journal of Moral Education 4* (1975): 129–161.

Bolt, R. *A Man for All Seasons*. New York: Random House, 1960.

Bovee, M. *Reasons for Abolishing Capital Punishment*. Chicago: Author, 1878.

Bradley, A. C. *Shakespearean Tragedy*. London: Macmillan, 1904.

Bradley, F. H. *Ethical Studies*. New York: Oxford University Press, 1962.

Brandt, R. B. *Ethical Theory*. Englewood Cliffs, N.J.: Prentice-Hall, 1959.

Brandt, R. B. *Value and Obligation: Systematic Readings in Ethics*. New York: Harcourt, 1961.

Brandt, R. B. "Toward a Credible Form of Utilitarianism." In M. D. Bayles, ed., *Contemporary Utilitarianism*. Garden City, N.Y.: Anchor Books, 1968.

Bronfenbrenner, U. "The Role of Age, Sex, Class, and Culture in Studies of Moral Development." *Religious Education 57* (1962a):3–17.

Bronfenbrenner, U. "Soviet Methods of Character Education: Some Implications for Research." *American Psychologist 17* (1962b):550–565.

Bronfenbrenner, U. "Soviet Methods of Upbringing and their Effects: A Social-Psychological Analysis." Paper read at conference on Studies of the Acquisition and Development of Values, National Institute of Child Health and Human Development, Washington, D.C., May 23, 1968.

Carr, D. B., and Wellenberg, E. P. *Teaching Children Values*. Freeport, Calif.: Honor Your Partner Records, 1966.

Child, I. "Socialization." In G. Lindzey, ed., *Handbook of Social Psychology*. Reading, Mass.: Addison-Wesley, 1954.

Colby, A., and Kohlberg, L., with Gibbs, J.; Candee, D.; Speicher-Dubin, B.; Power, C.; and Lieberman, M. *The Measurement of Moral Judgment*, Vols. I and II. New York: Cambridge University Press, forthcoming.

Coleman, J. S. and others. *Equality of Educational Opportunity*. Washington, D.C.: U.S. Department of Health, Education and Welfare, Office of Education, 1966.

Cunningham, V. L. "Moral/Values Development and Education: The Ten-Year Perspective in Ontario—1968–1978." Mimeographed. Toronto: Ministry of Education of the Province of Ontario, Research and Evaluation Branch, 1978.

Curley, E. M. *Spinoza's Metaphysics: An Essay in Interpretation*. Cambridge, Mass.: Harvard University Press, 1969.

DeLubac, H. *The Religion of Teilhard de Chardin*. New York: Image Books, 1968.

DeVries, R., and Kohlberg, L. "Relations Between Piaget and Psychometric Assessments of Intelligence." In L. Katz, ed., *Current Topics in Early Childhood Education*. Vol. I. Norwood, N.J.: Ablex, 1977.

Dewey, J. "The Primary-Education Fetish." *Forum*. Washington, D.C.: U.S. Government Printing Office, 1898.

Dewey, J. *The Logical Conditions of a Scientific Treatment of Morality*. Chicago: University of Chicago Press, 1903.

Dewey, J. *Moral Principles in Education*. Boston: Houghton Mifflin, 1911.

Dewey, J. *Character and Events*. New York: Holt, 1929.

Dewey, J. *Liberalism and Social Action*. New York: Putnam's, 1935.

Dewey, J. *Art as Experience*. New York: Minton, Balch, 1937.

Dewey, J. *Democracy and Education.* New York: Macmillan, Free Press, 1944. (Originally published 1916.)

Dewey, J. *Experience and Education.* New York: Collier, 1963. (Originally published 1938.)

Dewey, J., and McLellan, J. "The Psychology of Number." In R. Archambault, ed., *John Dewey on Education: Selected Writings.* New York: Random House, 1964. .

Dewey, J., and Tufts, J. H. *Ethics.* Rev. ed. New York: Holt, 1932.

Dodder, C., and Dodder, B. *Decision Making: A Guide for Teachers Who Would Help Preadolescent Children Become Imaginative and Responsible Decision Makers.* Boston: Beacon Press, 1968.

Durkheim, E. *Sociologie et Philosophie.* Paris: Alcan, 1924.

Durkheim, E. *Moral Education: A Study in the Theory and Application in the Sociology of Education.* New York: Free Press, 1961. (Originally published 1925.)

Elfenbein, D. "Moral Stages in Societal Evolution." Unpublished bachelor's thesis, Harvard University, 1973.

Erdynast, A. "Improving the Adequacy of Moral Reasoning: An Exploratory Study with Executives and with Philosophy Students." Ph.D. dissertation, Harvard University, 1973.

Erikson, E. *Childhood and Society.* New York: Norton, 1950.

Erskine, H. "The Polls: Capital Punishment." *Public Opinion Quarterly 34* (1970):290–307.

Eysenck, H. J. *Handbook of Abnormal Psychology: An Experimental Approach.* New York: Basic Books, 1961.

Feuer, L. S. *Psychoanalysis and Ethics.* Springfield, Ill.: Thomas, 1955.

Flugel, J. C. *Man, Morals and Society: A Psycho-Analytical Study.* New York: International Universities Press, 1955.

Fowler, J. "Stages in Faith: The Structural Developmental Approach." In T. Hennessey, ed., *Values and Moral Development.* New York: Paulist Press, 1976.

Fowler, J. "Mapping Faith's Structures: A Developmental View." In J. Fowler and S. Keen, eds., *Life Maps: Conversations on the Journey of Faith.* Waco, Texas: Word Books, 1978.

Fowler, J., and Vergote, A., eds. *Toward Moral and Religious Maturity.* Morristown, N.J.: Silver-Burdett, 1980.

Frankena, W. K. *Ethics.* Englewood Cliffs, N.J.: Prentice-Hall, 1963.

Freud, A. *The Ego and the Mechanisms of Defense.* London: Hogarth Press, 1937.

Freud, S. *Civilization and Its Discontents.* London: Hogarth Press, 1930.

Gilligan, C. "In a Different Voice: Women's Conceptions of Self and Morality." *Harvard Educational Review 47* (1977):481–517.

Gilligan, J. "Psychoanalytic Theory and Morality." In T. Lickona, ed., *Moral Development and Behavior.* New York: Holt, Rinehart and Winston, 1976.

Gold, L. "A Psychiatric Review of Capital Punishment." *Journal of Forensic Sciences 6* (1961):465–477.

Gorsuch, R., and Barnes, M. "Stages of Ethical Reasoning and Moral Norms of Carib Youths." *Journal of Cross-Cultural Psychology 4* (1973):283–301.

Grimley, L. "A Cross-Cultural Study of Moral Development." Ph.D. dissertation, Kent State University, 1973.

Grinder, R. "Parental Childrearing Practices, Conscience, and Resistance to Temptation of Sixth-Grade Children." *Child Development 33* (1962):802–820.

Grotberg, E. *Review of Research, 1965 to 1969.* Office of Economic Opportunity Pamphlet 6108-13. Washington, D.C.: Research and Evaluation Office, Project Head Start, Office of Economic Opportunity, 1969.

Haan, N., Langer, J., Kohlberg, L. "Family Patterns of Moral Reasoning." *Child Development 47* (1976): 1204–1206.

Haan, N., Smith, M. B., and Block, J. "Political, Family and Personality Correlates of Adolescent Moral Judgment." *Journal of Personality and Social Psychology 10* (1968):183–201.

Hall, G. S. "The Ideal School Based on Child Study." *Forum.* Washington D.C.: U.S. Government Printing Office, 1901.

Hare, R. M. *The Language of Morals.* New York: Oxford University Press, 1952.

Hare, R. M. *Freedom and Reason.* New York: Oxford University Press, 1963.

Hartshorne, H., and May, M. A. *Studies in the Nature of Character.* Vol. 1: *Studies in Deceit.* Vol. 2: *Studies in Self-Control.* Vol. 3: *Studies in the Organization of Character.* New York: Macmillan, 1928–1930.

Havighurst, R. J., and Taba, H. *Adolescent Character and Personality.* New York: Wiley, 1949.

Hobhouse, J. T. *Morals in Evolution: A Study in Comparative Ethics.* New York: Holt, 1923. (Originally published 1906.)

Holstein, C. "Parent Consensus and Interaction in Relation to the Child's Moral Judgment." Ph.D. dissertation, University of California at Berkeley, 1969.

Homans, G. T. *The Human Group.* New York: Harcourt, 1950.

Hoover, J. E. "Statements in Favor of the Death Penalty." In H. Bedau, ed., *The Death Penalty in America: An Anthology.* Rev. ed. Garden City, N.Y.: Doubleday, 1967.

Hume, D. "Of Tragedy," in *Four Dissertations.* London: printed for A. Millar, in the Strand, 1757.

Jackson, P. W. *Life in the Classroom.* New York: Holt, Rinehart and Winston, 1968.

Jacquette, D., and Carrick, R. "The Relationship Between Moral Judgment and Prejudice." Unpublished manuscript, Harvard University, 1971.

Jencks, C., and others. *Inequality: A Reassessment of the Effect of Family and Schooling in America.* New York: Basic Books, 1972.

Jones, V. *Character and Citizenship Training in the Public School.* Chicago: University of Chicago Press, 1936.

Josselyn, I. M. *Psychosocial Development of Children.* New York: Family Service Association, 1948.

Kamii, C. "Evaluating Pupil Learning in Preschool Education: Socio-Emotional, Perceptual-Motor, and Cognitive Objectives." In B. S. Bloom, J. T. Hastings, and C. Madaus, eds., *Formative and Summative Evaluation of Student Learning.* New York: McGraw-Hill, 1971.

Kant, I. *Fundamental Principles of the Metaphysics of Morals.* New York: Liberal Arts Press, 1949.

Kant, I. *Religion Within the Limits of Reason Alone.* In C. J. Friedrich, ed., *The Philosophy of Kant.* New York: Random House, 1949.

Kant, I. *Foundations of the Metaphysics of Morals.* Trans. L. Beck. Indianapolis: Bobbs-Merrill, 1959. (Originally published 1785.)

Kaufman, W. *Tragedy and Philosophy.* Garden City, N.Y.: Doubleday, Anchor, 1969.

Ketto, H. D. F. *Greek Tragedy.* London: Methuen, 1961.

Kinsey, A. C., and others. *Sexual Behavior in the Human Female.* Philadelphia: Saunders, 1953.

Koeninger, R. "Capital Punishment in Texas, 1924-1968." *Crime and Delinquency 15* (1969):132-141.

Kohlberg, L. "The Development of Modes of Moral Thinking and Choice in the Years Ten to Sixteen." Ph.D. dissertation, University of Chicago, 1958.

Kohlberg, L. "The Development of Children's Orientation Toward a Moral Order: I. Sequence in the Development of Moral Thought." *Vita Humana 6* (1963a): 11-33.

Kohlberg, L. "Moral Development and Identification." In H. Stevenson ed., *Child Psychology.* 62nd Yearbook of the National Society for the Study of Education. Chicago: University of Chicago Press, 1963b.

Kohlberg, L. "Psychological Analysis and Literary Form: A Study of the Doubles in Dostoevsky." *Daedalus 92* (1963c): 345-363.

Kohlberg, L. "The Development of Moral Character and Ideology." In M. Hoffman and L. Hoffman, eds., *Review of Child Development Research.* New York: Russell Sage, 1964.

Kohlberg, L. "Cognitive Stages and Preschool Education." *Human Development 9* (1966a):5-17.

Kohlberg, L. "Moral Education in the Schools: A Developmental View." *School Review 74* (1966b):1-30.

Kohlberg, L. "The Child as a Moral Philosopher." *Psychology Today 1* (1968a):25-30.

Kohlberg, L. "Early Education: A Cognitive-developmental View." *Child Development 39* (1968b):1013-1062.

Kohlberg, L. "Stage and Sequence: The Cognitive-developmental Approach to Socialization." In D. A. Goslin, ed., *Handbook of Socialization on Theory and Research.* New York: Rand McNally, 1969.

Kohlberg, L. "The Moral Atmosphere of the School." In N. Overley, ed., *The Unstudied Curriculum: Its Impact on Children.* Monograph of the Association for Supervision and Curriculum Development. Washington, D.C.: 1970a.

Kohlberg, L. "Reply to Bereiter's Statement on Kohlberg's Cognitive-Developmental View." *Interchange 1* (1970b):40-48.

Kohlberg, L. "From *Is* to *Ought*: How to Commit the Naturalistic Fallacy and Get Away with It in the Study of Moral Development." In T. Mischel, ed., *Cognitive Development and Epistemology*. New York: Academic Press, 1971a.

Kohlberg, L. "Stages of Moral Development as a Basis for Moral Education." In C. Beck, B. Crittendon, and E. Sullivan, eds., *Moral Education: Interdisciplinary*. Toronto: University of Toronto Press, 1971b.

Kohlberg, L. "Cognitive-Developmental Theory and the Practice of Collective Moral Education." In M. Wolins and M. Gottesman, eds., *Group Care: An Israeli Approach: The Educational Path of Youth Aliyah*. New York: Gordon & Breach, 1971c.

Kohlberg, L. "Continuities in Childhood and Adult Moral Development Revisited." In P. B. Baltes and K. W. Schaie, eds., *Life-Span Developmental Psychology: Personality and Socialization*. New York: Academic Press, 1973a.

Kohlberg, L. "Stages and Aging in Moral Development: Some Speculations." *Gerontologist 13*, (1973b):497–502.

Kohlberg, L. "Moral Development and the New Social Studies." *Social Education 37* (1973c):368–375.

Kohlberg, L. "Contributions of Developmental Psychology to Education: Examples from Moral Education." *Educational Psychologist 10* (1973d): 2–14.

Kohlberg, L. "Moral Development and Juvenile Justice." Unpublished manuscript, Harvard University, 1974.

Kohlberg, L. "The Young Child as a Philosopher: Moral Development and the Dilemmas of Moral Education." In M. Wolman, ed., *Taking Early Childhood Seriously: The Evangeline Burgess Memorial Lectures*. Pasadena, Calif.: Pacific Oaks, 1979.

Kohlberg, L., and Kramer, R. "Continuities and Discontinuities in Childhood and Adult Moral Development." *Human Development 12* (1969):93–120.

Kohlberg, L., and Turiel, E. "Moral Development and Moral Education." In G. Lesser, ed., *Psychology and Educational Practice*. Chicago: Scott Foresman, 1971.

Kohlberg, L., LaCrosse, J., and Ricks, D. "The Predictability of Adult Mental Health from Childhood Behavior." In B. Wolman, ed., *Handbook of Child Psychopathology*. New York: McGraw-Hill, 1971.

Kozol, J. *Death at an Early Age: The Destruction of the Hearts and Minds of Negro Children in the Boston Public School*. Boston: Houghton Mifflin, 1967a.

Kozol, J. "New Ways of Teaching." *New York Times*, magazine section, October 29, 1967b.

Krebs, R. L. "Some Relationships Between Moral Judgment, Attention, and Resistance to Temptation." Ph.D. dissertation, University of Chicago, 1967.

Kuhn, D., Langer, J., Kohlberg, L., and Haan, N. "The Development of Formal Operations in Logical and Moral Judgment." *Genetic Psychology Monographs 95* (1977):97–188.

Langer, J. *Theories of Development.* New York: Holt, Rinehart and Winston, 1969.

Lehrer, L. "Sex Differences in Moral Behavior and Attitudes." Ph.D. dissertation, University of Chicago, 1967.

Lifton, B.J. "Shepherd of the Ghetto Orphans." *New York Times,* magazine section, April 20, 1980.

Loevinger, J. *Ego Development.* San Francisco: Jossey-Bass, 1976.

Loevinger, J., Wessler, R., and Redmore, C. *Measuring Ego Development.* San Francisco: Jossey-Bass, 1970.

Malinowski, B. *The Sexual Life of Savages.* New York: Halcyon House, 1929.

McClosky, H. "Consensus and Ideology in American Politics." *American Political Science Review 58* (1964):361–382.

Mead, G. H. *Mind, Self and Society.* Chicago: University of Chicago Press, 1934.

Mead, G. H. *Movements of Thought in the Nineteenth Century.* Chicago: University of Chicago Press, 1936.

Milgram, S. "Behavioral Study of Obedience." *Journal of Abnormal and Social Psychology 67* (1963):371–378.

Neill, A. S. *Summerhill.* New York: Hart, 1960.

Nietzsche, F. *The Birth of Tragedy from the Spirit of Music,* bound in *The Philosophy of Nietzsche.* New York: Random House, 1971.

Olson, E. *Tragedy and the Theory of Drama.* Detroit: Wayne State University Press, 1966.

Oser, F. "Stages of Religious Judgment." In J. Fowler and A. Vergote, eds., *Toward Moral and Religious Maturity.* Morristown, N.J.: Silver-Burdett, 1980.

Outka, G. *Agape: An Ethical Analysis.* New Haven, Conn.: Yale University Press, 1972.

Parikh, B. "Moral Judgment Development and Its Relation to Family Environmental Factors in Indian and American Urban Upper Middle Class Families." Ph.D. dissertation, Boston University, 1975.

Peters, R. S. *Ethics and Education.* Chicago: Scott Foresman, 1968.

Peters, R. S. "Moral Development: A Plea for Pluralism." In T. Mischel, ed., *Cognitive Development and Epistemology.* New York: Academic Press, 1971.

Piaget, J. *The Moral Judgment of the Child.* New York: Free Press, 1948. (Originally published 1932.)

Piaget, J. "The General Problem of the Psychological Development of the Child." In J. M. Tanner and B. Inhelder, eds., *Discussions on Child Development: A Consideration of the Biological, Psychological, and Cultural Approaches to the Understanding of Human Development and Behavior.* Vol. 4. New York: International Universities Press, 1960.

Power, C., and Kohlberg, L. "Religion, Morality, and Ego Development." In J. Fowler and A. Vergote, eds., *Toward Moral and Religious Maturity.* Morristown, N.J.: Silver Burdett, 1980.

Prothro, J., and Grigg, C. "Fundamental Principles of Democracy: Bases of

Agreement and Disagreement." *Journal of Politics 22* (1960):276–294.

Raphael, D. D. *Moral Judgment*. London: Allen & Unwin, 1955.

Raphael, D. D. *The Paradox of Tragedy*. London: Allen & Unwin, 1960.

Ratner, J., ed. *Intelligence in the Modern World: John Dewey's Philosophy*. New York: Random House, 1939.

Rawls, J. "The Sense of Justice." *Philosophical Review 72* (1963):281–305.

Rawls, J. *A Theory of Justice*. Cambridge, Mass.: Harvard University Press, 1971.

Reich, C. A. *The Greening of America*. New York: Random House, 1970.

Rest, J. "Developmental Hierarchy in Preference and Comprehension of Moral Judgment." Ph.D. dissertation, University of Chicago, 1968.

Rest, J. "The Hierarchical Nature of Moral Judgment." *Journal of Personality 41* (1973):86–109.

Rest, J., Turiel, E., and Kohlberg, L. "Relations between Level of Moral Judgment and Preference and Comprehension of the Moral Judgment of Others." *Journal of Personality 37* (1969):225–252.

"Revival of the Eighth Amendment: Development of Cruel-Punishment Doctrine by the Supreme Court (Comment)." *Stanford Law Review 16* (1964):996–1015.

Ross, W. D. *The Right and the Good*. New York: Oxford University Press, Clarendon, 1930.

Royce, J. *The Religious Aspect of Philosophy: A Critique of the Basis of Conduct and Faith*. Boston: Houghton, 1885.

Scheffler, I. "Anti-Naturalistic Restrictions in Ethics." *Journal of Philosophy 1* (1953).

Schwartz, S., Feldman, K., Brown, M., and Heingartner, A. "Some Personality Correlates of Conduct in Two Situations of Moral Conduct." *Journal of Personality 37* (1969):41–57.

Scriven, M. *Primary Philosophy*. New York: McGraw-Hill, 1966.

Sellin, T. *The Death Penalty*. Philadelphia: American Law Institute, 1959.

Selman, R. L. "The Relation of Role-Taking to the Development of Moral Judgment in Children." *Child Development 42* (1971):79–91.

Shawver, D. J. "Character and Ethics: An Epistemological Inquiry of Lawrence Kohlberg's Cognitive Theory of Moral Development." Ph.D. dissertation, McGill University, 1979.

Shulik, R. "Faith Development, Moral Development, and Old Age: An Assessment of Fowler's Faith Development Paradigm." Ph.D. dissertation, University of Chicago, 1979.

Sidgwick, H. *Methods of Ethics*. London: Macmillan, 1887.

Simon, S. "Value-Clarification vs. Indoctrination." *Social Education 35* (1971):902.

Simpson, E. L. "Moral Development Research: A Case of Scientific Cultural Bias." *Human Development 17* (1974):81–106.

Skinner, B. F. *Walden Two*. New York: Macmillan, 1948.

Skinner, B. F. *Beyond Freedom and Dignity*. New York: Knopf, 1971.

Smith, A. *Theory of Moral Sentiments*. In *Smith's Moral and Political Philosophy*. New York: Hafner, 1948. (Originally published in 1759.)

Spinoza, B. *Ethics.* In J. Wild, ed., *Spinoza Selections.* New York: Scribners, 1930.

Sprinthall, N. A., and Mosher, R. L. "Psychological Education in Secondary Schools: A Program to Promote Individual and Human Development." *American Psychologist 25* (1970):911–924.

Sullivan, E. V. *Kohlberg's Structuralism: A Critical Appraisal.* Toronto: Ontario Institute for Studies in Education, 1977.

Sumner, W. G. *Folkways.* Boston: Ginn, 1906.

Teilhard de Chardin, P. *Letters from a Traveller.* New York: Harper & Row, 1962.

Teilhard de Chardin, P. *The Phenomenon of Man.* New York: Harper & Row, 1965.

Teilhard de Chardin, P. *The Divine Milieu.* New York: Harper & Row, 1968.

Thrower, J. "Effects of Orphanage and Foster Home Care on Development of Moral Judgment." Ed.D. dissertation, Harvard University, 1970.

Tillich, P. *The Courage to Be.* New Haven, Conn.: Yale University Press, 1952.

Tillich, P. *Love, Power and Justice: Ontological Analyses and Ethical Applications.* New York: Oxford University Press, 1966.

Toulmin, S. *An Examination of the Place of Reason in Ethics.* Cambridge, England: Cambridge University Press, 1950.

Tullock, G. "Does Punishment Deter Crime?" *Public Interest 36* (1974):103–111.

Turiel, E. "An Experimental Test of the Sequentiality of Developmental Stages in the Child's Moral Judgment." *Journal of Personality and Social Psychology 3* (1966):611–618.

Turiel, E. "Developmental Processes in the Child's Thinking." In P. Mussen, J. Langer, and M. Covington, eds., *New Directions in Developmental Psychology.* New York: Holt, Rinehart and Winston, 1969.

Turiel, E., Edwards, C. P., and Kohlberg, L. "A Cross-Cultural Study of Moral Development in Turkey and the United States." *Journal of Cross-Cultural Psychology 9* (1978):75–87.

Unamuno, M. *Tragic Sense of Life.* New York: Dover, 1954.

Unger, R. *Knowledge and Politics.* New York: Free Press, 1975.

Van den Daele, L. "Preschool Intervention with Social Learning." *Journal of Negro Education 39* (1970):296–304.

Van den Haag, E. "On Deterrence and the Death Penalty." *Journal of Criminal Law, Criminology, and Police Science 60* (1969):141–147.

Vidmar, N., and Ellsworth, P. "Public Opinion and the Death Penalty." *Stanford Law Review 26* (1974):1245–1270.

Vygotsky, L. S. *The Psychology of Art.* Cambridge, Mass.: M.I.T. Press, 1971.

Weber, M. *The Methodology of the Social Sciences.* New York: Free Press, 1949.

Westermarck, E. *Ethical Relativity.* 1932. Patterson, N.J.: Littlefield, Adamo, 1960.

Wheeler, M. "Toward a Theory of Limited Punishment: An Examination of the Eighth Amendment." *Stanford Law Review 24* (1972):838–873.

Whitehead, A. N. *Process and Reality*. New York: Humanities Press, 1938.

Wolff, R. P. *Understanding Rawls: A Reconstruction and Critique of A Theory of Justice*. Princeton, N.J.: Princeton University Press, 1977.

Zeisel, H. *Some Data on Juror Attitudes toward Capital Punishment*. Chicago: University of Chicago Law School, Center for Studies in Criminal Justice, 1968.

Bibliography of Writings by Lawrence Kohlberg

Kohlberg, L. "The Development of Modes of Thinking and Choices in Years 10 to 16." Ph.D. dissertation, University of Chicago, 1958.

Kohlberg, L. "The Development of Children's Orientations Toward a Moral Order: Sequence in the Development of Moral Thought." *Vita Humana 6* (1963a):11–33.

Kohlberg, L. "Moral Development and Identification." In H. Stevenson, ed., *Child Psychology*. 62nd Yearbook of the National Society for the Study of Education, Part I. Chicago: University of Chicago Press, 1963b.

Kohlberg, L. "Psychological Analysis and Literary Form: A Study of the Doubles in Dostoevsky." *Daedalus 92* (1963c):345–363.

Kohlberg, L. "The Development of Moral Character and Ideology." In M. L. Hoffman and L. W. Hoffman, eds., *Review of Child Developmental Research*, Vol 1. New York: Russell Sage, 1964.

Kohlberg, L. "A Cognitive-Developmental Analysis of Children's Sex-Role Attitudes." In E. Maccoby, ed., *The Development of Sex Differences*. Stanford, Calif.: Stanford University Press, 1966a.

Kohlberg, L. "Cognitive Stages and Preschool Education." *Human Development 9* (1966b):5–17.

Kohlberg, L. "Moral Education in the School." *School Review 74* (1966c):1–30.

Kohlberg, L. "Moral and Religious Education, and the Public Schools: A Developmental View." In T. Sizer, ed., *Religion and Public Education*. Boston: Houghton Mifflin, 1967.

Kohlberg, L., and Zigler, E. "The Impact of Cognitive Maturity upon the Development of Sex-Role Attitudes in the Years Four to Eight." *Genetic Psychology Monographs 75* (1967):89–165.

Kohlberg, L. "The Child as a Moral Philosopher." *Psychology Today 7* (1968a):25–30.

Kohlberg, L. "Early Education: A Cognitive-Developmental View." *Child Development 39* (1968b):1013–1062.

Kohlberg, L. "Montessori with the Culturally Disadvantaged: A Cognitive-Developmental Interpretation." In R. Hess and R. Bear, eds., *The Challenge of Early Education: Current Theory, Research and Action*. Chicago: Aldine Press, 1968c.

Kohlberg, L. "Moral Development." In *International Encyclopedia of the Social Sciences*. New York: Crowell, Collier and Macmillan, 1968d.

Kohlberg, L. "Stages in Moral Growth." *International Journal of Religious Education 44* (1968e):8–9.

Grim, P. F., Kohlberg, L., and White, S. H. "Some Relationships Between

Conscience and Attentional Processes." *Journal of Personality 8* (1968):239–252.

Kohlberg, L., Hjertholm, E., and Yaeger, J. "Private Speech: Four Studies and a Review of Theories." *Child Development 39* (1968):691–736.

Kohlberg, L. "Stage and Sequence: The Cognitive-Developmental Approach to Socialization." In D. A. Goslin, ed., *Handbook of Socialization Theory and Research.* Chicago: Rand McNally, 1969.

Kohlberg, L., and DeVries, R. "Concept Measurement Kit: Conservation: Review." *Journal of Educational Measurement 6* (1969):263–266.

Kohlberg, L., and Kramer, R. "Continuities and Discontinuities in Children and Adult Moral Development." *Human Development 12* (1969):93–120.

Rest, J., Turiel, E., and Kohlberg, L. "Level of Moral Development as a Determinant of Preference and Comprehension of Moral Judgments Made by Others." *Journal of Personality 37* (1969):225–252.

Kohlberg, L. "Development of Moral Character." In *Developmental Psychology.* Del Mar, Calif.: CRM Books, 1970a.

Kohlberg, L. "Education for Justice: A Modern Statement of the Platonic View." In T. Sizer, ed., *Moral Education: Five Lectures.* Cambridge, Mass.: Harvard University Press, 1970b.

Kohlberg, L. "The Moral Atmosphere of the School." In N. Overley, ed., *The Unstudied Curriculum: Its Impact on Children.* Monograph of the Association for Supervision and Curriculum Development. Washington, D.C.: 1970c.

Kohlberg, L. "Moral Development and the Education of Adolescents." In R. F. Purnell, ed., *Adolescents and the American High School.* New York: Holt, Rinehart and Winston, 1970d.

Kohlberg, L. "Reply to Bereiter's Statement on Kohlberg's Cognitive-Developmental View." *Interchange 1* (1970e):40–48.

Kohlberg, L., LaCrosse, J., and Ricks, D. "The Predictability of Adult Mental Health from Childhood Behavior." In B. Wolman, ed., *Handbook of Child Psychopathology.* New York: McGraw-Hill, 1970.

Kohlberg, L. "Cognitive-Developmental Theory and the Practice of Collective Moral Education." In M. Wolins and M. Gottesman, eds., *Group Care: An Israeli Approach: The Education Path of Youth Aliyah.* New York: Gordon & Breach, 1971a.

Kohlberg, L. "From *Is* to *Ought:* How to Commit the Naturalistic Fallacy and Get Away with It in the Study of Moral Development." In T. Mischel, ed., *Cognitive Development and Epistemology.* New York: Academic Press, 1971b.

Kohlberg, L. "Indoctrination Versus Relativity in Value Education." *Zygon 6* (1971c):285–310.

Kohlberg, L. "Moral Education, Psychological View of." *International Encyclopedia of Education.* Vol. 6. New York: Macmillan and Free Press, 1971d.

Kohlberg, L. "Stages of Moral Development as a Basis for Moral Education." In C. Beck, B. Crittendon, and E. Sullivan, eds., *Moral Educa-*

tion: Interdisciplinary Approaches. Toronto: University of Toronto Press, 1971e.

Kohlberg, L. and Gilligan, C. "The Adolescent as a Philosopher: The Discovery of the Self in a Post-Conventional World." *Daedalus 100* (1971):1051–1086.

Kohlberg, L., and Turiel, E. "Moral Development and Moral Education." In G. Lesser, ed., *Psychology and Educational Practice.* Chicago: Scott Foresman, 1971.

Gilligan, C., Kohlberg, L., Lerner, J., and Belenky, M. "Moral Reasoning About Sexual Dilemmas." Technical Report of the Commission on Obscenity and Pornography, Vol. 1 (No. 52560010). Washington, D.C.: U.S. Government Printing Office, 1971.

Kohlberg, L. "The Cognitive-Developmental Approach to Moral Education." *Humanist 32* (1972a):13–16.

Kohlberg, L. "The Concepts of Developmental Psychology as the Central Guide to Education: Examples from Cognitive, Moral, and Psychological Education." In M. C. Reynolds, ed., *Psychology and the Process of Schooling in the Next Decade: Alternative Conceptions.* Minneapolis: University of Minnesota Press, 1972b.

Kohlberg, L., and Mayer, R. "Development as the Aim of Education." *Harvard Educational Review 42* (1972):449–496.

Kohlberg, L., and Selman, R. L. "Preparing School Personnel Relative to Values: A Look at Moral Education in the School." Washington, D.C.: ERIC Clearinghouse on Teacher Education, 1972.

Kohlberg, L., and Whitten, P. "Understanding the Hidden Curriculum." *Learning Magazine 1* (1972):2.

Kohlberg, L., Hickey, J., and Scharf, P. "The Justice Structure of the Prison: A Theory and Intervention." *Prison Journal 51* (1972):3–14.

Kohlberg, L. "The Claim to Moral Adequacy of a Highest Stage of Moral Judgment." *Journal of Philosophy 70* (1973a):630–646).

Kohlberg, L. "Continuities in Childhood and Adult Moral Development Revisited." In P. B. Baltes and K. W. Schaie, eds., *Life-Span Developmental Psychology: Personality and Socialization.* New York Academic Press, 1973b.

Kohlberg, L. "Contributions of Developmental Psychology to education: Examples from Moral Education." *Educational Psychologist 10* (1973c):2–14.

Kohlberg, L. "Moral Development and the New Social Studies." *Social Education 37* (1973d):369–375.

Kohlberg, L. "Moral Psychology and the Study of Tragedy." In S. Weintraub and P. Young, eds., *Directions in Literary Criticism: Contemporary Approaches to Literature.* University Park: Pennsylvania State University Press, 1973e.

Kohlberg, L. "Stages and Aging in Moral Development: Some Speculations." *Gerontologist 13* (1973f):497–502.

Kohlberg, L., and Boyd, D. "The *Is-Ought* Problem: A Developmental Perspective." *Zygon 8* (1973):358–371.

Kohlberg, L. "Comments on the Dilemma of Obedience." *Phi Delta Kappan* 55 (1974a):607.

Kohlberg, L. "Discussion: Developmental Gains in Moral Judgment." *American Journal of Mental Deficiency* 79 (1974b):142–144.

Kohlberg, L. "Education, Moral Development and Faith." *Journal of Moral Education* 4 (1974c):5–16.

Kohlberg, L. "The Cognitive-Development Approach to Moral Education." *Phi Delta Kappan* 61 (1975a):670–677. Also in D. Purpel and K. Ryan, eds., *Moral Education: It Comes with the Territory*. Berkeley, Calif.: McCutchan, 1976a.

Kohlberg, L. "Counseling and Counselor Education: A Developmental Approach." *Counselor Education and Supervision* 14 (1975b):250–256.

Kohlberg, L. "Moral Education for a Society in Moral Transition." *Educational Leadership* 33 (1975c):46–54.

Kohlberg, L. "The Relationship of Moral Education to the Broader Field of Values Education." In J. R. Meyer, B. Burnham, and J. Cholvat, eds., *Values Education: Theory, Practice, Problems, Prospects*. Waterloo, Ontario: Wilfred Laurier University Press, 1975d.

Blatt, M. M., and Kohlberg, L. "The Effects of Classroom Moral Discussion upon Children's Level of Moral Judgment." *Journal of Moral Education* 4 (1975):129–161.

Kohlberg, L., and Colby, A. "Moral Development and Moral Education." In G. Steiner, ed., *Psychology in the Twentieth Century*. Zurich: Kindler Verlag, 1975.

Kohlberg, L., and Elfenbein, D. "The Development of Moral Judgments Concerning Capital Punishment." *American Journal of Orthopsychiatry* 45 (1975):614–640. Also in H. A. Bedau and C. M. Pierce, eds., *Capital Punishment in the United States*. New York: A.M.S. Press, 1976.

Kohlberg, L., Kauffman, K., Hickey, J., and Scharf, P. *Corrections Manual, Parts I and II*. Cambridge, Mass: Moral Education Research Foundation, 1975.

Kohlberg, L., Kauffman, K., Scharf, P., and Hickey, J. "The Just Community Approach to Corrections: A Theory." *Journal of Moral Education* 4, (1975):243–260.

Kohlberg, L. "Moral Stages and Moralization: The Cognitive-Developmental Approach." In T. Lickona, ed., *Moral Development and Behavior: Theory, Research and Social Issues*. New York: Holt, Rinehart and Winston, 1976a.

Kohlberg, L. "The Quest for Justice in 200 Years of American History and in Contemporary American Education." *Contemporary Education* 48 (1976b):5–16.

Kohlberg, L. "This Special Section in Perspective." In E. Fenton, ed., *Social Education* 40 (1976c):213–215.

Gibbs, J., Kohlberg, L., Colby, A., and Speicher-Dubin, B. "The Domain and Development of Moral Judgment: A Theory and a Method of Assessment." In J. Meyer, ed., *Reflections on Values Education*. Waterloo, Ontario: Wilfrid Laurier University Press, 1976.

Haan, N., Langer, J., and Kohlberg, L. "Family Patterns of Moral Reasoning." *Child Development 47* (1976):1204–1206.

Kohlberg, L. "The Implications of Moral Stages for Adult Education." *Religious Education 72* (1977a):183–201.

Kohlberg, L. "Moral Development, Ego Development and Psychoeducational Practice." *Pupil Personnel Services Journal 6* (1977b):25–40.

DeVries, R., and Kohlberg, L. "Relations Between Piaget and Psychometric Assessments of Intelligence." In L. Katz, ed., *Current Topics in Early Childhood Education*, Vol. 1. Norwood, N.J.: Ablex, 1977.

Kohlberg, L., and Hersh, R. H. "Moral Development: A Review of the Theory." *Theory into Practice 16* (1977):53–59.

Kuhn, D., Langer, J., Kohlberg, L., and Haan, N. "The Development of Formal Operations in Logical and Moral Judgment." *Genetic Psychology Monographs 95* (1977):97–188.

Colby, A., Kohlberg, L., Fenton, E., Speicher-Dubin, B., and Lieberman, M. "Secondary School Moral Discussion Programmes Led by Social Studies Teachers." *Journal of Moral Education 6* (1977):90–111.

Kohlberg, L. "The Cognitive-Developmental Approach to Behavior Disorders: A Study of the Development of Moral Reasoning in Delinquents." G. Serban, ed., *Cognitive Defects in the Development of Mental Illness.* New York: Brunner-Mazel, 1978a.

Kohlberg, L. Foreword to *Kohlberg's Theory of Moral Education in Practice,* by R. Hersh, D. Paolitto, and J. Reimer. New York: Longman Press, 1978b.

Kohlberg, L. "Moral Development." *Synthesis: The Realization of the Self, 5* (1978c.)

Kohlberg, L. "Moral Education Reappraised." *Humanist 38* (1978d):13–15.

Kohlberg, L. Preface to *New Directions in Child Development.* Vol. 1, No. 2: "Moral Development," ed. W. Damon. San Franscisco: Jossey-Bass, 1978e.

Kohlberg, L. Preface to *Readings in Moral Education,* ed. P. Scharf. Minneapolis: Winston Press, 1978f.

Kohlberg, L., Wasserman, E., and Richardson, N. "Die Gerechte Schul-Kooperative: Ihre Theorie und das Experiment der Cambridge Cluster School." In G. Portel, ed., *Socialisation und Moral: Neuere Ansatze zur Moralishen Entwicklung und Erziehung.* Wienheim, Basel: Beltz Verlag, 1978.

Turiel, E., Edwards, C. P., and Kohlberg, L. "A Cross-Cultural Study of Moral Development in Turkey and the United States." *Journal of Cross-Cultural Psychology 9* (1978):75–87.

Kohlberg, L. Foreword to *Developments in Judging Moral Issues,* by James Rest. Minneapolis: University of Minnesota Press, 1979a.

Kohlberg, L. "From Athens to Watergate: Moral Education in a Just Society." *Curriculm Review 18* (1979b):8–11.

Kohlberg, L. "Justice as Reversibility." In P. Laslett and J. Fishkin, eds., *Philosophy, Politics and Society.* Fifth Series. Oxford: Blackwell, 1979c.

Kohlberg, L. "The Relations Between Piagetian Theory and Educational

Practice: Perspectives from Moral Education." In *Piagetian Theory and the Helping Professions, Eighth Annual Conference.* Los Angeles: University of Southern California Press, 1979d.

Kohlberg, L. "The Young Child as a Philosopher: Moral Development and the Dilemmas of Moral Education. In M. Wolman, ed., *Taking Early Childhood Seriously: The Evangeline Burgess Memorial Lectures.* Pasadena, Calif: Pacific Oaks, 1979e.

Kohlberg, L. "The Future of Liberalism as the Dominant Ideology of the West." In R. Wilson and G. Schochet, eds., *Moral Development and Politics.* New York: Praeger, 1980a.

Kohlberg, L. "High School Democracy and Educating for a Just Society." In R. Mosher, ed., *Moral Education: A First Generation of Research.* New York: Praeger, 1980b.

Kohlberg, L. "The Meaning and Measurement of Moral Development." Heinz Werner Lecture. Worcester, Mass: Clark University Press, 1980c.

Kohlberg, L. "Moral Education: A Response to Thomas Sobol." In *Educational Leadership 38,* no. 1. (1980d).

DeVries, R., and Kohlberg, L. "Don't Throw Out the Piagetian Baby with the Psychometric Bath: Reply to Humphreys and Parsons." *Intelligence 4* (1980):175–177.

Power, F. C. and Kohlberg, L. "Religion, Morality, and Ego Development." In J. Fowler and A. Vergote, eds., *Toward Moral and Religious Maturity.* Morristown, N.J.: Silver-Burdett, 1980.

Kohlberg, L., and Wasserman, E. "The Cognitive-Developmental Approaeh and the Practicing Counselor: An Opportunity for Counselors to Rethink Their Roles." *Personnel and Guidance Journal* (May 1980):559–565.

Bar-Yam, M., Kohlberg, L., and Naame, A. "Moral Reasoning of Students in Different Cultural, Social, and Educational Settings." *American Journal of Education 88* (1980):345–362.

Kohlberg L. *Essays in Moral Development.* Vol. 1: *The Philosophy of Moral Development.* San Francisco: Harper & Row, 1981.

Kohlberg, L. "Reply to Owen Flanagan." *Ethics,* in press.

Jennings, W., and Kohlberg, L. "Effects of Just Community Program on The Moral Level and Institutional Perceptions of Youthful Offenders." *Journal of Crime and Delinquency,* in press.

Kohlberg, L., and Power, C. "Moral Development, Religious Development, and the Question of a Seventh Stage." *Zygon,* in press.

Colby, A., and Kohlberg, L., with Gibbs, J., Candee, D., Speicher-Dubin, B., Power, C., and Lieberman, M. *The Measurement of Moral Judgment,* Vols. I and II. New York: Cambridge University Press, forthcoming.

Colby, A., Gibbs, J., Lieberman, M., and Kohlberg, L. *A Longitudinal Study of Moral Judgment: A Monograph for the Society of Research in Child Development.* Chicago: The University of Chicago Press, forthcoming.

Index